LETTERS OF
ARNOLD BENNETT

Volume I

Letters to J. B. Pinker

ARNOLD BENNETT

in New York, 1911

LETTERS OF ARNOLD BENNETT

Edited by
JAMES HEPBURN

VOLUME I

LETTERS TO J. B. PINKER

LONDON
OXFORD UNIVERSITY PRESS
NEW YORK   TORONTO
1966

Oxford University Press, Ely House, London W.1

GLASGOW NEW YORK TORONTO MELBOURNE WELLINGTON
CAPE TOWN SALISBURY IBADAN NAIROBI LUSAKA ADDIS ABABA
BOMBAY CALCUTTA MADRAS KARACHI LAHORE DACCA
KUALA LUMPUR HONG KONG

Printed in Great Britain by R. & R. Clark Ltd., Edinburgh

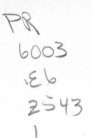

CONTENTS

	Page
ACKNOWLEDGEMENTS	ix
CHRONOLOGY	xiii
INTRODUCTION	
1 The Collection	1
2 Arnold Bennett's Early Literary Career	6
3 James Brand Pinker	22
I EARLY YEARS: 1901–1908	29
II FAME AND WEALTH: 1908–1914	113
III WAR YEARS AND LATER: 1914–1922	209
IV AFTER J. B. PINKER'S DEATH: 1922–1931	305
INDEX	413

LIST OF ILLUSTRATIONS

Arnold Bennett in New York, 1911
  (photograph Pirie MacDonald, Hon.F.R.P.S.)   *frontispiece*

J. B. Pinker at about the time when he started
  his Agency   *facing page* 22

Facsimile of Letter to Pinker, 6 January 1908   *page* 99

Facsimile of Letter to Pinker, 27 October 1918   *page* 269

ACKNOWLEDGEMENTS

This collection of Arnold Bennett's letters is published with the generous permission of Mrs. Dorothy Cheston Bennett. I am particularly grateful to Mrs. Bennett for her helpfulness and forbearance in the selecting of letters. I am also very much indebted to the editors of the Oxford University Press, whose advice and encouragement brought this first volume through considerable difficulties. I have special obligations to three other people: to Professor T. E. M. Boll of the University of Pennsylvania, with whom I first read Bennett; to Professor Gordon S. Haight of Yale University, whose interest in the collection helped to bring it into being; and to my wife, who shared much of the work.

It is with the kind permission of the authorities of University College, London, that most of the letters in this volume have been made available to me. I owe special thanks to the librarian, Joseph W. Scott, and to the deputy librarian, Ian Angus, for their courtesy and helpfulness. The University of Texas has allowed me to use letters from the collection of Bennett-Pinker material held there. I should like particularly to thank Mrs. Ann Bowden and Mrs. Mary M. Hirth, former and present librarians of the Academic Center of Texas, for their assistance. Dr. Lafayette Butler of Hazleton, Pennsylvania, whose generosity to me has extended over several years, has permitted me to use some of the Bennett-Pinker letters in his fine private collection. Much of the annotating for this volume derives from Dr. Butler's collection. Northwestern University has allowed me to use several letters from its collection of Pinker material; and I am especially obliged to Richard D. Olson, Curator of Rare Books, for his helpfulness. All the letters on the Pinker side are published with the kind permission of Eric S. Pinker. Mr. Pinker provided many of the details in the biographical account of his father.

I would like to thank John Ford of the Stoke-on-Trent Library and Ian Willison of the British Museum for providing me with information on many occasions. Other people to whom I am similarly obliged are Mr. Augustus Baker; Miss Violet Barton, J. B. Pinker's secretary for many years; Mr. George Beardmore; Miss Patricia Butler; Professor Helmut E. Gerber; Mr. Rupert Hart-Davis; Mr. James Keddie, Jr.; Professor James G. Kennedy; Miss Mary Kennerley; Mr. Reginald Pound; Mr. Thomas R. Roberts;

Miss Sybil Rosenfeld; Mr. Bertram Rota; Mr. Eric Salmon; Mr.
Frank Singleton; and Mr. Frank Swinnerton. Miss Winifred
Nerney, Arnold Bennett's secretary, helped me on several occasions
before her death.

I am obliged to the directors of Chatto and Windus for allowing
me to see their file of Bennett contracts and for providing information on other contracts; to the Society of Authors for allowing me
to use their files; and to the Society for Theatre Research and the
British Film Institute for providing information. I would like also
to express my appreciation to the staffs of several libraries where I
did much of my research: the British Museum in Bloomsbury and
the British Museum Newspaper Library at Colindale, the Beinecke
and Sterling Memorial Libraries of Yale University, the Houghton
and Widener Libraries of Harvard University, the New York
Public Library, and the Library of the University of Rhode Island.

Incidental letters and portions of letters by the following persons
are used by permission of the people, firms, and institutions indicated.

Arnold Bennett to Richard Bennett (from *Arnold Bennett's Letters
   to His Nephew*, 1935): William Heinemann and Harper and
   Row.

Arnold Bennett to William Morris Colles: Henry W. and Albert
   A. Berg Collection of the New York Public Library.

Arnold Bennett to Louis N. Feipel: Mr. Louis N. Feipel.

Arnold Bennett to E. V. Lucas: Mrs. Charles Shaw.

Arnold Bennett to the Editors of *The Times*: The Times Publishing Company.

Golding Bright: Midland Bank Executor and Trustee Company.

Mrs. Patrick Campbell to Arnold Bennett: Bartlett and Gluck-
   stein and the Trustees of the Estate of Mrs. Patrick Campbell.

Mrs. Patrick Campbell to George Bernard Shaw (from *Bernard
   Shaw and Mrs. Patrick Campbell: Their Correspondence*, ed. by
   Alan Dent): Curtis Brown Ltd. and the Trustees of the Estate
   of Mrs. Patrick Campbell.

Joseph Conrad (from G. Jean-Aubry's *Life and Letters*, 1927):
   J. M. Dent and Sons and the Trustees of the Joseph Conrad
   Estate.

Archibald Constable: Constable and Company.

Robert H. Davis: Mrs. Robert H. Davis.

George H. Doran: Doubleday and Company.

Sir Newman Flower: Dr. Desmond Flower.

Ford Madox Ford (from Douglas Goldring's *The Last Pre-
   Raphaelite*): David Higham Associates.

Harley Granville-Barker: Trustees of the Granville-Barker Estate.

C. L. Hanson: Charles L. Hanson, Jr., and Helen B. Hanson.

Sir Ernest Hodder-Williams: Paul Hodder-Williams.

Edward Knoblock: Actors' Benevolent Fund, Beefsteak Club, Hospital for Sick Children, Royal Literary Fund.

D. H. Lawrence (from *The Collected Letters of D. H. Lawrence*, ed. by Harry T. Moore, © 1962 by Angelo Ravagli and C. Montague Weekley, 1932 by the Estate of D. H. Lawrence, 1934 by Frieda Lawrence, © 1933, 1948, 1953, 1954 and each year 1956–62 by Angelo Ravagli and C. Montague Weekley): Laurence Pollinger Ltd., the Estate of the late Mrs. Frieda Lawrence, and Viking Press.

Sir Algernon Methuen: Methuen and Company and Messrs. Russell-Cooke, Potter, and Chapman.

Frank A. Munsey: Metropolitan Museum of Art, New York.

A. R. Orage: Mrs. Jessie Orage.

Eden Phillpotts: Mrs. Robina Phillpotts and The Times Publishing Company.

J. B. Pinker to Miss Violet Barton: Miss Violet Barton.

John Reburn: National Press Agency.

Paul Reynolds, Sr.: Paul R. Reynolds, Inc., 599 Fifth Avenue, New York 17, New York.

George Bernard Shaw (from *Bernard Shaw and Mrs. Patrick Campbell: Their Correspondence*, ed. by Alan Dent): Curtis Brown Ltd. and the Trustees of the Estate of Mrs. Patrick Campbell.

Arthur Waugh: the late Evelyn Waugh.

H. G. Wells to Arnold Bennett (from *Arnold Bennett and H. G. Wells*, ed. by Harris Wilson): Rupert Hart-Davis.

H. G. Wells to the Editors of the *Author*: A. P. Watt and Son and the Estate of H. G. Wells.

Thomas B. Wells: Harper and Row.

Henry James Whigham: Mrs. Sybil W. Young.

Unidentified editors of Tillotsons, Cassells, and *Pears' Annual*: Tillotsons, Cassell and Company, and Gibbs Proprietaries.

Other material used includes passages from uncollected articles, reviews, and stories by Arnold Bennett, reprinted by permission of A. P. Watt and Son; passages from *The Journal of Arnold Bennett*, copyright 1932, 1933, 1960, 1961 by the Viking Press, Inc., reprinted by permission of the Viking Press, Inc., and also of A. P. Watt and Son; passages from *The Truth About an Author* by permission of A. P. Watt and Son and Doubleday & Company, Inc.

The photograph of Arnold Bennett was taken by Pirie

MacDonald, Hon.F.R.P.S., and is used by permission of his daughter, Mrs. Patricia MacDonald Tutchings.

The two facsimile letters are reproduced by permission of the C. K. Ogden Library, University College, London.

The photograph of J. B. Pinker is used by permission of Eric S. Pinker and Miss Violet Barton.

Lastly I should like to thank the American Council of Learned Societies and the University of Rhode Island for grants that helped me to prepare this volume.

J. H.

CHRONOLOGY

1867	May 27	Birth at 90 (now 92) Hope Street, Hanley, Stoke-on-Trent. Eldest of nine children of Enoch and Sarah Ann Bennett.
1875		Family moves to Dain Street, Burslem. Arnold attends Wesleyan Infants' School, Burslem.
1876		Family moves to 175 Newport Lane, Burslem. Enoch Bennett becomes a solicitor.
1877		Enters Burslem Endowed School. Wins poetry and short story contests during first years here.
1878		Family moves to what is now 198 Waterloo Road, Cobridge.
1880		Family moves to 205 Waterloo Road (the new house in *Clayhanger* and now the site of the Arnold Bennett Museum).
1882		Enters Middle School, Newcastle-under-Lyme.
1883		Leaves school and enters father's law office.
1884–1885		Attends night-school at the Wedgwood Institute.
1885		Passes matriculation examination for London University.
1887		Writes two stories during this or the following year; fails to sell them.
		Fails legal examinations.
1888		Fails legal examinations again.
	November 17	Begins writing weekly notes for the *Staffordshire Knot*.
1889	March 2	Comes to London to be a shorthand clerk in the law offices of Le Brasseur and Oakley.
		Takes rooms at 46 Alexandria Road, Hornsey.
1891		Issues (apparently early in the year) the first of two second-hand book catalogues, *A Century of Books for Bibliophiles*.
	January or later	Lives briefly in Raphael Street, Knightsbridge, and (apparently at this time) Cowley Street, Victoria.

1891	Spring	Moves to 6 Victoria (now Netherton) Grove, Chelsea.
	December 19	First London publication, a parody in *Tit-Bits* of Grant Allen's *What's Bred in the Bone*.
1892		Probably issues the second catalogue of *A Century of Books for Bibliophiles*.
		Buys a small yacht.
1893	Summer	Writes first serious work, the story 'A Letter Home'.
	Christmas	Abandons the law office.
1894	January 1	With financial aid of father, becomes Assistant Editor of *Woman*.
1895	April	Begins writing first novel, *A Man from the North*.
	July	First serious work published, 'A Letter Home', in *Yellow Book*.
1896	May 15	Finishes writing *A Man from the North*.
	August	Visits Belgium.
	November	Becomes Editor of *Woman*.
1897	August	Visits France.
	October	Visits Paris.
1898	February	Goes to live at 9 Fulham Park Gardens.
		A Man from the North published.
	March	*Journalism for Women* published.
	June	First signed article for the *Academy*.
	September	Decides to take up writing fiction for a living; begins writing first sensational novel, *Love and Life* (*The Ghost*).
	Autumn	Rents country house at Witley for weekend visits with friends.
1899	February	Writes first dramatic piece, a duologue for a private entertainment.
	November	*Polite Farces*, three one-act plays, published (imprint 1900).
1900		Writes *The Chancellor* (play) with Arthur Hooley, and dramatizes Eden Phillpotts' *Children of the Mist* with Phillpotts. This year or next writes *A Wayward Duchess* (play) with Hooley. (None of this work ever published or produced.)
	March	Becomes literary adviser to Pearson's.
	September	Resigns editorship of *Woman*.
	October	Goes to live at Trinity Hall Farm, Hockliffe, Bedfordshire.

1901	September	*Fame and Fiction* (essays) published.
	December	J. B. Pinker becomes his agent.
1902		This year or earlier helps to dramatize Violet Tweedale's novel, *Her Grace's Secret*. (Collaborator unknown; never published or produced.)
	January	*The Grand Babylon Hotel* published.
	January 16	Father dies.
	February	Begins collaboration with H. G. Wells on a play, *The Crime*. Never finished.
	September	*Anna of the Five Towns* published.
	November 14	Begins year-long series of essays in *T. P.'s Weekly: Savoir Faire Papers*. (Never collected.)
	December	Abandons reviewing for the *Academy*.
1903	January	Gives up Trinity Hall Farm. Goes to Algeria for perhaps more than a month; on return to London at the end of February lives with friends at 7 Halsey House, Red Lion Square.
	February	*The Gates of Wrath* published.
	March 15	Leaves England for France, living first at the Hôtel du quai Voltaire, Paris.
	July	*The Truth About an Author* published anonymously.
		Visits England for two months or more.
	September	*How to Become an Author* published.
		Goes to live at 4 rue de Calais, Paris.
	October	*Leonora* published.
	November 13	Begins long series of essays in *T. P.'s Weekly: A Novelist's Log-Book*. (Never collected.)
	November 18	Conceives idea for *The Old Wives' Tale*.
	December	Visits Burslem briefly.
1904	January 14	Goes for a month to Menton to write *Christina* (play) with Phillpotts. (Never published or produced.)
	May	*A Great Man* published.
	August	Goes to Scotland for treatment for his speech impediment.
	October	*Teresa of Watling Street* published.
		Rents rooms at Les Sablons, near Moret, for occasional use.
	November	Begins writing *An Angel Unawares* (play) with Phillpotts; finished 3 January. (Never published or produced.)
	December 20	Goes to England for six weeks.

1905	January	*Tales of the Five Towns* published.
	June	*The Loot of Cities* (stories) published.
	Summer	Lives at Les Sablons.
	September	*Sacred and Profane Love* published.
	December	Visits England briefly.
	December 1	Begins long series of articles in *T. P.'s Weekly: Savoir Vivre Papers.*
1906	January	*Hugo* published.
	April 20	Goes to England briefly.
	June 15	Becomes engaged to Eleanor Green, sister of novelist Julian Green.
	August 3	Engagement broken off.
	August 4	Goes to England for four weeks.
	October	*Whom God Hath Joined* published.
	November	*The Sinews of War* published. (Written with Phillpotts.)
	December	*Things That Interested Me* (journal extracts) published privately.
		Moves to 3 rue d'Aumale, Paris.
		Visits England briefly.
1907	January	Meets Marguerite Soulie.
		The Ghost published.
	February	Spends holiday in San Remo during the month and most of March.
	March	*The Reasonable Life* (pocket philosophy) published.
	June	Visits Burslem.
		The Grim Smile of the Five Towns (stories) published.
	July 4	Marries Marguerite Soulie. They live at Les Sablons until late November.
	August	Writes first play to be produced: *Cupid and Commonsense* (dramatization of *Anna of the Five Towns*).
	September	Writes *The Sole Survivors* (play) with Phillpotts; finished 4 October. (Never published or produced.)
	October	*The City of Pleasure* published.
	October 8	Begins writing *The Old Wives' Tale*.
	December	*Things Which Have Interested Me, Second Series* (journal extracts) published privately.
	December 4	Goes to England for three months.
1908	January	Interrupts *The Old Wives' Tale* to write *Buried Alive*; finished 27 February.

1908	January 26–27	*Cupid and Commonsense* produced by the Stage Society at the Shaftesbury Theatre.
	March	*The Statue* published. (Written with Phillpotts.)
	March 21	Begins long series of 'Books and Persons' articles in the *New Age*, signed 'Jacob Tonson'.
	April 23	Moves into the Villa des Néfliers near Fontainebleau.
	June	*Buried Alive* and *How to Live on Twenty-Four Hours a Day* (pocket philosophy) published.
	August 30	Finishes writing *The Old Wives' Tale*.
	September	Makes a cycling tour of France.
	October	*The Old Wives' Tale* published.
	November	*The Human Machine* published.
	December	*Things Which Have Interested Me, Third Series* (essays) published privately.
	December 14	Goes to Switzerland for three months.
1909	March	Goes to England early in the month for rehearsals of *What the Public Wants*; stays until 11 May.
	May 2	*What the Public Wants* produced at the Aldwych Theatre by the Stage Society; new production at the Royalty on the 27th.
	July	*Literary Taste* (essays) published.
	October	*The Glimpse* published.
	November 27	Goes to England for four months.
1910	January 1	Goes to live at the Royal York Hotel, Brighton, for two and a half months.
	January 5	Begins writing *Clayhanger*.
	March	*Helen with the High Hand* published.
	March 18	Goes to Switzerland and Italy for two months.
	June 23	Finishes writing *Clayhanger*.
	July 1	Begins six-week holiday in Brittany.
	September	*Clayhanger* published.
	October 29	Takes a new flat in Paris at 59 rue de Grenelle.
1911	February	*The Card* published.
	April 8	Goes to England for two months.
	June	Returns to Villa des Néfliers in the middle of the month, stays until the end of August, and decides then to give up this home.
	August 31	Goes to England for a month.
	September	*Hilda Lessways* published.
	October	*The Feast of St. Friend* (pocket philosophy) published.

L.A.B.—B

1911	October 6	*The Honeymoon* opens at the Royalty Theatre.
	October 7	Sails for America. In six weeks visits New York, Washington, Boston, Chicago, Indianapolis, and Philadelphia.
	November 30	Sails from America.
	December	After brief stay in England and Paris, goes to live at Cannes for four months.
1912	January 31	Suffers attack of gastro-enteritis, or possibly typhoid fever.
	March	*The Matador of the Five Towns* (stories) published.
	March 5	*Milestones* (written with Edward Knoblock) begins its run of more than six hundred performances at the Royalty Theatre.
	April	Visits Paris briefly, and at the end of the month comes to England to live permanently. Stays mainly at Brighton until July, then goes to live at 14 St. Simon's Avenue, Putney, for seven months.
	June	Buys the yacht *Velsa*.
	September	Sailing in Holland.
	October	*Those United States* (travel sketches) published.
	December	Visits Paris briefly at the end of the year.
1913	February 24	Moves into his home, Comarques, Thorpe-le-Soken, Essex.
	March 25	*The Great Adventure* (dramatization of *Buried Alive*) opens for a long run at the Kingsway Theatre.
	September	*The Regent* published.
	October	*The Plain Man and His Wife* (pocket philosophy) and *Paris Nights* (travel sketches) published.
		Goes to the Continent for about three weeks in the middle of the month.
1914	February 17	*Helen with the High Hand* (dramatized by Richard Pryce) opens at the Vaudeville Theatre.
	March 13	Goes to the Continent for eight weeks; sails off the French and Italian coasts.
	August 24	Begins long series of political articles for the *Daily News*. (Never collected.)
	Autumn	Appointed military representative on the Thorpe Division Emergency Committee.

1914 October *The Price of Love* and *Liberty!* (essays) published.
November 23 Mother dies.
December *From the Log of the 'Velsa'* (travel sketches) published in America. (English publication 1920.)

1915 Comes to London frequently throughout the year for war work; stays at Berkeley Hotel.
Becomes a director of the *New Statesman*.
June 21 Begins twenty-five-day tour of battle front for the government.
October *The Author's Craft* (essays) published. (Imprint 1914.)
November *These Twain*, last of the Five Towns novels, published in America. (English publication January 1916.) *Over There* (war reporting) published.
December Goes to the Midlands and Scotland for two weeks.
December 13 First showing of the film *The Great Adventure*, apparently the first of Bennett's works to be filmed.

1916 Adopts as his son his nephew Richard Bennett.
July At the end of the month goes to Scotland for a brief holiday.
September *The Lion's Share* published.
October 28 Begins his anonymous 'Observations' in the *New Statesman*, series running throughout war, signed 'Sardonyx' and later 'Onyx'. (Never collected.)

1917 Lives mainly at the Royal Thames Yacht Club during visits to London throughout year.
January Resumes *Daily News* articles after lapse of eight months.
July *Books and Persons* (essays) published.

1918 April *The Pretty Lady* published.
May Becomes Director of British Propaganda in France.
May 19 Begins series of articles in *Lloyd's Weekly Newspaper*. (Never collected.)
July 20 *The Title* opens at the Royalty Theatre.
September Becomes Director of Propaganda, Ministry of Information.
September 10 Goes on holiday to Clevedon, Somerset, until the 26th.

1918	December	*Self and Self-Management* (pocket philosophy) published.
	December 24	First production at the Lyric Theatre, Hammersmith, under the directorship of Bennett, Nigel Playfair, and Alistair Tayler.
1919	January	*The Roll-Call* published (imprint 1918).
	April 30	*Judith* opens at the Kingsway Theatre.
	May or June	Takes a flat at 12B George Street, Hanover Square.
	November 10	*Sacred and Profane Love* (dramatization of the novel) opens at the Aldwych Theatre.
1920	January 29	Goes to Portugal for a month with Frank Swinnerton.
	June 5	*The Beggar's Opera* (adapted by Bennett) begins three-year run at the Lyric, Hammersmith.
	August	Buys yacht *Marie Marguerite*.
		Begins writing first film story, *The Wedding Dress*. (Never produced.)
	September	Occasionally sailing off the English coast, and then visiting Scotland until early October.
		Our Women (essays) published.
1921		Sailing off the English and French coasts much of the year.
	January	*Things That Have Interested Me* (essays) published.
	January 26	Begins series of articles on the theatre in the *Daily Express*. (Never collected.)
	October 20	Formal separation from wife agreed to.
	December	Early in the month goes on yachting cruise for two months.
1922	January	First showing of film version of *The Old Wives' Tale*.
	March	Meets Dorothy Cheston.
	March 21	*The Love Match* opens at the Strand Theatre.
	April	First showing of film version of *The Card*.
	May	*Mr. Prohack* published.
	May 6	Begins year-long series of articles in *John Bull*. (Never collected.)
	June	Sailing off the English coast throughout June, July, and August.
	September 11	*Body and Soul* opens at the Euston Theatre of Varieties.
	October	*Lilian* published.

1922	October 10	Begins writing *Riceyman Steps*.
	December	Moves into his new home at 75 Cadogan Square.
1923	February	*Things That Have Interested Me, Second Series* (essays) published.
	March 17	Finishes writing *Riceyman Steps*.
	March–April	Spends some time in Paris.
	May	*How to Make the Best of Life* (pocket philosophy) published.
	June	Sailing off the English coast and the Continent throughout June, July, and August.
	October	*Riceyman Steps* and *Don Juan* (play) published; the latter never produced.
1924	April	Visits Spain.
	June 4	*London Life* (written with Edward Knoblock) opens at Drury Lane.
	Summer	Sailing off the English and French coasts much of the time.
	October	*Elsie and the Child* (stories) published.
	October 19	Begins long series of articles in *Sunday Pictorial*.
	December	Goes to Italy in the middle of the month for thirty days.
1925	February 15	*The Bright Island* produced by the Stage Society.
	June	Sailing off the English coast during most of the month; at the beginning of July goes to Austria and Germany for a month and a half.
	November	Writes libretto of comic opera, *The Bandits*, with Eden Phillpotts; music by Frederic Austin. (Never produced.)
	December 14	Goes to Italy and France for three months.
1926	April	*Things That Have Interested Me, Third Series* (essays) published.
	April 13	Birth of daughter Virginia.
	May	At the end of the month goes for holiday to Amberley, Sussex, for seven weeks.
	August 31	Goes to Italy for two weeks.
	October	*Lord Raingo* published.
	November 18	Begins his 'Books and Persons' series in the *Evening Standard*; continued until his death.
	November 25, 29	*Riceyman Steps* (dramatized by Michael Morton) produced at the Ambassadors Theatre.

1927	January 2	First showing of the German film *Faust*, with English subtitles by Bennett.
	January 20	Goes to France, Austria, and Italy for seven weeks.
	April	Goes to Sicily in the middle of the month; sails in the Mediterranean with Otto Kahn until late May.
	June	*The Woman Who Stole Everything* (stories) published.
	July 28	Goes for holiday to St. Leonard's-on-Sea until 4 September.
	August	Facsimile edition of the manuscript of *The Old Wives' Tale* published.
	September	Visits Berlin in the middle of the month with Max Beaverbrook.
	Autumn	*The Vanguard* published in America. (English publication, as *The Strange Vanguard*, January 1928.)
	October 19	*Flora* opens at the Rusholme Theatre, Manchester. (No London production.)
	November	Becomes Associate Editor of *World Today* and for eight months writes an article on 'Men and Events'.
	November 16	*Mr. Prohack* (written with Edward Knoblock) opens at the Court Theatre.
1928	May	*The Savour of Life* (essays) published.
	July	Spends the month in France on holiday.
	September	Begins writing film story *Punch and Judy*. (Never produced.)
	September 1	*The Return Journey* opens at the St. James's Theatre.
	September 4	Goes to France for a fortnight.
	November	*Mediterranean Scenes* (travel sketches) published.
1929	January	*Accident* published.
	January 30	Begins writing last play; completed 13 June. (Never published or produced.)
		First showing of *Piccadilly*, film story by Bennett.
	March	*The Religious Interregnum* (essay) and *Piccadilly* (film story) published.
	March 26	Goes to France for a month.
	June 25	*Judith* (opera, music by Eugene Goossens, libretto by Bennett) produced at Covent Garden.

1929	June 30	Goes to France and Italy for six weeks, and then goes to Russia with Max Beaverbrook; returns home at the end of August.
	September 25	Begins writing *Imperial Palace*, longest and last major novel.
1930	June	*Journal, 1929* published.
	July	Goes to Cornwall in the middle of the month for six weeks; then goes yachting until the middle of September.
	July 5	Finishes writing *Imperial Palace*.
	October	*Imperial Palace* published.
	November 9	Moves to 97 Chiltern Court.
	November 25	Begins writing his last novel, *Dream of Destiny*; never finished.
	December 29	Goes to France for three weeks.
1931	January	Contracts typhoid fever in France.
	February 2	Writes last 'Books and Persons' article for *Evening Standard*.
	March 27	Dies at Chiltern Court.

(1931: *Venus Rising from the Sea*—long story; *The Night Visitor*—stories. 1932: *Dream of Destiny*. 1932–33: *Journals*. 1935: *Arnold Bennett's Letters to His Nephew*; *Arnold Bennett, A Portrait Done at Home*, together with *170 Letters from A. B.* 1937: *Don Juan*—opera, music by Eugene Goossens, libretto by Bennett—produced at Covent Garden 24 June. 1959: *Arnold Bennett and H. G. Wells*—letters. 1964: *Correspondance André Gide—Arnold Bennett*.)

INTRODUCTION

1. *The Collection*

It is pleasantly appropriate that the first volume of Arnold Bennett's letters should be devoted to those to his literary agent, the Pinker firm. One does not think of such a writer as D. H. Lawrence writing business letters except in moments of exasperation and need; one hardly thinks of Lawrence's letters to Edward Garnett as business letters. But Arnold Bennett was the business-man of letters. What should he do but write regularly to his agent? In fact, he once wrote five letters in a single day to J. B. Pinker, the chief figure of the firm, who was also for a time Lawrence's agent. On several occasions he wrote two and three times a day, and the whole surviving correspondence numbers above 2,600 letters. What is pleasant is not only that the collection is a valuable record of a writer's economic career and of the literary and artistic world about him, but also that it displays the energy and wit that Bennett brought to every aspect of his writing.

Bennett professed to be an indifferent writer of letters. In 1912, he wrote to an American woman: 'When I contemplate the sheer brains that . . . [George Meredith] puts into his letters I marvel, but have no desire to imitate. I have merely a desire to write no letters whatever. When my letters are collected and published—and nothing that I can do will stop that happening—my posterity will certainly be disappointed and feel itself aggrieved.' Many years later, he wrote to his second wife, Dorothy Cheston Bennett: 'I can't write long letters like you can. I only want to say a certain amount, très simplement, and then I don't want to spoil it.' In point of fact, he seems to have written letters as compulsively as he wrote novels, articles, and journals. Apart from the letters to the Pinker firm, which averaged one every three or four days for twenty-nine years, he wrote to his mother every day during the last twelve years of her life; he wrote every week to his nephew Richard Bennett for more than ten years; he wrote almost once a week to Pauline

Smith, the South African novelist, to Harriet Cohen, the pianist, and to Frank Swinnerton. Winifred Nerney, who was his secretary from 1912 onwards, said that he wrote twenty letters a day. Perhaps on one day he had a desire to write no more letters.

Many were the briefest of notes. Especially among the Pinker letters are dozens that say no more than '*Commission*. Many thanks for your letter. All right.' (Letter of 22 March 1921.) In the main, though, the letters avoid saying too little as well as too much. They reflect the fact that Bennett was shy and had a bad stammer, and preferred to conduct part of his life by letter. Pauline Smith tells of a note that he wrote her when they were first acquainted. She was playing bridge, and Bennett was sitting near by reading. Her partner spoke to her angrily about a mistake. Presently Bennett slipped to her a scrap of newspaper on which he had written: '*I* know why you play badly. You are thinking of something you are trying to write.' He could not easily have said so aloud. On many occasions he chose to conduct his quarrels with his first wife by letter. Once when he was being honoured in the Potteries and was asked to speak, he rose and said only, 'Ladies and gentlemen, I don't speak, I write.'

There was also his kindness. He was Uncle Arnold to many people, offering them the steadiness of his vision, and invariably responding to need. The letters to Pauline Smith were written in such a spirit. In the last year of his life he wrote to chide her for not working, and urged her to light a fire and a lamp and begin. She replied: 'No heat of fire and no light of lamp bring me such warmth and radiance as do your letters, and after twenty-two years of friendship I say it.' The kindness extended to hundreds of unknown people who wrote to him about his books. In 1924 Louis N. Feipel of New York City wrote to say how much he had enjoyed *Riceyman Steps* and also to point out that there were a multitude of misprints and spelling inconsistencies in the American edition of the novel. These mistakes were detailed on four single-spaced typewritten pages. Bennett replied:

Dear Mr. Feipel,

Very many thanks for your letter of the 10th January. Your industry staggers me. In order to save trouble I have made a number

of brief remarks on your letter itself, and I return it to you herewith
for you to study. Of course I am very careless in about 10,000 details
of proof correcting and even of writing. But life is so short and I have
so much to do, and moreover I have not sufficient application to do
what you have so exhaustively done.

Believe me,

Cordially yours,

Arnold Bennett

Bennett's brief remarks consisted of individual notes on fifty-
seven items and general comments on everything else. He was
equally kind when someone wrote to ask what happened to
Cyril Povey after the end of *The Old Wives' Tale*.

The Pinker letters, of course, are not primarily personal, and
their abundance has a distinct practical cause, a cause that
provides their special interest. They begin in 1901, six years
after Bennett had begun writing his first serious novel and
before he had finished writing his second. They show his sometimes brash confidence in his power, his sense of its variety, his
certainty of success. He knows how much he is worth as a
journalist (about two guineas for a thousand words); he takes
pleasure in bargaining with editors and publishers; and he
admires the agent who is generous and astute enough to lend
him £50 a month for several years. Twenty-five years later he
is worth two shillings and more a word; he still delights in the
poker game he plays with editors, publishers, actresses, and
impresarios; and he earns £20,000 a year. And now he writes
with the authority of an assured position. The letters make it
clear—as is not evident from other sources—that he suffered
no decline in energy or earning power in his last years, when the
Depression was beginning. They throw more light on certain
aspects of his creative habits than any other information.

The Pinker letters are additionally interesting as a record of
a relationship between an author and his agent at a time when
the agent had just appeared on the literary scene. The series
is perhaps unmatched in the correspondence of other important
writers. Small groups of letters from Edith Wharton to the
American agent Paul Reynolds, and from Stephen Crane,
Joseph Conrad, and Ford Madox Ford to J. B. Pinker have
been published. Ford had a correspondence with Pinker that
spanned as many years as Bennett's, but it numbers perhaps only

four hundred and fifty letters. There are at least two unpublished collections of probable importance: Somerset Maugham's to Pinker and A. P. Watt, which covers twice as many years as Bennett's, and Rider Haggard's to A. P. Watt, which is almost as extensive. But neither writer was involved year after year in multifarious creative and journalistic activities as was Bennett. Of the two writers of Bennett's time whose interests were as diverse and extensive as his, George Bernard Shaw was largely his own agent and H. G. Wells employed agents sporadically.

The following selection of letters represents about one-seventh of the surviving correspondence to the Pinker firm. In the first nine years, the surviving letters average about fifty a year; between 1913 and 1920 they average a hundred and twenty-five. There is no doubt that very many letters from the first years have been lost. Since part of the aim of the selection is to provide a continuous account, the proportion of surviving letters used from the earlier years is relatively high. Otherwise the letters have been chosen for intrinsic interest, variety, and internal coherence and clarity. There has been little censorship except on these grounds. Sixteen letters from the original selection had to be omitted, and six letters are printed with deletions. The deletions are indicated. Except in one instance, these losses do not at all affect the picture of Bennett that is given in the collection. A few letters from the Pinker firm are printed, along with some exchanges between Bennett and other people when Bennett considered the exchange to be part of his dealings with the Pinker firm. Unfortunately, very few letters on the Pinker side are known to have survived from before 1910. Deletions from letters to Bennett are likewise shown.

Bennett wrote all or nearly all his letters by hand, but after 1912 most of the letters received by the Pinker firm were type-written. The explanation is that at this time Bennett hired as his secretary Miss Winifred Nerney, who transcribed the short-hand or longhand drafts he thereafter wrote for his business correspondence. One book of his shorthand drafts survives, and was given by Miss Nerney to the Arnold Bennett Museum at Stoke-on-Trent. In a letter to Sir Arthur Quiller-Couch in 1925, Bennett responded to Quiller-Couch's apology for having typed his letter by saying that he himself regarded typing as efficient and respectable. Nevertheless, he too occasionally apologized to friends when he sent them typewritten letters; and throughout his life most of his personal letters were sent in his own hand. He wrote many of his letters at night, during his frequent attacks of insomnia.

The sort of person that he was—fastidious and formal—makes part of the task of editing his letters easy. His grammar, syntax, punctuation, and spelling are conventional. He rarely makes mistakes. When these mistakes are a repeated word, an *of* for a *to*, an omitted mark of punctuation, and the like, they are silently corrected. Two dozen such instances occur in this volume. Anything that he crosses out is ignored unless it seems worth showing. Omitted words and dates are placed within brackets; a question mark preceding them indicates editorial uncertainty. A bracketed question mark alone indicates an unreadable word. The addresses from which Bennett wrote are given in full the first time, and thereafter abbreviated; no distinction is made between printed and written addresses. Presumed addresses and signatures on letters reproduced from copies are placed within brackets. In a few instances the presumed address is a substitute for an obviously wrong letterhead address. Punctuation and the printing of titles of short stories, novels, and periodicals have been standardized. The spelling of a few names—e.g. Knoblock (also Knoblauch)—has been made consistent.

Except for one letter and a few fragments of others none of the letters printed in this volume has hitherto been published. Most of the letters have been drawn from the major collection of 2,000 letters held at University College, London. Others come from the collection of 1,000 Bennett-Pinker manuscripts held at the University of Texas. Most of the letters from the Pinkers to Bennett and a few from Bennett are drawn from the collection of several thousand Bennett-Pinker letters owned by Dr. Lafayette Butler. A few miscellaneous letters come from Northwestern University, which holds the main portion of the general files of the Pinker firm. Bennett-Pinker letters held by other libraries were examined but not used. The symbol U.C., TEXAS, BUTLER, or NW. at the head of each letter identifies its owner. The symbols MS. (manuscript), TS. (typescript), A.C. (autograph copy), A.C.C. (autograph carbon copy), T.C. (typed copy), or T.C.C. (typed carbon copy) indicate the character of the text printed from. There is no reason to doubt the authenticity or general accuracy of the typed copies and typed carbon copies. All the footnoted information for a letter is given in a single note that bears the same number as the letter itself. Some letters have no notes, and relevant information may be found in succeeding letters and notes.

2. *Arnold Bennett's Early Literary Career*

(Arnold Bennett himself told part of the tale of his early literary career in his delightful little book *The Truth About an Author*, written in 1902 when that phase of his career was just ending. Latter-day critics have often looked askance at the book, regarding it as a piece of froth produced in a spirit more commercial than truthful; and because the book was published anonymously, and with dates and names and places missing, they have been pleased to think that much of the detail was embroidered and exaggerated. But on investigation the book shows itself to be an essentially accurate record. It may still offend people who want the truth about an author to be exalted; but that is another matter.)

Arnold Bennett came to London from the Potteries when he was almost twenty-two years old. The date was 2 March 1889. He mentions in *The Truth About an Author* that some vague literary desire lay in the back of his mind; but his main thought was simply to escape from the Potteries, and he came to London prepared to be a shorthand clerk in the law offices of Le Brasseur and Oakley. He had behind him a grammar-school education, some training in his father's law office, an interest in history, architecture, painting, and literature, and a brief and slight success as a local journalist. In later years he said: 'I am a writer, just as I might be a hotel-keeper, a solicitor, a doctor, a grocer, or an earthenware manufacturer.' No doubt he was thinking of the accidents by which he fell into writing and of the talents he bent to writing that he could have used otherwise. At any rate, his attitude at twenty-one and his view in later years do not support the conventional image that Max Beerbohm traded on in depicting him in his old self–young self series of caricatures. There the paunchy and prosperous Bennett looks at the raw youth and says, 'All gone according to plan, you see', and the youth looks up at him unawed and says, '*My* plan, you know'. Of course there is truth in the Beerbohm caricature. Bennett was a person of the most orderly habits, and he possessed great will-power. Much was planned. He could intend to write 160,000 words of a novel in six months, and then do so. He could predict that by the time he was forty he would have a mansion by the sea, and be wrong by only five years. In a more serious way, too, it is hard to escape the Beerbohm view. The flow of words was a rising, unstoppable flood. But when Bennett was twenty-one, he did not know what was to be his destiny; and the ensuing years showed him repeatedly surprised at the talents and energies that were emerging.

On another occasion late in life Bennett wrote: 'I have not had a clear and fixed ambition. I began to write novels because my friends said I could. The same for plays. But I always had a strong feeling for journalism, which feeling is as strong as ever it was.' The first years of his literary life were given mainly to journalism. At home in the Potteries he won two schoolboy contests for poems and short stories; and after he left school he wrote two stories, submitting the first to the *Staffordshire Sentinel* and the second to the *Staffordshire Knot*, both unsuccessfully. The second story, which he describes as 'a sinister narrative to illustrate the evils of marrying a drunken woman' (written under the influence of Zola), perhaps survives as the original form of the story of Daniel Povey in *The Old Wives' Tale*. After a lapse of a few months or longer, the editor of the *Knot* invited him to do a column of local gossip for the paper. The invitation reflected the fact that Bennett's father was backing the paper financially, and the writing was to be done for nothing. But the venture worked out happily all round. Since the notes were anonymous, and Bennett's account is inaccurate on a minor detail or two, it is difficult to say exactly when he began; but it would seem to be with the issue of 17 November 1888, when for the first time the local notes are headed 'Burslem', 'Hanley', and so forth, and are signed 'Ready', 'Centre', 'Hawk', and the like. Bennett says that he was employed to write the notes for his own town, Burslem, but he evidently wrote those for Hanley some or all of the time, and may have helped with the others. According to *The Truth*

About an Author, the first note was concerned with the local trams; but no such item seems to be in the paper, and presumably Bennett's recollection at a distance of thirteen years was faulty. But he also recalls an item on the local coffee house, and such an item appears in the issue of 1 December, under Hanley rather than Burslem. He mentions too a difference of opinion with the sub-editor of the *Knot*—supposedly with regard to the tram note:

In due course I called at the office to correct proof, and I was put into the hands of the sub-editor. It was one of those quarters-of-an-hour that make life worth living; for the sub-editor appreciated me; nay, he regarded me as something of a journalistic prodigy, and his adjectives as he ran through the proof were extremely agreeable. Presently he came to a sentence in which I had said that such-and-such a proceeding 'smacked of red tape'.

'Smacked of red tape?' He looked up at me doubtfully. 'Rather a mixed metaphor, isn't it?'

I didn't in the least know what he meant, but I knew that that sentence was my particular pet. 'Not at all!' I answered with feeling. 'Nothing of the sort! It *does* smack of red tape—you must admit that.'

And the sentence stood. I had awed the sub-editor.

The sentence appears in the 1 December issue, in an item on a complaint by a local judge that the police were failing to keep order in his court. The police responded laconically. 'Chief Superintendent Hill told his Honour a few weeks ago that there was a reason, but he did not give it. We suspect it smacks of red tape.'

The notes are lively, those of Hanley and Burslem particularly so, but they are in the conventional vein of breezy journalism, and they could hardly be recognized as Bennett's early writing on internal evidence alone. Nevertheless, the clear and easy style of the mature Bennett has obvious roots in them. They enjoyed considerable success, and beginning with the issue of 19 January 1889, they were transferred to the front page, with the amount of space given to them much enlarged. During that January local interest centred on an election to the county council. The contest was between Spencer Lawton, town official for many years, and W. W. Dobson, proprietor of most of Burslem's pubs. The young Bennett was on the side of virtue, which proved to be the losing side, and he was instructed to write a column making fun of the winner. He says in *The Truth About an Author* that at the declaration of the poll he noticed that the hat of the triumphant brewer 'was stove-in and askew'. The evening afterwards was the evening before the paper, a weekly, went to press; and it also proved to be the evening when Bennett's grandfather was dying:

The doctor descended at intervals and said that it was only a question of hours. I was absolutely obsessed by a delicious feeling of the tyranny of the press. Nothing domestic could be permitted to interfere with my duty as a journalist.

'I must write those facetious comments while my grandfather is dying upstairs!' This thought filled my brain. It seemed to me to be fine, splendid. I was intensely proud of being laid under a compulsion so startlingly dramatic. Could I manufacture jokes while my grandfather expired? Certainly: I was a journalist. And never since have I been more ardently a journalist than I was that night and morning. With a strong sense of the theatrical, I wrote my notes at dawn. They delicately excoriated the brewer.

The curious thing is that my grandfather survived not only that, but several other fatal attacks.

Bennett's column on Dobson in the *Knot* describes the declaration of the poll:

Everyone could tell from the jaunty and satisfied way in which Mr. Dobson came forward that he was an easy winner. With his light brown hat, the crown knocked in, perched on one side of his head, his fancy check jacket and very latest style of overcoat, he certainly looked the beau ideal of a staid and dignified County Councillor.

And then, as Bennett concludes the account in *The Truth About an Author*: 'a few weeks later, my newspaper was staggering under the blow of my migration to London.'

The next two and a half years went by without Bennett's doing much, if any, further writing. Reportedly he wrote an account of the Oxford and Cambridge Boat Race in March 1891, but where it was published is unknown. Most of his time was spent at the law office, where he was soon earning £200 a year, and much of the remainder of his time he gave to book-collecting. He bought a book a day, mainly old and rare, and often in a language that he did not understand. Around 1891 and 1892 he issued two catalogues describing some of these

L.A.B.—C

books. One of his customers was Augustine Birrell. In the meantime, in the spring of 1891, he moved into a flat in Chelsea, in the home of a family of artists, and a place where other artists and musicians frequently gathered. The experience was crucial; for these people not only took art seriously, in a manner he had not witnessed before, but they also took him seriously. When he eventually said to himself, 'By heaven! I will write a novel', he was yielding to what they had been urging on him for perhaps more than two years. They assumed that any man of talent ought to do something large with his life, and they applauded even his most tentative and pedestrian efforts to find his way. The first occasion came in November 1891. The popular weekly magazine *Tit-Bits* offered a twenty-guinea prize for a humorous condensation of Grant Allen's *What's Bred in the Bone*, a light serial story that had begun in the magazine the previous Christmas. Bennett decided to enter the contest, and his friends encouraged him to believe that parody was a legitimate form of art. They expected him to win, and he did win. His condensation appeared in *Tit-Bits* on 19 December. It began thus:

> Once upon a time a pony was carrying a young lady to the railway station. If that pony hadn't jibbed you would never have experienced this happy moment.
> But it did, and the young lady nearly missed the train. If she had, the world would have lost a great book (and, we must also add, a most diverting condensation thereof). But she didn't. A porter managed to insert her sylph-like form in a second-class carriage, just as the train commenced its mad career, and she found herself 'alone—with an artist'. . . .
> She knew at once that he was an artist. Not by his raiment (for he was not arrayed like one of these), but by her woman's intuition. She had that badly.

This modest success was followed by a few others, but none so encouraging for another two years. The editor of *Tit-Bits* offered to consider articles by Bennett, and paid him ten shillings apiece for the two that he submitted. They were a few hundred words long, and were published anonymously, one of them, 'How a Case is Prepared for Trial', appearing on 27 February 1892, and the other, 'Lawyers and their Costs', on 28 January 1893. The two articles were presumably written at the same time, early in 1892, and Bennett remarks that his well of inspiration thereupon dried up: he could think of nothing more from his legal experience to write about. But he concocted articles and notes on other subjects during the rest of the year, and some of these were published. *Tit-Bits* and the evening paper the *Star* were now or later paying him half a crown for anonymous paragraphs, and other unknown journals apparently published more substantial pieces. He was, he says, earning threepence an hour at such work.

It was at this time that his friends began to talk of his writing a novel, and more to please them than himself he finally agreed to write a short story. *Tit-Bits* paid a guinea every week for a prize story, and Bennett's story won the guinea for the issue of 6 May 1893. 'The Artist's Model' is about a starving artist, a lovely model, a threatened illness that will wreck both art and love, and a happy ending. All the same it displays a stylistic grace creditable in a young man who had written four stories in the space of thirteen years or so. In a way it is close to the parody of *What's Bred in the Bone*. The best passage occurs at a point when the artist and his model are taking a walk together. She has been sitting for a portrait of 'Claire Ingelow', the heroine of a novel that the artist is illustrating. The artist has yet to propose to her.

During one of these walks Mary remarked that the portrait was nearly completed.

'Of course you will call it "Claire Ingelow"?' she said.

'Yes; I suppose I must,' was the reply, 'but I could suggest at least two better titles.'

'Indeed! And may I ask what they are?'

'Well, one is "The Dearest Girl in the World", and the other: "Portrait of the Artist's Wife".'

She was silent. It was dark, and the road was deserted. His arm crept round her waist. She looked up, and her lips met his, descending to meet them.

And so it was arranged.

This story was followed by several others, all within a few months. One of them was a tragic tale about a courtesan, and was published in an apparently short-lived monthly magazine. It has not been found. Most of the others, some of which Bennett describes as 'political skits in narrative form', were

published in the daily evening newspapers. There were ten
principal evening papers at the time. Almost all the writing in
them was unsigned, and Bennett's work is mainly unidentifi-
able. Three signed stories by him did appear in 1893 in one of
these papers, the *Sun*, on 29 July, 5 August, and 25 August
(signed A. B., A. Bennett, and Enoch Arnold Bennett, as elsewhere during these years he signed himself E. A. B., E. A.
Bennett, and Arnold Bennett). The stories are slight, but
indicative of things to come. The first, 'The Advanced Woman',
prepares the way for other advanced women such as Sophia
Baines and Gracie Savott, a preoccupation of Bennett's
throughout his career, and one that appears in many essays,
notably in *Our Women*. The situation—a humorous one concerning an apparently bogus marriage—was to become part of
the plot of *The Honeymoon* of sixteen years later. The second
story, 'In a Hospital', is a piece of sentimental realism: an over-
worked nurse who is about to abandon her drudgery for
marriage is brought in to attend a suicide case. The man is her
fiancé, and before he dies he mutters four words indicating that
he has lost money gambling. Bennett would do better than this
very shortly. The third story, 'Restaurant Spooks', is a complaint about London restaurants. A young man sitting in a
cheap and unappetizing restaurant imagines himself having an
interview with the French proprietor of a chain of sixty cheap
and appetizing restaurants. The lavish meals in *The Grand
Babylon Hotel* and *Imperial Palace* were doubtless in a corner of
the young man's mind.

None of this writing pleased the young Bennett. Some of it
he regarded with loathing. But it appears to be true that he
learned from the worst of his writing as well as from the best,
and that one of his keys to serious energy was to indulge his
light and superficial self. The writing of *The Old Wives' Tale*
followed immediately upon the writing of two potboilers with
Eden Phillpotts, and was interrupted for the writing of *Buried
Alive*. In any event, in the summer of 1893 a piece of writing
took Bennett by surprise:

Then, one day, one beneficent and adorable day, my brain was
visited by a Plot. I had a prevision that I was about to write a truly
excellent short story. I took incredible pains to be realistic, stylistic,

and all the other *istics*, and the result amazed me. I knew that at last
I had accomplished a good thing—I knew by the glow within me,
the emotional fatigue, the vista of sweet labour behind me.

The story was 'A Letter Home', and it was good enough to be
published in the *Yellow Book* in July 1895. It describes the death
of a young tramp. Before he dies he writes a letter to his mother
in the Five Towns, and the letter is entrusted to a fellow tramp
who presently uses it to light his pipe. The ironies of the story
are still too close to those of 'In a Hospital' to be very effective,
but the carefully drawn scene survives them. Bennett here
achieves something of the style that will mark his best novels,
and he also for the first time—so far as is known—touches upon
the Five Towns. It may have been immediately thereafter that
he said to himself, 'By heaven! I will write a novel.' But he did
not sit down to that task until April 1895.

By the end of 1893, though, he had made a beginning in
most of the sorts of writing that were to occupy his life. The
fiction displays the range of humorous, sensational, and realistic
writing of the later novels and plays; and the notes and
political skits are forerunners of the thousand and more articles
on the social-political scene. There was also some early book-
reviewing to anticipate the 'Books and Persons' columns in the
New Age and the *Evening Standard*. *The Truth About an Author* is
least helpful in its details on this point. Very probably, though,
the first reviewing was done in the *Illustrated London News*,
over the initials A. B., on 18 November 1893 and 24 March
1894.

The end of 1893 was also the end of Bennett's legal career,
and the beginning of several years of full-fledged journalism.
He learned during the year that the assistant-editorship of the
weekly magazine *Woman* was available to someone with talent
and also money with which to buy shares in the firm. The
position itself paid £50 less a year than he was earning at the
law office. He consulted his father, and with help from him
obtained the position, beginning work on the first day of the
new year. The journal was then in its fifth year, and was edited
by Fitzroy Gardner. Its motto was 'Forward but not too fast'
(subject of amused comment), and its preoccupation was with
kitchen, clothes, social notes, and chit-chat about the arts.

Bennett was apparently encouraged enough by his newspaper writing during 1893 to feel few qualms about taking the post; and Gardner once told another employee that after the first day Bennett had nothing to learn. Much of *Woman* was in fact prepared by women: the articles on cookery and cosmetics, the fashion drawings, some of the stories. The rest was written by Gardner and Bennett. Except for the stories, most of the writing was done over pseudonyms; and not only the pseudonyms but the style too sometimes survived the writers. 'Smartness' was the note, Bennett says in *The Truth About an Author*, and occasionally there was collaboration in producing a single smart note. It is thus difficult to know exactly what work individual writers did. Gardner apparently wrote the social gossip, over the name 'Marjorie', with occasional assistance from Bennett. In his memoirs he recalls once receiving a proposal of marriage from a male reader. Bennett was several people. After little more than a month he took over the book-reviewing column of 'Barbara', and in the following November he began sharing the music and drama columns with Gardner, signing his items 'E. A. B.' to Gardner's 'Cecile'. He was also 'Sarah Volatile', writer of stories and adviser on journalism for women, in all the appearances made by that lady in the journal. And at weekends, at one time or another, he sat at home reading French newspapers and was 'Our Own Correspondent' in Paris.

The Paris correspondent had a characteristic task:

On Monday last Madame Pierson gave a brilliant matinée musicale in her charming house in the Rue Lesner. Of course half of the Parisian *crème* was present, and Madame Pierson, with her usual charming ways, made everyone happy and at home. This popular lady seems to defy Time, and to grow younger instead of older. Really, the other day, in her pretty gown of black chiffon over heliotrope *faille*, and with her hair dressed high *à la Pompadour*, she looked quite a young woman—and a very charming one, too. Among the guests I noticed. . . .

Barbara did better:

The first story in Mr. Henry James's new volume of *Embarrassments* . . . is one of the best he has given us for many years. It is exceedingly subtle and exceedingly clear, and the effective simplicity of the narrative arrangement could not possibly be bettered. The remaining stories, it seems to me, will delight only that select circle of admirers (of whom, be it understood, I am one) which regards him as a great, though peculiar, master. For myself, my adoration is placid, and, therefore, discriminating; and, although I still worship, I can plainly see that the great man's mere ingenuity, not only of construction, but of expression, must strike the absolutely unprejudiced as tedious. . . . But at the worst there aren't two Henry Jameses; though many have imitated the cut of his mantle, he has never been approached.

Bennett says in *The Truth About an Author* that Barbara's reviews (of which the above sample is unquestionably his own) were unsuitable for *Woman*, but also that they attracted the attention of literary people and brought in publishers' advertisements. They did not stand in the way of his being made editor in November 1896, when Gardner resigned.

A sketch of Bennett at this time appears in the memoirs of Mrs. C. S. Peel, who was on the staff and later was editor.

He was a plain young man, a raw young man and afflicted by a violent stammer, but one who already knew what he meant to do. Under his direction *Woman* was a brilliant little paper.

I entered his room one day with an article. He took it, read a few sentences; then looked up at me. He leant back in his chair and his limbs stiffened, as happened when his stammer overcame him. 'W . . . w . . . w . . . why do you not l . . . l . . . l . . . learn to write?' he enquired. Probably by then I was earning considerably more than Mr. Bennett, but I had the sense to know that I could not write, and that he could. I replied humbly that I would gladly learn. How did he think that I should begin? 'I will teach you,' said he. Presently, 'Did you not learn grammar?' 'I think I know the difference between a verb, an adjective and an adverb.' He sighed . . . no, it was a hiss rather than a sigh. He hissed with exasperation. 'You must learn and I certainly shall not try to teach you. I know a Miss So and So who might be able to give you lessons. . . .'

He said that women were idle and would not take the trouble to learn their jobs, that authorship was a trade as well as an art, and that authors who wrote what no one wanted to read and muddled contracts and excused their foolishness on the plea of artistic temperament deserved to go hungry and generally did.

(I believe, however, that in spite of his fierce words he was a generous helper of those who needed help.)

Shortly after he became editor of *Woman* Bennett began to write regularly for other journals. He joined the staff of *Hearth and Home* (published by the same firm) apparently some time in 1897, beginning on 23 September a literary column signed by Sarah Volatile. In 1898 he began writing for the *Academy*, then edited by C. Lewis Hind. In *Authors and I*, published in 1921, Hind recalls reading Barbara's column in *Woman* and being so impressed by it that he sought out the writer. In *The Truth About an Author* Bennett recalls that he himself approached Hind. His first signed appearance in the *Academy* came with an interview with an American editor on 18 June 1898. During the next four years he was one of the principal contributors, sometimes publishing as many as four separate articles and reviews in a single weekly issue. Most of his work was unsigned. Apart from *The Truth About an Author*, which began publication in the issue of 3 May 1902, his most important writing for the *Academy* was a series of essays on modern writers, among them Turgenev and George Gissing. These essays, and similar ones published elsewhere, gave him his first opportunity to express publicly his fundamental views about writing:

Everyone is an artist, more or less; that is to say, there is no person quite without that faculty of poetising, which by seeing beauty creates beauty.

_____

Every work of art must have a moral basis.

_____

The realism of one age is the conventionality of the next.

_____

. . . from life at its meanest and least decorative . . . [can] be drawn material grand enough for great fiction.

In several of the essays Bennett discussed popular writers such as James Lane Allen and Charlotte M. Yonge, and justified their great popularity on literary or quasi-literary grounds. He wrote to a friend about the whole group of essays, which he published as *Fame and Fiction* in 1901: 'In its curious mixture of worldliness and passionate feeling for pure literary art, it is as exact an expression of myself as I am likely to arrive at.'

In his memoirs, at least, Hind was very appreciative of the

young Bennett. His writing never needed correction; his opinions were always original. 'He was the most valuable member of the staff. I knew it. He knew it. So I was not surprised when one day he demanded a 50 per cent. increase of pay. Of course I meekly assented. . . .' Bennett also recalls the moment in *The Truth About an Author*. But neither man recalls what was apparently the conclusion of their relationship. Bennett seems to have made another request for a rise (having first gone from ten shillings a column to fifteen). As remembered by a friend of Bennett's, Hind responded to this effect:' We think that you do not recognise the advantage it is to a young writer like you to have your articles appearing in a paper like the *Academy*.' Bennett's reply was: 'On the contrary, it seems to me that you do not appreciate the advantage it is to a paper like the *Academy* to have articles by a writer like me; but in any case, you will not have any more of them.' This was late in 1902.

Bennett's activities on the staffs of three papers did not consume all his energy. In his first year on *Woman* he wrote four more stories for the *Sun* (published 22 February, 10 April, 2 May, and 22 May 1894), and undoubtedly published several others elsewhere, including one unsigned story in the *St. James's Gazette* on 7 April. The following year he began his career as a novelist. He was then twenty-seven years old; and eight years of extensive reading had given him opinions about what a novel should be—and diffidence about his ability to write such a work. His models were Turgenev, Flaubert, de Maupassant, the Goncourt brothers, and, alone among English writers, George Moore. His style was to be elegant and colourful; the very physical appearance of paragraph, page, and chapter was to be consciously composed; and the tale itself should be prosaic, unsentimental, and true. 'It was to be the Usual miraculously transformed by Art into the Sublime.' And beginning in April 1895, he laboured for several months, describing a young man from the North who works as a law clerk and has intimations of being a writer. He made his hero a failure, though, having him succumb to marriage, ease, and security, and abandon writing. And after several months, in which to his critical eye the Usual did not transform itself, he experienced an evening in which it did, and he thereupon wrote the whole novel again in such a vein. His satisfaction lasted until the novel was finished, at which point he thought that the writing was probably hysterical. Five years later he wrote to H. G. Wells: 'There is much in it that is not authentic, merely fanciful and quasi-sentimental—I can see that now. But I seriously meant all of it at the time.'

The account in *The Truth About an Author* of his intentions in writing *A Man from the North* makes clear Bennett's concern for style and form. It also touches upon his first reservations about the creed of realism. He remarks that all of the stylistic elegance of the novel was to be achieved without any sacrifice of truth: 'Life being grey, sinister, and melancholy, my novel must be grey, sinister, and melancholy.' And then he adds: 'As a matter of strict fact, life deserved none of these epithets; I was having a very good time; but at twenty-seven one is captious, and liable to err in judgment.' But the significant aesthetic concern in *The Truth About an Author* is not for style or content but for beauty. It is this subject with which the book opens and closes:

I . . . who am so morbidly avaricious of beauty that I insist on finding it where even it is not. . . .

Say another thirty years of these emotional ingenuities, these interminable variations on the theme of beauty. Is it good enough?

In the middle of writing his next novel Bennett had an experience of beauty that made him a novelist.

A Man from the North was finished on 15 May 1896 and was accepted on the 28th of the same month by John Lane on the recommendation of one of his readers, the young John Buchan. It then lay untouched in Lane's office for eighteen months, and was published only after some dickering between Lane and Bennett. Before he finished writing *A Man from the North*, Bennett began thinking about the next novel, *Anna of the Five Towns*, and in September 1896 he started to write it. He soon left off. In January he took it up again, and abandoned it again. Later he wrote a whole draft, and then rewrote that. In all he spent four and a half years on the book. There were reasons. He became editor of *Woman* two months after beginning the novel. 'The office dogs me everywhere, night and day,' he wrote in his journal shortly thereafter. And when the editorship was under control, he had other things to consider. After a lapse of nearly three months in keeping his journal, he recorded on 12 September 1898:

In the meantime, partly owing to the influence of [Eden] Phillpotts, I have decided very seriously to take up fiction for a livelihood. A certain chronic poverty had forced upon me the fact that I was giving no attention to money-making, beyond my editorship, and so the resolution came about. Till the end of 1899 I propose to give myself absolutely to writing the sort of fiction that sells itself. My serious novel 'Anna Tellwright' with which I have made some progress is put aside indefinitely—or rather until I have seen what I can do. To write popular fiction is offensive to me, but it is far more agreeable than being tied daily to an office and editing a lady's paper; and perhaps it is less ignoble, and less of a strain on the conscience. To edit a lady's paper, even a relatively advanced one, is to foster conventionality and hinder progress regularly once a week. Moreover I think that fiction will pay better, and in order to be happy I must have a fair supply of money.

He thereupon sat down and wrote the first of his sensational novels, *The Ghost*. He had begun such a novel early in October 1894, before he began writing *A Man from the North*, but had given it up to write a series of seven stories on the occult for *Woman*. These stories appeared over Sarah Volatile's name in the first months of 1895, and they apparently encouraged him to make the new sensational novel of the same stuff. According to *The Truth About an Author* he composed each of the twenty-four chapters of *The Ghost* on each of twenty-four mornings (non-consecutive) as he walked to work along the Thames Embankment; and in the late afternoon of each of those days he wrote out each chapter, some 2,500 words. The novel was completed on 23 January 1899, and sold for £75 to the Tillotson syndicate for serial publication. Before he finished it, Bennett noted in the journal that his facility in writing had greatly increased in the preceding year. And he was so encouraged by this material success that he returned immediately to *Anna of the Five Towns* and by Easter completed a first draft, writing at the rate of 8,000 or 10,000 words a week.

The more serious problem in getting on with *Anna of the Five Towns* had to do with Bennett's gradual awakening to his own view of life and his own aims as a novelist. *A Man from the North* was a *tour de force* by a young man whose technical knowledge and skill were in advance of his understanding. So was *The Ghost* in its own way. At the outset of writing *Anna of the Five Towns* Bennett had a glimmering of what he wanted to do in a serious novel, and a year later he knew. In October 1896 there is a journal entry that stands alone: 'Essential characteristic of the really great novelist: a Christlike, all-embracing compassion.' Eleven months later, at the beginning of September 1897, this thought and the first thoughts about *Anna of the Five Towns* must have come together. Bennett was holidaying in France, and was called home by the news of the death of the fiancé of his youngest sister, Tertia, to whom he was closest of all his family. He wrote in his journal on 10 September:

> During this week, when I have been taking early morning walks with Tertia, and when I have been traversing the district after dark, the grim and original beauty of certain aspects of the Potteries, to which I have referred in the introduction to 'Anna Tellwright', has fully revealed itself for the first time. . . . It is *not* beautiful in detail, but the smoke transforms its ugliness into a beauty transcending the work of architects and of time. Though a very old town, it bears no sign of great age—the eye is never reminded of its romance and history—but instead it thrills and reverberates with the romance of machinery and manufacture, the romance of our fight against nature, of the gradual taming of the earth's secret forces. And surrounding the town on every side are the long straight smoke and steam wreaths, the dull red flames, and all the visible evidences of the immense secular struggle for existence. . . .

The first formal expression of this sense of beauty came with an anonymous article on the Potteries that he published in the 12 March 1898 issue of *Black & White*, of which Phillpotts was then assistant editor. And shortly before the article was published, he transformed this sense of beauty into the aesthetic principle that *Fame and Fiction* and *The Truth About an Author* touch upon:

> The day of my enthusiasm for 'realism', for 'naturalism', has passed. I can perceive that a modern work of fiction dealing with modern life may ignore realism and yet be great. To find beauty, which is always hidden; that is the aim. If beauty is found, then

superficial facts are of small importance. But they are of *some* importance. . . . My desire is to depict the deeper beauty while abiding by the envelope of facts. . . .

Such an illumination must have governed the writing of *Anna of the Five Towns* that followed in the next three months; but Bennett was not satisfied with the result, and rewrote the book in 1900–1.

By the end of 1900 Bennett was doing more work of more sorts than seems credible. He was editor (until September) of one journal, and a mainstay of two others. He was reviewing books at the rate of more than one a day, and also writing literary criticism of a high order. He counted the number of articles he wrote during the year as 196. Also during the year he wrote six short stories, one one-act play, two full-length plays (collaborating with Eden Phillpotts and Arthur Hooley), one sensational novel (*The Grand Babylon Hotel*, soon to have a sensational success), and most of the final draft of *Anna of the Five Towns* (which was to please the serious critics almost as much as *The Grand Babylon Hotel* pleased the public). In addition, he advised the C. Arthur Pearson organization on fifty manuscripts of books. His earnings for the year were £620: £6 a day, he said, for serial writing, and a self-imposed rate of productivity that guaranteed a minimum of ten shillings an hour for any commercial writing, a fair rise from the three-pence an hour he was making in 1893. He was obviously in need of a good literary agent, someone who during the next twenty years would supervise the rise to £55 a day, £20,000 a year.

He had already had an indifferent one. In May 1898 he became a client of William Morris Colles, who headed the Authors' Syndicate. Colles was one of the best-known agents of the time, perhaps mainly because his Syndicate, founded by him about 1889, began under the sponsorship of the Society of Authors. The early advertisements of the Syndicate mention that the management was voluntary and unpaid, that commissions went entirely into operating expenses, and that the Syndicate's services were available only to members of the Society of Authors. The situation must have changed by 1898, since Bennett was not a member of the Society of Authors until many years later. As editor of *Woman* he had corresponded with Colles in 1896, and he presumably came to him through Eden Phillpotts, for whose literary affairs Colles was then chief or sole agent. A description of Colles appears in Frederic Whyte's book on William Heinemann: 'a big, burly, bearded lawyer, with a wheezy infectious laugh—a sort of well-spoken, decent-minded, entirely reputable, nineteenth-century Falstaff'. Bennett himself was favourably impressed by Colles at their first meeting in May 1898. But the few surviving letters between them indicate that Colles never satisfied him thereafter. Colles failed to acknowledge receipt of stories, failed to sell them, had to be advised by Bennett where to sell them. Colles himself admitted his inadequacies. Their relationship ended in February 1902 with Bennett's saying: 'I cannot agree to you being my agent at all.' By this time Bennett was well-known enough for A. P. Watt to make an overture to him. But in the preceding December he had taken the advice of his friend H. G. Wells and gone to J. B. Pinker.

3. *James Brand Pinker*

The background of the founder of the Pinker firm is obscure. He was born in England in 1863 of parents in modest circumstances. His schooling was slight, and he appears to have earned his first wages as a clerk at the Tilbury docks. By 1887 or 1888 he was in Constantinople in the employ of the *Levant Herald*. He remained there three years, his work for the paper concerned mainly with the diplomatists in the city. Meanwhile, his fortunes had so risen that in one of these years Elizabeth Seabrooke, of a much more substantial family than his, sailed out from England to marry him. In 1890 or 1891 the couple returned to London, and Pinker took up duties as assistant editor of the illustrated weekly *Black & White*, which began publication on 6 February 1891, under the editorship of C. N. Williamson. During the first years of its existence, *Black & White* was a notable addition to the literary scene, printing articles and stories by Thomas Hardy, Robert Louis Stevenson, and Henry James. Among the members of its staff were M. H. Spielmann, the art critic, W. A. Mackenzie, author of *Rowton House Rhymes*, Eden Phillpotts, Violet Hunt, and Mrs. Belloc

J. B. PINKER

at about the time when he started his agency

Lowndes. One imagines that even in the most successful days
of the magazine Williamson and his assistant editor talked
about the pleasures of another sort of life; for presently
Williamson abandoned editing to help his wife write *The
Lightning Conductor* and other popular fiction, and presently
Pinker became a literary agent. The two men remained intimate friends over the years, and Pinker served as the Williamsons' agent.

While he was on the staff of *Black & White*, Pinker was also
a reader for a publishing house; and before he took the plunge
as an agent, he was briefly editor of *Pearson's Magazine*, a new
journal which began publication in January 1896. The aim of
Pearson's was to entertain the great public; and the fact that
Pinker was its first editor suggests that his capacities were presumed to range widely. His most profitable client of later
years, Arnold Bennett himself, was to prove extraordinarily
adept at moving between the *New Statesman* and the *Sunday
Pictorial*, and Pinker was apparently well prepared to handle
him. It is possible that he became editor of *Pearson's* with no
further intention than to help to launch the journal; at any
rate he quit his post before the first issue appeared. In the
middle of January 1896 he established himself as an agent, with
offices in Granville House, Arundel Street, and with H. G.
Wells (friend and neighbour at their homes in Worcester Park)
as one of his first clients. Within twenty months his reputation
was sufficiently large to bring Oscar Wilde to him in the hope of
finding an American editor to publish *The Ballad of Reading
Gaol*. Wilde was in the utmost distress, and for two or three
weeks he pinned absurd hopes on Pinker. Then, when Pinker
proved to be unable to sell the poem, Wilde wrote to Leonard
Smithers that Pinker was 'not to be trusted'. The poem was
placed in other hands. The episode seems mainly to suggest
that Pinker did not become an agent without first having made
himself well known in both London and New York. He was
in fact one of the first agents to have formal international
connexions.

His progress was rapid. He was the agent whom Stephen
Crane sought out in London in 1898, and by 1901 he acted for
Henry James, Joseph Conrad, and Arnold Bennett. James was
a great figure at the time; and his coming to Pinker after some

experience with A. P. Watt, the leading London agent, was an immediate measure of success. But Conrad and Bennett were uncertain quantities. That Pinker obtained them indicated the shrewdness and generosity which were to distinguish him as an agent. In the pages of the *Literary Year-Book* of these years is a description of his characteristic approach: 'Mr. Pinker has always made a special point of helping young authors in the early stages of their career, when they need most the aid of an adviser with a thorough knowledge of the literary world and the publishing trade.' The parallel description of Watt remarks incidentally that Watt is interested in helping young writers, but it is mainly given over to Sir Walter Besant's recommendation of him and to a list of more than fifty famous clients. The sort of risk that Pinker ran with Conrad is well expressed by Conrad's letter to him of 23 August 1899: 'My method of writing is so unbusinesslike that I don't think you could have any use for such an unsatisfactory person. I generally sell a work before it is begun, get paid when it is half done and don't do the other half till the spirit moves me. I must add that I have no control whatever over the spirit—neither has the man who has paid the money.' Pinker undertook to be one of the men who paid. For the next quarter of a century he advanced considerable sums of money to Conrad. In 1908 Conrad owed him £1,600. For several years Pinker managed Conrad's finances, paying for hotel rooms, cigars, and milk. When Mrs. Conrad wanted a new coat, Conrad wrote to Pinker to ask if it were possible. When Conrad had his pocket picked, he wrote to Pinker. In 1907 Conrad was urging Pinker to help him to 'settle down ... on an economical basis' and hoping that in three years he would be secure, and in 1919 he was needing Pinker to pay the expenses of his wife's illness.

Such a situation would have its irritations even if the author produced his novels and stories on time. In 1909 Pinker and Conrad quarrelled. Pinker suggested that he could advance no more money unless the writing of *Under Western Eyes* proceeded more satisfactorily, and Conrad threatened to throw the manuscript into the fire. The quarrel did not last. At one point or another, Pinker tried to solve the problem of moving Conrad's spirit by paying him so much per thousand words of delivered manuscript, rather in the manner of Dr. Johnson's publishers.

That the scheme produced books which otherwise would not have appeared may seem doubtful, but Conrad's sense of Pinker's importance to his creativity is unmistakable. In 1904 he heard that it was being said that Pinker treated him shabbily, and he wrote to Edmund Gosse to discountenance the rumour. Gosse had attacked the profession of literary agency more than once, and he very likely had had a hand in the rumour. Conrad wrote of Pinker:

He has stepped gallantly into the breach left open by the collapse of my bank: and not only gallantly, but successfully as well. He has treated not only my moods but even my fancies with the greatest consideration. . . . He cannot take away the weariness of mind which at the end of ten years of strain has come upon me; but he has done his utmost to help me to overcome it by relieving the immediate material pressure. . . . How much can he expect in return for these services? I don't know. But I fear I am not a 'profitable' man for anybody's speculation.

Pinker's risk with Conrad had, of course, the reward of such a letter as this. The warmth it displays survived the crisis of 1909, and a few years later Conrad wrote that his books 'owe their existence to Mr. Pinker as much as to me'. In these later years the two men became close personal friends. The 'dear Pinker' of earlier letters was now 'dearest Pinker', and the Pinker family were frequent guests at Capel House and Oswalds. Mrs. Conrad has described the pleasure to her and her husband of a visit of Pinker and his wife to the Conrads in Corsica in 1921. She has also described Conrad's shock at Pinker's sudden death in 1922. Conrad wrote to Pinker's son Eric of 'our sense of irreparable loss'.

With Arnold Bennett the situation was different. Bennett was entirely confident that one day he would be a valuable commodity to Pinker, and he produced his work with unusual promptitude. Pinker ran less of a risk, and he had the reward of many ten per cent. commissions. Nevertheless, he subsidized Bennett for nine years, during several of those years lending him £50 a month irrespective of Bennett's income. He charged five per cent. interest on a debt that stood above £1,000 at one time or another. He never won Bennett as a personal friend, as he did Conrad; but he won from him a similar admiration.

Both Bennett and Conrad began by treating the efficient businessman with a certain condescension, especially with respect
to his literary taste; and both came to see—in Conrad's words
—'qualities which were not perhaps obvious to the world'.

Pinker was sometimes less successful with his clients. Among
the files of the firm is a letter to him from an unknown correspondent who wishes to sever connexions. The relationship has
been unprofitable, and Pinker has done nothing to make it
profitable. Pinker's business manners exhibit an 'indifference so
curt as to be almost insulting'. Indeed, says the writer, 'I know
no one of less tact than yourself', and then he adds 'or greater
probity'. Letters from 1904 to 1911 from the Irish writer
Seumas MacManus reveal another connexion that was never
satisfactory and was finally broken off, this time by Pinker. The
most notable of Pinker's failures was with D. H. Lawrence.
Pinker appears to have made an approach to Lawrence in 1912
or later, very likely at the suggestion of Bennett, who was an
early admirer of Lawrence. Lawrence on his side expressed a
desire to have someone to conduct his business negotiations.
The relationship was never easy. Pinker had to trouble Lawrence with Methuen's request for deletions from *The Rainbow*
and with later objections to *Look! We Have Come Through*.
Lawrence had to trouble Pinker for money. In 1917 Lawrence
wrote to Lady Cynthia Asquith: 'I *can't* go on living here on a
miserable pittance which Pinker . . . will allow me. I can't take
a pittance from Pinker: it is too insulting.' Bennett was paying
part of the pittance. Almost three years later Lawrence broke
with Pinker: 'You told me when we made our agreement that
we might break it when either of us wished. I wish it should be
broken now. What bit of work I have to place, I like to place
myself.' He subsequently put his work into the hands of Curtis
Brown and Laurence Pollinger.

Long before he broke with Pinker, Lawrence described him
to a friend as 'that little parvenu snob of a procureur of books'.
From a lofty standpoint, the description must be true. Pinker
was not Lawrence or Conrad or Bennett. The memorials he
left behind him were not his own work, and the estate he left
behind was valued at £40,000. Perhaps the closest he came to
personal creativity was to collaborate with Conrad on a film
scenario of *Gaspar Ruiz*, and to supply Bennett with information

that Bennett used in his 'Observations' in the *New Statesman*. At the same time he was rather impressive in an ordinary human way, as the reminiscences of Arthur Waugh, Ford Madox Ford and Frank Swinnerton testify. Swinnerton, who was a friend and client for many years, describes him thus:

He was short, compact, a rosy, round-faced clean-shaven grey-haired sphinx with a protrusive under-lip, who drove four-in-hand, spoke distinctly in a hoarse voice that was almost a whisper, shook hands shoulder-high, laughed without moving, knew the monetary secrets of authors and the weaknesses of publishers, terrified some of these last and was refused admittance by others, dominated editors, and of course enjoyed much power. If he lied, as was said, he lied with an unchanging expression of composure; and I do not remember that he ever lied to me.

On the contrary, he repaid my unsentimental ingenuousness with occasional confessions, how far calculated I cannot now judge, of his likes and dislikes. He said candidly to one publisher, over a contract made direct with the author: 'But this is swindling!' 'Oh!' protested the publisher, 'that's a very strong word!' Pinker fixed those immovable eyes upon his victim. 'What other do you suggest?' 'Well', said the publisher, 'I admit it was sharp practice.' And so the contract was destroyed.

One other person who recollects Pinker with great affection is his former secretary, Miss Violet Barton. A letter from him to her perhaps gives the best direct glimpse into his character. The letter was written when Miss Barton was ill, and less than a month before Pinker's own death.

14 Jan 1922

My dear Miss Barton,

I am sorry to have such bad news from you—sorry for your sake first, and for my own and not only from the business point of view. I miss you and shall be glad when you come back. But you must not come until it is safe, because we manage to struggle on without too much hardship. Don't come back looking too thin, will you, because Miss Dyson seems to me to grow more fragile, and if you too look a shadow I shall be suspected of some subtle form of cruelty to my women folk.

Yes I have been ill, and I don't feel very fresh now, but I am

going to America on the 28th and hope the voyage will do me good.
    With best wishes and kindest regards, I am,
                                        Very sincerely yours,
                                                James B. Pinker

There is no doubt, though, that it is the literary agent rather
than the man who will be chiefly remembered; and for him
Conrad—not Lawrence—devised the right epithet: 'the Pinker
of agents'.

I

Early Years

1901–1908

In the autumn of 1900, Arnold Bennett resigned his editorship of Woman, *and left London to settle with his parents at Trinity Hall Farm in Bedfordshire. He was still on the staff of the* Academy *and* Hearth and Home, *and he was reading manuscripts for C. Arthur Pearson. It was perhaps as representative of one of these organizations that he wrote to J. B. Pinker the earliest known letter of their correspondence, the following letter of 5 January 1901. In December of 1901, H. G. Wells brought Bennett to Pinker as author to agent. The second known letter comes on 30 January 1902.*

TEXAS / MS. / 1

Trinity Hall Farm
Hockliffe
Bedfordshire
5th Jan 1901

Dear Mr. Pinker,

I will call on you tomorrow, Monday, at 12 o'clock. I hope you will be in then, as I shall not have too much time on my hands.

Yours very truly, E. A. Bennett

U.C. / MS. / 2

Trinity Hall Farm
30 Jan 1902

Dear Pinker,

A line to say that *Anna of the Five Towns* has *not* been seen by Lucas. It has been refused by Harpers American house for America.

Yours sincerely, E. A. Bennett

2. E. V. Lucas (1868–1938), an associate of Bennett's on the *Academy*, was a reader for Methuens, of which he eventually became chairman. *Anna of the Five Towns* was rejected by several firms before it was taken by Chatto and Windus, who published it in September 1902. See the comments on the book in the Introduction, pages 18–21.

u.c. / ms. / 3

Watling St. 35th mile stone
England
Trinity Hall Farm
24 Feby 1902

Dear Pinker,

Dent has sent me a prospectus of a new magazine *The Country*, edited by Harry Roberts (don't know him). I enclose *in duplicate* the first of a projected series of true & quietly humorous articles entitled *My Wild Adventures in Watling Street*, which should suit the said magazine or some other magazine. All the recent flood of effusions on the country that I have seen have been by experts in country lore. This series describes the experiences & sensations of a town-dweller, absolutely ignorant of the country, who suddenly went to live 3 miles from a railway station & is still enjoying it. I actually *do* live on Watling Street, & the articles are to describe fact. I have vast masses of more or less amusing experiences to draw from. If you will kindly read this first article & see what you think. . .! I expect the succeeding ones would be better, because one gets into this sort of thing; but I will stand or fall by this first one (3,000 words). If you think the notion ain't commercial, please say so.

Anyhow, I don't propose to do any more unless you can place a series on the strength of this first one. I have ten in mind, but I suppose all the lot would scarcely go into one magazine? I was thinking Dent might contract to publish in book form afterwards. They must appear as a book, or it isn't worth my while.

It seems to me that magazines are not so done up with light, amusing stuff, written in a distinguished style, and jewelled here & there with good stories, that this series ought to go begging long. But perhaps I am prejudiced.

Yours sincerely, E. A. Bennett

3. J. M. Dent (1849–1926) published *The Country* only in 1902. It was a polite country magazine, and had no room for Bennett's wild adventures. Apparently Bennett did not continue the series. In 1911 he published 'Watling Street: A Memory' in the *English Review*, and remarks therein: 'To me it was a wonderful road—more wonderful than the Great North Road, or the military road from Moscow to Vladivostock. And the most wonderful thing about it was that I lived on it. After all, few people can stamp the top of their notepaper, "Watling Street, England." It is not a residential thoroughfare.' (The essay appears in the collection of travel sketches *Paris Nights*, published in 1913.)

Harry Roberts (1871–1946) was a teacher, doctor, writer, and gardener as well as an editor.

TEXAS / MS. / 4

Trinity Hall Farm
3rd July 1902

Dear Pinker,
Touching McClure, I shall be in town one day next week &
will call on you. The matter is one for you to deal with of
course; but it seems to me that if McClure buys a book in the
dark—he buys it in the dark. As a business man he must have
known that he ran a risk. I didn't expect he would like the book;
but Chatto's imprint on this side ought to be sufficient assurance
to him that he isn't absolutely making a spectacle of himself in
publishing it. If a firm like his can't make such arrangements
as will ensure them against actual loss on *any* novel that they
choose to handle specially, I am a Dutchman.
                              Yours sincerely, E. A. Bennett

I enclose a cutting that Hind has just sent me.

U.C. / MS. / 5

Trinity Hall Farm
16th Augt 1902

Dear Pinker,
I enclose a short story, 'Nocturne at the Majestic' (6,300
words), which is meant to combine the virtues of the popular &
the rather high-class short story. I shall be glad if you will read
it, & let your acumen play upon it, & tell me whether it is the
sort of stuff you can sell in good places.
                              Yours sincerely, E. A. Bennett

4. S. S. McClure (1857–1949), founder of the McClure Syndicate, contracted
to publish *Anna of the Five Towns* in America. The book was issued by McClure,
Phillips in 1903. In his autobiography, McClure wrote that he 'judged a story with
my solar plexus rather than my brain'.
   C. Lewis Hind (1862–1927) was editor of the *Academy*, for which Bennett had
written his most important journalism of the previous three years, notably the
series of critical articles that were later collected under the title *Fame and Fiction* and
the autobiographical sketches of *The Truth About an Author*.
   5. The story appeared in the *Windsor Magazine* in May 1904. It was later published in *Tales of the Five Towns*.

u.c. / ms. / 6

Trinity Hall Farm
16th Oct 1902

My dear Pinker,

Do not fail to get the Literary Supplement to the *New York Times* for Oct 4th & see W. L. Alden's extraordinary appreciation of *Anna*. He says it is the best novel of the sort since *Esther Waters*. (It is.) You should lay it before McClures with your compliments & mine.

Yours sincerely, E. A. Bennett

I have sent my cutting to Chatto.

u.c. / ms. / 7

Trinity Hall Farm
28 Dec 1902

My dear Pinker,

I am much obliged for the super-prompt cheque for £100.

The other day I called merely to tell you that I had chucked all my journalism except *T. P.'s Weekly*, which pays me well. I could not stand Hind any longer, & in a fit of infinite disgust I took a cab & went round to sundry editors & gave them notice. I lose £5 or £6 a week over it; but I am extremely glad I did it. The relief is enormous. I am sick of reviewing. I shall have more time for fiction, & I shall trust to you to see that this plunge of mine does not land me in the Bankruptcy Court.

I have done *The Truth About an Author*, & Service will receive it on Dec 31. when his cheque will be due to you. I think the book is the best of its sort. Forgive this modesty.

With kindest wishes,

Yours sincerely, E. A. Bennett

6. William L. Alden (1837–1908) wrote in his 'London Letter' column:
    'I have read every novel of importance that has been published in England for the last ten years, and, of its kind, *Anna of the Five Towns* is certainly the best piece of work since *Esther Waters*. . . . Work so good as that which Mr. Bennett has here done can hardly fail of its reward. . . . We shall hear more of him as time goes on.'
7. In addition to his work for Hind on the *Academy*, Bennett was reviewing for *Hearth and Home* and may still have been reading manuscripts for C. Arthur Pearson. He relied on Pinker not only to sell his writing but also to lend him £50

TEXAS / MS. / 8

Hôtel du quai Voltaire
Paris
27 Mch 1903

My dear Pinker,

Thank you for your letter & the copy letter from Messrs. Constable.

With regard to titles, I do not object to *The Apprenticeship of an Author*, but I think strongly that my title is a much better selling title, & unless Messrs. Constable can make other suggestions I should part with it with regret. The three other titles which they give do not seem to me to be satisfactory.

As regards the close of the book this change of key is very deliberately intentional. There is a great deal more in the book than 'pleasant irony', & I particularly want the reader to feel that he has not merely been assisting at a circus. The close of the book, as it stands, will 'bring him up all standing,' & this is the effect that I desire. I feel sure that Messrs. Constable will see my argument.

By the way, in negotiating, when you give way on anything, you should exact as a quid pro quo that the book is issued at once.

Yours sincerely, E. A. Bennett

---

every month irrespective of his income. On this detail and on Hind see the Introduction, pages 16–17, 25–26.

F. Stanley Service was manager of the book publishing department of the Pearson organization, and Bennett was delivering *How to Become an Author* (not *The Truth About an Author*) to him. A letter of the following day makes the same slip. Pearsons published *How to Become an Author* the following September.

8. In an article entitled 'The Desire for France' Bennett recalls how from the time he was eighteen he was drawn to the literature of France. He was now free to live where he chose, and he made France his home for the next nine years. The Hôtel du quai Voltaire was his residence until he settled into his flat at 4 rue de Calais in September.

Constable suggested other titles for *The Truth About an Author*, including *A Man and Author*, by One; *The Journeyman Author: or Writing Revealed*, by an Adept; and *The Literary Ladder*, by a Climber. (The book was published anonymously.) Constable thought that 'the book would have expired more appropriately in a light shower of chaff or to the accompaniment of a salvo of cynical crackers, aphorisms or epigrams'. Bennett's ending to his delightful and true account reads:

'And sometimes I would suddenly halt and address myself:

"You may be richer or you may be poorer; you may live in greater pomp and luxury, or in less. The point is that you will always be, essentially, what you are now. You have no real satisfaction to look forward to except the satisfaction of

u.c. / ms. / 9

Hôtel du quai Voltaire
10 April 1903

My dear Pinker,

In returning proofs of some old commissioned work to Lever
Tillotson a few days ago, I referred to the prices I was getting
from *T. P.*, *Windsor*, etc, and asked why his firm shouldn't find
it remunerative to pay me the same prices, reversing their
decision of last year to offer me not more than £2 a thousand—
an offer which I declined. In his reply he offers me a definite
commission of 12,000 words of short stories at £2. 10/- a
thousand. Kindly tell me whether I ought to accept this, as of
course I shall not act contrary to your opinion. He *might* be
screwed up to a little more, but I doubt it, & if I tried for more
in vain & then accepted the original sum my dignity would not
glitter. Remember this is for world's serial rights. They sell my
stuff to the *Sphere* & to the *Queen* in London, & I fancy they also
place it in America.

I may see Lever Tillotson in Paris during the next few weeks;
he is getting married & going to Italy for his honeymoon.

It is only fair to say also that if I accept this commission (4
stories) I shan't be able to let you have any elaborate short
stories to offer to magazines for about six months.

What thought you of my 'Hungarian Rhapsody' in *T. P.*?

Yours sincerely, E. A. Bennett

---

continually inventing, fancying, imagining, scribbling. Say another thirty years
of these emotional ingenuities, these interminable variations on the theme of
beauty. Is it good enough?"

And I answered: Yes.

But who knows? Who can preclude the regrets of the dying couch?'

9. James Lever Tillotson (1875–1940) was in these years head of the fiction
bureau of the provincial newspaper syndicate of Tillotsons. The syndicate had
connexions in America with S. S. McClure. The *Sphere* published the story 'The
Episode in Room 222' on 17 January 1903; the *Queen* published 'The Police
Station' on 15 September 1900 and 'The Farrls and a Woman' on 17 October
1903. The first two stories were republished in an edition of *The Loot of Cities*
published by Thomas Nelson in 1917; the third does not appear in any of the short
story collections.

'The Hungarian Rhapsody' appeared in *T. P.'s Weekly*, 10 April 1903. It was
later published in *Tales of the Five Towns*.

Hôtel du quai Voltaire
9th May 1903

My dear Pinker,

Thank you for your letter of the 7th. I should like to do a series of stories in the vein of 'Nocturne at the Majestic'. I contemplated such a series nearly a year ago, & offered it to Tillotsons but they would not pay enough. Further, these would serve well to get me into the vein of my *big* book, which I shall do next year, called *The City of Pleasure*, the whole of which moves in the hotel-restaurant-Covent Garden ball atmosphere. I shall therefore be glad—apart from financial considerations—if you can fix the matter up.

In the autumn I am going to do a high class serial (à la *Grand Bab.*) upon whose quality I think you can rely. If *T. P. Weekly* cotton to it, so much the better. But if they don't, I have no doubt you will be able to place it elsewhere.

My weekly article in *T. P. W.* has 'caught on' so that they have asked me to enlarge it. They were giving me 2 guineas for 2 cols (1000 words). I tried for 3½ guineas for 1300 words, but I have not been able to get more than 3 guineas, for the present. This will do.

Anna is better appreciated by French people than English I find. Marcel Schwob, who is about the first authority on higher literature in France, has written me that it is the most impressive novel he has read for years. The French translator of Stevenson & Gissing, Georges Art, is going to translate it; Schwob has offered to write an introduction, & they seem to think they may place it first as a serial in some first-class French newspaper or periodical, such as the *Débats* or the *Revue de Paris*. Imagine *Anna* as a serial in England!

One of Putnam's home editors, a man named Jessup, has written me from America asking me to write an introduction to a volume of translations of de Maupassant which they are publishing. This was on the strength of my articles on the 'Short Story' in the *Academy*. He offered 20 dollars a thousand. But the fool writes from America on April 20th & says the volume must be in the printers' hands on June 1st! And he has not yet even chosen the stories. So I have had to write him that I can't do the introduction without an extension of time.

I feel pretty sure that *Leonora* will be completed by 30th June. I shall then return to England. I am going to spend part of the summer with Phillpotts on Dartmoor. I still think I can gently influence him to come over to you bodily.

Yours sincerely, E. A. Bennett

P.S. I shall come back to Paris in the autumn.

U.C. / MS. / 11　　　　　　　　　　　　　　Hôtel du quai Voltaire
24 June 1903

My dear Pinker,

Many thanks for your letter. I am glad to hear you have arranged with Tauchnitz for *The Gates of Wrath*. We have now, I hope, done finally with that wretched production.

As you predicted, Lever Tillotson has given way about the terms for short stories, & he has ordered 12,000 words length of stories at 36 guineas. Kindly credit yourself, in our accounts, with whatever percentage you think proper in this matter. If the *Windsor* decide on the six short stories, do not fix up dates until I have perpended upon my creative power during the next few months. Tillotson wants two stories in August.

Yours sincerely, E. A. Bennett

10. The stories like 'Nocturne' are presumably the group of six that were published in book form in 1905 under the title *The Loot of Cities*. They were written in the autumn of 1903 and appeared in the *Windsor Magazine* the following summer and autumn. *The City of Pleasure*, Bennett's best sensational novel, was not written until the spring of 1905. The high-class serial was not written at all. The weekly article, *Savoir Faire Papers*, written anonymously by 'The Man Who Does', ran from 14 November 1902 to 6 November 1903 in *T. P.'s Weekly*.

Georges Art (b. 1872) was a professor at the conservatory at Nantes. Marcel Schwob (1867–1905) is described elsewhere by Bennett as 'my literary godfather in France'.

Putnam's offer came to nothing. Bennett's articles on the short story appeared in the *Academy* on 16 August and 11 October 1902.

Leonora was a serious novel in the vein of *Anna of the Five Towns*. Bennett began writing it towards the end of 1902 and apparently finished it before 30 June.

Eden Phillpotts (1862–1960) had been Bennett's friend since 1897. From 1900 to 1907 the two men collaborated on several plays and at least two sensational novels. Phillpotts' chief or sole agent at this time was William Morris Colles (see page 21). He did not come to Pinker.

Bennett planned to come to England for the summer. He was perhaps just now deciding firmly that Paris would be his home.

* 11. *The Gates of Wrath* was the second sensational novel that Bennett wrote. Chatto and Windus published it earlier in the year.

U.C. / MS. / 12

> c/o Eden Phillpotts Esq.
> Eltham
> Torquay
> 10th Sept 1903

My dear Pinker,

I shall be in London a week today, for one day, 17th inst, & will call on you in the morning, as I wish to discuss with you what work I am to do next after the *Windsor* short stories. I have two things ready to work at (1) a serious novel, better than *Leonora*, study of a woman, only the first chapter in the 5 Towns, the rest in London & Paris, very dramatic, but impossible for a serial. (2) a book on the lines of the *Grand Babylon*, but better, & primarily intended for a serial. I am counting on a book of short stories being issued in the spring, but it has occurred to me that another novel ought to be ready for book publication in the autumn of 1904, so as to keep hammering at the British public. Now if I do the serial first, I should have no novel ready for the autumn, as it would not get through in time. (At the earliest I couldn't finish it before June 30th. I have arranged to write a play with Phillpotts in the spring, which will take at least six weeks.) I would as soon do the serial first, but it occurs to me that perhaps I had better do the serious novel first. Kindly consider this. I shall be guided by you.

Please get for me at trade price 3 copies of *Truth about an author*, & 2 extra copies (besides free copies) of *How to become an author* (which Service says is to be issued middle of this month) & have them sent to my flat on or before Thursday.

I hope you enjoyed your brief holiday.

> Yours sincerely, E. A. Bennett

12. The serious novel was *Sacred and Profane Love*, which Bennett deferred writing until November 1904. Instead of a serial, Bennett began writing *A Great Man* in December 1903. His first collection of short stories, *Tales of the Five Towns*, was not published until 1905. The play with Phillpotts, *Christina*, was duly written, but never produced or published.

U.C. / MS. / 13

4 rue de Calais
Paris
25 Oct 1903

My dear Pinker,

Many thanks for your letter & cheque for £25.

With regard to Methuen, I do not, personally, see how we can do anything with him, at any rate at present. The next novel anyhow is contracted for with Chatto. And I don't think he can sell more copies of a book than Chatto. That, however, is a point for you. The only drawback of Chatto is that my serious books seem always rather lonely & peculiar in his lists, between Frank Barrett, & Fred Whishaw & Co.

The *Savoir Faire Papers* finish in *T. P.'s Weekly* next week. (I am going to take up another feature for them by way of change, which I hope will be equally successful.) There will be 52 papers, but the last two I might probably prefer to leave out of a book. Total about 60,000 words. Can you do anything with this now? If so, kindly get the complete file from Whitten. My idea is a 1/- book (pseudonymous), & if 60,000 words is too much, some papers might be omitted not unadvantageously. The thing has certainly been a marked success in the paper, & has elicited an extraordinary amount of correspondence, mostly enthusiastically favourable.

Yours sincerely, E. A. Bennett

U.C. / MS. / 14

4 rue de Calais
22nd Nov 1903

My dear Pinker,

I shall finish the *Windsor* stories next week, (they ought to be pleased with them), & the week after that I shall have done the

13. A flat at 4 rue de Calais was Bennett's home for the next three years.

A. M. S. Methuen (1856–1924), sometime schoolmaster and textbook-writer, made his publishing name in 1892 with Kipling's *Barrack-room Ballads*. Andrew Chatto (d. 1913), who headed the firm of Chatto and Windus, was the successor of John Camden Hotten, the founder. Frank Barrett (1848–1926) had *The Sin of Olga Zassoulich* to his credit. Fred Whishaw wrote historical romances dealing with Russian life; he was also an early translator of Dostoievsky.

The new feature, *A Novelist's Log-Book*, began on 13 November. It was unexpectedly discontinued the following May, apparently for reasons of economy.

Wilfred Whitten (d. 1942), a former colleague of Bennett's on the *Academy*, was at this time an editor of *T. P.'s Weekly*; later he became John O'London.

other two stories for Tillotsons, so that I shall then be clear of commissions. I have just had an idea for a humorous novel (purely humorous), just long enough for 6/-, which, after I had begun it I could do in about 5 or 6 weeks. I have, however, to devote a certain amount of time to the play with Phillpotts. I would like you to ascertain from Chattos the latest date at which they could receive the manuscript, for publishing in the spring season (*not* autumn). And also whether they would be prepared to label the book in the advertisements as distinctly *humorous* & to advertise it rather specially. It might do well. I would guarantee that it would set the journalists writing about it.

Also this: I have a really fine idea for a 16,000 or 20,000 serious but dramatic & powerful story, called 'The History of Two Old Women'. You understand, it is as serious as *Leonora*, but it has a serial interest. Do you think there is any chance of serialising that? It happens that Whitten wrote me only the other day & said that they might ask me for a stop-gap 4 instalment story to be used after Christmas. I replied that if they did want it they must let me know, & not 'rush' me, as they tried to do over that other serial which came to nothing on the question of terms. Do you know anything of how they are fixed? Perhaps you might, without giving the least hint that I have said anything to you, ascertain what the situation is.

I have got a perfect fever for work now, & am in excellent form. But I don't think my next serious novel, *Camilla*, will be sufficiently 'stewed' for me to begin writing it for some time to come. You said I had better do a serial next. (I don't count the humorous novel as work; it would be pastime for me.) Supposing I do a serial, what about it? From what you have seen of the *Windsor* stories, do you think that series is likely to put my price up? You know I would write books like *Leonora* for pleasure & nothing else; but I don't precisely write serials for fun, & when I do them I want to get the last penny out of them.

By the way the reviews of *Leonora* in *Athenaeum*, *Sketch*, & *T. P.'s Weekly* have much pleased me. The swine on the *Chronicle* hadn't read the book, & refrained from saying anything very definite.

Bear with all these details, my dear Pinker. I write because

I see from that admirable book, *How to become an author*, that an author should keep his agent fully abreast of his ideas.

> Yours sincerely, E. A. Bennett

Whitten is more than satisfied with my new series of articles in *T. P. W.*

Why in hell hasn't H. G. W. sent me 12 stories & a nightmare. It is the nightmare I want to read.

TEXAS / MS. / 15

> 4 rue de Calais
> 28 Nov 1903

My dear Pinker,

Many thanks for yours, which did not arrive till last post last night, and as I believe that you are not in town on Saturdays I did not trouble to telegraph this morning.

I should much like to do the tale, in 4 instalments if possible. See my last letter for particulars. Whitten is *extremely* keen on *Leonora*, & might welcome something in the same key. This projected story deals with the entire life history of two sisters, & does not end unhappily. My negotiations with *T. P. W.* for a serial last year broke down because I would not take a penny less than 15 guineas per instalment. Whitten told me privately he thought he could have got me 12 guineas. So you know how things stand. I will not do this story now, except on a definite commission. But you may safely guarantee it will be my very best work, & full of plot. The idea came to me all of a sudden— & that sort of idea is always fine and inspiring.

> Yours sincerely, E. A. Bennett

14. The humorous novel was *A Great Man*. The fine idea was ultimately *The Old Wives' Tale*. Camilla became Carlotta, the heroine of *Sacred and Profane Love*. (Bennett was soon to use the name Camilla in one of his sensational novels.)

H. G. Wells (1866–1946) had recently published *Twelve Stories and a Dream* ('A Dream of Armageddon'). He and Bennett became friends in 1897, when Bennett was reviewing his books in *Woman*. The lifelong friendship between the two men is recorded in the collection of their correspondence edited by Harris Wilson in 1959: *Arnold Bennett and H. G. Wells*. Included therein is an article on Wells written by Bennett in 1902.

15. *Leonora*, like much of *The Old Wives' Tale*, deals with the life of a middle-aged woman.

4 rue de Calais
2nd Dec 1903

My dear Pinker,

Many thanks for your letter, received tonight. It was Whitten who just wrote to me about a short serial. I replied, as to that, & as to other things, & am still awaiting a letter from him. I don't care to write him again on that till I hear from him. But I am quite sure that his influence will be used to the utmost without any prompting from me. So go ahead.

As to the humorous novel, my notion was that it should be published middle of May—surely a good time; or even later. I should not care to promise the MS. before the end of March. Please see if this cannot be arranged. I much want to do the novel, anyhow, but one reason for wanting to do it is to have a book out in the spring. I attach importance to this, though I don't think you do. I have no 'views' as to terms; this is your department. But don't forget that we are under contract to give Chatto another book for £75 down. If you can persuade him that this humorous novel is special & demands more, and give him a volume of short stories to fulfil the contract, so much the better. There is a volume of *Tales of the Five Towns* ready. But if I do the serial for *T. P. W.*, I would include that in the volume of tales, as the two heroines will be born in Bursley.

Certainly the two books which Chatto has in hand *must* be suppressed, in England, at all costs. If he will take a volume of short stories in the place of the two (neither is long enough for a 6/- novel), I shall be satisfied; but perhaps you can arrange something better than this, something that will not mean money out of my pocket next year.

I have now finished all the *Windsor* stories, & they are being typewritten. I think they are a bit more than all right, & I shall have no artistic objection to their being published as a book. I fancy Ward Locks would like to do them & would pay pretty well, & you could tell Chatto that I preferred in future to keep that sensational line *out* of his list. But this is a matter entirely for you.

Also I have done the two remaining stories of my contract with Tillotsons, and am delivering today, with a request to them to pay the money to you. The sum is 18 guineas & is due at the end of the month.

Kindly also collect 12 guineas from *Hearth & Home* for story, 'Phantom', in their Christmas Number.

It is of course, as you indicate, of much importance that the *T. P. W.* serial question should be decided at once. This week I am working on the play which I am doing with Phillpotts, but I should like to know by Monday or Tuesday at latest definitely about the serial. If it is 'off' I shall proceed instantly with the humorous novel. You might wire me if it is arranged (I mean the serial). I happen to be in tremendous form for work.

Yours sincerely, E. A. Bennett

TEXAS / MS. / 17

Hôtel d'Italie
Menton
1st Feby 1904

My dear Pinker,

Many thanks. I think it's scarcely good enough. As Tillotson is already paying me £3/3/- a thousand for short stories, I don't see why he should give less for a serial. Moreover he wants *all* the Continental rights, usually, & that means £30 at least for a good sensational serial. I know he made £40 out of continental rights of *Grand Babylon*. And another early serial of mine, which he bought, is just beginning in *La Sera*, of Milan. I had the advertisement today. I have little doubt in my own mind that you will have no difficulty in getting £3/3/- a thousand for English rights for the serial that I shall do, as it will be a good

16. The humorous novel, *A Great Man*, was begun on 10 December and finished on 13 March. It was published on 19 May.

Tales of the Five Towns was published in 1905, and did not include the tale of the two sisters, which was deferred until October of 1907.

Andrew Chatto had in hand two early sensational serials, *Love and Life* and *Teresa of Watling Street*.

Ward Lock published the *Windsor Magazine*, in which the series of stories *The Loot of Cities* appeared. Alston Rivers, not Ward Lock, published the collection in 1905.

The Tillotson stories were probably 'The Railway Station' and 'Saturday to Monday'. Information on periodical publication is unavailable, except that the latter story appeared early in November 1904. It also appeared in an expanded edition of *The Loot of Cities* published by Thomas Nelson in 1917. The other story has not been republished in any collection of Bennett's short stories.

'Phantom' appears in *Tales of the Five Towns*.

The Phillpotts play, *Christina*, was written from about 20 January to 5 February of the following year. Bennett was probably at this point sketching some ideas.

one. Whereas, if I knew I was doing the thing as a cheap-ish commission for Tillotson I might be inclined to scamp it. In any case you can plant it on to Tillotson after you have actually seen it, if you think Tillotson is good enough for it. Anyhow, the decision, as always, is with you.

Yours sincerely, E. A. Bennett

TEXAS / MS. / 18

4 rue de Calais
[postmarked 14 March 1904]

My dear Pinker,

By concurrent registered parcel post I send you the complete MS. of *A Great Man*. It is almost exactly the length I predicted, 60,000 words. Kindly acknowledge receipt.

You will no doubt remind Chatto that he has promised to give the book special attention & to advertise it as 'a humorous novel'.

As regards America, I assume that in any case you will secure the formal copyright there. Personally I can't see how anyone can read the book without laughing; but one never knows.

It will be well for you to instruct Chatto's *printers* how to send the proofs over here. Otherwise I shall be let in for a lot of excess postage. I prefer to have all the proofs at once; I would undertake to correct them in two days.

I see Chatto is advertising a 3/6 edition of *Grand Babylon*.

I will return proofs of *Windsor* story in a few days.

Yours sincerely, E. A. Bennett

17. Bennett spent a working holiday at Menton from 14 January to 12 February. Phillpotts was with him.

The Grand Babylon Hotel was written in 1900, published serially in the *Golden Penny*, beginning 2 February 1901, and published in book form in 1902. It had a considerable success.

La Sera was publishing *Love and Life* (later revised and called *The Ghost*), Bennett's first sensational work, written in 1898–9.

18. *A Great Man* was not published in America until 1910 (see page 94n.).

The *Windsor* story was 'Nocturne at the Majestic', which appeared in the May issue.

TEXAS / MS. / 19

4 rue de Calais
[postmarked 8 April 1904]

[no salutation]

Many thanks for cheque safely received.

I have sold the French translation of *Anna of the 5 Towns* serially to *Le Temps*, the most serious & important newspaper in France. As this is a rather rare thing for a sternly serious novel like that, perhaps you could impart the fact to some literary paragraphist. The price is *nothing*, but I will account for it to you in due course.

E. A. B.

U.C. / MS. / 20

4 rue de Calais
18 Apl 1904

My dear Pinker,

Enquiries about the publication of *Savoir Faire Papers* in book form still persist from readers of *T. P.'s Weekly*. Also *A Novelist's Log-Book* comes to an end in about 3 weeks time, & this feature too has had a great success, & enquiries about its publication in book form are frequent. Anyone who wants to know what sort of effect these things have had on a solid regular public of 150,000 a week has only got to enquire at the editorial department of *T. P.'s W.* I am now getting anxious to have them both published, & by Chatto & Windus. It seems to me that if you see Mr. Chatto, & explain to him that I am keen on these things personally, because I do not want them to be wasted, & point out to him that so far as I am concerned our connection is to be a permanent one, he will agree to some arrangement.

1. *Savoir Faire Papers*. I really believe this would sell, if issued cheap (say 1/- in paper) with a proper sub-title. I think it would sell well.

2. *A Novelist's Log-Book*. I do not think this is a gold mine, & I merely want it published (like *The Truth about an author*) for

19. The translation of *Anna of the Five Towns*, by Georges Art (see pages 37–38), was apparently published in *Écho de Paris*, not in *Le Temps*. Files of the journal were not available.

the satisfaction of myself & a few admirers. It is an intensely personal thing, & I believe it to be good, and original too. *I do not care 2d about terms.* All I wish is that it should exist as a book. It is rather longer than *The Truth about an author,*—about 33,000 words. The *Savoir Faire* stuff, when I have edited it, will be about 55,000 to 60,000 words.

There should not be too much delay in publishing, for internal reasons of the matter.

Mr. Chatto has *Love & Life* & *Teresa*, which I want him definitely to suppress—both of them. I should like to deal with him perfectly frankly & fairly in the way of exchange. It has occurred to me that he might take these other two books in exchange, and if, when he has published them, he finds that they have not done sufficiently well to make the exchange a just one, I shall be quite willing to consider the affair further. This is my rough idea, & if you like you can read this letter to Mr. Chatto; but that is your business, & I shall be glad to have your views if they are different from mine. Only you clearly understand that I wish these two *T. P's* books to be published, & by C. & W.

I want a volume entitled *Tales of the Five Towns* to be published in the autumn. All the stuff has appeared except 'Nocturne at the Majestic', which I expect the *Windsor* will publish in May or June.

Kindly reimpress on C. & W. that I want *A Great Man* to be persistently labelled in the advertisements as *a humorous novel*. I notice they have not yet done so. And will you please point out to them that advertisements of this novel in *T. P's W.* as 'by the author of *Savoir Faire Papers* and *Novelist's Log-Book*' will beyond question be remunerative. T. P. is always being asked to reveal my name in order that readers may obtain my novels. The name will be revealed in three weeks time, & Whitten will engineer a special log-roll for me, with particular reference to *A Great Man*. As the book will be issued just afterwards, this will be good. The suggestion is not mine at all, but Whitten's.

I am happy to say that I have begun a sensational serial compared to which the *Grand Babylon Hotel* is nothing. Its title is simply & majestically

'HUGO'

It will be immense.

Yours sincerely, E. A. Bennett

U.C. / MS. / 21

4 rue de Calais
24 Apl 1904

My dear Pinker,

Many thanks for your letter. I wish I could talk to you so that we might understand each other better. I expect you have some good reasons for what you say but I do not understand them. Personally I am very strongly of opinion that it is a great mistake to pile up books in waiting for another book which is intended to make a boom. I think it is best to go on in the ordinary way, & let the 'selected' book do what it can when it does appear but not to let it interfere with the general course. *No* one knows or can prophesy what will boom. One has only

20. Chatto nevertheless published *Teresa of Watling Street* before the end of the year and *Love and Life* (as *The Ghost*) in 1907. In a letter of 1924 to E. V. Lucas, Bennett says, 'I always regard *Teresa* as the world's worst novel'.

Bennett was revealed as the author of the *Savoir Faire Papers* and *A Novelist's Log-Book* when the latter series came to an end on 6 May. On 8 July the book review column began: 'Readers of this journal who have so constantly testified to their appreciation of the author of the *Savoir Faire Papers* and *A Novelist's Log-Book* will welcome the appearance of *A Great Man*, by Arnold Bennett.' The publisher of *T. P.'s Weekly* was T. P. O'Connor (1848–1929), who later became a Member of Parliament. He was founder of several journalistic enterprises, including the daily newspaper, the *Star*.

Hugo appears in a different light in Violet Hunt's recollections of Bennett in his early Paris days:

'He told me he wrote four books a year. One shocker, two populars and one to please himself. He would scold me for reading the shockers:

"I distinctly told you *not* to read *Hugo*. It is astonishing that I cannot keep my friends from reading the un-literature which I write solely in order to be in a position to offer myself a few luxuries."'

to look back at the books which have founded reputations during the last ten years & to ask one's self how many publishers, or even agents, would have backed them before publication to succeed. I fully believe that *Hugo* will come up to expectations, but I much object to it interfering with my normal course. No good work that intervenes between the present time & its publication can possibly vitiate its chances. And after all the surest way to consolidate one's position is to keep on steadily producing sound work. One cannot produce too much sound work. One can only produce too much scamped work. And no one who knows anything of the subject can say that any of my work is not well & honestly done. I am absolutely certain that the publication of any of the books you have in hand can do nothing but good to my position; it can't do harm.

Moreover we must not get into arrear with publication. You must remember that my normal rate of production is about 5 books of all sorts in two years. There is *The Loot of Cities*, which will make a good 3/6 book, besides these others. You will have *Hugo* at the end of July, but you cannot count on its publication as a book until next summer at the earliest.

Lastly I regard it as very important that the book of 'Five Towns' stories should appear in the autumn, because they are serious work, in the vein by which (whatever happens in the meantime) I shall ultimately make the most money. What with *A Great Man, Loot of Cities,* & *Hugo* the public would stand a good chance of losing sight completely of the author of *Leonora*. This must not be. It cannot be too clearly understood that though one may do lighter work for the sake of a temporary splash etc. & for relief, it is the *Leonora* type which is & will be the solid foundation of the reputation. It is *Leonora* & *Anna* which will be talked of 20 years hence, when people will wonder why they attracted so little notice at the time. This is certainly my opinion, but it is also the opinion of a number of other persons well able to judge, as you are no doubt aware.

Anyhow, I don't see how the two *T. P.* books affect my fictional side at all. A novelist has by long custom the right to throw off by-products which do not affect his novels either way.

I am in a rather influenzic state of health, & perhaps not over-clear, but you will have gathered my trend. I am firmly

of opinion that the *Tales of the Five Towns* & at least one of the
T. P. books should be issued this year.

Yours sincerely, E. A. Bennett

P.S. You will not forget my suggestions about advertising *A
Great Man* to Chatto.

u.c. / ms. / 22

4 rue de Calais
27 Apl 1904

My dear Pinker,
  Many thanks for your letter. I entirely disagree with your
theory. I should like to have an instance of a man who spoiled
his reputation by too rapid production of good work. I can't
think of any. Here is Phillpotts producing regularly three books
a year; his work is certainly not improving, but the point is that
his income steadily *is* improving. I am perfectly certain you are
wrong & that Chatto would be wrong. According to your idea,
I shall never be able to publish certain books, because there will
never be space for them in a year. By the end of this year I shall
have finished another serious novel, *Carlotta*. You will then have
*Carlotta, Hugo, Loot of Cities, Savoir Faire Papers, Novelist's Log-
Book*, & a volume of literary criticism, all of which are decidedly
worth publishing in book form, & ought to be so published.
You would be under a false impression if you imagined that I
am working at pressure. I am not. I could do lots more. I have
vast leisure. When I think that I wrote the *Grand Babylon Hotel*
in less than a month & that I am taking over 3 months with
Hugo, I ask myself, Why? You don't yet realise what an engine
for the production of fiction you have in me. I could take long
holidays & still produce as much as you would require from
me, but the fact is I am never content unless I am turning out
the stuff. I have much the same objection to holidays that you
have. I ruined my summer last year by 3 months idleness. You
must accustom yourself to these facts & do what you can to
meet them.
  However, with regard to the particular point at issue, I am
nothing if not logical, & it would appear to me very illogical
for me to fly in the face of your last two letters. It is absurd to

pay an expert for advice & then only to take the advice when it agrees with your own views. You will therefore have your way as regards the output for this year. And of course I shall not keep on telling you that I think you are wrong. I accept your advice.

But there is to be no mistake about that volume of short stories, which from every point of view is most important. Chatto can have the stuff as soon as he likes.

And you might just hint to Chatto what has passed between us. It will prepare his mind for the exciting & eventful future.

The public & the reviewers always have given way, & always will give way, to the idiosyncrasies of an author who is strong enough to make them. The history of literature is nothing but the performance by authors of feats which the best experience had declared could not be performed. You say, & experience would perhaps support you, that the public cannot be made to buy more than an average 2 books a year by one author. I say it can, & I am as certain that I shall make it as I am certain, my dear Pinker, that I am yours always,

E. A. Bennett

You think me a blustering person, Pinker, but I am not. The truth is you twist me round your little finger.

U.C. / MS. / 23

4 rue de Calais
21st May 1904

My dear Pinker,

In reply to your letter of the 19th, I do not want to appear wrongheaded to Chatto or to you, but I am nevertheless convinced of the soundness of my attitude. However, I fully recognise Chatto's rights in the matter, & I will make the following proposition. The plot of *Love & Life* has always seemed to me better than the book itself. So far as any plot can be original, it is decidedly so, & very strong too. I have always regretted that I thought of it before I knew how to handle it adequately. I will

22. In 1899, after a visit to Phillpotts, Bennett wrote in his journal: 'I left Torquay. . . with the main idea that in 10 years Phillpotts would be one of the biggest, if not the biggest, novelist in England and America.'

write that book again; I should enjoy doing so; & I will lift it to the same plane as the *Grand Babylon Hotel* or even *Hugo* (I am sure I can do this), if Chatto, instead of owning the book, will consider that he has paid me £60 on account of royalties (It is one of four, & by no means the best as it stands, for which he paid £250). I know I can make *Love & Life* into something very striking & thrilling indeed, & at the same time good. This would be much more satisfactory than issuing the book as it stands, & would in the end pay Chatto himself better.

Further, I am definitely convinced that my next book to be issued ought to be a serious one; & also that no year ought to elapse without a serious book being issued. It is for this reason that I want *Tales of the Five Towns* issued in the autumn. Indeed I have set my heart on that, & *shall be extremely disappointed & dissatisfied if it is not arranged*. It may not be *quite* as remunerative to Chatto (on the other hand it may easily be more so) as, say, *Teresa*, at the moment, but I am sure it will be better for the solid side of my reputation, & Chatto is just as much interested in that as I am. A number of the tales in the volume are as good as anything I have done, & the best papers will certainly say so. Now if *Tales of the 5 Towns* were issued *early* in the autumn, I would agree to *Teresa* being published quite early in 1905 (The *Grand Babylon* was issued on Jan 9th, which *I* think the best time of all the year for books not by established favourites), provided Chatto will issue another book towards the end of May or beginning of June. He has issued two books of Frank Richardson in one half year, & I do not see why he should not do the same for me. This other book would be either *Hugo* or my new serious novel *Carlotta*, which will be finished by the end of March; that would depend on the serial arrangements of *Hugo*. These two books will beyond doubt be the two best books I have done, each in its own line. I may tell you that *Carlotta* will be somewhat sexual (but never indiscreetly so), & I will bet anybody £5 it sells as many as *Anna* & *Leonora* put together. The thing would therefore be thus:—

Tales of Five Towns	Sept. 1904
Teresa	Jan. 1905
Carlotta or *Hugo*	May 1905

My strong reason for getting in an extra book is that I really cannot do with my books being piled up. (But I have explained this to you before.)

After *Carlotta* I should rewrite *Love & Life*. And you would then have for publication

Carlotta or *Hugo*, whichever was postponed from spring.

Love & Life

The Loot of Cities.

As all these things will certainly be complete by the end of June 1905, I think I shall have to spend the remainder of that year in travelling & do a new sort of humorous travel book, *pour me changer un peu*, as you would be well supplied with fiction till the autumn of 1906.

I earnestly entreat you, Pinker, to get this arrangement through, or something closely akin to it. I think it meets the difficulties & is a fair compromise.

You can point out to Chatto that he got better than his bargain in one respect. He bought *The Gates of Wrath* when it was 28,000 words. I enlarged it to 42,000 & much improved it.

Yours sincerely, E. A. Bennett

P.S. From all I can hear, *A Great Man* is by no means the only book with a disappointing subscription this season.

2nd P.S. Monday

I have sent *Hugo* part I to typewriter. Thanks for your note.

23. *Love and Life* (later re-titled *The Ghost*) treats of the love of two men for the same woman. The first man is destroyed by the ghost of a former fiancé, who had died of brain fever years before; and the second man is saved from destruction only by the intercession of the woman. The action takes place in the present, and the second man, the hero of the novel, is simply forced to acknowledge the reality of the ghost. In 1907, when the novel was published, Bennett wrote in his journal: '*The Ghost* was built on a great sensational spiritual idea—no doubt a very old one, but I thought of it for myself! I can remember to this day the excitement I felt when it formed itself in my mind. The mischief was that I lacked the skill to develop it and handle it. I frittered the lovely thing away through sheer ignorance of the technique of development.'

Teresa of Watling Street was published in October 1904. In 1905 came *Tales of the Five Towns* (in January), *The Loot of Cities* (in June), and *Sacred and Profane Love* (in September). Bennett did not finish writing *Sacred and Profane Love* until July 1905;

u.c. / ms. / 24

4 rue de Calais
6th July 1904

My dear Pinker,

In returning proofs of the last of the stories for Tillotsons I asked them to let me know in good time if they wanted any more stories. I enclose their reply. Will it be best for you or me to deal with it? As a matter of fact I have a very good idea for a serial which I could do some time next year—say by August or September. That is to write an exciting yarn 'round' an Exhibition like Earl's Court, dealing with the Exhibition as an entity, as I deal with the Hotel & with Hugo's Stores. The material would be simply superb—all the amusements, orchestras, cafés, machinery, Great Wheel, gardens, Welcome Club, railways, etc etc. It is a long time since I had such an inspiration. There is not the slightest doubt Tillotsons would like the yarn. The question is the price. If they will give a definite commission, taking delivery say in September, I suppose 3 guineas a thousand will do, & I think they would pay that. I mean for *serial rights only*. The translation rights of such a yarn, according to the experience of the *Grand Babylon Hotel*, would be worth £30 at least, as they have good reason to know. I mention this because they usually try to get translation rights thrown in. Kindly instruct me.

I expect to finish *Hugo* at the end of next week. It is panning out very well. I don't expect you have done anything with *T. P's W.*, & I didn't think you would. There are too many palates in that concern; & I feel pretty sure that T. P. himself, in addition to having a sort of prejudice against me because Whitten has always rammed me down his throat, is determined

---

he called the later American edition *The Book of Carlotta. Hugo* was deferred until 1906, although Bennett finished writing it in the summer of 1904. It shared the stage that year with the serious divorce novel *Whom God Hath Joined* and with the sensational novel *The Sinews of War*, which Bennett wrote in collaboration with Eden Phillpotts. 1907 brought the drastically revised *Love and Life* (as *The Ghost*), along with *The City of Pleasure*, a second collection of short stories entitled *The Grim Smile of the Five Towns*, and a pocket philosophy, *The Reasonable Life*. The *Savoir Faire Papers* and *A Novelist's Log-Book* were never published in book form, nor was the volume of literary criticism mentioned in the letter of 27 April.

Frank Richardson (1870–1917) published three novels with Chatto and Windus in 1903.

to cut down prices at any cost. But I expect you to sell the story in London.

Shortly I am going to do some purely humorous stories with a view to magazines—style of 'His Worship the Goosedriver'. What magazines had I better keep in my mind's eye while writing? And do you prefer 'Five Towns' stuff or more general stuff? The stories will be *really* good, as well as 'magaziny'.

Yours sincerely, E. A. Bennett

Did you notice I got the *Pall Mall* to review *A Great Man* twice over? I wrote to Straight about the first review, & his reply was certainly a most pleasing surprise.

24. The exciting yarn is still *The City of Pleasure*, and Tillotsons did not like it, perhaps because the sensationalism is sometimes treated so lightly as to seem satirical, as in the description of the band conductor of the City of Pleasure:

'It was said that he was capable of conducting the Eroica Symphony of Beethoven with his left foot—and who shall deny it? "God Save the King" was child's play to him. Moreover, he showed a certain reserve in handling it. He merely conducted it as though in conducting it he himself were literally saving the King. That was all. But with what snap, what dash, what *chic*, what splash and what magnificent presence of mind did he save the King! The applause was wild and ample.'

On 6 September 1906 Tillotsons wrote to Pinker: 'We should like to publish further work from Mr. Bennett's pen, but naturally it must be such work as we can sell. *The Grand Babylon Hotel* hit the mark with our clients, but *The City of Pleasure* was unacceptable to them, and we have lost considerably on the story, while the majority of those who did publish it say they will not publish another from the same pen.' The novel began running in the *Staffordshire Sentinel* on 6 January 1906 and in four other papers at the same time. By the end of the year a total of at least thirteen papers had taken it.

On 'His Worship the Goosedriver' see pages 79–80.

Bennett wrote in his journal:

'I wrote to Sir Douglas Straight the other day to complain of a review of *A Great Man* in the *Pall Mall Gazette*. It had grossly misrepresented the plot, and so I explained my conception of the negative duties of a reviewer who did not read a book. Straight's answer is to review the book again, very favourably, under the title "Second Impressions". At the end of the review he says, after stating that he has read it twice: "There is hope for civilised mankind so long as it can appreciate the interest of light and clever writing like the present story. . . . We say this the more readily because in first acknowledging the book, we recorded what was, after all, a superficial impression, and in making amends now we have said no more than any fair-minded reader will admit it deserves." This is decidedly handsome. But many people will think I am a friend of Straight's and that the first review slipped in without his knowledge.'

The first review had said only: 'Light, modern, humorous. It is the story of Henry Knight, who starts life as a draper's manager and winds it up as a literary man of repute. Part of the author's humour is to make the hero forty years of age when the story opens; but there are (as need be) better instances of his humour than this.' Straight (1844–1914) was editor of the *Pall Mall*.

TEXAS / MS. / 25

4 rue de Calais
[postmarked 7 July 1904]

[no salutation]

Touching those short stories, I have had an idea for a series of six, with a central character who would be decidedly droll & would constantly be saying funny things, & with a series of situations in themselves comic. Would you prefer a series thus, or would you prefer disconnected stories? You can rely on them in either case being funny in the magazine way (like 'His Worship the Goosedriver', but moving in more polite circles, & not at all 5-Townsy). Kindly send me a line. You will receive the complete typescript of *Hugo* on Thursday or Friday next.

E. A. B.

U.C. / MS. / 26

The Hotel
Ardentinny
Loch Long
N. B.
20 Augt 1904

My dear Pinker,

I enclose the Tillotson document signed. It is not witnessed, as it is inconvenient for me to get a witness here; but that does not invalidate it in the least. You can witness it if you like.

I shall not be in London before the middle of September. I think it will be well for you to send me one copy of *Hugo* here with the passages marked. I am extremely surprised to find I have put in anything to which exception can be taken, & I rack my brains in vain to think what on earth it can be. However, it certainly can't be anything fundamental, & I will alter it at once.

I have no ideas for a particular destination for the Wells article. H. G. said to me that what he wanted was a really well informed review of himself in some good medium, & as I fancied from his manner that he would like me to do the thing, I at once offered to do so if it could be fixed up. I do not *want* to do it; I would much sooner spend the time at fiction; but I shall be very glad to tell the British Public what it ought to think concerning Wells if the matter can be arranged.

Yours sincerely, E. A. Bennett

P.S. I am glad you like the story. I will do a series. Six, I presume.

TEXAS / MS. / 27

Grand Hotel
Aberdeen
1 Sept 1904

My dear Pinker,

Thanks for your letter & the enclosure. I return the MS. altered as you wish. I have emphasised the housekeeper; changed the cabinet de toilette into the housekeeper's room; and suppressed the change of costume, merely making Tudor give Camilla the hat & the cloak as a present. I expect this will meet all objections completely.

What is the matter with me is that my mind is too pure. It never occurred to me for a moment that anyone could twist that chapter into an indecency. However, there is no doubt that it can be so twisted. I can see it when it is pointed out. At the [same] time, I regard T. P's explanation that they refused the story on account of that chapter as grotesque. When a paper has four editors of equal authority it is capable of stupendous folly, but it would not go so far as to refuse a story for a thing that could be altered in two minutes. T. P. must have had some other reason.

Yours sincerely, E. A. Bennett

26. Bennett was at his Scottish address for two or three weeks while he obtained treatment there from a Frenchman for his speech impediment. There were no results.

Bennett visited Wells before he went to Scotland. The new article on him seems not to have been written (see page 42n.).

The series of stories bore the title *The Adventures of Jack Stout*. Bennett's letter of 13 January 1909 suggests that they may never have been published serially. They were not collected in any of the later volumes of short stories.

27. In Chapter V of *Hugo* the heroine Camilla relates how she visited the apartment of her former fiancé with the intention of preventing him from committing suicide. Her behaviour there was decorous; his was designing. The novel as a whole is lightly flavoured with sex.

L.A.B.—F

u.c. / ms. / 28

4 rue de Calais
Sunday [30 October 1904]

My dear Pinker,

Many thanks. I enclose contract signed. The next thing will be to get a starting royalty of 20% out of Chattos. I ought to have it. The reviews of *Teresa* have been better than I expected, much better. And I could not honestly quarrel with even the severe ones. I am working in the country for a week, near to Davray, on the edge of the forest of Fontainebleau.

Yours sincerely, E. A. Bennett

u.c. / ms. / 29

4 rue de Calais
26 Nov. 1904

My dear Pinker,

I shall be glad if you will pay the December cheque into my bank at Fulham. At the end of the year I calculate that, unless you have received any sums of which I am unaware, I shall owe you about £400. Against this you will have adequate security, I imagine. *Hugo* will be worth, I suppose, altogether about £300, even assuming it has no more success than ordinary. You have also the six short stories, & the book rights on these & on the *Loot of Cities*, not to mention any good luck you may have in America (which I trust may soon occur). I have lived like a trappist monk this year, but the family matters which I mentioned to you have been such a drain on me that I am no better off than I was before. And I shall really be very much obliged to you if you will continue the arrangement for another year. After that, in any case, I shall not ask you to do so. You will I think be well secured altogether. There will be the *Tales of the Five Towns, Sacred & Profane Love (Carlotta*—this book is

28. Bennett's starting royalty with Chatto was, and continued to be, 2*d.* in the shilling, with the publishing price at 6*s.* Royalties rose to 20 per cent. after sales of 5,000 copies.

Henry D. Davray (1873–1944) was in these years editor of the Collection of Foreign Authors for *Le Mercure de France.* His translation of *The Ballad of Reading Gaol* appeared there shortly after the English publication. In 1905 he translated into French a two-act play Bennett had written. The play is known only by its French title, *Que Faire?* It was never produced.

great), the serial already sold to Tillotsons, & if you care I can let you have another set of six stories in the autumn. There is also *Love & Life*. Of course my part of the agreement will be that I let you have the stuff on the proper dates.

I have not mentioned to you theatrical matters lately, because I have been too disgusted by the capriciousness & uncertainty of the theatrical world. Things, however, are always moving there. I was almost quite sure, in April, that I should have two plays running at once, one at the Haymarket & the other by Mary Moore at the New Theatre. However, both were postponed & are still waiting. Besides these I have two other plays sold. And besides these I have written during the last twelve months two comedies in collaboration with Eden Phillpotts. One of these was an experiment, but the second is a bit of all right & I think Harrison will have it. I do not see how next year can pass without seeing *one* play of mine, unless God specially intervenes against me.

I know a lot of Americans in Paris & they have all read *A Great Man*, & they all agree that it would succeed in America. Has any special effort been made with it there?

Yours sincerely, E. A. Bennett

P.S. I hope you are quite restored to your usual Herculean health. E. A. B.

29. The family matters may have involved his brother Frank (1868–1938), who was visiting him earlier in the month. His mother (1840–1914) was ill earlier in the year.

Bennett's dramatic career, which was eventually to become a major source of income, hung fire for several years. Beginning in 1894, he wrote occasional dialogues that appeared in *Woman*. In 1899 he wrote a duologue, 'The Music Lesson', for performance at a private party among friends; and, encouraged by its success, he wrote in six days the three one-act plays that comprise *Polite Farces*, which was published late in the year. In 1900 he collaborated with his friend Arthur Hooley on a melodrama, *The Chancellor*, which was accepted by a producer; and in that year or later, he and Hooley wrote a farce, *A Wayward Duchess*. Also in 1900 he wrote a curtain-raiser, 'The Post Mistress', which was accepted by Frederick Harrison for the Haymarket Theatre; and in the same year or later he helped in a dramatization of Violet Tweedale's novel *Her Grace's Secret*. He also found time in 1900 to collaborate with Eden Phillpotts on a dramatization of Phillpotts' novel *Children of the Mist*. In 1902 he and H. G. Wells worked together on a play called *The Crime*, and he was asked by Harrison to adapt an old English comedy for the Haymarket. In 1904 he and Phillpotts collaborated on *Christina* (*A Credit to Human Nature*) and *An Angel Unawares*. None of this work was ever produced except for one

u.c. / ms. / 30

4 rue de Calais
9 Mch 1905

My dear Pinker,

Many thanks for your letter & the enclosure, which I return signed. I suppose the date left blank will be filled in so as not to clash with my autumn book.

No doubt you have paid my cheque into my London bank as usual.

I enclose two letters which I have received from Alfred Nutt, whom I do not know except by repute. In answer to the first I replied that the idea certainly appealed to me, & that the subject was one which I well understood on its legal side owing to my legal experience. I also said that I was fully engaged for some time to come & that in any case I should want to be assured of a *minimum* certain remuneration. My ideas about the thing frankly are that, first, it appeals to me & that I could make it very striking & documentary etc; second that it might be a good thing for me to do a sort of 'purpose' novel; third that Nutt is evidently somewhat keen on the subject and on me, & might probably go out of his way to push such a book & pay me rather more than I could ordinarily get. Of course there would be no question of him issuing any other book by me. I see he is now advertising a list of four or five novels. You see what he says about the success of his translation of Bourget's novel. Before replying to the second letter I await your advice. I am as usual entirely willing to be guided by you. Do you know Nutt? If so you might see him. I shall be

> Chez M. Lebert aîné
> Les Sablons
> près Moret
> S. & M.
> France

---

of the polite farces, which ran for a few nights in 1914. Except for the polite farces, none of the plays was ever published. Bennett's first produced play was *Cupid and Commonsense*, 1908.

Mary Moore (1861–1931), one of whose successes was the role of Roxanne in *Cyrano*, was mainly associated with Sir Charles Wyndham at the Criterion Theatre. Harrison (d. 1926) managed the Haymarket Theatre for three decades, beginning in 1896.

until next Thursday. If you do not see any sense in the notion
I shall name some preposterous terms to Nutt & tell him I am
not free for two years.

                              Yours sincerely, E. A. Bennett

U.C. / MS. / 31

                                        4 rue de Calais
                                        5 Apl 1905
My dear Pinker,

Many thanks for your letter. The price offered by *Today* is
extremely depressing, but you must act as you think best. I
should have thought the Northern Newspaper Syndicate even
would have given more than that. I won't write any more
serials except on commission. I'll go & live in Canada first. If
Today gets the thing, kindly point out to them that it is written
to be printed in *twelve instalments, & the effect will be marred if the
divisions are changed.* I should like the book to be issued either
early in July or late in August; I have a great notion of books
being issued in off-seasons. I particularly want to know what
Tales of the Five Towns has done. Kindly ascertain & let me
know. I do not want more time for completing *Carlotta*. It will
be finished in ample time for the autumn season, but of course
if we issue *Hugo* in July or August, *Carlotta* mustn't be issued till
January. It is a pity. However, I am nothing if not a philo-
sopher.

Nutt's offer is of course grotesque. Considering that he asked
me to write the book, why does he condole with himself about
not a line of the book being written? As I have now practically
decided in my own mind to write the book, don't give way to
him the least bit. What I want is to be published by Methuen.

---

30. Alfred Nutt (1856–1910) directed the firm that his father, David Nutt, had
founded in 1829. He was a writer on folklore and the Celtic revival. His proposal
to Bennett materialized as the divorce novel *Whom God Hath Joined.* He published
Un Divorce, by Paul Bourget (1852–1935), in 1904. The two letters from him to
Bennett do not survive.

After his few days in the country with Davray the previous October, Bennett
wrote in his journal: 'I liked the country so much that I determined to go there a
great deal more, and I arranged to have a little first-floor suite in the house of a
gardener named Lebert at the rate of 2 fr. a day whenever I wanted it.' Lebert and
his wife later provided information on the Siege of Paris for *The Old Wives' Tale.*

How soon can I get there? Chatto's list gives me appendicitis.
I wish we could have *Hugo* published by Methuen.

Yours sincerely, E. A. Bennett

U.C. / MS. / 32

4 rue de Calais
26 April 1905

My dear Pinker,

Many thanks for your letter. I thought Nutt would try again,
as I have heard indirectly that his notion of my work & future
is considerably more lofty than the sufficiently enthusiastic
terms of his first letter would indicate. By all means accept
£125 if you cannot get more. After all, with a 20% royalty, a
difference of £25 in the advance is not much. I think I would
sell the copyright, except translation rights, for £350. If a
definite date for the publication of the book is not fixed in the
agreement, a particular season ought to be fixed. This season
ought to be the autumn of 1906 in my opinion. I can definitely
agree to furnish the MS. on the 31st July 1906. I am getting to
the end of my Tillotson serial, with which they ought to be
acutely pleased. I shall then finish off *Carlotta*. It will be complete during July. It is *Carlotta* & not *Hugo* that I want to be
published in the autumn, the early autumn. I have a belief in
Carlotta. It will certainly get talked about. You might let me
know when you next write what you ultimately did with *Hugo*,
& also the sales of *Tale 5 T*.

Yours ever, E. A. Bennett

I propose to amuse myself during August & September by
writing a few really good short stories.

31. *Today* was a cheap weekly, soon to be absorbed by *London Opinion*. *Hugo*
began appearing in it on 3 May.
32. 'Yours ever' and 'Bennett' are in shorthand.
Whom God Hath Joined was finished in July 1906; it was published in the
autumn. Bennett wrote the Tillotson serial, *The City of Pleasure*, during April and
May. Not until the end of September did he begin writing stories.

U.C. / MS. / 33

> 4 rue de Calais
> 11 June 1905

My dear Pinker,

I have finished the Tillotson serial & shall deliver it in a day or two direct to them by registered post.

I think I have got you a new client in the person of W. Somerset Maugham. At any rate, after some weeks of my discourses on agents, he demanded from me your address yesterday & said he meant to write to you. I have lately got to know him quite well. He seems to me to be a man who will make his way. He has already got a very good contract with the Curzon group for a play. He says they tell him it is a certainty for the autumn. If you could also manage his plays for him it would be a decent thing.

> Yours sincerely, E. A. Bennett

U.C. / MS. / 34

> 4 rue de Calais
> 31st Oct. 1905

My dear Pinker,

I send you by registered book post the three other humorous stories. Of the six, 'The Lion's Share' is the best, and 'The Silent Brothers' the next best. 'The Baby's bath' might please some feminine audience.

I shall send you the *Bystander* story probably in less than a week. I will make it as near 2,500 as possible.

I sent the Chatto agreement yesterday.

Private

You know all about Violet Hunt. She manages her own affairs, & I have explained to her the folly of attempting to do so, & that she ought to go to you. She wishes now to come to you, & has asked me to write to you & commend her to you.

---

33. Maugham (1874–1965) came to Pinker for a time, and then went on to A. P. Watt. His theatrical 'certainty' evaporated, and he waited another two years before his first play was produced in the West End. His extraordinary success with *Lady Frederick* in 1907, and with *Mrs. Dot* and *Jack Straw*, was emulated a few years later by Bennett with *Milestones* and *The Great Adventure*.

But you used to be in the same office, hadn't you, in the middle ages? If you don't want her, send me a line by return (& see that it is posted in good time—your letters still reach me 12 hours late), as I shall probably see her on Thursday night. I can then put her off again if necessary. She is quite free, & has just got a novel finished. By the way Courlander has to give 6 months notice to a firm whose name I forget—Something & Cazenove, I fancy, but I am not sure. I am looking after him.

Kindly send my cheque direct to me.

Yours sincerely, E. A. Bennett

U.C. / MS. / 35

4 rue de Calais
7 Dec. 1905

My dear Pinker,

Phillpotts has got a great notion for a mystery story of 60,000 words, & he has asked me to collaborate with him in it some time next year. The thing is to be rather exceptionally strong. He has arrangements which enable him to make sure, in England & America, of at least £900 out of such a story, of which he did one last year. He offers me halves and personally guarantees me a minimum of £450. He will draft the entire book, & I shall write it. He has always praised my work enthusiastically but this is the greatest compliment he has ever paid me. I have naturally accepted. I do not suppose the thing will clash with Tillotson, but if by chance it should ultimately seem likely to do so, I shall depend on your famous diplomatic

34. The three good stories were collected in *The Grim Smile of the Five Towns*. On their serial publication see page 84n. The *Bystander* story, 'The Letter and the Lie', appeared on 20 December; it was republished in *The Matador of the Five Towns*.

Bennett had just met Violet Hunt (1866–1942) in Paris, where she was living. Her next published work was *White Rose of Weary Leaf*, issued by Heinemann in 1907. In *I Have This to Say* she writes:

'My literary agent . . . was . . . J. B. Pinker, prince of agents, kindest friend to his clients and a great rider to hounds. I have sat with him in his office and observed the back of his head green with some nasty fall he had had. "Jy B" I had known as a boy in the office of *Black & White*, and he and I used to race to get the foreign stamps out of the editor's wastepaper basket for our collections.'

Alphonse Courlander (1881–1914) was a novelist and journalist; his firm was the Literary Agency of London, managed by G. H. Perris (1866–1920) and C. Cazenove (d. 1915). The Agency was founded in 1899 and shared offices at 5 Henrietta Street, Covent Garden, with Curtis Brown, who took over the firm around 1917.

powers to arrange things smoothly. There will only be a month's work in the book for me.

Yours sincerely, E. A. Bennett

U.C. / MS. / 36

4 rue de Calais
17 Jan. 1906

My dear Pinker,

Many thanks for your letter of yesterday. I telegraphed to you today strongly objecting to more than 80,000 words. Counting 100,000 words, the price works out at £4. 10/- a thousand, which is decidedly insufficient for this combination. I go halves with Phillpotts, but I do most of the work. Moreover the original suggestion to the *Tribune* was 60,000, & I had heard of no change. Secondly, a serial of over 80,000 is a mistake. The *author* may keep up the pace, but he can't prevent the reader from getting fatigued. Lastly, *T.P's* will get the same serial in any case, whether it is 80,000 or 100,000, & you can tell them from me it will be much better, necessarily, in 80,000 than in 100,000 words. I suggest as a limit twenty instalments of 4,000 words each—in *their* interest quite as much as in mine. As you have already accepted the offer at 100,000, I shall of course stand by it if you cannot alter it without too much difficulty. *But I do most decidedly object to it,* & I think you will be able to secure the modification. Please wire me tomorrow the number of instalments & length of instalments as finally settled, & send me a copy of the scenario.

You have now to carry out your promise to arrange matters with Tillotsons. I am leaving this entirely to you. It would suit me infinitely better to postpone the serial due to them in July for a year. Sheppard asked me, on his own initiative, whether I could do this, & I said I thought I could. He then said he wouldn't know for a few weeks whether he would want to ask me to postpone it, & that he would let me hear. With this as a beginning you can probably set about arranging a postpone-ment. They will certainly get a better serial next year than this. I am, as you know, a great worker, but even for me, to do two

35. Phillpotts and Bennett began working on *The Sinews of War* on 26 January 1906 and finished on 7 April. T. Werner Laurie published the novel later in the year.

serials and finish the Divorce book by August will be more than is good for the soul. I have completed a scenario of Tillotson's serial.

At Phillpotts' request I called to see Curtis Brown just before leaving London, as to the serial in America. Phillpotts had sent him his copy of *Hugo*, together with a highly enthusiastic letter, & Brown had read it, & suggested that he would very probably be able to place the book in the States. I agreed that he should try and thanked him, while making it perfectly clear to him that you were my regular agent. If he does anything with the book the money will of course pass through your hands according to our arrangement. Assuming he *can* create an opening for me there, there is no reason why we shouldn't let him, is there?

When I have heard from Phillpotts I shall write you again about the difficulty between you & him.

Yours sincerely, E. A. Bennett

U.C. / MS. / 37

4 rue de Calais
19 Jan. 1906

My dear Pinker,

Thank you for yours of yesterday. The draft contract is quite satisfactory. The story will have to be copyrighted in America. What is necessary for this? But I don't see why Curtis Brown shouldn't have the bother of this, as he is supposed to handle it. I will ask Phillpotts.

36. The *Tribune* was a London daily. *T. P.'s Weekly*, not the *Tribune*, serialized *The Sinews of War*. As published by Laurie, and probably *T.P.'s Weekly*, the novel was 80,000 words long.

The proposed serial for Tillotsons apparently came to nothing, unless it was transformed into *Helen with the High Hand*, which was written in the spring of 1907. Robert Sheppard (1870–1934), known to his Tillotson colleagues as 'the hurricane', had met Bennett in the late eighties, before Bennett left the Potteries. At that time Sheppard was a traveller for the firm, and he arranged that the youthful Bennett should meet him at the station in Burslem wearing a large white flower in his buttonhole. After the war, Sheppard became a director of Tillotsons.

Curtis Brown (1866–1945) was a transplanted American, and apparently had better connexions in America at this time than did Pinker. He acted for Bennett on several occasions there. Through his efforts, *The Sinews of War* (under the title *Doubloons*) was published by McClure, Phillips at the same time that Laurie published it.

With regard to *Hugo*, Brown asked me if it had been offered in America, & I told him that so far as I knew it had not but I distinctly told him I could not say positively (as none of my books has been placed in U.S. since *Anna*). If you are on friendly terms with him, as no doubt you are, would it not be well for you to see him & talk the matter over? I do not want him to come to me with a contract & then have to tell him the thing is already arranged. I enclose a letter from him that wants answering. Perhaps you can let me have the information. Act as regards Brown as you think best, but I naturally wish to be perfectly open with him.

Apropos of my short stories I observed to you: 'You have sold the best.' This is not so. The best—& one of the most humorous I have ever done—is 'The Lion's Share'. Can you not plant this on the *Tribune*? It ought to go somewhere good, as it is classy.

Yours sincerely, E. A. Bennett

u.c. / ms. / 38

4 rue de Calais
6th Feby 1906

My dear Pinker,

Many thanks for your letter of yesterday & the enclosure. I am of Phillpotts's opinion. If the *Tribune* can't form a sufficient idea of what the novel would be, from the play, then no synopsis would give them a sufficient idea. Of course if you seriously think you can get a £500 commission for 60,000 words I don't mind doing a synopsis, though it seems to me silly. In any case the MS. couldn't be delivered *before* the end of the year. I had the idea of rewriting *Love and Life* in the autumn. I know I can make that a worthy successor to *Hugo*. It will be well for us to keep in mind what I have now maturing for publication. To wit:

Whom God hath joined (Nutt)
The City of Pleasure (Chatto)

37. Apparently through Brown's agency, *Hugo* was published by Buckles in America later in the year.

'The Lion's Share' was published in the *Pall Mall Magazine* in June 1907. Bennett placed the story first in the collection *The Grim Smile of the Five Towns* that Chapman and Hall published later in the year.

Love & Life (Chatto)
Sinews of War (with Phillpotts)

And a volume of short stories. It seems as if we should make
£1,000 apiece out of *The Sinews of War*, & if these contracts
work out right, & if *Hugo* sells pretty well (the reviews are
excellent) I shall want at least a clear six months next year for
another absolutely serious book.

I shall send you tomorrow, in proof, the first instalment of
The Sinews of War for copyrighting in America. Kindly let me
know how much of the whole thing you will want for purposes
of copyright. I take it you & Brown will arrange the copyrighting & that I can tell Phillpotts we have nothing to bother
about.

Kindly ask Chatto to send me a couple of copies of the 6d.
edition of the *Grand Babylon Hotel* when it appears.

Yours sincerely, E. A. Bennett

u.c. / ms. / 39

4 rue de Calais
21 Feby 1906

My dear Pinker,
I notice that Chatto is leaving *Hugo* out of his advertising
list. He probably has some reason for this, but I should like to
know what it is. The book has been out just a month. The
reviews have been exceptionally favourable—some quite
remarkable. Moreover *Sacred & Profane Love* went into a second
edition. He has a permanent advertisement in today's *Tribune*.
Now the review (3/4 col.) of *Hugo* in the *Tribune* was one of the
very best, & I should have thought that the *Tribune* would
therefore have been a good place to advertise it, especially as
I contribute to the *Tribune*. But he has left *Hugo* out of the
advertisement. It was also left out of his advt in the *Times* on
Friday. Perhaps you can ascertain the reason.

Yours sincerely, E. A. Bennett

38. The *Tribune* was considering a transformation of *Christina* in lieu of *The
Sinews of War*. Nothing came of the proposal.

39. Andrew Chatto, Sr., was nearing the end of his career, and he did not elicit
from Bennett the enthusiasm with which some earlier writers had regarded him.
In 1884, Robert Louis Stevenson wrote to him, 'If you don't know that you have a
good author, I know that I have a good publisher. Your fair, open and handsome
dealings are a good point in my life.'

U.C. / MS. / 40

4 rue de Calais
27th Feby 1906

My dear Pinker,

Many thanks for your letter. I accept Chatto's statement with very great reserve. I have seen four of Chatto's advertisements, during the last few days (since Friday), in none of which *Hugo* appeared, though books are included which were issued only a few days after mine. The usual, almost the universal practice is that a publisher has a definite season's list & sticks to it—unless of course he is one of these publishers who advertise specially certain books, which Chatto never does. One never sees Methuen cut his list in pieces. Moreover Chatto has previously advertised my books (& others) steadily for 10 or 12 weeks. Thus his autumn list (including *S. & P. Love* published in September) was being advertised on Dec. 30, fourteen weeks. He has never before dropped a book of mine after a month, or after two months. And it seems to me absurd to do so. If he has spent 2/- per copy in a month, what has he been doing with the money? That he advertises without distinction in display, and chooses his 'review-quotes' badly is notorious. I sent him a list of review-quotes but I have seen no result. This, however, is beside the point. His *method* of advertising has to be accepted for what it is. But that he should reduce the *quantity* for a book like *Hugo*—the book that he has been asking for for years—strikes me as singular.

With the example of certain of my fellow authors before me, I am extremely slow to make charges against publishers, & I should doubt if Chatto would cut off his nose to spite his face. Still, a paragraph did appear in the *Tribune* about my divorce book & Nutt, and *Hugo* departed from Chatto's lists just afterwards. The coincidence suggested to me an idea which may or may not be absurd.

I sent you the Laurie contracts yesterday, signed. It is a very good contract.

Kindly send my cheques direct to me in future.

Yours sincerely, E. A. Bennett

Certainly *Love and Life* can't be put in type yet. Chatto hasn't even sent me the copy to rewrite. It can't be put in type for a long time yet.

U.C. / MS. / 41

4 rue de Calais
6th Mch 1906

My dear Pinker,
  Many thanks for your letter. I am glad the serial is a success. It ought to be. Immediately Phillpotts saw my opening instalments he suggested another one for next year. I enclose a letter I received from him which sufficiently declares his attitude. You know of course how this serial is done. The scenario, except the last trick of bringing the Russo-Japanese war into the story, was entirely Phillpotts'. The whole of the writing, except one or two descriptions of scenery, is mine. If you compare the scenario with the finished thing you can judge my share of the business. On the other hand, it was Phillpotts' own suggestion that we should go halves (indeed I wouldn't have accepted any other terms), & as the whole affair will take me just 2 months and four days, I shall be very well paid. Four days would cover all Phillpotts' work on the thing, which means he will ultimately get about £250 a day for his trouble. Do not disclose to anyone the manner of our collaboration, as it is just as well to keep these things dark. We shall almost certainly do another serial next year, so you can bear that in mind.
  I don't think McClure's objection to Phillpotts's output is quite honest. He certainly never issues more than one novel in a year. Of the five books mentioned by McClure one is a booklet of poems, containing at most *one* thousand words, another is a sixpenny book of stories issued by Newnes, & I expect another is his garden-book. It is the *business* of a publisher to handle the stuff of an author in bulk. Phillpotts's work is never scamped. What would some modern publishers say if they had to deal with the output of Dumas père, or Sir Walter Scott? Another thing, no publisher of Phillpotts has ever lost money by advance on royalties. Phillpotts assures me that in every case the royalties have surpassed the advance. So I do not see what complaint a publisher can have. An author isn't a Bradford mill, to shut down whenever the middleman thinks it profitable to do so.
  I send by registered book post instalments 8, 9, 10, and 11 of the serial. Please have them typed in duplicate, & send *both* the copies to me. I will return one to you for America.
                                    Yours sincerely, E. A. Bennett

TEXAS / MS. / 42

[Paris or Moret]
[about 11 March 1906]
My dear Pinker,

I have told Nutt that you will see him in reference to this letter. I fancy the contract says that MS. is to be delivered 'about July'. It certainly won't be delivered before then. The novel is in three parts, & the first part is quite finished; the other two parts are not in a fit state to be seen; moreover I object to my stuff being exhibited half-done. Nutt can have the first part (30,000 words) at once if he wishes, but there is nothing to guarantee that I shall not make minor alterations in it later on. It seems rather queer on Nutt's part to be asking for the MS., or portions of it, before Easter. While maintaining a perfectly genial attitude you may as well indicate to him that I don't want to be unduly worried.

Yours sincerely, E. A. B.

U.C. / MS. / 43

4 rue de Calais
18th June 1906
My dear Pinker,

I have just become engaged to be married, to an American young lady who has lived all her life in Paris (& thus combines the best qualities of two nations).

A sum of about £400 will be necessary to my operations between now & the autumn, & I hope I can rely on you to let

41. The success of *The Sinews of War* was determined by the first instalment, which appeared in *T. P.'s Weekly* on 2 March.

Phillpotts proved Bennett wrong in 1906. In addition to *The Sinews of War*, he published two novels with Methuen (a Dartmoor novel, *The Portreeve*, and *The Poacher's Wife*) and the garden book and the collection of short stories with Newnes (*My Garden* and *The Unlucky Number*). The poetry collection Bennett refers to is *Up-Along and Down-Along*, published in 1905.

42. This letter is written on a blank side of Alfred Nutt's letter to Bennett of 8 March. Nutt asks about the progress of the novel and whether any of it will be ready before Easter. The contract called for delivery by 1 August. Bennett's journal indicates that he may have gone for a few days to Moret (see pages 60–61).

me have this; I shan't want it all at once. As regards the pro-
duct of 1906, the following figures seem to represent it.

Sinews of War	£775
City of Pleasure (Tillotsons)	£87
,, ,, (Chatto)	£75
Hugo	£75
Divorce novel	£150
7 or 8 short stories etc.	£100
	£1262

All these, I believe, are minimum figures, & take no account
of any good luck that may occur, nor of other things that you
have in hand. I overdrew about £650 against the actual cash
you had in hand at the end of last year; so that if this year you
let me have my £50 a month (£600) & another £400, making
£1000 altogether, I shall still be £250 better off with you at the
end of 1906 than I was at the end of 1905.

The next year's serial by Phillpotts & myself is already completely planned out, & you have also *Christina*.

No one can possibly be more surprised at my approaching
marriage than I am. But there it is, & I am immensely excited
about it. I cannot easily conceive any other event which would
cause me to come down on you like this for millions.

Anything to be done now with my *Savoir Vivre Papers* in book
form? What about the *P.T.O.* serial?

Yours sincerely, E. A. Bennett

43. The American young lady was Eleanor Green, one of the sisters of the
novelist Julian Green. She was about twenty-four. On his thirty-seventh birthday
in 1904, Bennett had written in his journal: 'I have now warned both the Mater
and Tertia that I shall get married before I am 40.'

The new serial was *The Statue*. It was completed by 31 October 1907.

The *Savoir-Vivre Papers* began in *T.P.'s Weekly*, 1 December 1905. They became
The Reasonable Life, the first of the pocket philosophies, published in 1907. *P. T. O.*
was another venture by T. P. O'. It merged with *M. A. P.* (mainly about people)
in 1908. The proposed serial is unknown.

u.c. / ms. / 44

4 rue de Calais
20 June 1906

My dear Pinker,

I was very much touched by your exceedingly kind and sagacious letter. I expect to be married in October. I think I am a prudent person. But up to now I have had no cause for prudence. The fault that hitherto I have committed is that I have given too much money away. I shall cease to do that. Of course I shall insure my life before my marriage, & for more than £750, & I shall have much pleasure in giving you a proper lien in the policy. It surprises me that you will have £600 *unsecured* against me at the end of the year, & I should say you are wrong. But that doesn't matter, as if you *are* wrong, so much the better for me. I imagine we know each other pretty well by this time, & have a mutual confidence. Anyhow I can't let this occasion pass without expressing to you my deep sense of your excellence as an agent & your good value as a friend. I do not often give vent to my feelings, but I am in a highly emotional state just now, & I use the chance to tell you what I think. Pinker, I will write you some *books* in the future!

Yours sincerely, E. A. Bennett

u.c. / ms. / 45

Duchy House
Princetown
Dartmoor
Tuesday [7 or 14 August 1906]

My dear Pinker,

A great calamity has overtaken me, & it is a good thing my book is done. I had made all arrangements for my marriage, taken a flat, bought a lot of furniture, and accepted various responsibilities, & given up my old flat, and now my engagement is broken off. A piece of pure ill-luck—or perhaps good-luck—who knows? Anyhow I had no alternative but to bring the affair to a sudden & definite end. I will tell you about it when I see you.

Which I expect to do about the end of the month, if you are to be in London. I shall still insure my life—I have arranged that—& turn the policy over to you, as this will be more satisfactory. I shall not want £400, but I have spent so much, & I have such other liabilities in connection with my vanished marriage, that I shall want £250.

I am in a pretty queer state, but I shall be better soon. And the book is done. Here I am with Phillpotts & his wife, scheming the new serial. Idleness is no good to me.

Yours sincerely, E. A. Bennett

u.c. / ms. / 46

4 rue de Calais
1st Oct 1906

My dear Pinker,

I have read through the 12 lessons of the Literary Correspondence College, & made a few corrections & suggestions, & I return them by parcel post. They are devilish good. But it is impossible to deny that they *are* my book. There is not, I think, a single sentence in all the lessons that is not my ipsissima verba. And beyond the chapters on journalism, verse, etc, there is nothing in my book which is not in these lessons. In a word, the twelve lessons are simply my book split up and typewritten.

I did not understand from you that this was to be so.

But I am perfectly agreeable that it should be so, provided the just consequences of it being so are recognised by the College. No student who had these lessons would want my book afterwards. If he bought it thinking he was getting something fresh, the disillusion on reading it would be apt to make him cross. Hence every student of these lessons is a reader lost of my book. Under these circumstances it appears to me that the College should pay me a royalty, say 1/6, on every copy of the lessons used. Such is my notion of fairness, but I am open to listen to any arguments against it. I am indeed open to leave the matter

---

45. One description of the relationship with Eleanor Green is presented by Reginald Pound in his biography of Bennett. Miss Green was never interested in Bennett and was unaware that he had proposed to her. When she necessarily broke with him, he could do little but stammer absurdities about her losing 'the respect of the 'ole world'. Pound's account came from Eleanor Green herself (Mrs. Kenneth Joll). Another version is offered by a sister, Anne Green, in her memoir *With Much Love*. She portrays Eleanor and her mother as wilfully deceiving Bennett, the one indifferent to his feelings and content for a while to lead him on, and the other responding in her daughter's name to Bennett's love letters. Neither account seems true. What is certain is that the event was a deep shock to Bennett.

to be decided by you as between the College & me. It is indisputable, on the face of the twelve lessons, that in regard to the theory of writing fiction I, and no other, *am* the College.

Yours sincerely, E. A. Bennett

u.c. / ms. / 47

4 rue de Calais

9th Nov 1906

My dear Pinker,

Many thanks.

The last contract which I *executed* for Tillotsons was for £175. The N. N. S. went higher than this—how much I forget, & then Tillotsons went to £200.

It really would not be quite fair to land the N. N. S. with the story which I outlined to you, this being an absolute novelty in the way of humorous fiction, which most of their clients would consider daring and unsuitable. I have, however, another plot for a humorous novel, which I *could* recommend to them, which I should enjoy doing, & which would be thoroughly artistic at the same time. As regards this one, we could safely promise a continuous interest with effective curtains etc—it being of course clearly understood that the story is a humorous story. In view of this can't you get them up to their original offer of a year ago?

The chief objection that I have, otherwise, to the draft contract, is the date for delivery. Anyhow the 1st of March is impossible. When you said 'March' I thought you would mean the 31st.

Further, they are not limited as to date for serial publication. They should be bound to finish it not later than a given date. *I want a date in late summer or autumn for delivery.*

I should like the contract arranged, if it can be. Because the opportunities of getting a serial run for anything that I consider artistic are very rare. The book would suit Methuens.

Nutt is really rather naive. He is just discovering that the press in general regards my serious novels with coldness. He ought to have known this long ago. What did he expect? He commissions a work which he asks shall be realistic on an unpleasing subject; he gets it, and is very pleased with it—he

---

46. The College was using *How to Become an Author*. It acceded to Bennett's notion of fairness.

wrote me he considered it 'really first-class'—and then he expects that such a work shall be enthused over in the average paper! He ought to know better. You will scarcely believe it, but he actually wrote and asked me to reply personally to a footling and inept criticism in the *Academy*. What he wants is a book as artistically serious as *Whom God hath joined*, and a newspaper reception such as is accorded to *The Sinews of War*. He is old enough to know that he might as well ask for the moon.

Yours sincerely, E. A. Bennett

P.S. Thanks for story.

u.c. / ms. / 48

4 rue de Calais
22 Nov 1906

My dear Pinker,

Many thanks for your letter & the cheque.

If you get an offer for *The Statue*, of the same sum as we got for *Sinews*, I will see that it is accepted. It would be folly to refuse it. So you can go ahead on that basis; but of course more if possible. As a matter of fact, certain people get it into their heads that they have a grievance against the entire band of editors & publishers, & they will find food for that grievance in everything. The whole idea that one gets less than one's value & receives unmerited neglect is ridiculous. If people, editors or public, are genuinely interested in one's stuff they will soon show it; & if they aren't—well, they aren't! And they have a perfect right not to be. There is no compulsion in these matters. When I reflect upon certain friends of mine who manage to extract some £3,000 a year out of the public, & still grumble the whole time, I smile, & my smile is somewhat sardonic.

I don't know what Nutt is doing in the way of advertisements. But I have seen no advertisements whatever since the

47. The daring novelty unsuitable for the Northern Newspaper Syndicate ultimately became the play *The Honeymoon*, a comedy of sex, marriage, and nationalism. In the first act, the honeymooning couple learn that they have been married by a bogus curate; the complications here are intertwined with the determination of the husband, a famous aviator, to prevent a German from being the first to fly over Snowdon. The other story was *Helen with the High Hand*.

Whom God Hath Joined was published in October.

first week. The poster I regard as a good idea spoilt. Nothing on it stands out sufficiently. And I don't know at all if sandwich boards have any effect on the sale of books; I believe in news-paper advertisement myself, & if I had the designing & arrange-ment of the advertising I could do something good at little cost. Nutt's advertisements have no individuality at all.

Please refuse the German offer. Anything is better than the 10 per cent dodge. Tell her we will take £10 cash. That is a fair price as things go.

Yours sincerely, E. A. Bennett

U.C. / MS. / 49

Grand Hotel Royal
San Remo
4th Mch 1907

My dear Pinker,

Many thanks for your letter of the 1st which reached me this morning.

I consider 2,500 copies of the *Ghost* as entirely an inadequate sale. Considering the notoriety they had as pioneers, & con-sidering that they sell to the 'Times Book Club', I cannot under-stand their being satisfied with it. The book, though it has no connection with my best work, is a perfectly good & well-done marketable work, & has had many excellent reviews. I should not have considered anything less than 5,000 as being adequate. They advertised '2nd large impression' on the day after publica-tion. I may tell you that I have for a long time suspected the absolute genuineness of C. & W.'s figures. And seeing that it is notorious how Macmillans cheated Charles Kingsley, and Chapman & Hall cheated Meredith, etc, I do not imagine that I shall shock you in expressing my suspicions. It is a fact that Chatto & Windus have paid Mrs. Alice Perrin £150 for her

48. One of the 'certain friends' was H. G. Wells, to whom popular success had come much more rapidly than to Bennett and for whom the public was 'the Beast'. Wells' income was above £1,000 in 1896, and ascended rapidly. Early in 1906 Bennett was writing in his journal about his own fortunes of the previous year: 'Genuine success seemed, as usual, to delay and postpone itself. But I find that I am much less interested in money than Phillpotts and Wells.'

A flat sum rather than a royalty was characteristic for translation rights. £20 was a common figure for a novel before the First World War. The work referred to here is unknown.

new novel *A Free Solitude,* and £50 for a book of short stories. Now at a royalty of 5d per copy, they would have to sell nearly 7,500 copies to get back their money on the novel. Whereas the royalties on 2500 copies of *The Ghost* will only be about £50. Why can they afford to be, comparatively, so generous when they buy outright as they do from Mrs. Perrin? This lady is a particular friend of mine & I am sure she told me the truth as to the price. They offered her £100, and it was I who urged her to stick out. If everything is quite on the square, the inference is that Mrs. Perrin's books sell three times as well as mine: which I do not believe. Of course *The Ghost* may continue to sell for a time, but the bulk of the sale is already over. I do not wish to get any prejudiced opinion into my head about C. & W., but the facts certainly need a great deal of explanation. I wish you would ascertain how many they sold to 'The Times Book Club'.

Anyhow we have done with C. & W.

As regards *The City of Pleasure,* there is a definite contract to publish it at 6/-. They will want to alter this. I will not alter it, but if they wish to cancel the contract they may do so. Or if they wish to buy the book outright for £200 they may do so. You may tell them, so as not to render your position with them delicate in any other matters which do not concern me, that these are my definite instructions to you, & that you have no discretion.

As regards Chapman & Hall, their 'shady' reputation in the past does not influence me at all. If one only did business with people who were righteous, one's business would be restricted.

But what about the rumours as to their financial unsoundness?

And what about the difficulty you had with them as to Maugham's novel?

I knew Waugh many years ago, & he always struck me as being a very decent chap. He wrote to me the other day, apropos of an affair of Eden's, expressing high admiration for *Whom God hath joined.*

I quite agree that if Methuen is not keen Methuen is not our man. I am quite willing to go to Chapman & Hall. But it must be clearly understood that there shall be no question raised as to the character of my books. I am not in the least prepared to take lessons from any publisher as to what is or is not 'proper'. I have written two very outspoken books, & I shall certainly write more. I shall produce various sorts of books, and one sort will be the outspoken sort. You cannot put this before them too plainly. It is no use mincing it.

As to the book of short stories, tell Chatto he can have it for £100 outright. He will no doubt decline this. You can then end the negotiations. If I cannot at this time of day get an advance on a book, I will retire and become a grocer. Other things being satisfactory, offer the book of short stories and one novel to Waugh. The novel will be humorous. I want the same royalty as I got from Nutt.

Now that I am changing publishers I want to change definitely. I have therefore written you at some length, & I want to have your views at length. The matter is extremely important to me.

By the way, what about Heinemann?

Eden is absolutely satisfied with Chapman & Hall. And when *Eden* is satisfied, miracles have occurred! He considers Waugh most 'sympathetic.'

The next two books I shall write are humorous. One will be suited for serialisation. And I do not wish to write it at all unless the serialisation is arranged for. The other will not be suited for serialisation, & will be decidedly 'daring.' I told you about it —*The Honeymoon* it is called. Let me know which I ought to do first.

Did you receive my letter about the Tillotson short stories? If so, please let me know what you decided.

'My best short story' (from the *Grand Mag's* point of view) is 'His Worship the Goosedriver', the first story in *Tales of the Five Towns*. I will send you the reasons in due course.

Yours sincerely, Arnold Bennett

P.S. What occurred to the *Tribune* article? If it appeared, please send me a copy of the paper in which it appeared.

49. San Remo was where Bennett was spending a holiday.
Chatto and Windus have provided the following information on *The Ghost*: '2500 copies were printed in December 1906 and published on January 24 1907. The book evidently subscribed well, for a second printing of 2500 was ordered

TEXAS / MS. / 50

[Grand Hotel Royal]
[about 6 March 1907]

[no salutation]
Please deal with this how you like. Copy of my reply is appended.

E. A. B.

---

before the end of January. . . . But only 500 of the second impression were bound at that time, and no more were required until 1910.' Of *A Free Solitude* Chatto and Windus write: '5000 copies of Mrs. Perrin's novel were printed in February 1907 and published on March 7. . . . 2500 copies were bound in February, and a further 1250 in March–April, but no more until 1909. *A Free Solitude* did, therefore, in fact sell more and faster than *The Ghost*, though certainly not three times as many. The fact that twice as many copies were printed in the first instance was doubtless due to A. B. having successfully urged Mrs. Perrin to push C. & W's offer up from £100 to £150.' Bennett had known Mrs. Perrin (1867–1934) from his days on *Woman*.

The Macmillan brothers, Daniel and Alexander, had their first great commercial success with Kingsley's *Westward Ho!*, for which they paid £300 for the first edition and a 10 per cent. royalty for a later edition. Such rates were common, if inadequate. Chapman and Hall's treatment of Meredith was similar. Arthur Waugh (1866–1943), who became managing director of the firm in 1902, acknowledges in *A Hundred Years of Publishing* that the firm's underpayment of Meredith for his work as reader and writer 'cost the house dearly . . . in credit'. The trouble over Maugham's novel, *The Bishop's Apron*, published in 1906, is unknown.

The short story collection was *The Grim Smile of the Five Towns*. The humorous serial, *Helen with the High Hand*, was begun in April.

'His Worship the Goosedriver' appeared in the *Grand Magazine* in May with a prefatory note by Bennett:

'Among all my short stories I like this the best, because more than any other, it gave me pleasure to write it. I remember that when I finished it I read it aloud to two friends, and I frequently stopped to laugh. The two friends also laughed, but perhaps that was only their politeness—one never knows. I think the story illustrates with truthfulness certain romantic aspects of life in my "Five Towns". Josiah Curtenty was taken from a real person. This person died not long since, so I may now admit my indebtedness. He drove a pig through the streets of the town of which he was mayor, but this was only one of his exploits, which are legendary in the district. Also I like the story because I very particularly like Clara. I would not have married Clara, but I would have committed follies for her, as Mr. Gordon did. Lastly, my chief reason for preferring this story is a Clara-ish reason: "I like it best because I like it best." '

John Ford, Deputy City Librarian, Stoke-on-Trent, identifies the original of Curtenty as Aaron Edwards, three times Mayor of Longton:

'On the occasion of a charity Bazaar he asked the Duke of Sutherland to present a pig as the traditional prize for climbing a greasy pole. The Duke of Sutherland said certainly he would give the pig if the Mayor would drive it from the ducal residence at Trentham to Longton. Unaware that he was behaving like a Bennett character, His Worship took up His Grace's challenge and complied with the condition.'

The *Tribune* article is unknown.

50. This note is written in the margin of the following letter to Bennett from Alfred Nutt.

TEXAS / MS. / 51
(*From Alfred Nutt*)

> 57-59 Long Acre
> London, W.C.
> 4th March 1907

Dear Mr. Bennett,

The full return of sales of *Whom God Hath Joined* are now lying before me for 1906, since the end of which year sales have practically ceased.

The sales have been as follows:

> 1254 at 6/-
> 150 (col. ed.) at 2/-

The agreed royalties: 20% on the 6/- ed.; 3d. a copy on Colonial, work out, if I mistake not, at £25.4 & £1.17.6 or together £27.1.6.

In paying an advance of £125 I find I thus considerably exceeded the legitimate advance based on the actual initial sale. As a simple matter of fact I am out of pocket by just about the difference between [what] I should have paid & what I actually did pay.

When the book was issued, I found myself seriously handicapped by my desire to leave you a perfectly free hand in the artistic working of the story. The failure to sell an American edition was entirely due, if I may trust the assurances given me, to the method of treatment. As far as England is concerned you will recall my criticism of the denouement & my pointing out that you would certainly be misunderstood & that your impersonal, objective way of leaving people to draw their own conclusion instead of drawing it for them would deprive the book of much of that propaganda, thesis, interest that might otherwise have been counted upon. The bulk of your reviewers did misunderstand and the sale was certainly prejudiced thereby.

Let me also say that I had looked to the Continent for part of my market and did not clearly realise it was excluded therefrom, a misapprehension which affected my calculation of the advance royalty.

I don't want to cry over spilt milk, but I think I have a right to play upon your doing what you can to help me to retrieve the situation in the only way in which it can be retrieved, namely by the issue of a cheap edition. This would of course not carry the same royalty as the present one; indeed I should not be prepared to offer more than 10%. This would [?necessitate] modifying the present agreement & if you are willing I will draft a new clause. You may take it as fact that no more sales at 6/- are to be looked for.

I should be sorry to feel that I can't afford to back you against the Philistine public (as would certainly be the case if you vetoed the cheap edition I propose) and then I should have to abandon the idea of any further business transaction. I sincerely trust you will agree with me as to the only course to be pursued.

Very faithfully, Alfred Nutt

TEXAS / A.C. / 52
(*To Alfred Nutt*)

[Grand Hotel Royal]
[about 6 March 1907]

Dear Mr. Nutt,

Many thanks for your letter. The book has had a far less circulation than any recent work of mine. But I think this said phenomenon might be explained in ways other than the ways you suggest. It is, however, futile to go into that.

I never had the slightest intention of making the book 'propagandist'.

I have never concealed the fact that I considered the spontaneous offer of a commission from you as the greatest compliment I could possibly receive in the world of publishers. But at the same time you as a man of business must have been precisely aware that a commission given to an author is & must be an affair of risks.

As to the continental rights, surely the agreement was perfectly explicit.

I am perfectly willing to agree to any reasonable terms for a cheap edition. Indeed I am quite as anxious as you are that you should come as well as possible out of the financial transaction. I have written to Mr. Pinker & given him full powers to negotiate with you & settle a new clause. I can conceive that ultimately you may be fairly well pleased that you commissioned

Whom G Hath J. I need not point out to a person of your immense knowledge of literary history that a certain kind of work has a habit of proving profitable in the end.

Believe me etc. [Arnold Bennett]

u.c. / ms. / 53

Grand Hotel Royal
23 Mch 1907

My dear Pinker,

City of Pleasure

Good. This is all right. But how does this strike you, as regards what I said as to C & W's accounts? I have never made more than £90 on royalties out of any book issued by them. And yet, when faced with the choice between giving £200 for a book, or losing it, they give £200. £200 at a 5d. royalty means about 10,000 copies, & yet they say they only sold something over 2,500 of *The Ghost*. This contrast seems to me to demand some explanation, & I particularly want to know what you person- ally think of it. I am not of a disposition to carp against pub- lishers, but frankly ça m'a donné furieusement à penser.

Short stories

As this book will contain some of my best work, I will not sell the copyright outright. I will sell the copyright for 7 years for £100. If they do not care for this, I trust you can place the book elsewhere—say C. & Hall. I would sooner take the chance of making less out of another publisher than accept less than £100 from C. & Windus. *But I want the book issuing during the summer*, towards the end of June. I can't promise that it shall be 85,000 words, but I can promise that it shall be at least as long as any of my novels that Chatto & Windus have issued. The *Pall Mall Magazine* & the *Windsor* have each a story which goes into the volume. No doubt you can arrange with the respec- tive editors that these shall appear before June. There is also another story which you have: 'A Five Towns Xmas'. Will you kindly get from Tillotsons pulls of all the short stories I have

52. This copy of Bennett's letter is written on a blank page of Nutt's letter. For the sequel to the exchange, see pages 195–6. When Nutt died in 1910, Bennett had kind remarks to make of him in his *New Age* column.

written for them & send them to me in Paris. I expect this puts them to trouble, so kindly express to them rather particularly my indebtedness for the favour. I will see if any of these are good enough for the book. I think one or two are. The principal story in the book I am just now writing. It is unsuitable for magazines (not because of any riskiness, but because it is too severe & too long.)

By the way, among various things which you have to reply to me about is the question as to Tillotsons recent request for short stories.

Yours sincerely, E. A. Bennett

I return to Paris on Easter Monday.

U.C. / MS. / 54

Grand Hotel Royal
27 Mch 1907

My dear Pinker,

Some words, which you may have seen, passed between Phillpotts & *The Times*, in *The Times*, about 2 months ago. Moberly Bell afterwards wrote to Phillpotts, in a very pacific strain. He wrote several long private letters, & ended by hinting what great things *The Times* could do if it had, say, an edition of 30,000 copies of a book of Phillpotts' to handle; & indicated that authors did not know their own business.

Phillpotts wrote in reply describing *The Statue*, saying that it was just being finished, and had been seen complete by no one, and asking Moberly Bell to say frankly what he would do with it if he had it.

Moberly Bell was away. There was no reply till this morning when a telegram came from him asking for the manuscript and for terms, & to be put in communication with our agent.

Phillpotts has written referring him to you.

53. On Chatto and Windus's accounts see pages 77–80.
All three stories mentioned went into *The Grim Smile of the Five Towns*. The *Pall Mall Magazine* published 'The Lion's Share' in June. The *Windsor Magazine* published 'The Silent Brothers' in July; they had also published in January another story, 'The Baby's Bath', that went into the collection. 'A Five Towns Xmas', whose periodical publication is unknown, was given a new title, 'Beginning the New Year'. The principal story of the collection was 'The Death of Simon Fuge', which is usually reckoned to be one of Bennett's best stories.

Please see him, or rather let him see you.

I have never discussed the Book Club question with you. I may tell you briefly my opinion (which is very largely shared by authors, and, secretly, by some publishers) is that though both parties are wrong, *The Times* is less wrong than the publishers. Also I think that it will soon be settled—and settled by compromise. *The Times* profess a great anxiety for the welfare of authors. I attach no importance whatever to this, but they want to get hold of an author or two, to prove what they can do. To this end they would most probably spend much more money than under ordinary circumstances.

We see with absolute clearness that nothing must be done which would afterwards prejudice our position with the 'publisher's trust'.

This may as well be explained frankly to Moberly Bell at the start. But we are inclined to think that something could be done with *The Times* which would *not* prejudice our position afterwards with the Trust. For instance, a firm like Sisleys or any other free firm could be used as an intermediary, the supposition being that *The Times* is willing to do something special to obtain the advantage of Phillpotts's name.

By diplomatic skill an immense & harmless advertisement might be arranged for us.

In the first place what you have to do is to listen to what Moberly Bell has to say and then think it over *with an open mind*. It might be as well to discuss it with Curtis Brown. This would be only proper towards Phillpotts.

I don't think that Moberly Bell wants the serial rights. What he wants is the book rights. I fancy *The Times* would buy them outright at a stiffish price, & that this might be done without giving the ring a handle against us. Anyhow you will see.

If Morley has refused the serial rights, of course they must come into any transaction.

Phillpotts will be at the Grosvenor Hotel, Victoria, from *6 p.m.* on *Tuesday next* till *10.15* a.m. on *Wednesday*. We shall be very much obliged if you will call & see him between those hours so as to give him your views & hear his.

Yours sincerely, E. A. Bennett

54. *The Times*, headed by Moberly Bell (1847–1911), began its Book Club as a means of restoring itself to economic health. The Book Club offered a lending

u.c. / ms. / 55

3 rue d'Aumale
Paris
2nd April 1907

My dear Pinker,

Many thanks for your letter of the 28th.

I will not give way to Chattos about the book of short stories. But I want the *City of Pleasure* contract to go through. Therefore if there is any chance of them wishing to cry off that if the short stories are not arranged for, say that I will consider the short story question & get the *City of Pleasure* contract signed in the meantime.

What you say as to Waugh and Chapman & Hall is very satisfactory. Kindly go ahead with that. The delay in publication of short stories serially is very annoying. However, Waugh will not insist on an 85,000 word book, & next week I shall have a 20,000 word story done for the volume. I will cut the *Pall Mall* story; but it is their lookout if the thing is seriously impaired. *I* don't care. I care only for the volume form.

I shall do the humorous serial at once. It will be finished by

---

library service of new books, with free delivery within London, and the sale of these books at a large discount within a very short period after publication. The latter practice was immediately objected to by both regular booksellers and publishers. The latter refused to supply books and withdrew their advertisements from *The Times*. *The Times* was forced to preface its reviews of many books with the following notice:

'The Publishers of this book decline to supply *The Times* Book Club with copies on ordinary trade terms, and subscribers who would cooperate with *The Times* to defeat the Publishers' Trust will oblige us by abstaining from ordering the book so far as possible, though we are prepared to furnish it even at a pecuniary loss if subscribers insist.'

Such a notice preceded *The Times* review of Phillpotts' *The Whirlwind* on 25 January, and elicited from Phillpotts the following letter:

'Sir, — I see incorporated with a review of my recent new book a request to your Book Club not to purchase it. You invite them to rob a British artist of his bread, that your revenues may reap some slight benefit.

"How are the mighty fallen!"

Is it too late to urge upon our greatest newspaper the unwisdom of its latest ways? . . .

Most faithfully yours, Eden Phillpotts'

No arrangement was made with *The Times* for *The Statue*. After eighteen months *The Times* was defeated by the publishers' trust.

Charles Morley (d. 1916) was on the staff of the *Pall Mall Magazine*, which likewise rejected *The Statue*.

the end of July. I shall then do a long serious novel, which will *contain a great deal of humour* as well as of tragedy. It will be at least 120,000 words long. It is all ready to do, and will be really the most ambitious & biggest thing I have done. If Waugh liked *Whom God hath joined* (& he spontaneously wrote me in praise of it), he will like this new one much more. Kindly tell him about this & explain that he can have the two books—the short story book & this one.

I repeat that I attach much importance to the publication of the short stories in the summer. They are artistic work, some of my best, & they must come between a potboiler like *Ghost*, & another potboiler like *City of Pleasure*. I cannot let 2 potboilers come together. Please therefore arrange the short story volume with C & H. unless C. & W. will give way, *at once*.

As regards the N. N. Syndicate I think it will be well to wake 'em up, & tell them they must either sign or cry off at once. They have dallied much too long.

The two things that I want to impress on you are, the importance of the short story volume, and the length, & general ambitiousness, & the blend of tragedy & humour in the new novel, which will be ready for publication next summer. This is not the *daring humorous* novel, but one which, though I have had it in my head for 4 years, I have not mentioned to you. It is a great work.

Tillotsons wrote asking for 2 short stories at 3 guineas a 1000. I wrote to you asking if I ought to accept this, & I sent you their request to answer. It is this letter that you have not had. They took my silence for consent, & I thought you had written to them, so now the matter is arranged anyhow. Don't trouble further with it.

Yours sincerely, E. A. Bennett

55. 3 rue d'Aumale was Bennett's Paris address after he left 4 rue de Calais at about the end of November 1906.

Chapman and Hall, and not Chatto and Windus, published *The Grim Smile of the Five Towns*. They paid Bennett the starting royalty of 20 per cent. that he had been unable to get from Chatto. 'The Death of Simon Fuge' is the long story. The *Pall Mall* story is 'The Lion's Share', which appears in the same volume. The collection appeared in June. *The Ghost* (Chatto) had appeared in January, and *The City of Pleasure* (Chatto) followed in October.

The humorous serial, *Helen with the High Hand*, was finished by 15 June. The Northern Newspaper Syndicate was interested in it. The long serious and great novel was *The Old Wives' Tale*. Pinker's report of it to Waugh brought an offer

u.c. / ms. / 56

Les Sablons
Près Moret
S & M.
[postmarked 16 April 1907]

My dear Pinker,

Our poor dear Eden is worrying over the *Statue*, & wants me to worry you: which I have declined to do. He has got into his head the idea that from the time you received the complete thing to the time you saw him at the Grosvenor, nothing was done with the thing at all. I have told him to do anything he wants to do through Brown, but he will doubtless continue to worry me. How *does* the thing stand with Morley? I understood that he had it to consider. As Eden's temperament is a hard fact with which we have to deal, you had better perhaps keep me informed of what goes on, instead of adopting your ordinary (and much better) procedure of saying nothing until there is something to say.

Yours sincerely, E. A. Bennett

u.c. / ms. / 57

3 rue d'Aumale
23 April 1907

My dear Pinker,

Eden was anxious to do all sorts of things with *The Statue*, including take it off *The Times* before they had done with it, & take it off you & hand it to Brown. I have definitely stopped him. In fact I have had a hell of a row with him, & I do not think that either you or Brown will be worried by impatient interferences in this matter any more. Under the circumstances it will be well if you report to Brown what goes on. Hint to him what has passed, & suggest that he keep Eden fully informed, so that he will have no excuse for complaining. I have un-

---

from Waugh in a letter of 8 April of a royalty of 20 per cent., rising to 25 per cent. after the sale of 5,000 copies, with an advance of £150. The novel proved to be 200,000 words long.

The Tillotson stories are unidentified.

56. On Les Sablons see pages 60–61.

On Morley see page 86n.

doubtedly left him extremely sore, but really a line has to be drawn somewhere, & I think I am the man to draw it.

I have had no copies of *The Ghost*.

Please pay my cheque into Cooks, Paris, on the 1st. I am *excessivement à court*.

Yours sincerely, E. A. Bennett

Many thanks for your letter about *The Statue*

You will receive in a few days the typescript of the novel of your new client, Mrs. Farley, 16 rue de la Paix. The important thing is to sell this quickly for cash on publication. Price doesn't matter. I simply want to get her encouraged to go on. If she is, she will produce regularly, and should prove a profitable small client to you. I should say Chatto, Ward Lock, or Sisleys. I have read through the novel, and had it altered to suit my notions several times. So you can take my guarantee that it is sound, quiet, capable, library fiction, quite up to the standard.

u.c. / ms. / 58

3 rue d'Aumale
2nd May 1907

My dear Pinker,

Many thanks for your letter received yesterday, the two letters received today, and the books.

Phillpotts and I are now on the most amicable terms after our row, and the *next* serial is about half done. But I think it will be better for all communications as to the business side of the *Statue* to go through Brown to him. As a matter of fact four people cannot manage a business affair; two are already more than enough.

57. Agnes Farley was the wife of an American dentist practising in Paris. She was introduced to Bennett by Violet Hunt, who in the preface to a joint translation of Casanova's *Memoirs* describes her as 'the great *piocheur* in localities and scandals in old Paris and London'. She in turn introduced Bennett to the family of Eleanor Green. Later in 1907 Chapman and Hall published her piece of library fiction, *Ashdod*. She seems to have produced nothing else of the sort. In 1911, under the pseudonym 'Vados', she published a book about French country life, *The Belmont Book*, with an introduction by Bennett.

I have already told Phillpotts that if the decision had been left to me I should have accepted £300 from Pearson long ago. He made no reply to this.

As to bookrights, he has reiterated to me positively that Methuen will give £600. If Laurie lost (on paper) £150 on *Sinews,* I think the fault is largely Laurie's; the reception of the book was all that could be desired. I certainly think Laurie's offer of £350 down ought to be refused. I am sure that £500 ought to be got at least, especially having regard to the success of the *Whirlwind*. This is my real opinion, & you know I am not prone to overvalue my wares. Brown must certainly deal with Phillpotts. I don't think he will have much trouble—as to the serial.

Yours sincerely, E. A. Bennett

U.C. / MS. / 59

3 rue d'Aumale
5th May 1907

My dear Pinker,
    I heard from Hughes Massie today.
    I cannot at the moment put my hand on your accounts, but I am sure there is at least one item (of a few pounds) in one of them for protecting one of my novels in America. This novel must have been *A Great Man, Leonora* or *Sacred & Profane Love.* I think it was the first. Kindly look into this & let me know by return. I was under the impression that all my serious books had been partially protected in America. I cannot too strongly insist to anyone who has anything to do with my serious work that there is money in it, ultimately, and those who persuade themselves to act on this assumption from the start will have least cause to kick themselves in the distant future. I am a classic writer. Ahem!

Yours sincerely, Arnold Bennett

58. The next serial was presumably *The Food of the Phagocytes.*
    The Whirlwind was a Phillpotts novel published by Chapman and Hall earlier in the year (see pages 84–86).
    59. Hughes Massie (d. 1921) was in these years associated with Curtis Brown. The partnership was dissolved before the First World War, and each man continued his own agency.

u.c. / ms. / 60

Les Sablons
here till Saturday next
2nd June 1907

My dear Pinker,

Many thanks for your letter. My plans do not depend on the N. N. S., as at the end of next week the book will be *finished*. I have not yet got a title for it; but I think you will agree that it is a very agreeable and amusing domestic serial, really humorous. You will arrange matters how you like. But I reckon that the English serial & book rights of the thing together must be worth together a *minimum* of £300. My own instinct is to tell the N. N. S. to go to hell. However, I much prefer you to act on your own instinct.

Yours sincerely, E. A. Bennett

P.S. Please pay my cheque into Cook's, Paris. I shall see you in London in about a fortnight.   E. A. B.

u.c. / ms. / 61

3 rue d'Aumale
11th June 1907

My dear Pinker,

This time I really *am* going to be married, to a French lady, and soon. It is a great shame that I should come to you twice in a year for money, on the plea of marriage. But the fact is that money spent in anticipation of one marriage will not obviate the necessity of spending money on another.

At the end of this week I shall have finished the humorous serial, and I think I am putting the value of that (£300 for everything), *The City of Pleasure* (£200) & my share of *The Statue* (£500), at somewhat less than their minimum if I say that in these three you have £1,000 worth of my stuff in hand at the moment. I shall be glad therefore if you can arrange to let me have an *extra* £100 within a month or so. I hope

60. The National Press Agency, not the Northern Newspaper Syndicate, finally handled *Helen with the High Hand*. It was published serially as *The Miser's Niece* in the *Star*, beginning 12 June 1909.

this will not be inconvenient to you. I particularly want a cheque for £50 to reach my sister, Mrs. W. W. Kennerley, 37 Clarendon Road, Putney, S.W., on the 1st July without fail.

I shall see you next week. I mean to come to London on Sunday.

Yours sincerely, E. A. Bennett

u.c. / ms. / 62

Les Sablons
3 Augt 1907

My dear Pinker,

I return the contract signed. As all the criticisms of it which immediately occur to me will doubtless have occurred to you and Curtis Brown, I need make no comment on it. Except that it is an absolute proof that Phillpotts' boast of a certainty of £600 for the book, which he repeated to Curtis Brown after he had made it to me, could not be substantiated.

The book is, I think, something like 80,000 words in length, not 70,000. Kindly explain to Cassells that it is written to appear in 16 or in 8 instalments.

It should be set up from the *MS.*, not from the typescript. Kindly insist on this.

61. Bennett met Marguerite Soulie in January, and shortly thereafter was nursed back to health by her from a case of food poisoning. Writing of her in his study of Bennett, Georges Lafourcade remarks, 'It is easy enough to understand what attracted him to his first wife: as a man, her beauty and personality; as an artist, her talent; as a native of the Five Towns, her Parisian characteristics; as a practical man, her domestic assets.' She wrote poetry, and published it; she also gave recitals of French poetry. None of her qualities, though, not even the domestic assets, guaranteed a successful marriage. Twenty-five days after the marriage, which took place on 4 July, Bennett was writing to his sister Tertia (Mrs. W. W. Kennerley: 1872–1949): 'The one difficulty that I have in marriage is to refrain from looking after everything. I am so used to controlling every department of my household, from the washing to the dusting, that I continually forget that it is no longer necessary for me to worry about such things.' The marriage is described by Reginald Pound in his biography; he summarizes the last years of it as 'a slowly gathering crisis of infelicities'. A separation was arranged in 1921. Mrs. Bennett died in 1960.

Mrs. Kennerley was Bennett's youngest sister. *The Old Wives' Tale* was dedicated to her husband.

I shall be glad if you will let me know exactly what the terms are for serial and for book rights in the United States.

I presume you received the MS. of the short story.

                                        Yours sincerely, E. A. Bennett

u.c. / ms. / 63

                                        Les Sablons
                                        8 August 1907

My dear Pinker,

Many thanks for your letter. I return the [?] form signed. I shall be much obliged if in writing to this man you will ask him to be good enough to send me, here, copies of any of my books which he has published or is to publish. I suppose he published *A Great Man*.

With regard to the serial, I entirely understand you. Of course, earlier in the proceedings, I also should have been disposed to refuse anything less than £300, having regard to the fact that £450 was got for the last one. But I would have willingly agreed to £300. As to the future, you have, as always, a free hand so far as I am concerned. I will have no direct communication with Phillpotts as to the business side of it. He must vent all his bad manners & unbusinesslike childishness on his agent, who must take the responsibility for it to you. If you are not satisfied with the conduct of the matter on Brown's side, you have my full authority to protest. My position with Phillpotts, as regards business, is now clearly defined. He has his agent; I have mine. Mine has unhampered powers from me, & I will have no communications from anyone about the serial except my agent. This seems to me perfectly logical.

I do not want to stop these serials until it suits me to do so. Even if they fail, as *The Statue* has done, they bring in £1,000 at least, all told, and my share of that amply repays me for five weeks' work. Moreover, on their plane, they are thoroughly sound & conscientious work, of which nobody need be ashamed. In any difficulty between me & Phillpotts as to them, I feel

62. The £600 for *The Statue* refers to book rights only. Cassell issued the book the following year. No serial publication is known.

sure that if I stood out he would give way. He is a coward, morally, &, moreover, not at all anxious to drop a minimum of £500 a year.

Yours sincerely, Arnold Bennett

P.S. If I were you, I should let Brown try to sell the serial rights of the next one. It is called *The Food of the Phagocytes*. You might suggest this to him. We should then see. . . .
Let them set up from the typescript.

u.c. / ms. / 64

Les Sablons
9th Sept 1907

My dear Pinker,

Many thanks for your two letters. I am very sorry you were not able to come; but I hope you *will* come, as soon as you can. A visit from you would give me very genuine pleasure.

I had better give you now an outline of my plans.

I have finished the 'Stage Society' play.

During this month I have to finish a play in collaboration with E. P., which is more than half done. There seems to be a good chance of *Children of the Mist* being produced at the 'Scala'. Anyhow after the play now in hand, neither E. P. nor I will touch any play until something has been produced. I have now, either singly or in collaboration, at least 8 long plays in hand, & it only needs the success of one to make the rest more marketable. Curtis Brown said he wanted a play. I gave him *A Wayward Duchess*. He was most enthusiastic about it, but—well, you know. . . .

Next month I proceed to the big novel for Chapman & Hall. This will be decidedly long, 120,000 words. Copyright of it *must* somehow be secured in the States. In every way it will be my largest work. I expect to have this finished at the end of

---

63. The supposed publisher of *A Great Man* is unknown. Presumably he was an American pirate—see the letter of 5 May. But no American edition of *A Great Man*, unauthorized or authorized, seems to have appeared until Doran's of 1910.
The Food of the Phagocytes seems never to have been finished.

May, unless E. P. worries me to finish our next serial, which is about half done.

Yours sincerely, Arnold Bennett

u.c. / ms. / 65

Les Sablons
14 Sept 1907

My dear Pinker,

Many thanks for your letter. I hope you will come as soon as you can. (Grapes ripe in a fortnight—best grapes in France.) This is only a country cottage affair, & not our real *home*, which is shut up as I find it impossible to tear myself away from the country; but we shall be able to keep life in you while you stay. We remain here till December.

When *The City of Pleasure* appears, kindly send *2* copies to F. C. Bennett, 1 Hill Street, Burslem, Stoke on Trent; and the rest here.

Conrad's book, though of course very distinguished, is not as good as his last.

My wife's meilleurs sentiments. I have explained to her that of all my friends you are the most essential to her happiness.

Yours sincerely, E. A. Bennett

u.c. / ms. / 66

Les Sablons
21st Sept 1907

My dear Pinker,

Many thanks for your letter. You must do as you think best with C. & W. Personally I see no reason whatever why we

64. Pinker had made a trip to France, and Bennett had pressed him to come to Moret.

The Stage Society play, *Cupid and Commonsense*, was a dramatization of *Anna of the Five Towns*. It was presented on 26 and 27 January 1908, at the Shaftesbury Theatre. On the other plays see page 59n.

65. Francis Clayton Bennett, a year younger than his brother Arnold, became a solicitor, as their father had been. In earlier years he did some reviewing for Arnold in *Woman*. He was active throughout his life in amateur musical and dramatic societies.

The Secret Agent, published earlier in the year, received an unsympathetic press. Bennett was comparing it with *Nostromo* rather than with *The Mirror of the Sea* of the previous year.

should oblige them. No light whatever has yet been thrown on the great mystery why, though I have never received even £100 as the proceeds of a single book, they are, when faced with the alternative of paying £200 for a book or losing it, prepared to pay £200. As it stands the whole affair is fishy. Perhaps they can explain it, but they have not done so. They published *The Ghost* at 2/6 solely to suit themselves, and in defiance of their contract with us, which we released them from out of sheer good-nature. Their experiment was a failure, & now they want us to make further sacrifices in order to help them. If we have anything to gain, let us meet them; but if we have not, why should we do so? These are my views. After considering them, you will act as seems to you advisable.

I am very glad you like *Love & Riches*. Of course I wrote this chiefly for serial use, and if it is not well placed serially I shall be extremely disappointed. I designed it to be something which would please the serial public without giving the *serious* public a chance to accuse me of 'playing down'—as in *The City of Pleasure*, etc. If there is any demand for humorous serials, this ought to sell. You might enquire from Curtis Brown if he has placed it yet in the U.S. He asked for it—he was not approached —and he cannot say that it isn't good sound stuff. So that if he doesn't place it he must withdraw his pretensions, and ought within a reasonable time to return the manuscript, and leave the field free to the less boastful.

Yours sincerely, E. A. B.

U.C. / MS. / 67

179 Waterloo Road
Burslem,
Stoke on Trent
20th Dec 1907

My dear Pinker,
I send you today by registered parcel post the MS. of the first book of *The Old Wives' Tale*, except the first two pages. A flat

66. On the Chatto and Windus mystery see pages 77–80.
Love and Riches was a tentative title for *Helen with the High Hand*. The serial title was *The Miser's Niece*. Before the book was published by Chapman and Hall, Bennett changed the heroine's name from Ellen to Helen, and before copies went out he discovered that the running heads read 'Helen of the High Hand'. One copy in that form survives. Brown did not place the novel in America.

parcel will arrive addressed to me care of you, from Liverpool. Please open it. It will contain the first 2 pages, which have been on exhibition at Liverpool, as an example of what MS. ought to be. Kindly have the stuff typewritten, in duplicate if necessary, and insist on my instructions that the *greatest possible care* must be taken in handling the MS., which is extremely precious.

I shall be glad if you will send me five £5 notes by registered post to the above address on Monday or Tuesday, & send a cheque for £25, on the *30th*, to Mrs. Kennerley 37 Clarendon Rd., Putney S.W. This will make up the £50 for the first of January.

There will be £42 due to me shortly from the *Dispatch*. On this & on all work I do for the *Dispatch* you have most richly earned your commission. But it is journalism money & if they send the cheque to you I shall be glad if you will pass it on to me, less your commission, as I count on journalism money. If they send it to me I will advise you.

From Dec 31st my address will be Ilchester Mansions Hotel, St. Petersburg Place, W., & my wife says you are to come to lunch with us as soon as possible, & fix your own date, provided it isn't later than the 7th January.

Best wishes,

Yours sincerely, Arnold Bennett

67. 179 Waterloo Road was the address at which Bennett's mother lived during her widowhood.

In a portion of the journal published in *Life and Letters* in 1929, Bennett describes the origin of the fine calligraphy which he developed for *The Old Wives' Tale* and his later novels. His sister Tertia and her husband, W. W. Kennerley, pointed out to him that he had no hobby. He took up calligraphy.

'Yesterday [23 July 1907] I began to perceive that my hobby of fine writing and illumination could not advance on sound lines unless I combined utility with beauty. . . . I have an idea that I can produce the most beautiful original manuscript of a novel that a novelist ever did produce. It will be the manuscript of *The Old Wives' Tale*. I suppose all this reflection and experimentation amounts to the sad death of a hobby. The hobby is no longer a hobby, but whether it is debased or ennobled God knows. I am a bit daunted at the prospect of writing a whole novel, and a long one, in a formal hand. It frightens me more than the composition. . . .'

The *Daily Dispatch* (Manchester) published articles by Bennett from 1907 to 1910 and perhaps later.

Bennett and his wife remained in London for the next two months.

u.c. / ms. / 68

> 3 Ilchester Gardens
> [London]
> 6 Jan 1908

My dear Pinker,

Many thanks for sending me the express letter. And all my excuses! The fact is, one is apt to forget that you are human. I think I ought to assure you that this irregular need of money on my part is in no way caused by personal affairs, but is due to my peculiar responsibilities as the head of a large family. I told you when I saw you that, under my wife's influence, I was now living in the most reasonable way possible, & this is the fact. I am spending much less than I used to, & the effect of this will soon be apparent. During my absence from Paris I have let the flat there, & we live here on £7 a week inclusive. I should be all right now even, were it not that one of our mutual acquaintances persists in owing me a sum of £100, which I can't get.

These explanations are due to you. They do not mitigate my need of money. Send me £10 tomorrow if you can. Anyhow we expect you on Wednesday at 1. And anyhow I am very much obliged to you.

> Yours sincerely, Arnold Bennett

u.c. / ms. / 69

> Les Sablons
> 15 Mch 1908

My dear Pinker,

Your letters of the 11th & 12th (2) & the two letters from the N. P. A. were addressed to Ilchester Gardens. They have reached me.

I return the two N. P. A. letters.

As to that of the 9th.

I never keep reviews. I throw them away every few months. I will see if I can put my hand on a few recent ones. Anyhow, opposite the title page of the 2nd edition of the *Grand Babylon Hotel*, there are a lot of real beauties, which might be copied out. I expect you have it, or C. & W. can furnish them. I will send a portrait.

3 Ilchester Gardens
6 Jan 1908

dear Pinker

Many thanks for sending me the express letter. And all my excuses! the fact is, one is apt to forget that you are human. I think I ought to assure you that this irregular need of money on my part is in no way caused by personal affairs, but is due to my peculiar responsibilities as the head of a large family. I told you when I saw you that, under my wife's influence, I was now living in the most reasonable way possible, & this is the fact. I am spending much less than I used to, & the effect of this will soon be apparent. During my absence from Paris I have let the flat there, — we live here on £7 a week inclusive. I should be all right now even, were it not that one of our mutual acquaintance persists in owing me a sum of £100, which I can't get.

These explanations are due to you. They do not mitigate my need of money. Lend me £10 tomorrow if you can. Anyhow we expect you on Wednesday at 1. And anyhow I am very much obliged to you.

yours sincerely
Arnold Bennett

As to that of the 11th.

Whoever has counted the book as 46,875 words has counted wrong. I have not the MS. here, but I have the details of the instalments in my diary, & they add up to 50,700 words. I always count all my work, word by word. I sent the stuff to you as being over 50,000 words. It is. Mr. Reburn is wrong in saying that the story can only be divided into 10 instalments. It is specially constructed to be divided into 12 instalments, the usual way, and it cannot be properly divided in any other way. (As to length, consult the typewriter's bill.) I can if necessary get the MS. from Paris, & furnish Mr. Reburn with particulars of the proper division. If he wanted 13 instalments he should have made this a condition. It is to be remembered that this story was not written specially for the N. P. A. You had it in hand and after reading it decided that it would do for them. Had I written it specially for them I should have interpreted between 50 & 60,000 words to mean 55,000. The actual length meets the letter of the contract. Of course I should like to meet the N. P. A. in any way that will not cause me too much trouble, and I would write in a complete chapter of a few thousand words if you think it advisable. I cannot possibly, however, 'strengthen' the first few chapters. The first few chapters are perfectly all right, & very interesting, & I cannot under any circumstances alter them. Does Reburn think he had commissioned a story by William Le Queux?

Buried Alive

I think you will like all this book. Anyhow I am very glad the opening appeals to you. As to disposing of it, do *exactly* as you think best. I wrote it because, as I told you, I wanted some money, & I threw it in as an extra. I now find I want temporarily more money than I anticipated. So long as you arrange this, I don't mind. As regards the serial, it is not a book that will 'keep'. If a serial opening can't be got at once, I should be inclined to sacrifice the serial, & get some publisher to specialise in it. I agree with you that it ought to go.

Yours sincerely, Arnold Bennett

69. The National Press Agency, of which John Reburn was commercial mana-ger, was handling *Helen with the High Hand*. Among his other complaints, Reburn noted that 'the first few chapters are not of sufficient interest to grip the

U.C. / MS. / 70

Les Sablons
21 Mch 1908

My dear Pinker,

I enclose a letter from the 'New Age Press', & copy of my reply. Kindly deal with the matter. On the evening before I left London, Orage, who runs this firm, & who is a friend of mine, urged me to let him have these articles to make 2nd & 3rd volumes in a new series which he has begun with Shaw's *Sanity of Art*. He says they can be practically sure of selling 5,000 of each book. They publish nothing but absolutely serious stuff. I know that you did not seem keen, some time ago, on my republishing these articles; but I think you were wrong, & I think that when you see them away from the vile headings & associations of the *Evening News*, you will change your mind. Anyhow, without exception you are the only friend who, having mentioned them, has not hoped that they would be republished. Orage, who is an ex-lecturer on English literature, is most enthusiastic as to them, merely as literature. Personally I think they are quite good & quite new. I should be sorry if they were lost.

This explanation is due to you.

Yours sincerely, Arnold Bennett

---

reader'. Bennett wrote a supplementary instalment of 5,000 words on 28 and 29 March. The serial began appearing in the *Star* on 12 June 1909.

Buried Alive, perhaps the best of Bennett's comic novels, was written in January and February. On 17 January Bennett wrote in his journal: 'Tomorrow I shall have finished a quarter of the whole. I am deliberately losing sight of the serial, and writing it solely as a book. I do this just a little under the influence of Pinker, with whom we lunched at the Gaiety on Wednesday. He was quietly pessimistic as to serial markets; and advised writing for book-form, and then seeing afterwards if a serial can be carved out of the book.' Bennett left off the writing of *The Old Wives' Tale* at the end of the previous November, when he finished Book I.

70. A. R. Orage (1873–1934) published *How to Live on Twenty-Four Hours a Day* and *Literary Taste* in 1908 and 1909 respectively. The former appeared in the *Evening News* beginning 6 May 1907 and had a remarkable success there. It was succeeded by several articles on book-buying. Bennett apparently reconceived the latter series after he wrote the present letter; he published the series that became *Literary Taste* in *T. P.'s Weekly* beginning 2 October 1908.

u.c. / ms. / 71

Villa des Néfliers
Avon S/M
17 June 1908

My dear Pinker,

The serious novel is proving terrific. It will be 200,000 words long. I shall finish it on the 15th September. Waugh can have the first 150,000 words at the end of July if he wants to begin setting up. The title is *The Old Wives' Tale*. I assume that a new contract must be signed. I suppose it can be published at the end of October.

I shall post the new story for *B. & W.* on Friday. With regard to the other story 'The Glimpse', if you have no destination for this, I think the *Albany Review* might take it. They wrote to me last year & asked me for stuff, but as they wouldn't give a definite commission I refused. They are much impressed by my work, & it would be well, if you offer the story, to explain frankly how it comes to be in the market.

Yours sincerely, Arnold Bennett

u.c. / ms. / 72

Villa des Néfliers
17 June 1908

My dear Pinker,

Many thanks for yours of the 15th & the copy correspondence.

I quite agree with you that the point is not a technical point at all. I think also that I have lost quite enough money through the eccentricities of my collaborator on *The Statue*. The serial rights would have been sold, most probably, by you for at least £200 had not Phillpotts absolutely declined to consider any such sum. And I only consented to this scorning of offers on the

---

71. The Villa des Néfliers near Fontainebleau was the Bennetts' country home for the next three years. Bennett obtained the place after failing to arrange with the Leberts to lease their home at Les Sablons.

The new story for *Black & White*, 'The Glimpse', was not accepted by them. Bennett expected that the story, which concerns a man at the point of death, would be 'much too good, too spiritual' for their taste. (See the note on the novel of the same name, page 151n.) In rejecting the story, the editor told Bennett that he himself liked it but his readers would not. It was published by the *New Age* on 4 November 1909, and republished in *The Matador of the Five Towns*.

strength of Phillpotts's reiterated positive statement to me that Methuens would give £600 for the book. There appears to have been no ground for this statement, and in the end Phillpotts, having made a general mess of the whole thing, insisted on accepting an offer which at best cannot be described as good. Moreover, having agreed to the publication of the book in March, he deliberately ruined the chances of the book by publishing a volume of his own in January and another in February.

It is impossible to protect one's self against all the acts of a collaborator with peculiar personal notions of what constitutes honourable conduct and business methods. In acceding to Phillpotts's request that I should collaborate with him, I took the risks which a collaborator must take, & I accept the consequences. But I can, & I think I ought to, defend my legal rights. If Phillpotts tries to make a present to Cassells of what does not belong to him, and if Cassell's idea of business is that they can accept such a present, either one or the other of them must suffer. The General Press cannot possibly have acquired any right which involves a modification of the agreement without my signature or yours. If *I* had consented to a modification of the agreement without consulting Phillpotts there would have been an immense uproar.

To me, the theory that Cassell's, by dint of calling themselves 'Cassells' General Press', can get something for nothing, seems grotesque. But of course if Phillpotts has made them a present he must so arrange that his generosity does not involve me in expense.

Yours sincerely, Arnold Bennett

P.S. I write to you in this strain so that you can show Brown a copy of the letter if you feel inclined to. A. B.

72. *The Statue* was published by Cassell in March 1908. Whether they obtained the serial rights and perhaps resold them to an American firm is unknown. Phillpotts' letters to Pinker about the quarrel display no rancour towards Bennett. They are concerned only to defend the propriety of his conduct.

U.C. / MS. / 73 Villa des Néfliers
26 June 1908

My dear Pinker,

Thank you for your letter. I return the contract signed.

As regards *Old Wives' Tale*, I cannot promise it before the 15 Sept., but I can promise it definitely for that date. Surely it can thus be published on Oct. 15th, which will be early enough. This book is 3 times as long as *Buried Alive* and it is a very big undertaking.

I hope something decent is going to be done with *Buried Alive*, & that Waugh will do all he possibly can. He must know that the book & its author are worth a special effort!

My *Human Machine* articles are just finishing in *T. P.'s Weekly*. They have made a sensation among the readers which Whitten describes to me in a letter as *immense*. He suggests that they would like to republish them at 1/-, through Hodder & Stoughton; I said I would accept a 2d royalty. I shall be glad if you will enquire what is being done. Whitten is very enthusiastic but he is so casual that no one can ever know what he is leaving undone. These articles are 22,000 words in length. They are really quite striking, & they undoubtedly have startled a lot of people. They are worth looking after. I think Waugh ought to read them.

Kindly pay my next cheque into Cooks, Paris.

Yours sincerely, Arnold Bennett

TEXAS / MS. / 74 Villa des Néfliers
9 July 1908

My dear Pinker,

Many thanks for your letter & Waugh's.

If I am asked whether I consider that a book of mine is worth £150 on account of royalties, I should be obliged to reply, honestly: 'I do not know'. As regards the bulk of my previous books, I have never been satisfied as to what the sales really were. ~~I make no accusations. I merely assert the existence of mysteries.~~ All that I can possibly state as a fact is that my

73. *The Old Wives' Tale* was finished on 31 August; it was published on 23 October. *The Human Machine* was published by Orage's New Age Press later in 1908.

previous publishers chose to pay a considerably larger sum than
£150 for a book infinitely inferior to anything that Waugh has
had, rather than lose it.

I strongly object to the introduction of *The Grim Smile* into
the argument. That book was not adequately advertised, & did
not have a chance. I do not in the least blame Waugh, as the
season was bad. I state the fact. It must also be remembered
that we refused £100 for the book in order to give it to Waugh.

As regards *Buried Alive*, I think it is rather too early to judge.
Waugh has here a humorous book, a book that pleases him, &
a book that pleases you. The reviews have been excellent. And
I don't think it can be argued that I am an unknown man. In
the phrase of the street, it seems to me that the situation is now
up against Waugh.

~~I leave you absolutely free to deal with this matter as you like.~~
I should be disgusted to think that a publisher was going to lose
over my books. But I think a publisher must take some risks.
The author takes risks. On certain occasions one has to speak
frankly of one's self, & so I will not disguise my opinion that I
am one of the future great prizes of the publishing world. I did
not form this opinion myself. It was forced on me by many people
known and unknown. It is very widely held by very good
judges. Waugh, and the directors of his company, must consider
this. ~~Do exactly as you like.~~ I need not tell you that the idea of
forcing a contract on an unwilling Waugh is distasteful to me,
~~& that I would not dream of trying to do it.~~ Waugh, however,
has more than once expressed his desire for this contract, since
he received *Buried Alive*.

Show him this letter if you like.

Yours sincerely, Arnold Bennett

u.c. / ms. / 75

Villa des Néfliers
8 Nov 1908

My dear Pinker,

In reply to your letter, I thought I had told you a long time
ago about Mrs. Perrin, I did my very best to put her in the way

74. Waugh paid Bennett £150 in advance on *The Old Wives' Tale*.

Buried Alive, Bennett had to acknowledge in 1911, 'was received with majestic
indifference by the English public, an indifference which has persisted to this day'.

of salvation; but she would not have it. She says she once went to you (apropos of *East of Suez*, I think) and that you snubbed her so effectually that she would never dare to approach you again. She must have *felt* hurt, whether she was or not. This is her version, to which I attach no importance; but she does. I expect you told her that there was no hope for short stories. In general there isn't. But it did just happen that *East of Suez* sold well, & brought her into prominence. With Kipling, Barrie, Crockett, Quiller-Couch, Arthur Morrison, Doyle, Jacobs, & sundry others she is an example of a reputation built on short stories—which publishers, who ought to know their business, will never touch if they can help it. If it is any consolation to you, she has no agent at all,—or had not when I last saw her.

Do you want Frank Harris? If so, I think I could bring him into the fold. I need not tell you that artistically, in the opinion of the very best judges, he stands extremely high. He knows everything except the business side of literature. His last book *The Bomb* (which is a most masterly thing) is published by Long (!) who gave him £75 in advance. He has two or three books unpublished; including one on Shakespeare which is probably the most penetrating book on Shakespeare ever written. I know nobody at all who understands literature and the craft thereof so well as he does. As for his reputation in the City, he is probably neither better nor worse than any average City man. I regard him as a sublime adventurer, capable of strong hatreds, but incapable of a meanness. He looks like a horsedealer, is forbidding at first, and ultimately becomes miraculously seductive, if he likes you. You may not care to touch him. He is, however, undoubtedly a genius, comparable to Conrad at his best. I should not mention him, did I not know that he has books ready. He was asking me about an agent. I did not mention you, as I was not sure if you would consent. He has a very great opinion of my views.

Please do not send 'The Glimpse' to the *English Review* until you hear from me. Hueffer considers *The Old Wives' Tale* a great masterpiece, & is having it reviewed in the second number of the *Review*. Wells writes me that in his opinion the book is strictly great & that no other writer 'could have come anywhere near it'. Phillpotts has broken a long silence in order to say that, though he regards our friendship as definitely broken, he feels he must tell me that *The Old Wives' Tale* stands on a higher plane than any novel of modern times. This may amuse you, but it pleases me.

Yours sincerely, Arnold Bennett

U.C. / MS. / 76

Villa des Néfliers
12 Nov 1908

My dear Pinker,

Many thanks for your letter.

I quite agree with you as to Harris. In your place I would not handle him. But I thought I would put him fairly before you.

It may interest you to know that Murray Gilchrist has at last *really* left Colles, and is quit of him. Lawyers came on the scene in the end! I think you might write to him. There is not much money in him, but there might be. Anyhow he lives on what he makes. And to have a genuine artist on your list always does you good.

I wish you would telephone to Waugh and ask if he has sent review copies to the *New Age*, the *Staffordshire Sentinel* (Hanley) and the *Mercure de France*. No review has yet appeared in the *Sentinel*, and I cannot understand it if a copy has been sent. The *New Age* (which is as likely as any paper to get me readers) complain that though they have asked for a copy it has been in vain, & they have had to *buy* a copy in order to get done a 3 column review of me & my work. This is a bit thick. The *Mercure de France* (26 rue de Condé, Paris) is also important to

---

75. On Mrs. Perrin see pages 77–78, 80.

Sometime editor of the *Fortnightly* and the *Saturday Review*, Frank Harris (1856–1931) was moving downwards along the path up which Bennett had come: he was presently to be editing *Hearth and Home*. His book *The Bomb* was published by John Long in 1908. Shortly thereafter, and for a brief time, he and Bennett became good friends. In October 1901, after losing his position on the *Candid Friend*, Harris himself asked Pinker to be his agent.

Ford Madox (Hueffer) Ford (1873–1939) did not have *The Old Wives' Tale* reviewed in the *English Review*, despite efforts by Ford's friend H. G. Wells. In 1903, in response to a letter from Wells criticizing *Leonora* severely, Bennett had written: 'I am conscious . . . of an intention to make you get down unconditionally on to your knees yet, in a future book.' Wells now wrote to him: 'A great book and a big book. . . . Nobody else could come anywhere near it. We are satisfied with our Bennett.'

me. Will you kindly make Waugh understand that he will oblige me by sending out these three copies if they are not sent. Frank Harris is anxious to do a long signed review in *Vanity Fair*, if Waugh will deign to send copy.

My humorous study of Harmsworthian manners and morals is going ahead. It is entitled: *What the Public Wants*. It is quite fair, and even sympathetic. And *I* think it will be very funny, and would make a most amusing serial, as there is a good square plot to it. Any chance of placing this? *Any* price would be a clear gain.

Yours sincerely, Arnold Bennett

U.C. / MS. / 77

Villa des Néfliers
13 Nov 1908

My dear Pinker,

Many thanks for your letter re Waugh.

First, you have an absolutely free hand.

These are my views:—as regards advts I presume that Waugh advertises in mediums not used by the run of publishers. I know this is his theory. I hope he does, for he certainly doesn't advertise in the usual places—for example, where Methuens advertise. Nor does he advertise with any originality of any kind.

I think a lot of Waugh. But unless he has the courage of his opinions about *me*, he isn't likely to do much good with me. I

76. The novelist Murray Gilchrist (1868–1917) was probably known to Bennett through his neighbour, Eden Phillpotts. Gilchrist apparently did not go to Pinker. William Morris Colles (1855–1926), who was Bennett's first agent (see pages 21–22), seems to have rounded off his career with legal troubles: he was soon to be involved in a court case with W. Somerset Maugham, whom he had served before Maugham came to Pinker. The case concerned Maugham's selling a play to a producer who had earlier rejected it when Colles was handling it. Colles won the case.

The *New Age*, Orage's journal, had been publishing since March a weekly column about books and persons. The author, 'Jacob Tonson', was Bennett.

What the Public Wants was conceived as a novel; it became a play. Its inspiration seems to have been the libel award of £50,000 that Lever Brothers, the soap manufacturers, won against the Harmsworth organization in 1907. Bennett wrote in his journal then: 'The spectacle of Lord Northcliffe raging around in the "impotent fury" of one of the foiled baronets of his own serials, and insulting all his staff from top to bottom—this spectacle is human, touching: it has the austere beauty of tragedy.'

believe that in common with a number of other people, he is convinced that my serious work is bound to last (I couldn't find the cheek to repeat the praises that half a dozen authors have written to me from England the last few days). Let him mark me off in some of his ads. Let him advertise the book in small spaces, separately. There is, according to what all the judges say, ultimate money in both *Buried Alive* & *The O.W.T.* He has too much sense of fairness to expect that I shall take all the risks of my work now, & the publisher come in later when the risks are over. There *are* risks, and when I spend 8 months in writing a book that brings in only £150 certain, I think I take a fair share of the risks. It is a good thing for me that I can work very quickly indeed on smaller things. I say all this to indicate my general attitude to C. & H. Ltd. I am in favour of sticking to them. But I am in favour of driving them to the utmost possible extent, and sticking out to the last for the highest possible advance.

If *The Old Wives' Tale* is pushed properly, it will assuredly do better than *Buried Alive*. I wish Waugh would let me arrange the form of the ads of it, and choose the quotations of reviews. Can you enter into the state of mind of an advertisement manager who advertises *The Old Wives' Tale* as by the author of *The City of Pleasure*? I can't.

There will be a spring novel. I have already told you about it. It will be ready on February 28. Slightly longer than *A Great Man*. And certainly better. A humorous book. You may count on this. Of course if you can serialise it, the programme will be changed.

You are at liberty to sell it serially or in volume how you like, at what price or advance you like.

I have sold *Buried Alive* in French for £15. Credit yourself therefore with £1. 10/-.

Yours sincerely, Arnold Bennett

P.S. I shall be glad if you will write specially to Tauchnitz about *The O.W.T.* It will mean two volumes, but I shall be very disappointed if he doesn't take it.   A. B.

77. The spring novel was *The Card*. Tauchnitz published several of Bennett's novels, including *The Old Wives' Tale*. A French edition of *Buried Alive* (*Enterré vivant*) was published by Monde Illustré in 1910.

U.C. / MS. / 78

> Villa des Néfliers
> 29 Nov 1908

My dear Pinker,

Many thanks for your three letters, & the enclosures.

Chapman & Hall

I return the contract signed. Certainly they have been doing more in the way of advertisement lately. I have heard from Waugh & replied. My own theory as to the sales of my various books is that in paying £200 for *The City of Pleasure* Chatto & Windus simply performed an act of idiocy, & lost heavily on it. Previously they had never given more than £75. Then Nutt gave £125, and lost on that. Then you got £150 out of C & H. I am inclined to think that on the whole the sales are steadily going up, though with the most damnable slowness. I am sure that the reception of the *Old Wives' Tale* will do me good, anyhow. The reviews have been extraordinary, & there are a lot more to come. I am not in the least discouraged, & I shall most decidedly continue to turn out the highest-class stuff I can do. At the same time we must do something special to meet this drop from £150 to £100. I know that I am at present one of your less important clients, but I equally know that I am bound to become one of the more important. I don't make any bones therefore about urging you to put yourself about to arrange something with a magazine, say, if you possibly can. A serial, or a series of short stories, in either case humorous. You never have much difficulty in selling my stories, & perhaps you could arrange a commission as you did with the *Windsor* ones; but humorous, or a serial like *Helen with the High Hand*. I know what you can do when you personally back a man with editors, & you know that you can depend on me for stuff that won't 'let you down'.

I am not coming to England for Christmas. It always costs me such a deuce of a lot. We are going to shut the house up for a couple of months, & live in a hotel in Switzerland at 13 fr. a day, for the two, & I have got free railway tickets thither. This is the French woman's answer to the lack of spontaneity shown by the British public towards *The O. W's Tale*!

English Review

I think something can be arranged here. On what terms are you with Hueffer? When it comes to the point can I tell him he must arrange prices with you? I don't think the Harmsworth novel will do for him, as he has already bought one serial dealing with the Yellow Press. But I have got *two* novels ready for writing, & the other will certainly do. I think I must write this other one first; then if by chance he cries off, it can still be published. But if he doesn't cry off, then the Harmsworth book will be thrown a little later. Both these books are short.

Correspondence College

I am not the author of *How to write for the Magazines*. I shall be quite willing for the College to handle *Journalism for Women*. I enclose the contract with Lane, which has run out. The outside price of the book ought to be 1/6. It is a good book.

Sorry to hear you have been ill.

Yours sincerely, Arnold Bennett

78. In his letters of 23 March 1907 and 21 September 1907 (pages 83 and 95) Bennett wondered how Chatto and Windus could afford to pay £200 for *The City of Pleasure* in advance on a 5*d*. royalty—which would require sales of 10,000 copies to cover the advance—when they had reported sales of *The Ghost* of only 2,500 copies. Chatto and Windus write concerning *The City of Pleasure*:

'2500 copies were printed in August 1907 and published on October 3 at 6/-. Only 1250 copies were bound initially, and a further 500 that year. In 1910 the price was reduced to 3/6; even so it took until 1919 to clear the remaining 750 copies. A. B. was therefore obviously right in surmising that in paying £200 for the copyright C & W "lost heavily on it". But it might have been more accurate —as well as more charitable—to describe this as an act of faith rather than "an act of idiocy". C & W's faith in A. B. as a writer worth persevering with was eventually justified, and . . . *The Grim Smile of the Five Towns* is in print on our list today (1965), along with *Tales of the Five Towns*.'

On Bennett's suspicions about *The Ghost* see pages 77–80. His letter of 21 September 1907 tacitly admits the unjustness of those suspicions.

Journalism for Women was a small book Bennett had published with John Lane in 1898.

II

Fame and Wealth

1908–1914

According to Marguerite Bennett, Arnold said to her on the day The Old Wives' Tale *was published: 'I shall never be able to do better.' The common opinion is that he never did as well. What is certain is that he chose not to write another* Old Wives' Tale. *His next serious novel,* The Glimpse, *was written as a first-person confession by a London aesthete who believed he had undergone a transforming adventure into life after death. In 1909 he began composing a romantic drama about Don Juan de Marana. When in 1912 he began writing a serious melodrama about the Five Towns,* The Price of Love, *he decided that he 'would not have a fine MS. of it: The regularity of the lines and handwriting does not seem to accord with style in which this novel is to be written. A freer style than before—a little more capricious and swinging.' If with* The Old Wives' Tale *he achieved his masterpiece, he perhaps knew this better than anyone else; but he also seems to have known that his talent was not the sort to thrive upon restriction and repetition. In the passage from* The Truth About an Author *quoted on pages 35-36 is to be found the truest statement about his creativity. He looks forward therein to thirty years of 'continually inventing, fancying, imagining, scribbling. . . interminable variations on the theme of beauty'. The mysterious process of genius would, on occasions both early and late in his career, raise a few of those variations to the realm of high art. 'I always write as well as heaven permits,' Bennett said.*

From November 1908 to August 1914, he wrote seven novels and five plays. For more than three of these years he wrote a regular (usually weekly) column for the New Age. *Numerous other articles and short stories were gathered into seven additional volumes. There was also the journal; there were countless letters.*

In these same years Bennett decided to, and did, return to England to live. 'The desire for France', as he phrased it, a desire moved by his acute aesthetic sensibility, gave way before a desire for England. In 1911, when he was still living abroad, he wrote: 'I am an Englishman and become daily more English.' In the midst of an attack on English literary censorship, he remarked: 'I am a tremendous admirer of England. I have lived too long in foreign parts not to see the fineness of England.' Some years afterwards he wrote: 'For several years there had been germinating in my mind the conviction that I should be compelled by some obscure instinct to return to England. . . . I had a most disturbing suspicion that I was losing touch with England, and that my work would soon begin to suffer accordingly. . . . I suppose I have a grim passion for England.'

TEXAS / MS. / 79

Hôtel Belvédère
Mont Pélerin
[Switzerland]
19 Dec 1908

My dear Pinker,

Thank you for your two letters.

All right about the tale.

As to Tillotsons, I cannot send you any of the novel yet. I am now doing a long short story for Hueffer, & after that it was my intention to do a 60,000 word novel for Hueffer as he has promised to keep August open for me, & I presume he would want to see the stuff as soon as possible.

After that I meant to do the other novel. But it will not be the Harmsworth-journalistic subject, as I can see that that would have no chance as a serial, & will do equally well later on. It will be a harmless humorous novel in the vein of the one I did for the National Press Agency. You will be quite safe in recommending it. I do not think I could deliver it much before June 30th, complete.

If you see any improvement in this programme kindly let me know. I thought that Hueffer was the most important, both artistically & financially; and certainly the most in my special line. He must be keen or he would not keep on writing to me.

The new play I have written has *electrified* the leading committee-men of the Stage Society so much that they want to arrange for a commercial production of it, if they can. I gather also that a production of another of my plays, by an ordinary West End commercial theatre, is nearly certain. This, for what it is worth.

Yours sincerely, Arnold Bennett

79. Bennett and his wife were in Switzerland until March.

Tillotsons wanted a serial, and Bennett intended *The Card*, the 'other novel', to go to them.

U.C. / MS. / 80

Hôtel Belvédère
20 Dec 1908

My dear Pinker,

The order is now made for the federation of the Potteries into one town, which will be the 12th largest town in the Kingdom. It takes effect in about a year's time I think, and will have a certain interest. I should like to do a special article for a monthly on this new town, with my own illustrations. I suppose it may be considered my particular subject. As to illustrations, I don't know whether you know of my activities as a rival of Rembrandt. But you can see four of my sketches, very badly reproduced, in this week's *Country Life*.

Can you arrange a commission for such an article on the new town?

Yours sincerely, Arnold Bennett

I could give you plenty of illustrated description travel articles to sell, but I don't know if you don't regard this sort of business as a worry.

TEXAS / MS. / 81

Hôtel Belvédère
30 Dec 1908

[no salutation]

I have this day sent direct to Hueffer the tale which he commissioned for the *English Review*. He specially asked me to make it long. It is between 11 & 12,000 words, rather shorter than Hy. James's story in the first number. I have told him to arrange the price with you. He wrote me to say he would pay 'a good price'. Title of story: 'A Matador of the 5 Towns'.

The new play, *What the Public Wants*, was written between 3 November and 3 December, and Bennett was apparently still intending to write a novel on the same theme. The play was produced by the Stage Society at the Aldwych Theatre on 2 May 1909. Charles Trood and Dennis Eadie took the leading roles. On 27 May it was produced at the Royalty, with Charles Hawtrey and Ben Webster starring.

80. 'The People of the Potteries' appeared in *Cassell's Magazine*, January 1911. Bennett did not do the illustrations. The article was never published in a volume of his essays.

I am now proceeding with story for Cassells, & with a novel that will do for a serial. I will send you opening chapters of this in due course. A Happy New Year from us both.

A. Bennett

U.C. / MS. / 82

Hôtel Belvédère
8 Jan 1909

My dear Pinker,

Many thanks for your letters.

I will attend to the Tillotson stories.

I should have sent you the opening chapters of the new book today, but I have had 3 days in bed & been delayed. You will have them next week. I am arranging it in 12 chapters of 5,000 words, each of which makes a complete story, while the whole makes a novel. It can be sold either as a novel or as a series of stories. I am doing this first as I prefer to let my serious novel mature a bit longer. I feel that after the extraordinary reviews of *The Old Wives' Tale* I really must make the next published book quite as fine in its own way. Is Waugh going to advertise again this month? He told me he expected the book to keep on selling. You might give him to understand that the eyes of Europe are upon him at this crisis, & point out to him the recent remarkable reviews in the *Daily News* and the *Graphic*, as mines of quotation.

With regard to the tale for the *English Review*, this of course can only be left to the conscience of Hueffer. The thing was written specially at his request, at his urgent & reiterated request, & by both its length and its literary quality, it is unsuitable for almost any other magazine. I have not his letters here, but I have them at home, and can produce them, and I will guarantee that one of them contains the phrase: 'I will pay you a good [or high] price for it.' There can be no getting away from this. I presume that Hueffer will not argue that two guineas

81. 'The Matador of the Five Towns' appeared in the *English Review* in April 1909. Henry James (1843–1916) shared the first issue with Hardy, Conrad, Galsworthy, Wells, W. H. Hudson, and Tolstoy. His story was 'The Jolly Corner'.

Cassell's Magazine published 'Why the Clock Stopped' in September 1910. The story appears in the collection *The Matador of the Five Towns*, published in 1912.

The serial, *The Card*, was begun on 3 January.

a thousand is a price so high that it must be specially referred to in a letter as an inducement. I am quite willing to accept my ordinary price, 3 guineas, and I really do not think that Hueffer will make a difficulty as to this. Anyhow I must leave the matter to you.

Yours sincerely, Arnold Bennett

TEXAS / MS. / 83

[Hôtel Belvédère]
[postmarked 11 January 1909]

[no salutation]

What Hueffer says is an absolute lie. He wrote to me *twice* asking for a story, before I suggested to him at all that perhaps later he might like a book which I was contemplating. It is entirely untrue that he suggested a short story because he could not accept my suggestion for a serial. I have all his letters at home, and they can be produced to him, to prove beyond any possible question that the overtures came from him, that he was urgent and insistent, and that he offered the inducement of a good price.

A. B.

U.C. / MS. / 84

Hôtel Belvédère
13 Jan 1909

My dear Pinker,

Many thanks for your letter of the 11th & the enclosure.

This debit balance must now be reduced, & I have little doubt that I shall appreciably reduce it this year—with your help.

I shall send you on Sunday the first quarter of the new novel. Kindly acknowledge receipt of it when it comes. I have called it, for a magazine or newspaper, *The Deeds of Denry the Audacious*. But this will not be the book-title. It is in 12 chapters, each practically containing an episode or story complete in itself. It is purely humorous and light, but it is true to life. It

82. The Tillotson stories may be the *Jack Stout* series. See page 57n.
The new serious novel was *The Glimpse*.

describes the adventures of a Five Towns youth who rose from nothing to the highest dignities of the Five Towns, entirely by his knack of doing picturesque things. Of course if this thing is not placed serially, I shall be seriously discouraged as a serial writer. But you can safely recommend it, & I expect that with your moral influence, & your appreciation of the great importance of bringing something off, *just now*, you will succeed.

Won't one or other of these new magazines buy *Jack Stout?* I hear Methuens are starting one.

If Tauchnitz has not taken *The Old Wives' Tale*, I wish you would send me the name & address of the official to whom you write, as I should like to write to him myself—unless you see an objection.

I rather regret that you closed with Hueffer before getting my answer to your second letter. There is no doubt that I have been swindled over that. I am not easily startled by instances of the depravity of authors in business, and their wonderful lack of straightness. But I admit that this one slightly startled me. I ought to have remembered that Hueffer is an author, and insisted on a price being fixed before I put pen to paper. It is strange that, for the sake of saving six guineas or so, he should think it worth while to tell you a gross untruth—and chance it not being found out in time. Personally I would not label myself a dishonest man for six guineas. I doubt if I would do it for seven. I should give myself the pleasure of writing to Hueffer with a bowdlerised version of my views as to his crookedness, only I regard this kind of pleasure as somewhat beneath one, and as serving no useful end. But I hope you will allow him to understand that though we have been 'done', we are not favourably impressed.

Waugh writes me that he has printed a third edition. Keep him up to the scratch with advts. I may tell you that the new novel (not the one mentioned above), though short, will be particularly striking.

Yours sincerely, Arnold Bennett

84. Bennett's debt to Pinker at the end of December was £1,003.
The Deeds of Denry the Audacious was *The Card*.

u.c. / ms. / 85

[London]
11 May 1909

My dear Pinker,

Very many thanks for letter & enclosures. I am thinking of letting Hueffer print *What the Public Wants* complete in one number of *English Review* (July). I told him I would *give* it him, but he said if it increased the sale he would pay me a royalty!!!

I like him! I think he can't help being devious.

Write me tonight (to Putney) if you see any objection to this.

Yours, A. B.

u.c. / ms. / 86

Villa des Néfliers
[? May 1909]

My dear Pinker,

Many thanks for your letter.

It is about time you took a holiday. I know you always have to be urged to do so.

There are two small matters for your attention.

I gather that though the *New Age* will continue, the 'New Age Press' publishing business is very likely to stop. I am one of the few authors out of whom they have made a bit of money. They took up my books *How to Live on 24 hours a day* and *The Human Machine* when nobody else cared to look at them, and these books have certainly brought me a new public. They spent *nothing* on advertising them. If they had been advertised I think these books would have sold immensely. I gave them *Literary Taste* on the distinct understanding that they should

85. Bennett was in London during most of March and April for the rehearsals of *What the Public Wants*. The play was published in a special supplement to the July issue of the *English Review*.

In an exchange of letters with Bennett over their difference, Ford wrote, 'I am running a philanthropic institution for the benefit of the better letters. I am perfectly resigned to bankruptcy and the sooner you bankrupt me the sooner my troubles with the *Review* will be over. I stand here to be shot at. Shoot! But not through Pinker!' He denied being commercial, 'but when a commercial gent comes to me I simply feel it sporting to beat him at his own game'. Ford was bankrupt by the end of 1909, and when he left the *Review* Bennett paid tribute in the *New Age* to his 'enterprise, audacity, and expertness'. Though one would not guess it from his letter, Ford himself had been using Pinker as an agent since 1904 or earlier.

Putney was where the Kennerleys lived.

L.A.B.—K

advertise it. Up to the present I believe that they have not done so. I shall be glad if you will wake Palmer up seriously, and ascertain what is going to happen to the concern. My idea is that these three books have still got a considerable sale before them if they are handled, and that they might be transferred to some more moneyed publisher now that their popularity has been modestly proved. The 'New Age Press' also has *Cupid and Commonsense*. But of course there is no sale for this, through any publisher. No contract for this has been signed. When it is signed the term for which the N. A. Press has the right to publish should be made as short as possible.

The *Sunday Stories Journal* (or some similarly named rag) has republished 'Nocturne at the Majestic', which originally appeared in the *Windsor*. Will you kindly let me know by what authority.

I enclose the usual from the Natl. Provident Institution.

Yours sincerely, Arnold Bennett

P.S. It is more than likely that I shall have a play done at the Haymarket under the Trench management.   A. B.

U.C. / MS. / 87

Villa des Néfliers
17 May 1909

My dear Pinker,

Many thanks for your letter.

I quite appreciate Methuen's motives, but I will not under

---

86. Frank Palmer (A. F. Palmer Phillips) was business manager of the *New Age*. The Press survived for several more years, the journal until the thirties. In a letter to the Kennerleys of the previous October, Bennett wrote that the *New Age* 'is too damnation clever to last long. I have the written certificate of the editor that commercially "Jacob Tonson" is the most important contributor to the paper. But the question in my mind is: How long am I going to continue making them a present of £150 a year, at least? There is no virtue in me, because I only do it for the amusement of self and a few others.'

The National Provident Institution was and still is a life assurance firm.

Herbert Trench (1865–1923), the theatrical producer, was director of the Haymarket Theatre in 1909. Bennett wrote *The Honeymoon* later in the year for him.

The evidence for dating this letter is somewhat contradictory. *Cupid and Commonsense* was published in May 1909; *Literary Taste* was published in July, after having appeared serially in *T. P.'s Weekly*. The republished 'Nocturne at the Majestic' could not be found.

any circumstances bind myself to produce only one novel a year—not even for one year.

In one year I wrote:

a. *The Old Wives' Tale* (three times as long as an ordinary novel)
b. *Buried Alive* (60,000 words odd)
c. *What the Public Wants* (a play, 27,000 words)
d. *The Human Machine* (25,000 words)
e. *Literary Taste* (25,000 words)
f. A series of introductory lectures for 'T. P.'s Correspondence College'.
g. and lots of articles and a few short stories, including a big one for the *English Review*.

I shall be glad if Methuen or any other competent critic (Lucas, for instance) will examine any of this work, and say if it bears any sign of haste or slovenliness. As a fact most of it has been praised in the very highest terms by those best able to judge.

Two months is my time for an ordinary novel. I know I am singular. But it is me that Methuen has to deal with, not another man. I have a very great deal to say, and I mean to say it. As for my work being taken seriously, we shall see about that. Suppose I do a novel in two months, & a play in one, what am I to do with myself in the other nine? I write fast, but Methuen ought to know that nearly all the classic English & French novels have been written & published at a greater rate even than I work. Even now Methuen does not realise that in me he has to deal with someone slightly out of the common. Anyhow, while quite sympathising with Methuen, I will not bind myself. The mere idea of doing so strikes me as simply monstrous. He must take me or leave me. He had the chance of having me eight years ago and refused it. If he refuses it again he will be the one to regret it. I shan't. I am not really interested in money, but I am interested in being free.

Yours sincerely, Arnold Bennett

P.S. Owing to the strike I only got your letter this afternoon.

87. On E. V. Lucas see page 31. George Webster, another member of the Methuen staff, had written to Pinker on the 10th, suggesting the following phrasing

BUTLER / TS. / 88
(*From J. B. Pinker*)

> Talbot House
> Arundel Street
> The Strand
> London WC
> 11th August 1909

My dear Bennett,

Many thanks for your letter of the 9th. I enclose the type-written copy of the concluding chapters of *The Glimpse*, and I shall be glad if instead of sending it to me when you have corrected it you will send it direct to Sears, (His address is

> Messrs. D. Appleton & Company,
> 35, West 32nd Street,
> New York, U.S.A.)

as I thought, in the circumstances, you would wish me to agree to the compromise. I have already sent him the proofs that I had. I note what you say about the date of publication, and will tell Waugh. We should be ready in ample time for that.

Yes, I am very glad indeed to have Mrs. Belloc-Lowndes. I have known her since the early *Black & White* days, as a very clever journalist, but to tell the truth I was surprised to find her such a clever novelist. It seems to me that she has great possibilities. She was talking about you only the other day, and she told me that you had said she ought to come to me. If she goes on as one expects we shall make money out of her work.

Yes, I think Curtis Brown is losing ground. I like him personally, and think he is an honest, capable man, but he is like all Americans and wants to make a lot of money in a very little time. I could always see that he thought my English way was slow and rather stupid, and I do not think he ever realised that the capacity for snapping up commissions does not make a Literary Agent. . . .

---

in their contract: 'Each of these novels shall be the author's only long novel of the year, but if the author finds it absolutely necessary that two of these three novels should be published in one year, the said Methuen & Co. shall so publish them.'

Methuen refused *Anna of the Five Towns* in 1902 (page 31n.) and was disinclined to take on Bennett in 1907 when Bennett left Chatto and Windus (page 78).

I have just come back from a couple of days in Paris, where I went to meet the author of *The Inner Shrine*, the novel that has made such a big sensation in America. I know you will rejoice to hear that he has become my client.

With kindest regards to Mrs. Bennett,

Sincerely yours, J. B. Pinker

TEXAS / MS. / 89

[Villa des Néfliers]
[6 October 1909]

[no salutation]

This is copy of my reply.

What arrangements are being made for *Helen with the High Hand* and *The Card*? The 3 novels for Methuen will be as important as I can make them, *and they will form a trilogy*. Should not these be arranged for in good time, somewhere?

E. A. B.

88. Talbot House was the place of business of the Pinker firm for four decades. Pinker began his business in Granville House, Arundel Street, in January 1896. By the end of the year he moved to Effingham House in the same street. At the end of 1906 he moved to Talbot House. The present letter is the earliest of any importance that has been preserved on his side of the correspondence. Several later letters from him are also included here. They are more conventional business letters than Bennett's. Occasionally when Pinker wrote in longhand from his home, he addressed Bennett as 'My dear Arnol''. Bennett's biographer, Reginald Pound, implies that this was an effort to establish greater familiarity, an effort rebuffed by Bennett. But it seems rather to have been a standard piece of informality on Pinker's part. There is no doubt that on the whole Bennett's letters are more personal than Pinker's. The two men simply never became close friends.

Mrs. Belloc Lowndes (1868–1947), sister of Hilaire Belloc, published more than a score of popular books after 1909. She and her husband, F. S. A. Lowndes (1868–1940), were friends of Bennett's for many years.

Curtis Brown, in the year 1966, is probably the largest of the literary agencies in England.

The Inner Shrine was by Basil King (1859–1928), author of several other books on religious subjects.

89. This note to Pinker is written on the copy of the following letter to George Doran.

The three novels are *Clayhanger*, *Hilda Lessways*, and *These Twain*. Methuen offered advances of £300, £350, and £400 on them.

TEXAS / MS. / 90
(*To George Doran*)

Villa des Néfliers
6th Oct 1909

My dear Sir,

Believe me that your letter gives me very much pleasure. I had written you about a week ago asking about the sales of *The Old Wives' Tale*, & I am glad to have your views.

With regard to your proposition you will doubtless be aware that Appletons are publishing my next novel. They came to me and asked for it. The sole reason why *The Old Wives' Tale* was not copyrighted in the United States is that no publisher to whom it was submitted would accept it. I leave the arrangements for publication of all my books in the hands of my friend and agent Mr. J. B. Pinker (Talbot House, Arundel Street, Strand, London). He has a free hand, & he knows much better how I stand with regard to contracts than I do myself. Will you therefore kindly address yourself to him or to his American correspondent Mr. Reynolds?

I shall always be delighted to hear from you and to assent to business being done if business is possible. And I fully appreciate your personal interest in my book & know how valuable it must be. As all American publishers seem to live chiefly in London you will doubtless soon be over in Europe, in which case I hope you will come and see me.

Believe me,

Yours very truly, Arnold Bennett

90. George Doran (1869–1956), who published in America for Hodder and Stoughton, had just started his own firm, and his first wise act was to publish *The Old Wives' Tale*. As he tells the story, he gave his wife half a dozen books to entertain her during an illness. The English edition of *The Old Wives' Tale* was one of them. She was entranced by it, and urged him to obtain American rights. He did so. His present letter to Bennett reported that he had sold out two editions of 1,000 copies each, and wanted to publish other Bennett novels. (Thirteen months later— see page 143—he reported sales totalling 12,000 copies. In a letter to Frank Swinnerton in 1924, Bennett says that Doran just told him that the novel had up till then sold 60,000 copies. In *Chronicles of Barabbas* Doran himself reports sales of 100,000 copies within the first three years.)

Until Doran took up his work, Bennett was known only slightly in America. He had been praised by William Dean Howells and Francis Hackett, but prior to 1909 *Anna of the Five Towns* and *A Man from the North* were the sole serious works of his that America knew. In March 1909, Paul Reynolds (1864–1944), who was one of the first of the American literary agents and was Pinker's American associate for a

U.C. / MS. / 91

Villa des Néfliers
27 Oct 1909

My dear Pinker,

Many thanks for your two letters, of 25th & 26th. I was just going to write to you in the sense of the second, when the second arrived. I quite agree that if Doran is solid (& I suppose he is, as the American edition bears Hodder & Stoughton's imprint) he ought to have the books if he will pay as good or better terms. I notice he says nothing as to advances. Kindly arrange the matter how you like.

Doran wrote to me the other day saying that he would write to you, but that he would have preferred to deal with me direct. In reply I indicated that this idea could not be entertained. I also gave him particulars of the trilogy, so that you need not trouble to give him particulars.

I want the copyright of *The Card* arranging for in the States. Kindly pay my cheque to Cook's *London*.

Yours sincerely, Arnold Bennett

P.S. Why is Waugh keeping back his advertisements?   A. B.

---

time, wrote to say that he had offered *The Old Wives' Tale* to Holt, Dutton, Scribner, and Dodd. He had tried Putnam twice, once after the English office had expressed interest in the book. All had rejected it. Reynolds concluded: 'As the book has been published for some time now and is very long and very English, I am afraid there is no chance of doing anything with it over here. I thought it was a remarkable book in many ways, but not the kind that is very popular here.' Appleton published *The Glimpse* in 1909. E. P. Dutton was sufficiently impressed by *The Old Wives' Tale* to make an offer to Pinker on the next three novels. Then Doran appeared on the scene.

91. In *Chronicles of Barabbas*, Doran recalls a later attempt on his part to deal directly with Bennett:

'I had one grand spat with Pinker. He was very jealous of hi. agent's prerogative. On a visit to Paris with Arnold Bennett I tentatively negotiated a small book with A. B. I made the blunder of naming terms, which A. B. promptly reported to Pinker. A day or two later I called on Pinker and such abuse I have never had before or since from living man. It was rather more than an American, free, white, and twenty-one, could take lying down. So I told Pinker I did not come to England to be reprimanded by him or any other living Englishman, that if a literary agency was not a perfectly legitimate and understanding partnership between author, agent, and publisher then I was for ever finished with his kind. The result was amazing and transforming. He had no case to bring before Bennett because I had resorted to no subterfuge. He became very genial, and

U.C. / MS. / 92

Royal York Hotel
Brighton
12 Jan 1910

My dear Pinker,
    Many thanks.
    I am going to do some journalism for the new proprietorship
of *The English Review*. They have got money. It will take the
form of descriptive sketches of the very newest & most spectacular manifestations of social life in London, & contrasting
similar sketches of Paris. Something new; certainly dealing
with matters not yet touched in the way of literature. It will
be about 15,000 words, in 3 instalments. Can you sell this blind
to some U.S.A. magazine, such as *McClure's* or *Everybody's*? It
would be no use for *Harper's* or any of the other old-fashioned
things, being too true & sincere for them. Ultimately it will
form part of a book on London & Paris which will be illustrated
by my friend E. A. Rickards, one of the best caricaturists now
going, and admitted to be *the* best architectural draughtsman
in England. He is a very successful architect & he and his
partner are now putting up the £250,000 building on the site
of the old Aquarium. The illustrations will be partly humorous
& partly architectural. An American magazine might or might
not care to have these illustrations, or it might or might not
prefer its own. But that is a minor point. I don't care to submit
my stuff in advance, nor to worry much about America, as
Austin Harrison will give me a definite commission for England.
It is probable that he will want to begin the series pretty soon,
as he seems very keen on having me. This is why I tell you
about the matter at once, before I have begun to write the stuff.
Don't trouble about the affair if you think it is not promising.

Yours sincerely, Arnold Bennett

---

his peace-offering was "Doran, I have *Marie-Claire* for you". . . . That book
immediately sold over 50,000 copies in America. . . .' (For more on *Marie-Claire*
see page 158.)
    92. The Royal York Hotel was Bennett's place of work from 1 January until
18 March. It is called the Royal Sussex in *Clayhanger*.
    Lord Alfred Mond (1868–1930) bought out the *English Review*. Austin Harrison
(1873–1928), former correspondent on the *Daily Mail*, became editor. Bennett's
sketches for it began appearing in the November issue; they are collected in *Paris
Nights*, published in 1913, with illustrations by Rickards. Rickards (d. 1920) and

u.c. / ms. / 93

Royal York Hotel
28 Jan 1910

My dear Pinker,

What the Public Wants

This seems all right. I return Palmer's letter. I expect no appreciable money; but I *do* wish the play to have a decent permanent form. He produced *Cupid & Commonsense* very well. The contract ought to include both plays, as no contract for the latter has been signed; but the terms for *Cupid & Commonsense* should be a proper royalty throughout, as there was no question of buying up another edition.

Daily Chronicle

I had better tell you what I have been doing in journalism that you don't know of. The Manchester *Daily Dispatch* wanted to reduce my price from 6 to 5 guineas. I refused, as reduction by one & the same paper is dead against my programme. So I have done no more work for them. The London editor put the blame on his directors & practically apologised for them. The *Sheffield Telegraph* asked me to state terms for a weekly article, & I said six guineas. They agreed. They were, however, to syndicate the article with one Scotch & one Irish paper, & they couldn't bring this off; so the thing fell through. The Manchester *Sunday Chronicle* recently asked me to do them an 1,800 word article. I asked ten guineas, which they agreed to. I did the article. I have an idea they wanted this as a sort of trial kite, but I have heard nothing since. Being an out & out radical, I would sooner have a pulpit in the *Chronicle*, & in London, than in these other sheets. And of course if Mr. Donald wants to have something seriously to rival Chesterton in the opposition shop, he ought to know that from me he will get it. I should suggest doing something that could be described as *Human Nature Notes*, one subject—topical—each week. I did a long series called *A*

his partner, Dr. H. V. Lanchester (1863–1953), were at that time engaged upon the Central Hall at Westminster. Rickards was a friend of Bennett's from his early days in London.

No American magazine seems to have published the sketches that went to the *English Review*, although in the summer of 1911 *Living Age* published some other sketches that were also collected in *Paris Nights*.

Novelist's Log-Book for *T. P.'s Weekly* in this vein some years ago. My philosophy has matured since then. I must be free to be humorous, but on the other hand I won't agree to take the edge off my (very moderate) opinions by being *merely* flippant, 'bright', 'readable', unprovocative, etc. I am a terrific optimist, but I will not shirk facts, and I will not hedge. I will do a preliminary series of four articles if this is clearly understood; in which case you might ask Mr. Donald to write me direct if he has anything editorial to say.

Of course if this comes off, the usual commission will be yours but I must have the cheques, as similarly before; as I shall give up other articles in order to do the stuff.

Of next month's cheque, kindly send me £30 in notes here, & pay £20 into Cook's London.

Many thanks about Olive Ledward.

Yours sincerely, Arnold Bennett

93. Frank Palmer formed his own publishing company. He issued *Cupid and Commonsense* in 1909 and *What the Public Wants* in 1910. The latter play was first issued in paper covers by Duckworth in 1909 as a special supplement of the *English Review*.

The *Daily Chronicle* was edited by Sir Robert Donald (1861–1933) from 1902 to 1918. The radicalism that Bennett was prepared to deliver to it is indicated by a manifesto that he had recently published in Burslem. Entitled *The Present Crisis: Plain Words to Plain Men*, the four-page leaflet attacked the House of Lords for its food taxation proposals in the following vein.

'WHY THEY RULE US.

Now the vast majority of the Lords enjoy and exercise their enormous privilege for one of the following reasons:—

  1.—Because their ancestors were royal bastards.
  2.—Because their ancestors openly robbed the church.
  3.—Because their ancestors bought their titles by open purchase from ancient kings.
  4.—Because their ancestors bought their titles by secret payments to the campaign funds of modern political parties.
  5.—Because their ancestors, being inconvenient to their own party in the House of Commons, were ennobled to get them out of the way. . . .

They will fight without scruple. They are fighting without scruple. They call themselves the gentlemanly party; but on the platform and in their reptile press they hesitate before no lie, no slander, no libel, no vulgar abuse. . . .'

The manifesto was also published in the *New Age* on 30 December 1909. The *Daily Chronicle* articles began appearing on 16 February. G. K. Chesterton (1874–1936) published his conservative liberalism in the *Daily News* and the *Illustrated London News*.

The Manchester *Sunday Chronicle* published Bennett's article 'Fiction and Happiness, the Supposed Influence of the Woman Novelist on Marriage' on 10 January.

Olive Ledward (Mrs. Olive Glendinning), a sister of the sculptor Gilbert Ledward, was a friend of Bennett's for many years. The reference to her is unexplained.

U.C. / MS. / 94

Royal York Hotel
2nd Feby 1910

My dear Pinker,

I return Waugh's letter. I quite coincide with your attitude towards him. If he agreed to the cheap edition I think you ought to hold him to his word. He is a born grumbler. The fact is, he is not a business man, but a second-rate artist by temperament, with his emotions undisciplined. I like him, to talk to, but on business I am sick of him. I don't think he will press the point, as he will not care to upset us. When he has given way, & ultimately learns that we have gone to Methuens after all, Henrietta St. won't hold him!

Yours sincerely, Arnold Bennett

P.S. It is ridiculous for him to say that the *Daily Mail* edition destroys 'all possibility' etc. He would never have touched the book again anyhow, unless some steady public demand forced him to do so.   A. B.

94. The Amalgamated Press issued *The Old Wives' Tale* in 1909 and *Buried Alive* in 1910 in its series of Daily Mail Sixpenny Novels. In his recollection of Bennett in *A Hundred Years of Publishing*, Waugh mentions the break with the firm:

'It is good also to remember that Chapman & Hall published the first edition of *The Old Wives' Tale*, even if it has to be confessed that nobody in the firm quite realized that we were attending at the birth of a masterpiece. If Mr. Bennett realized it himself, he never pressed his faith upon his publishers. A couple of years later he passed from the firm's list—a great loss, leaving a genial and incisive memory behind him.'

Waugh wrote to Pinker on 4 February 1910:

'I wish you would come and see me at the office one day next week. I must say I don't much appreciate the tone of your last letter, in which you seem to adopt the manner of a schoolmaster lecturing a small boy—as though it were *my* fault that the public don't want more of Arnold Bennett's books! I think a little talk might clear the air.'

He wrote to Pinker again on 21 March.

'I do not want to write, believe me, with any sort of bitterness, but do you not think that, considering the relations which have obtained between Arnold Bennett and myself (to say nothing of those, which have never been disturbed, between myself and you), it would have been more gracious, more considerate, more in accordance with the courtlier traditions of publishing if you had said some word to me before taking Bennett away, and placing three books with another house? I am very conscious of having given Bennett and his books more than the usual amount of thought and attention. You also are aware that several of them have failed to earn the advances paid. I should have thought you would have said something before posting off to Methuen. I am writing to Bennett somewhat in the same tone. Little instances like this rather disturb one's belief in the possibility of establishing, nowadays, cordial relations between authors and publishers.'

u.c. / ms. / 95

Royal York Hotel
6 Feby 1910

My dear Pinker,
I seem to be doing nothing else today but writing letters to you. I have finished the first part of the first Methuen novel. It will be called *Clayhanger*. The whole thing will be finished on June 30th. I shall not have the second novel of the trilogy ready for publication before autumn 1911. Perhaps this news will comfort Methuen. In the meantime there is *The Card*, which begins in *The Times* this week. I have just finished the proofs of it, & I think it is a *good* humorous work with two weakish chapters in the middle. Ought not this to be sold separately for publication in spring 1911? I am told that Murray is more determined than ever to make a speciality of fiction & is offering higher prices than ever, but I expect you know more about that than I do.

Yours sincerely, Arnold Bennett

P.S. *Clayhanger* will be a bit of all right. There will be about 90 chapters to it.   A. B.

u.c. / ms. / 96

Royal York Hotel
9 Feby 1910

My dear Pinker,
Many thanks for your letter. By all means mention *The Card* to Methuen first. But I do not think it will be advantageous to refrain from issuing a light book between two volumes of the trilogy. I think the reverse. One can't always be producing big books. Moreover I have always produced all kinds of work, & mean to continue to do so. The mild success of *The O. W. Tale* does not mean, to me, that I must now only produce heavy artillery. After three years of heavy artillery the public would

---

95. *Clayhanger* was begun on 5 January and finished on 23 June. It has sixty-eight chapters. *Hilda Lessways* was finished on 13 June of the following year.
   The Times Weekly Edition began publishing *The Card* on 4 February.
   John Murray published little fiction until 1908, when they took over Smith, Elder, which had a distinguished list.

have forgotten the author of *Buried Alive* etc. It is, in my opinion, much better that *The Card* should be issued next spring. At the end of *Clayhanger* I propose to put a note stating the title of the second work of the trilogy & that it will be issued in the autumn of 1911. I particularly want you to take the line with Methuen that he must expect all sorts of different things from me, & plenty of them; and that it should be his business to make the best of it. The question is not whether my method of producing is the best way commercially or artistically—it is the only way I have of producing. It is not the slightest use any publisher trying to cork me up, or to keep me to one line.

I cannot rewrite anything in *The Card*. I never rewrote any portion of any book. My first draft is always also the final writing. I would much sooner write a complete fresh novel than rewrite two chapters of an old one.

Yours sincerely, Arnold Bennett

U.C. / MS. / 97

> Pension White
> Piazza Cavalleggieri
> Florence
> 9th April 1910

My dear Pinker,
    Many thanks for your agreeable letter.

Helen

I return the agreement signed. This extra £5 is an excellent symptom. I may mention that since the publication of the book I have not seen *a single advertisement* of it. The reviews have been without exception effusive.

McClures

No, I didn't know. Mrs. Bisland told me vaguely that they meant to publish 'The 19th Hat'. She also said they were thinking of publishing the two stories I wrote last for Tillotson. This I absolutely forbade her to arrange, on pain of eternal enmity. I do not want these two stories published in America.

96. Methuen issued *The Card* in February 1911, between *Clayhanger* and *Hilda Lessways*.

I quite agree with you that they ought to pay £10—or nothing. You will doubtless be able to convey to them that if they want to keep on intimate terms with their latest darling discovery they will pay £10. A story like 'The Death of Simon Fuge' is worth either £10 or 3¾d. *I would much prefer them to begin with* '*The Lion's Share*'. Kindly urge this. Also I would like to suppress one or two of the stories and give them 'The Matador', out of *The English Review* instead. If you can arrange this, I will buy a Tauchnitz copy of *The Grim Smile* here, and look through it. I forget the stories. I want *McClures* only to issue stuff at which editors of the leading papers, like the *Boston Transcript* etc., who have written me sending me copies of their signed articles on *The O. W. Tale*, cannot turn up their noses. Both 'The Death of Simon Fuge' & 'The Matador' will give them something to think about.

Truth about an author

Is this transfer arranged with Constable?

Clayhanger

Going strong. Two thirds done.

Yours sincerely, Arnold Bennett

u.c. / ms. / 98

Pension White
24 Apl 1910

My dear Pinker,

Clayhanger

I don't want to discourage you, but I doubt if you will place it serially. It is 160,000 words long. Three quarters of it is done.

97. Bennett and his wife travelled in Switzerland and Italy during April and much of May.

In his journal Bennett noted that 'the reviews of *Helen with the High Hand* are exceedingly polite and kind, but they do not gloss over the slightness of the thing'. Chapman and Hall had published it in March.

Mary Bisland managed McClure's London office. The stories that *McClure's Magazine* published were 'The Nineteenth Hat' and 'From One Generation to Another', which had been collected in England in *The Grim Smile of the Five Towns*. They appeared in the May and July issues, 1910. The Tillotson stories are unidentified.

The Truth About an Author was reissued with Bennett's name in 1914 by Methuen.

Over a hundred thousand words can be seen, but I hesitate about trusting the unique MS to the post. 60,000 words are typewritten. I will send these off tomorrow, Monday, morning. They will probably be enough to discourage any editor.

There is nothing in it to shock prudes, as there was in the *O.W.T.* Not even a confinement. It ends happily.

Kindly pay my next cheque to Cook's, Paris.

Have you received anything for Italian serial rights of *The Statue*? I bought it in Italian here today.

Yours sincerely, Arnold Bennett

U. C. / MS. / 99

Villa des Néfliers
26 May 1910

My dear Pinker,

The Honeymoon

Many thanks. I should say the play would suit a magazine excellently. Though I say it, it really is very funny, & it is also a genuine social criticism. I have reserved of course all the book & serial rights etc. for you to deal with (having disposed only of the dramatic rights for England for 10 years), but I do not think it would be fair for the play to be printed in America before it is produced in England, at the Haymarket. (Trench is under contract to produce it before Christmas, but the immense success of *The Blue Bird* will put him in a hole.) So that any arrangement you make should provide that publication shall await production. You will of course also take care that publication in U.S.A. does not in any way forfeit or impair dramatic rights in U.S.A. It is a play which will suit all countries.

I have only the original MS., which I have lent to a friend. I have asked him to post it direct to you. If you have it typed please get it done in duplicate & send one copy to me.

Has anything been done as to *H. with H.H.* with Doran? Or as to serial of *Clayhanger*?

Yours sincerely, Arnold Bennett

99. *McClure's Magazine*, which had published *What the Public Wants* in three instalments earlier in the year, was interested in *The Honeymoon*, and published it in 1911.

Villa des Néfliers
25th June 1910

My dear Pinker,

Clayhanger

I send the last part of the MS. by concurrent book post registered. You will receive it on Monday morning. I shall be glad if you will take measures to have the typescript despatched from your office to me not later than *Thursday*. (The MS. can follow.) I shall then return to you the complete typescript at once. I want to get everything clear before I go away about July 3rd. The typescript of vol 8 of MS has not yet reached me.

Will you kindly explain to Duttons & Methuens that I only want page proofs, that I shall return the proofs as quickly as sent, and that there will be no corrections except of slips.

Morning Leaders

Many thanks for your letter. I will do the article. 5 guineas.

Yours sincerely, Arnold Bennett

Hôtel de la Plage, Carantec
Finistère
11 July 1910

My dear Pinker,
Many thanks.
Proof of story, & *MS.* of play not yet arrived. Typescript arrived.

On 4 January Bennett wrote in his journal: 'I . . . [had] a letter from Herbert Trench asking me to alter tremendously the third act of *The Honeymoon*. My soul revolted, but of course I gradually gave way and then wrote him that I would.' On 17 February he wrote: 'I wrote to Trench . . ., telling him definitely I wouldn't alter the last act of *The Honeymoon*.' Trench accepted the play as it stood, but then did not produce it.

Doran published *Helen with the High Hand* in 1910. *Clayhanger* was not serialized.

100. Dutton published the first two novels of the *Clayhanger* trilogy, Doran the third.

Bennett began a series of articles for the *Morning Leader* on 3 August.

Clayhanger. This title shall stand.

W. L. George. He is a perfectly serious young man. His wife writes also. He is one of the few men who really *do* write & speak French like French people. He served in the French army. Socialist. Idealist. Like most of these people, inclined to sentimentality. Wrote a good little book on modern France. This is all I know of his work, except newspaper articles. He has written a novel, which I gather is considered improper. But I know that he is ready to put that on one side, and write another one. *He is a quite honest artist,* & I should say would do very good work that never quite reached the absolutely first rate. Probably about the level of F. M. Hueffer as a writer. He has means, & I think his people are wealthy. This is about the extent of my knowledge. If you are thinking of taking him on, I should (respectfully) suggest that you made him promise to produce for you at least one novel each year. I told him to consult you if he meant to work steadily, but not otherwise. You never know with these private-means authors!

Yours sincerely, Arnold Bennett

u.c. / ms. / 102

Hôtel de la Plage
30 July 1910

My dear Pinker,

Many thanks for your letter. I see no objection to Doran publishing all my novels (*not* the fantasias) that have not yet been issued in U.S.A. As to terms I leave all that to you, but I should really like to see him about other aspects of the undertaking. He wrote me asking where he could see me. I replied that I should be delighted if he could come here, as my arrangements wouldn't let me leave here before August 15th. I have had no word from him since. I wish you would ask him whether

101. Bennett was on holiday in Brittany. He wrote in his journal on 15 August:
'I have now taken, what nearly everybody said I was incapable of taking and never would take, a long holiday. From July 2nd to yesterday I did nothing whatever in the way of work except 3 short articles for the *New Age*, which I was obliged to do. Of course I had to attend to my correspondence; but I kept that as short as possible. I wrote an illustrated journal at Carantec, and I also did a number of paintings and sketches.'
W. L. George (1882–1926) came to Pinker. He published a novel a year thereafter.

L.A.B.—L

he could meet me in Paris on August 11th or any following day; or come to my house at Fontainebleau on any day or days on or after the 14th. Ask him to wire me here. I have not his address. There are a lot of things I want to explain to him.

He ought to issue *The Human Machine* & *How to Live on 24 hours a day*. I have received dozens of press-cuttings about these books in the U.S., although they have not been issued there. They are just the sort of book for the American public. Also my plays. And I want a book of essays doing there, and in England too—not that I expect any money from it. I think *A Man from the North* is now free from Lane's clutches. Please look at agreement. If so, I would like that republished in U.S.A.

Yours sincerely, Arnold Bennett

George D. Dutton writes me that he prefers *Clayhanger* to anything else I have written!

U.C. / MS. / 103

Villa des Néfliers
13 August 1910

My dear Pinker,

I enclose the agreement with Lane for *A Man from the North*. It is out of print, & the agreement expired in 1904. Will you therefore do what is necessary formally to take it out of Lane's hands. As this is one of my best books I hope that a new edition of it will be done in England as soon as Methuen thinks it is worth while. I particularly want it included in the United States series.

What about *The Truth about an author* for the United States?

How to live on 24 hours a day. That well-meaning ass Palmer writes me that this is out of print, & that he omitted to keep the stereo plates, & will therefore have to set up again. Perhaps the news that Doran will buy sheets will wake him up. Will you kindly rouse him? Over six months ago he was getting out an illustrated pamphlet or leaflet about all my books that he has. I sat for a portrait for it in January. It has not yet appeared.

---

102. John Lane (1854–1925) issued *A Man from the North*, Bennett's first novel, in 1898 in both London and New York.

George D. Dutton was apparently head of the Dutton firm at this time.

I think it is not even written. I bet he has not yet spent the agreed sum on advertising.

I am writing to Doran, but as it is only to give him my ideas of the relative importance of the books he is handling, I needn't trouble you with details. By the way, I see no reason why you should give him first refusal of anything.

Buried Alive. In any case nothing useful could be done with this in U.S. unless by friendly arrangement with Brentanos. If the book succeeded, & they considered themselves aggrieved by anything we did with Doran, they could reprint on their own. I am in favour of telling them straight that a uniform edition is contemplated and asking them to give up if & when they have sold their thousand. The notices in U.S. of this book have been quite remarkable.

It seems to me about time you took a holiday, my dear Pinker.

Yours sincerely, Arnold Bennett

U.C. / MS. / 104

Villa des Néfliers
17th Sept 1910

My dear Pinker,

A Man from the North

Many thanks for your letter. I think there is an ultimate public for this book at the price of at least 3/6. Therefore I should prefer not to cede indefinitely the right to publish it at 3/6 & upwards. I am thinking of Methuens. For twelve years I have consistently stuck up for this book, as having a quality which none of my other books has, & of course now that some interest is being shown in it, I am more in love with it than ever. This is natural, but excusable. I should prefer, speaking without any special knowledge that you may have, to let Hodder & Stoughtons have the right to publish it at a bob subject to our right to issue it after an agreed interval (say 2 years) at 3/6 or more. In other words, I think their edition should be a distinctively cheap edition—not in cloth. As to 1/- or 6d, I should say

103. Doran was issuing uniform volumes of several of the novels. The friendly arrangement was made with Brentano's.

it is more a 1/- than a 6d. sort of novel, but I don't mind which price is chosen.

It would not be a bad thing to have some slight connection with H. & S., because such a connection would undoubtedly influence Claudius Clear's criticisms. I have the greatest contempt for them as an artist, & I never lose an opportunity, & I never will, of going for him. But the effect of his criticisms is undeniable. He has already publicly proclaimed his opinion that I am a 'great' writer, to which proclamation my response was to 'go for' him again, with the very natural result that he has kept an august silence for some time. But his canny skill in getting on the top of the wave will probably lead him to repeat his view, and this suggested connection may hasten the process. I am wondering whether he will say anything about *Clayhanger*. I write all this of course purely as a commercial man. No commercial consideration would induce me to spare him in the press, in his quality of critic.

Yours sincerely, Arnold Bennett

P.S. I have received a very nice, pathetic letter from Waugh about *Clayhanger*.   A. B.

U.C. / MS. / 105

Villa des Néfliers
14 Oct 1910

My dear Pinker,

Many thanks for yours of the 12th. So far there has been no delay in the posts. Waugh does not come with credit out of this.

104. Claudius Clear (Sir W. Robertson Nicoll, 1851–1923), who ran Hodder and Stoughton's *British Weekly*, wrote of *The Old Wives' Tale*, 'There is no book in the fiction of recent years that I should rank as equal to it.' Bennett on his part, in his role as Jacob Tonson of the *New Age*, wrote about Nicoll a few weeks before: 'I would give much to prevent him from afflicting the intelligent when the solemn annual moment arrives for him to make the reputation of a novelist.' In an essay on A. C. Benson, written about a month after *The Old Wives' Tale* appeared, Nicoll doubted that any essayist could write on such a subject as 'Work and Worry' without being dull. The following week in the *New Age* Bennett offered to make the attempt. He would contribute £5 to the London Hospital if he failed, and thought that Nicoll might contribute such a sum if he succeeded. He regarded Nicoll's opinion as a defence of a tediousness in Benson that Bennett himself had previously attacked. The essay was written, printed in the *British Weekly*, and judged by the reading public, only some of whom thought it succeeded. Bennett said later in the *New Age* that all he had wanted to do was 'to cause fury'. And Nicoll praised *Clayhanger* highly.

Nevertheless I had a very friendly letter from him the other day, about *Clayhanger*, to which I replied in the same vein. I certainly think *The O.W.T.* ought to be kept in print. I know from my own bookseller there is a demand for it, just as there is still a demand for *A Man from the North*.

Would not Methuens take it up? If so, would it not be better to get all the decent books so far as possible together, in the hands of one firm? You will in any case reserve (in dealing with H. & S.) the right to publish *A Man from the North* later at its original price. We have *Anna* under our own control. And I expect *Whom God hath joined* could be obtained. Why should not Waugh give up all the books he has, if he is doing nothing with them? Supposing one of my forthcoming books had a more considerable success, the difficulty of getting hold of the earlier ones would be at once increased very much. So why not do what can be done now, in this way? What are the advantages of H. & S. over Methuens? By the way I had a very appreciative letter from Methuen himself the other day. You ask me for my views, but this letter consists mainly of questions!

I wrote to Dr. Otto about a fortnight ago, but have had no reply. Perhaps he is sitting up at nights and counting the words himself.

Yours sincerely, Arnold Bennett

u. c. / ms. / 106

Villa des Néfliers
26 Oct 1910

My dear Pinker,
Many thanks for your letter. I return the enclosures.

Chatto

I should say he most certainly had the right to sell his copies. Of course he will pay royalties on them. There is nothing in his letter to indicate that he has any other intention.

105. Waugh had allowed *The Old Wives' Tale* to go out of print.
Methuen issued *A Man from the North* in 1912.
Dr. Curt Otto was a Tauchnitz representative. He thought *Clayhanger* to be longer than it was.

Lane

Damned rascal. I enclose a letter to the Society of Authors. Kindly forward it with a copy of the agreement.

Tauchnitz

I enclose letter from the excellent Otto, to which I have suitably replied. I cannot cut this book down.

Yours sincerely, Arnold Bennett

U.C. / MS. / 107

59 rue de Grenelle
Paris
12 Nov 1910

My dear Pinker,
    Kindly note address.
    Many thanks for your letter.

Honeymoon

I will see about copyright performance & let you know shortly.

Chatto

It is an astounding thing that Chatto's can dispose of their copies without paying any royalty. I hope that by means of sixpenny editions or something we shall soon be able to cut the ground from under their feet. Also that in any future leasing contract, we shall be able to guard against being done in the same way. Of course the financial aspect is not important, but the principle is. I don't suppose any firm would be able to dispose of 500 copies of *Anna* in five years.

Old Wives' Tale

Certainly if Methuens don't want it, I should be inclined to let Hodder & Stoughton have it. So far as my opinion is worth anything, I should say the price ought to be 3/6, not 2/-. As

106. Chatto and Windus wished to dispose of copies of *Anna of the Five Towns* after their licence had expired.
    According to Pinker, John Lane in London gave assurances that there was nothing to hinder Doran from issuing *A Man from the North* in America, since Bennett's contract with Lane had run out; but the Lane firm in New York insisted that Doran must pay a royalty. The Society of Authors offered legal advice on such matters.

regards Methuens, I may tell you that *Clayhanger* has been received better than I expected. After all, a book like that *is* a stiff dose for the public. Doran writes me he has sold about 12,000 of *O.W.T.* I am writing new prefaces for *The Truth about an author* and *Sacred & Profane Love.*

Yours sincerely, Arnold Bennett

P.S. You have to credit yourself with commission on 25 guineas for a story in *T. P.'s Weekly.* Also among my complex *New Age* transactions I find I have received a sum of £23.9.5 which is vaguely supposed to be for royalties on books before Palmer took over the 'New Age Press'. You are therefore entitled to commission on this. Has Palmer done that advertising, and issued that 4 pp leaflet which it was part of his agreement to do?

U.C. / MS. / 108

59 rue de Grenelle
8 Dec 1910

My dear Pinker,
　　Many thanks for your letter.

The Card

I do not like the change of title, but I will accept it.
　　As to price, there are dozens of novels no longer than this published at 1½ dollars in the United States. For example *His*

107. The Bennetts moved into a flat at 59 rue de Grenelle at the end of October.
　　No information is available on the copyright performance of *The Honeymoon.* The regular production opened on 6 October 1911 at the Royalty Theatre under the management of Marie Tempest. Miss Tempest and Dion Boucicault, the producer, played the leading roles.
　　Hodder and Stoughton began publishing *The Old Wives' Tale* in 1911. They also issued Bennett's new pocket philosophies.
　　Clayhanger received high praise in the *Times Literary Supplement* and the *Spectator.* The *Athenaeum*, which Bennett occasionally attacked in the *New Age* for its stuffiness, observed that 'the psychology of Edwin Clayhanger . . . could . . . have been suggested . . . by a master of art in a quarter of the space'.
　　The prefaces for *The Truth About an Author* and *Sacred and Profane Love* first appeared in Doran's American editions of these works in 1911. The American title of the latter book was *The Book of Carlotta.*
　　The story 'Mimi' is doubtless referred to. It appeared in *T. P.'s Magazine*, a new monthly started by O'Connor, in October 1910. It was republished in *The Matador of the Five Towns* in 1912.

Hour (Elinor Glyn), which is shorter. My feeling is against change of price; but I leave the matter entirely to you.

John Lane

Thring writes me that the Society's Solicitors are instructed to take up this case. It is exceedingly agreeable to be able to have a row with this damned rascal at somebody else's risk.

Yours sincerely, Arnold Bennett

U.C. / MS. / 109

59 rue de Grenelle
18 Dec 1910

My dear Pinker,

Many thanks for your letter. I like the idea of furnishing the plot of a 25,000 word story by return of post. It shows your confidence in me. The difficulty about the *London* is this. 25,000 words would be no use afterwards except in a book of short stories, & I couldn't put them in a book of short stories unless they were 25,000 absolutely high-class words. And high class is not what the *London* wants.

I could base a story on the play *The Honeymoon*. It would be very easy to do. You have the play, or you know the plot. So that you could tell them what it is. Of course I should use as much of the dialogue as I could. I should change all the names. I presume that with these . . . Harmsworth people, it would be necessary (a) to get an absolutely definite commission (b) for British serial rights only—and to be used only once (c) without prejudice to my right to publish the play itself afterwards in a periodical. Do they want to publish the story complete in one number, or is it to be divided?

I am now busy with *Hilda Lessways*.

108. America preferred *Denry the Audacious* to *The Card. The Deeds of Denry the Audacious* had been Bennett's working title and the title under which the book was originally copyrighted in America. Dutton published it.

G. Herbert Thring (1859–1941) was for many years Secretary of the Society of Authors. The case against Lane ultimately turned upon the fact that he had obtained no copyright in America for *A Man from the North*. The solicitors of the Society of Authors advised Bennett that Lane had been under no contractual obligation to obtain copyright, and that anyone was now free, without consulting either Lane or Bennett, to reissue the book in America. Doran issued it in 1911.

Doran is coming over to see me next Saturday. Is there any special line to be taken about anything?

Will you kindly let me know how many copies of *Clayhanger* have been sold to date.

Yours sincerely, Arnold Bennett

BUTLER / TS. / 110
(*From J. B. Pinker*)

Talbot House
19th December 1910

My dear Bennett,

I have just received your letter of yesterday. I will see what can be done with the *London*, and let you know the result. They would want to publish the story complete in one number.

I expect Doran's chief concern is to get you to make him a promise as to the future. I have told him that you do not like the idea of promising to give him the refusal of all your future books, and that my own opinion is that it is not reasonable for a publisher to ask such a promise. I have told him that in my experience you are the sort of man to give full weight to any obligation, and that if he wants you to feel attached to him his policy is to show how well he can do with the books that he has. He has got plenty of scope for his skill and energy, don't you think so? I should imagine that *Clayhanger* would entirely justify Dutton's enterprise, and I expect you will think it is not worth while making agreements for American rights still further ahead unless on very swagger terms. Over here *Clayhanger* has sold about 5,800 of the 6/- and 700 Colonial, and Methuen tells me the book still shows a lot of life.

I shall be passing through Paris on my way to see the Williamsons next month, and if there were anything you would like to talk over I could perhaps arrange to leave here in the morning instead of the evening, and so get time for a talk with you.

Sincerely yours, J. B. Pinker

P.S. I have seen the editor of the *London Magazine* and explained about *The Honeymoon*. I had not a copy of the play in the office, so that I could not show it to him, but he will definitely commission a story of 25,000 words, to be written from the play, as you suggest, and will pay £130 for the British serial use. He wants to know whether you could let him have the MS. by January 20th. Is this possible from your point of view?   •

u.c. / ms. / 111

> 59 rue de Grenelle
> 27 Dec 1910

My dear Pinker,

   Doran made no attempt at all to get any promise about future novels. I made, however, the following arrangement with him about some journalism on the subject of Christmas, & I shall be glad if you will attend to the contract for the book publication of it. I am to supply him with 10,000 words on the subject of Christmas by 1st September. He is to publish it as a booklet at 50 cents and to pay £100 (500 dollars) in advance of a 15% royalty. He said he thought Hodder & Stoughton would like to publish it in England. But I said I was not sure that I cared for it to be published in England; not because the stuff will not be perfectly serious & in my best philosophic vein, but because the English public is liable to misunderstand a realistic novelist publishing booklets of a Christmas nature. What do you say? (I also don't fancy myself in H. & S's Christmas advertising. This may seem absurd to you, but it is so.)

   You remember those 2 children's books of my sister's? I have persuaded Doran to publish one of them in America on a 10% royalty, & he may arrange with H. & S. to do it in England also. I don't know whether you would care to bother yourself with this trifling contract; but having regard to the large amount of trouble you generously put yourself to, the least I can do is to leave the contract & commission to you if you would like it. Otherwise I can do it myself. If you take charge of it, kindly accept broadly whatever Doran suggests (the royalty is

---

110. The *Clayhanger* sales were from 15 September, when the novel was published.

   C. N. and A. M. Williamson (1859–1920; 1869–1933) were living in France. They were old friends of Pinker's (see pages 22–23).

arranged), as there is no disguising the fact that he is doing the book solely in order to oblige me.

We expect you soon.

Yours sincerely, Arnold Bennett

U.C. / MS. / 112

59 rue de Grenelle

5 Jan 1911

My dear Pinker,

Many thanks for yours of yesterday & the enclosures. Far be it from me to teach my grandmother to suck eggs; but do you not think I ought to get six guineas? I have put my journalistic prices up this year. *The English Review* will take all the journalism I care to give them, and more, at six guineas a thousand, which is equal to seven guineas a newspaper column. With this advantage, that the stuff I do for them is good for a book afterwards. Also I told Tillotsons my price for column articles would be six guineas. They declined to pay it at first, but immediately afterwards they changed their minds, and ordered two articles instead of one. I shall be charmed to work for the *Chronicle* at six guineas. Till I hear from you I will keep the enclosures. The idea is good for one really striking article, but no good for a series. Moreover the notion of a consecutive series appearing in a daily *once a month* is ridiculous.

Yours sincerely, Arnold Bennett

P.S. Any reason why that Xmas 10,000 words should not appear *serially* in England? Serial stuff doesn't count, & prejudices nobody, not even the author. A. B.

111. *The Feast of St. Friend* (also called *Friendship and Happiness*) was published by both Doran and Hodder and Stoughton in 1911. It recommends an agnostic celebration of the Christian mystery: 'The discoveries of science have at once quickened our imagination and compelled us to admit that what we know is the merest trifle. The pagan in his ignorance explained everything. Our knowledge has only deepened the mystery, and all that we shall learn will but deepen it further.' Hodder and Stoughton were important publishers of conservative religious literature.

One of Tertia Bennett's children's books, *Gentleman Dash* (in which Arnold figures as 'the editor'), was published by Doran and Hodder and Stoughton in 1912. Another, *Tiptail*, was published earlier, in 1900, by Lamley. A third, *The Mysterious Uncle*, was published in 1924 by Wells Gardner, Darton.

112. The letter is misdated 1910.

The *English Review* published Bennett frequently from 1910 to 1913. See pages 128-9 and 180n. The Tillotson articles are unknown. No new *Chronicle* series could be found.

u.c. / ms. / 113

59 rue de Grenelle
23 Feby 1911

My dear Pinker,

Many thanks for your letters. I enclose the Doran agreement for *Buried Alive*, signed.

In a letter about going over to America he tells me he has written you about a contract for a new book. I am coming to the conclusion, from the way in which he diplomatises with me, that Doran is one of the acutest men of business of my acquaintance. And I know a few! When I have finished this heavenly trilogy, I am going to do a book in the vein of *Buried Alive*. It seems to me that Doran might have this book (1913) on the condition that he binds himself to do what he says he is doing and can do.

(1) generous terms for the book.

(2) serialisation. He says this is a practical certainty at a high figure. Let him buy the serial rights for America.

(3) a definite sum to be spent on campaigning with the books he already has. Say £1,000.

I think Doran deserves at any rate one new book if only for his cleverness & enthusiasm. He tells me he has sold 5,000 copies before publication of the new revised edition of *Sacred & Profane Love*. Is not this rather good? It was all his idea. When he came here he even took away one of my water-colour drawings to use as coloured wrappers for this book, & the result is quite pleasing.

———————

I see that despite Methuen's objection to two books a year *The Card* is not going to be an absolute frost.

Yours sincerely, Arnold Bennett

113. Doran was urging Bennett to visit America. Bennett made the trip in October. According to Doran in *Chronicles of Barabbas*, the trip was sponsored by Harper's. This was not so.

The book in the vein of *Buried Alive* was never written. Bennett did write the humorous novel *The Regent*, a sequel to *The Card*, in 1912. Subsequent letters (of 14 March 1911, 10 June 1911, and 29 June 1917) indicate a possible confusion between the two novels on Bennett's part.

BUTLER / TS. / 114
(*From J. B. Pinker*)

Talbot House
24th February 1911

My dear Bennett,

Many thanks for your letter of the 23rd enclosing the contract with Doran for *Buried Alive*.

Yes, Doran wrote to me a diplomatic letter about the question of a contract for a new book. I told him in reply that I did not think anything had occurred to change the situation since we discussed it last, but that if he had changed his views, and now particularly wanted a contract, I would submit the question to you again; but I told him that I thought it was no good my raising the question with you in a general way, but that we must arrive at a definite proposal to be submitted to you. I quite agree with you that Doran is very acute, and the only doubt I have of him is as to whether he is not also a little flighty. He is certainly most attentive, and is honestly keen on your work, and it is impossible altogether to resist the effect of his diplomacy. If he is willing to give generous terms for the book, and to buy the American serial rights at a good figure, then I agree with you it would be worth while making a contract with him; but I am anxious not to do anything at the moment that might check his enthusiasm. If we start bargaining with him, and either make him pay terms that he thinks too stiff, or fail to come to an arrangement, he would be left, perhaps, a little chilled.

Another important consideration is that I told Dutton you did not intend to contract for further books ahead until you saw how the trilogy was going, so that the race was open to him too. It would lead him perhaps to be more economical in advertising if he heard that the first book succeeding his lot was to go somewhere else.

For all those reasons, therefore, I would suggest that I delay getting to close quarters with Doran about the new book, and just continue gently with the discussion, blaming your reluctance to bind yourself. I think he has done well with *Sacred and Profane Love* and he deserves encouragement. I am writing to him again today, telling him what you have just told me about the book in the vein of *Buried Alive*, so as to keep things nicely simmering.

I am not sure about your proposal for a definite sum, say, £1000, to be spent on campaigning with the books he already has. Even if he were willing to bind himself to spend such a sum, it is impossible to check the expenditure, and to be satisfied that the specific sum has been utilized. What I have been telling him is that his best claim for new books will be a proof that he has done well with those he has.

Yes, I think *The Card* is going to do all right here. Methuen is very pleased, I am not quite sure whether it is with you, himself or me, over the business, but he told me one day that he thought you were probably the best writer I had. This is very amusing to me, because when I suggested you to Methuen, he scorned the idea, and actually said that he did not think you were ever going to be much good.

Sincerely yours, James B. Pinker

U.C. / MS. / 115

59 rue de Grenelle
1st March 1911

My dear Pinker,

Many thanks for your letter of yesterday. Certainly I should like the Dutton contract to be transferred to Doran. I have always thought, & I have several times suggested to you, I think, that it was unfair to the Dutton books to crowd the market with the old books, & I should be inclined to take Dutton's view of the matter.

By the way, when I saw Doran he told me he had offered £1,000 down on the trilogy (so much per book), but that the offer was not accepted. I said there was certainly some mistake there, but he did not seem to be convinced. Of course I did not tell him what Duttons were paying.

If Doran could take over *The Glimpse* from Appletons (is it?) I should be glad. I am absolutely certain there is still a remunerative public for this book in America. Had it been published there after *The O.W.T.* it would have made a stir. The vast spiritualistic public in the States would not understand it, but it would pretend to. Kindly perpend upon this matter.

Glad to hear about Locke.

No, I have not seen *Harper's*, & know nothing of it.

Yours sincerely, Arnold Bennett

P.S. Typewriting received. Thanks.

U.C. / MS. / 116

59 rue de Grenelle
6th Mch 1911

My dear Pinker,

Many thanks for your letters.

Money

It is evident that the financial situation is about to become quite embarrassing. I think you had better keep the balance in hand, until you are sure that you will have enough to pay me £50 a month to the end of the year without overdrawing. *When you are assured of this you might let me know.* I want the £50 a month arrangement to continue. It forces me to earn the difference between that & £1,000 a year (which I need altogether) by journalism & plays. Fundamentally I am an idle man & have to be spurred on. It is rather wonderful that you have contrived to pay off an overdraft of over £1,000 in a year, & I congratulate you, while offering you once more the assurance of my thanksgiving for your sweet reasonableness in finance during the last ten years.

---

115. Bennett reported in his journal on 27 October 1909: 'Today I heard from Pinker that Dutton's had offered £250 down and a good royalty on each of my 3 next novels for U.S.A. This shows how enormously one's prospects can change there in a year. A year ago no American publisher would publish my work on any terms.' By March 1911 the Dutton *Clayhanger* was competing with earlier works issued by Doran at the rate of almost one a month.

The Glimpse describes a man at the point of death. The perceptions, or fantasies, about reincarnation and psychic forces that Bennett gives to him are drawn in part from theosophical writings. H. G. Wells expressed the common view when he called the novel 'a glimpse into an empty cavern in his [Bennett's] mind'; Bennett himself thought that most of it was 'as good as the best I can do'. Appleton published it in 1909. No edition by Doran is known.

W. J. Locke (1863–1930), popular author of sentimental fiction (*The Morals of Marcus Ordeyne, The Beloved Vagabond*), had praised Bennett's work.

In *Harper's*, in the March issue, appeared a very favourable notice of Bennett by William Dean Howells.

Short stories

Certainly. Ten guineas a thousand, & stick to it. I have just made Hammerton pay me 8 guineas for a thousand words in *Everybody's Weekly*. I could do one or two stories in the late summer.

Yours sincerely, Arnold Bennett

u.c. / ms. / 117

59 rue de Grenelle
12 Mch 1911

My dear Pinker,

Will you kindly reflect upon the following:—I want Methuens to issue a book of short stories next spring, & I want to have 'The Death of Simon Fuge' from *The Grim Smile* included in it. Will Waugh agree? This story, 20,000 words, is still one of the best things I have done. The principal story in the new volume would be 'The Matador of the 5 Towns' (which might serve as a title), quite as good as 'Simon Fuge'. 12,000 words. I have about 15 other stories to choose from for the rest of the volume.

Yours sincerely, Arnold Bennett

P.S. Many thanks for the copies of *O.W.T.* Did you notice they have engraved Nicoll's sickly praise on the actual binding of the book itself. I do think this is a bit thick!   A. B.

P.P.S. Do you know of any good furnished rooms near S. Kensington? We shall come to London about April 6th & stay for 2 or 3 months.   A. B.

116. Pinker reported on 1 March that his ledgers showed a balance of £195 in Bennett's favour. On 30 June of the preceding year, Bennett owed Pinker £1,157.

In a letter of the 2nd, Pinker suggested that since Bennett was not interested in writing stories at present, the time was propitious for raising the rate.

Everybody's Weekly, edited by J. A. Hammerton (1871–1949), published a series of comments by authors on 'Why I Don't Live in London'. Bennett's appeared on 1 April. It was not republished in any of his essay collections.

117. Methuen issued *The Matador of the Five Towns* in 1912 without ' The Death of Simon Fuge '. The American edition, which is radically different from the English, does have the story in it.

Nicoll's sickly praise is quoted on page 140n.

u.c. / ms. / 118

59 rue de Grenelle
14 Mch 1911

My dear Pinker,

Thanks for your letter of yesterday. I will talk to you about the volume of short stories when I see you next month. In the meantime you might mention to Methuen that there is such a thing.

O.W.T.

I have no doubt that H. & S. have arranged the binding to help the sale of the book. But I think they have been ill-advised. Anybody with any feeling for books as books must object to it. Moreover the same end might have been obtained by printing the quotation on the paper-cover. My own feeling is so strong that I prefer not to put it into words. If you can arrange with Mr. Hodder-Williams to omit the quotation from the binding when the copies already bound are exhausted, I shall be very much obliged. As you know, I never try to interfere in matters that primarily concern the publisher, but in this instance, so exceptional, I think you will be justified in mentioning my opinion to the firm.

Doran

The offer for the book seems all right. But there is £500 difference between £1,000 & £500, & I don't think it would be wise to accept the offer for the serial. Whatever may be my situation in the States, I am at any rate notorious there. My U.S.A. press cuttings are most extraordinary. The biggest New York papers will print 3 columns of extracts from *The Truth about an author*, under the title of a personal sketch of me. How would it be if you suggested £500 minimum, & 50 or 60% of anything he got over that?

I thought perhaps you might know of rooms in S. Kensington. One large, or two small, bedrooms & a large sitting room, with meals only as ordered—*good* meals. Personal recommendation is the only thing.

Yours sincerely, Arnold Bennett

118. Ernest Hodder-Williams (1876–1927) was head of Hodder and Stoughton. Doran was offering a royalty of 20 per cent., with £500 on account, for a novel.

L.A.B.—M

u.c. / ms. / 119

59 rue de Grenelle
21 Mch 1911

My dear Pinker,

Many thanks for your letter of yesterday. I am much obliged for all your trouble with the *Daily Chronicle*. I think I had better refuse. I announced to several journalistic connections at the beginning of the year that my signed stuff could not be bought by anybody at less than six guineas, & on the strength of this I have got six guineas & over. Therefore I cannot fairly go below it; and, as you say, there is no reason why I should.

Yours sincerely, Arnold Bennett

butler / ts. / 120
(*From J. B. Pinker*)

Talbot House
5th April 1911

My dear Bennett,

I have just read in *The Bookman* your preface to the American edition of *An Old Wives' Tale*. You naturally do not there mention what I always recollect as a remarkable history of the novel, so far as my office was concerned. I remember you coming into the office one day, and telling me in your customary manner that you were going to write 'a great novel'. You told me the exact date on which you would begin it, and the exact date on which I should have the MS., and the length of the novel. In my experience it is remarkable for an author to begin a novel exactly on the day he fixes; it is still more remarkable for him to finish it on the day he fixes, but the astonishing thing was that the novel was a great novel, and that we both knew it would be.

Sincerely yours, J. B. Pinker

He had backed down from £1,000 to £500 on the sum he might get from the *Saturday Evening Post* for the serialization of *Hilda Lessways*. The negotiations with the *Post* fell through.

119. For the beginning of the *Chronicle* negotiations see page 147.

120. This letter is reproduced in Reginald Pound's biography with slight omissions and changes, the only noteworthy one being a correction of the title to *The Old Wives' Tale*. The letter must have touched Bennett, and it is true enough—despite the fact that Bennett first told Pinker the 200,000-word novel would be

U.C. / MS. / 121

2, Whitehall Court
S.W.
17 May 1911

My dear Pinker,

Many thanks. Aren't there any other novels Newnes can publish at 6d? How much do I get out of Chatto's edition?

With regard to Methuens & *The O.W.T.* There seems to be something mysterious about their office. Whom do you deal with there? I ask this because of the following singular incident. You originally tried to get Methuens to publish a cheaper edition of *The O.W.T.* And when they refused & you closed with Hodder & Stoughton you said you were glad the latter had taken it as it would show Methuens their mistake of judgment. The other day Lucas made a humorous reference to me being published by Claudius Clear. I told him what had passed with Methuens. He said he had heard nothing of it. He lunched with me today; he said he had just left Methuen himself, who assured him that he had no recollection of having had the refusal of *The O.W.T.* & that he would have been delighted to have it. I don't mind Methuen coming up to his office only once a week, but I strongly object to his gardening leading to this sort of thing, & I shall be much obliged if you will get an official explanation out of the firm. I would infinitely rather have had the book published by Methuens.

Yours sincerely, Arnold Bennett

U.C. / MS. / 122

2, Whitehall Court
19 May 1911

My dear Pinker,

Many thanks. I understand, & I shall let Lucas know exactly. Now can't we make Methuens take something else for their 2/-

---

'at least 120,000 words'. However, Bennett must have noticed the mistake in the title—he who proof-read some of H. G. Wells's books in order to improve Wells's spelling and syntax. What he thought about it is indicated by his letter on page 296.

121. 2 Whitehall Court was and is the address of the Authors' Club. The Bennetts came to England on 8 April.

Newnes wished to issue a sixpenny edition of *Hugo*. Arrangement had already been made with Chatto and Windus.

On E. V. Lucas see page 31n.

editions, for which, according to Lucas, they want good stuff? For instance *Whom God hath joined*. Probably you could get this absorbing work away from Nutt. I know you don't like it. But on the other hand I know a number of people who read it again & again.

Will you come to lunch on Monday week the 29th at 1.15?

Yours sincerely, Arnold Bennett

u.c. / ms. / 123

2, Whitehall Court
10th June 1911

My dear Pinker,

Many thanks for your thrilling letter. I very heartily congratulate you on your achievements this week. There are several rather important points that I must discuss with you, & I propose to call about 4 on Monday. I hope this hour will suit you, as I am just finishing *Hilda* & very much engaged. But if it won't, perhaps you will telephone me. Don't telephone, please, if it does suit.

I will certainly accept the Harper proposition for the articles, serially & in book form.

It will be absolutely impossible for me to begin to write the Hearst serial before my return from America. But between you & me when I begin I shall do it very quickly. You can promise it for early in March at latest. This serial has got to be an A1 thing, & it would be quite out of the question for me to do an A1 vivacious thing immediately on the top of *Hilda*. Kindly tell the purchasers that it is in their interests as well as in my own that they must wait. It surely isn't sense to order an expensive thing & then urge for delivery under unfavourable conditions! Anyhow they can't have it.

Yours sincerely, Arnold Bennett

P.S. We are very sorry we can't accept your wife's most kind invitation.

122. Pinker had confirmed that he had urged Methuen to take up *The Old Wives' Tale* and that Methuen had refused.

123. Harper's had offered £800 for serial rights to six articles on Bennett's American impressions, and a £100 advance on them in book form, with a royalty of 15 per cent., rising to twenty after the sale of 5,000 copies. Harper's had also

U.C. / MS. / 124

Villa des Néfliers
21 June 1911

My dear Pinker,
   Many thanks for your letters & cablegram.

Hilda Lessways

It was particularly arranged between you & me that the typescript of the last part of this book should not be sent to me, but straight to the publishers, to save time, & that only one copy would be necessary. Two copies have been made, & both sent to me, & moreover in the same parcel as the MS., which is always dangerous owing to risk of loss in post. I have sent one copy back to you at once. By this mistake a week of somewhat precious time will have been lost, as of course this week ends today. I hope they will hurry up.

Harpers

I have arranged with Wells that this novel shall be 100,000 words long, & that it shall be a Five Towns tale with movement in it & humour; also that no other serial shall run concurrently with it, & no other book be published in U.S.A. concurrently or until the spring following book publication in the autumn of 1914. I am to furnish part of the MS. in April 1913 & all of it by August 1913, & serial publication is to commence in the autumn of 1913. He didn't ask for anything else. It will perhaps be well if you formulate these conditions in writing to him as a preliminary to the contract. He asked for the refusal of the next book after that. I referred him to you. I found that the book

---

indicated that they would contemplate paying £3,000 for serial rights to a new novel, and £1,000 advance on the book, with a royalty of twenty per cent. Pinker was told by Harper's that should the latter arrangement be made, it would mark the highest sum Harper's had ever paid for a serial. The impressions were published in *Harper's* beginning in April 1912, and were published in book form later in the year. The American title, *Your United States*, became *Those United States* in the English edition issued by Secker. The serial was *The Price of Love*.

Hearst publications included *Cosmopolitan*, *Hearst's International*, and *Harper's Bazaar*. On 9 June Bennett wrote in his journal: 'Pinker . . . sold my next humorous serial to the Hearst combination for £2,000, all serial rights. This means at least £3,000 for the novel, or 1s. a word. I was justly elated.' The novel Bennett had in mind may have been either the sequel to *The Card*, *The Regent*, or the unwritten novel in the vein of *Buried Alive*.

couldn't be the third Clayhanger book, as this would mean a delay of three years between publication of *Hilda* & publication of Clayhanger III—too long.

Honeymoon

I should insist on a payment down of £50. I suppose publication in a monthly is off.

Audoux

Her friend & mine has not yet heard from her in reply. I have done all I can to prevent her from making a fool of herself. Your position has been made perfectly clear.

Odd volume story

I shall deliver this at the end of the month.
In great haste.

Yours sincerely, Arnold Bennett

u.c. / ms. / 125

Villa des Néfliers
28 July 1911

My dear Pinker,
Many thanks for your letter & the enclosures.

Harper's

I return the agreements signed. I have added the necessary phrase to the clause about 'no other articles'. As it stood this

---

124. Thomas B. Wells (1875–1941) was an editor at Harper's. Bennett started writing *The Price of Love* on 4 November 1912, and finished (after an interruption of three months or more) on 29 September of the following year. It began in *Harper's* that December.

On the adaptation of *The Honeymoon* for a monthly, see pages 144-6.

Marguerite Audoux (1863–1937) was a Parisian seamstress who wrote an account of her girlhood in a Catholic orphanage and as a shepherdess. The book, *Marie-Claire*, won a literary award in France, and became a best-seller there and in England and in America. Bennett wrote the introduction to the English translation. The author had sold the English and American rights to the book for the absurd sum of £16 or £20, and was apparently at the moment compounding her folly.

The Odd Volume was a charity annual, with stories contributed by popular writers—Barry Pain as well as Bennett. Bennett's story was 'Jock-at-a-Venture', which later was republished in *The Matador of the Five Towns*.

clause would prevent me from publishing anything whatever non-fictional until they issued the book.

I am not disposed to agree to Harper's suggestion for other novels. I will if they like give them *one* other novel for £4,000 total, the manuscript to be delivered not sooner than two years after the delivery of the first one, i.e. not earlier than 1915. One chief reason why I will not bind myself to Harper's for 1914 is that in 1914 I shall write my London novel (history of the son of Hilda Lessways) & that this novel will be of a quite un-serial quality, & will be done deliberately in an un-serial way. I will *not* write it with the idea that Harper's might want it for a serial. I particularly want Doran to have this book. I think it will be good business to keep him encouraged with a big book, and to see what he can do with it. Of course it was impossible for me to talk comfortably to him while keeping dark about the Harper contract, & so I told him frankly at once. He will be ready to give £1,500 down for the next book he takes, & if he will sign a contract on these terms, he can have the London book.

By the way the 3rd Dutton book will not be published in autumn 1912, as Wells said, but in spring 1913. Please arrange this.

Cosmopolitan

I am glad they show shame. Certainly in your place I should utterly refuse to recommence negotiations. I hope it will come off.

Doran

I am quite agreeable to no serialisation of the Xmas book. He likes the book. The other book is *not* a birthday book but a calendar. He is quite ready to take it. I have told him he mustn't do the sensational books. Has he paid his cheque? Has that £200 been repaid?

Yours sincerely, Arnold Bennett

Doran wished to say if I was writing that he wants to see you on Tuesday and will call at three.   A. B.

125. The London novel, *The Roll-Call*, was not written until 1916–17.
The third book intended for Dutton was *These Twain*, the last novel of the Clayhanger trilogy. It was taken over by Doran.

u.c. / ms. / 126

Villa des Néfliers
14 Augt 1911

My dear Pinker,

I enclose a letter just received from Macrae. It seems rather satisfactory. I have asked him to lunch or dine with me in London, where I shall be early in September. But of course I shall not discuss business with him. Nor do I see any chance of him getting another book, unless he is prepared to wait a long time & pay a fantastic price. Please return the letter.

You will remember that when I first came to you (about 1900, I think), I informed you with my usual confidence that I expected ultimately to make a great deal of money, & that I wanted an arrangement by which your percentage should be somewhat smaller beyond a certain sum per annum. We agreed upon terms, of which you took note but I didn't. I have completely forgotten what they were, but it appears to me that next year they are likely to become applicable.

Yours sincerely, Arnold Bennett

BUTLER / TS. / 127
(*From J. B. Pinker*)

Talbot House
17th August 1911

My dear Bennett,

I have your letter of the 14th with its enclosure, which I return. Macrae's report is most encouraging. I imagine you will not wish Duttons to have more books?

I have looked up the papers relating to our arrangement. What you have in mind, I think, is the arrangement we made for dramatic work. Our arrangement was embodied in a letter from me to you, dated December 23rd 1903, and it provides for a straight 10% commission with 5% interest on any over-

---

Cosmopolitan (Hearst) backed out of its informal commitment to publish the new humorous serial.

The Arnold Bennett Calendar was compiled by Bennett's brother Frank. Doran issued it and *The Feast of St. Friend* in 1911.

126. John Macrae was an editor at Dutton's. His letter probably reported satisfaction with the proofs of *Hilda Lessways*.

draft. This is confirmed in a letter from you dated December
24th 1903. I can send you copies of these if you wish. Attached
to these is a pencilled memorandum as follows:—

> Terms arranged with Bennett for dramatic work. Where
> I negotiate the play 10% on the first £2,000, 5% up to
> £4,000 and 2½% afterwards. If author negotiates the play
> 5% up to £2,000 and 2½% afterwards.

I think this must be what you had in mind. There was never
any suggestion that I should have less than my usual 10% on
fiction etc. I remember you discussed the thing with me before
you made your first arrangement with Lee Mathews for a
certain number of years, and at your suggestion it was arranged
I should stand aside so far as dramatic work was concerned
during that time, and after that time take up the work on the
terms that we fixed. It was at that time we discussed the modification, and you quoted to me the large sums that were made
out of plays, and suggested this modification of the commission
on dramatic work.

Sincerely yours, James B. Pinker

u.c. / ms. / 128

2, Whitehall Court
6th Sept 1911

My dear Pinker,

G. B. Hotel

Many thanks for your letter. I think Doran is apt to over-
estimate the risk of unauthorised editions. Perhaps you had
better cable him to await letter. I should prefer the book not to

127. Dutton published nothing more of Bennett's.

Bennett's memory had perhaps fastened upon some words he wrote about the
literary agent in *How to Become an Author* of 1903: 'The remuneration of agents,
10 per cent. on gross receipts, may at first sight appear large, but actually it is not
excessive, especially on small incomes. When an author's income reaches two
thousand a year, the agent should be willing to accept 5 per cent. on all sums
exceeding two thousand; but these details are not for the aspirant.' A new contract
that Bennett negotiated with Pinker in 1913 provided for a straight 10 per cent.
commission on all work except dramatic, on which the commission was a straight
7½ per cent. For other details of that contract see page 333n.

William Lee Mathews (d. 1931) was a businessman whose personal interest was
the theatre. He was an intimate friend of Bennett's, and had acted as his dramatic
agent since 1903 or earlier.

be included in uniform edition. If it is necessary to publish it
to stop competition, I should like it *not* uniform with the others,
and I *must* have in it a note conceived more or less in the
following terms

*This book, written about 1899, was one of the first stories which the
author composed specially for serial publication, and which he has
classified as 'fantasias', to distinguish them equally from his realistic
novels and from his satiric novels. It is now reissued in order to obviate
the risk of unauthorised editions.*

Yours sincerely, Arnold Bennett

P.S. As a matter of fact, editions of minor work seem to be
pretty well ignored by the press. For example *The Ghost*, which
has raised no protest whatever.   A. B.

U.C. / TS. / 129

George H. Doran Company
35 West 32nd Street
New York
October 21, 1911

My dear Pinker:

Many thanks for your letter of the 11th, and the enclosures. I
return the two contracts, duly executed.

I quite agree with all that you say about the new agreement
with Methuen. Please do exactly as you think best.

I have made a provisional contract through Mr. Paul
Reynolds with the *Metropolitan Magazine* for eight essays, which
are to begin immediately after the conclusion of the articles in
Harper's, at the price of £150 each *for America only*. I have also
sold to him the American serial rights of the Novel of London,
of which the book rights have already been sold to Mr. Doran.
I told him that I had refused £2,500 from Messrs. Harper's,
and he asked me if I would accept £3,000. I agreed. Although
this business was done through your agent, Mr. Paul Reynolds,
the entire verbal negotiations were conducted by myself.

In confirmation of my cable the other day, Mr. Doran has

---

128. Bennett came to England on 31 August. He was to leave for America on
7 October.
Doran issued *The Grand Babylon Hotel* in 1913.

sold the American serial rights of the Humorous Novel to the *American Magazine* for £2,000.

If you can do anything with these things in England, of course I shall be only too pleased.

Yours sincerely, Arnold Bennett

P.S. I have just received your second letter and the contract with Messrs. George Newnes, which I enclose, duly executed.

U.C. / TS. / 130

George H. Doran Company
35 West 32nd Street
October 31, 1911

My dear Pinker:

Mr. J. S. Phillips of the *American Magazine*, has just showed me the letter which he has written to you embodying the

---

129. Bennett was in America from 13 October to 30 November. The visit was a huge and exhausting public success. He spent most of his time in New York, and travelled briefly to Washington, Boston, Chicago, Indianapolis, and Philadelphia. In his journal are recorded the multitude of details that fascinated him about American life: 'The flexibility of arrangements for business and social affairs; ingenuity expended in getting things to fit in for comfort . . .'; 'Tunnel under Hudson; very neat, regular, and well lighted. . . .' He also found the country uninteresting in the sense that Matthew Arnold had several decades before, seeing little that was beautiful or distinguished. In the Capitol Building in Washington, he noted the 'astounding collection of ugly statues'; the Washington Monument was 'phallic, appalling'; Washington generally seemed a 'plantation of public edifices amid a rather unkempt undergrowth of streets'.

George Doran, who was Bennett's host much of the time, tells an amusing anecdote about their parting:

'Just before his departure Arnold sat for Pirie MacDonald for a portrait photograph which is the most exact likeness and finest picture interpretation of Bennett in existence. He was greatly pleased with it and so was I. In giving me a print he wrote beneath it: "To George H. Doran from whom in the United States the Almighty, Himself, shall not separate me." My publishing instinct must momentarily have transcended my friendship, for I told him I would feel so much safer if he would substitute "my literary agent" for the "Almighty".'

When Bennett arrived back in Paris, he noted that the total expenses of the American tour were £252 5s. 8d. The material reward for going was more than twenty times that sum.

The *Metropolitan* series began with four articles on *The Case of the Plain Man* in October 1912. It was published in book form in 1913 as *The Plain Man and His Wife* (also as *Married Life* and as *Marriage: The Plain Man and His Wife*). On Reynolds see page 126n.

Newnes issued 6d. editions of *The Gates of Wrath* and *Teresa of Watling Street* in 1912.

arrangement with regard to the short humorous book which I have to write in the early part of next year. I enclose a copy of my answer. Can you place this in England?

You will doubtless hear direct from Paul Reynolds as to the contract with the *Metropolitan Magazine* for a series of essays, and also for the *American* serial rights of the novel which I shall write after I have written the novel for Messrs. Harpers.

I have arranged with Mr. Roland Phillips of the *Cosmopolitan Magazine*, to write for him a series of four short stories of about five thousand words each, the first to be delivered in October, 1913, and the others at intervals of two months afterwards. The price is twenty cents per word for the entire serial rights. I respectfully beg you to observe, my dear Pinker, that this means £200 per short story, and that I have obtained this price by simply asking for it.

Will you please keep a careful note of all these engagements?

Will you kindly send a check for £10 : 10 to Alexander Webster, Esq., Hampden Club, N.W., posting it on November 9th?

Yours sincerely, Arnold Bennett

P.S. I see no reason why Messrs. Newnes should not have *Teresa of Watling Street* on the same terms as *The Gates of Wrath*. I enclose also correspondence with *Cosmopolitan*.

u.c. / ms. / 131

The Blackstone
Michigan Boulevard
Chicago
16 November 1911

My dear Pinker,

Many thanks for your letter of the 3rd & the enclosures. I return the two agreements signed.

The *Metropolitan* novel is the London novel (about the son

130. John S. Phillips (1861–1949), former partner of S. S. McClure, published the *American Magazine*. He bought *The Regent*.

Cosmopolitan (Hearst) once again backed out of its contract. See pages 201–2. Roland Phillips is not otherwise identified.

Alexander Webster (d. 1919) was an old friend. Bennett lived with him briefly after leaving Trinity Hall Farm in 1903.

of 'Hilda') which I said could not be serialised. The *Metropolitan*, however, have particularly asked for the highest class stuff I can produce.

I hope you will arrange with the *Strand* for the sequel to *The Card* in England. The *American* propose to begin the serial in October or November.

My instructions as to Palmer remain in their fullest force, please.

It might be prudent to keep the *Cornhill* in tow, in case we had need of them. But my feeling is very strongly against both *Cornhill* & Smith Elders. I am very sure they wouldn't really like a serial of mine (unless purely humorous) even if they bought it.

Chicago is the city of superlatives, & it has decided that I am one of the superlatives.

Yours sincerely, Arnold Bennett

u.c. / ms. / 132

The Bellevue-Stratford
Philadelphia
22 Nov 1911

My dear Pinker,

Kindly pay in £100 to my account with Cook *Paris* at once. I will give you a cheque in payment of this when I see you in London. On the arrival of the Lusitania (about Dec 4th) I shall spend one night in the Five Towns, & then come to London, & I shall ask you to make an effort to keep an appointment with me which I will make by telegraph. It will not be in the evening, but it *might* be between 5 & 6. You know how I hate to derange you in your habits, but I do it as little as I can, don't I? I am anxious to fly to Cannes at once, so as to begin my work. I am now on the last lap of my tour. Great time.

Yours sincerely, Arnold Bennett

131. The *Metropolitan* novel proved to be not *The Roll-Call* but *The Lion's Share*, a light novel.

The sequel to *The Card*, *The Regent*, was serialized in the *London Magazine* beginning in November 1912, and in the *American Magazine* beginning in December.

Frank Palmer published *The Arnold Bennett Calendar* in England in 1911. Bennett was dissatisfied with its sales. Palmer issued nothing more of his.

Bennett said of the *Cornhill*, in an article in the *New Age* in 1909, that it 'still admirably fulfils its apparent purpose of appealing to people who object to thinking about anything that is worth thinking about'.

TEXAS / MS. / 133

[Hôtel Californie]
[Cannes]
3–2–12

[no salutation]
The title of the new humorous novel will be

THE REGENT

which I think is a pretty good sounding title. It has no reference to any character in the story. It is the name of the Regent Theatre (in Regent St.) which Denry Machen, hero of *The Card*, comes to London to build. You can impart these interesting details to the *London*, or not, as you deem wisest. My own experience is that when an editor having bought something without knowing what it is, is *told* what it is, his instinct is to exclaim that it is the very last thing he desired.

By this post I am delivering to *Harper's* the 5th & 6th articles of the contract, & money will therefore be now due, which kindly collect.

Still in bed & enfeebled; up tomorrow.

A. B.

U.C. / MS. / 134

Hôtel Californie
27 Mch 1912

My dear Pinker,
Many thanks. I am returning the H. & S. agreement signed. It seems quite all right—indeed very strict on them. Apparently *The Feast of St. Friend* remains in abeyance.

133. The Bennetts stayed at Cannes from the middle of December until the middle of April. Just before going to America, Bennett had decided to give up the Villa des Néfliers at Avon, and presently he decided to return to England to live permanently.

In 1922, when Bennett's play *Body and Soul* was produced at the Euston Palace of Varieties, the theatre was temporarily renamed the Regent. Bennett wrote to his nephew Richard (son of his brother Frank): 'a great sensation, seeing the name "Regent" in vast gilt letters over the super-card's theatre!'

On 31 January Bennett suffered an attack of what was diagnosed as gastroenteritis. It left him weakened during the rest of the year, and was responsible for a delay in his writing the third Clayhanger novel. In 1931, when he lay mortally ill with typhoid fever, there was suspicion that this earlier illness was a lighter attack of typhoid.

Milestones. If you have written formally to Miss Kauser, I think your responsibility, so far as the inter-relation of book rights & dramatic rights is concerned, is discharged. Knoblock is coming here on Saturday.

I am on the last lap of *The Regent.* I shall send one copy direct to America on or before the 15th April, and another to you.

I see *A Man from the North* has achieved a third edition. In view of this success, couldn't Methuens issue another old book at 6/- in the autumn, as they will have nothing new? The sun seems to be shining; let the hay therefore be made. I staggered myself by a calculation yesterday which showed that my *minimum* earnings from the book & serial work which I *do* this year will be £11,000. This leaves plays out of account entirely. *Milestones* is a *real* success. A small theatre, but my net share of the royalties (after deducting 10% commission) is over £60 a week. This during the worst strike in history!

Yours sincerely, Arnold Bennett

P.S. I shall be glad if you can find me a secretary for about middle of May. I want a thoroughly first class presentable man, who can see people for me if necessary, & who will move about (e.g. to Brighton), and I am quite ready to pay a proper salary.

134. Hodder and Stoughton, so Bennett thought, were displeased with the religious sentiments of *The Feast of St. Friend,* and were not advertising it. A letter from Ernest Hodder-Williams of 19 March says: 'We were extremely proud that Mr. Bennett allowed us to publish it, and I can assure you that we all did our utmost to make it sell. The result has been frankly disappointing, the total sales reaching 1,500 copies.'

Milestones was written by Bennett in collaboration with Edward Knoblock (1874–1945), author of the recent success *Kismet.* Miss Alice Kauser (d. 1945) was Knoblock's American dramatic agent; several years earlier she seems to have decided against acting for Bennett. *Milestones* opened at the Royalty Theatre on 5 March. The general coal strike began on 26 February and lasted until 6 April. *Milestones* lasted more than a year. The cast included Dennis Eadie, Lionel Atwill, Haidée Wright, and Gladys Cooper.

Bennett's secretary for a brief spell was Archie de Bear, later a theatrical manager. He had a succession of secretaries until he found Miss Winifred Nerney, who came to him later in the year and remained with him until his death. In *Background with Chorus,* Frank Swinnerton says of her relationship with Bennett: 'Miss Nerney began by detesting him; she ended, as all who knew him well did, by regarding him with amused, discreetly adoring affection.'

TEXAS / MS. / 135

[Hôtel Californie]
13–4–12

[no salutation]

I have this day despatched to you in two book packets, a copy of *The Regent*. You may take it positively from me that this book is all right. I have read nearly all of it aloud to friends, with enormous success. Phillips writes that he hopes to make a joint arrangement for illustrations. I have sent Phillips his copy. This other one is for Harmsworths.

Also, without consulting you, I have ventured to send to your office addressed to you, a case of books, collected here, carriage forward. I hope you won't mind housing it till I am able to relieve you of it. I really didn't know where else to send it. I expect the carriage will be fairly stiff.

The Regent is 78,000 words long.

Our address till April 29 is Hôtel du Rhin, Place Vendôme, Paris.

A. B.

U.C. / MS. / 136

Hôtel du Rhin
4 & 6 Place Vendôme
[Paris]
17 Apl 1912

My dear Pinker,

Many thanks for yours of 15th & the enclosures. I heartily congratulate you on the *Strand* success. It is certainly better so, & always it is better to leave these editors regretting that they could not spring to your prices. It does good! Now it remains to sell the book; and also, incidentally, for me to write the essays. You have also the United States book to sell in England.

I sincerely hope Craig will *not* illustrate the serial. He has no humour, & his work is the highly finished, unoriginal, & utterly mediocre stuff which suits the magazines & which ought to be discouraged. I have indicated a goodish man to Phillips— one Solon, *native of the Five Towns*, & I hope he will take him, as he lives in N.Y. now. Raven Hill would be a very good man—

135. The Harmsworth organization published the *London Magazine*.

an original & distinguished artist. Craig's illustrations to my U.S.A. articles are damnable. See his lifeless imitation of 10,000 previous drawings of New York skyscrapers by night, & his types of steamer people & 'strong clean healthy young men'! Odious stuff! Here I go & do a really original description of a steamer, & he goes and slobbers all over it with his detestable banality. He is a nice chap, but I knew he was a damned bad artist from the way he talked. This is the first work of his I have seen.

I enclose a letter about a 2,000 word article I wrote recently for the *Youth's Companion*. It may encourage you in sticking up for prices. It is the only instance I have ever known of an editor being enthusiastic, in writing, immediately on receipt of an article.

I think it would be very unwise for you to say or hint in any way that you are in the future to be my dramatic agent. My scheme in life is to be able to look people in the face, & Lee Mathews is a great friend of mine. I shall have a quite sufficiently difficult time with him as it is, without the situation being complicated by his hearing from other people that you are to supplant him. In fact I am not at all looking forward to it! Although I emphatically do not think highly of Lee M as a business man, he is extremely human beneath his massive & rather comic exterior, & his enthusiasm & immense & quite sincere admiration also touch my heart, & I feel sure you will agree with me that his amour-propre ought to be exposed to no unnecessary risks. Considering that you have only recently gone into the dramatic business seriously, & that I have been in it for 12 years, the explanation of you not acting for me will not be difficult for you to find. I am glad you are going ahead. You have evidently impressed Selwyn.

Yours sincerely, Arnold Bennett

136. The Bennetts had a flat at the Hôtel du Rhin for about two weeks.

The *Strand* paid £200 for four articles of the series *The Case of the Plain Man* (*The Plain Man and His Wife*) after Cassells had declined to pay more than £150.

Frank Craig, popular magazine illustrator, was offered by the *London Magazine* as 'the greatest black and white artist in England'. They soon had to write to Pinker that they were 'sorry that Mr. Bennett does not like Frank Craig'. Craig, Léon Victor Solon (b. 1872), and Leonard Raven-Hill (1867–1942) yielded to C. H. Taffs.

Youth's Companion wrote to express complete satisfaction with 'Clay in the Hands of the Potter' and to note the promptness with which the manuscript was delivered.

L.A.B.—N

u.c. / ms. / 137

> Poste Restante
> Brightlingsea
> 11–6–12

My dear Pinker,

For nearly 2 years I have been off & on in negotiation for the purchase of a Dutch barge named 'The Velsa'. She was sold over my head once. Then the new owner, after spending a lot on her, wanted to sell her again, & I was just buying (last year) when his wife refused to let him sell. He began again this year, & the negotiations again came to a stop just before I came away here. Immediately I came away his agent (Andrew Thomson, 50 Pall Mall) telegraphed accepting my offer. £550. (I have bit by bit got the price down from £1,100!) But he wants to complete at once. As the negotiations had broken down I invested on Friday last £600 which I had been keeping for this affair. Hence my telegram to you this morning. I have paid a deposit of £55, leaving £495 to be paid, & I have told Thomson that you will complete on Tuesday next. As to checking the inventory I will write you later. The boat is up at 'Thames Ditton', & it may be necessary to send a clerk up there. You might telephone to Thomson. He is a well-known yacht agent & I have told him that I will accept his assurance as to the inventory if he can give it.

> Yours sincerely, Arnold Bennett

P.S. Health incredibly improved. Probably you have got the £500 from Phillips by this time.

The article, which concerns the Five Towns, was never published in any collection of Bennett's essays.

On Lee Mathews see page 161. Edgar Selwyn (1875–1944) was Bennett's American dramatic agent. He was a former actor and playwright, and now headed Selwyn and Co., theatrical producers and theatre-owners.

137. Brightlingsea was where Bennett eventually kept the *Velsa*. His friend J. B. Atkins (1871–1954), assistant editor of the *Spectator*, apparently kept a yacht there as well, and Bennett was probably sailing with him at this time.

U.C. / TS. / 138

Royal Albion Hotel
Brighton
June 25th, 1912

My dear Pinker,

Many thanks for your letter of the 24th. We shall be delighted to see you for lunch on Thursday. Will you kindly let me know the time of your arrival?

I will now write to Thomson myself as to the future insurance of the yacht.

I enclose a form for insurance of the chauffeur, filled up. It is a very ambiguous form.

I am extremely sorry to hear that *Milestones* has been sold serially in the United States for £200. Doran was, in my opinion, quite ill-advised to urge the acceptance of such a sum, and when I see him I shall certainly inform him of my view. *Milestones* is at least 20,000 words in length and it is easily the greatest theatrical success of the year. I have actually refused blind commissions in more than one quarter at the rate of one shilling a word. I have a contract for short stories at £200 each, and here is one of the most valuable items of the age being sold at less than 5 cents a word, which is no more than the price paid by a high class American magazine to an ordinary contributor for an ordinary contribution. As you are aware I received £200 a couple of years ago for *The Honeymoon* which is a considerably shorter play and which had no extrinsic value at all.

Please send on or before the end of the month the following cheques:—

F. C. Bennett Esq., Solicitor, Hanley, Stoke-on-Trent. £13.
Mrs Emily Edge, 57, Redcliffe Road, S.W.: £15.
Mrs. W. W. Kennerley, 'Glenholme', Cobbs Road, Lyme Regis: £25.

Yours sincerely, [Arnold Bennett]

138. *Milestones* was published in *Munsey's Magazine* in October 1912.

Mrs. Emily Edge (1871–1953) was one of Bennett's sisters. She was a year older than Tertia (Mrs. Kennerley).

u.c. / ts. / 139

14 St. Simon's Avenue
Putney, S.W.
August 8th. 1912.

My dear Pinker,

Many thanks for your letter of yesterday. The question of the essays is extremely awkward. Since I last wrote to you I have been struck down with an abscess in the middle ear which has prevented me from doing any work at all. I may possibly be able to finish the second essay by Monday, when I have made all my arrangements for going away, but it is not by any means sure. Quite possibly all your great powers as an agent may have to be brought into play, but I will let you hear definitely on Monday morning.

Yours sincerely, Arnold Bennett

u.c. / ms. / 140

Yacht Velsa
The Hague
3rd Sept. 1912

My dear Pinker,

I enclose Insurance notice. Tomorrow I shall send you the second article of *The Plain Man* Series. It is not so much late after all. Please have it typed (& most carefully checked by two intelligent persons, one reading aloud to the other) in duplicate & send one copy to the *Metropolitan*. This article completes the subject raised in the first one; and an interval in publication can now occur without damage to the Series. I am all right, & can work excellently on this liner. Please acknowledge receipt to Poste Restante, Amsterdam, & tell me any interesting news. Marguerite arrives this afternoon from France. It has rained *every* day. But today is lovely and chilly.

Yours sincerely, Arnold Bennett

139. The Bennetts lived mainly at 14 St. Simon's Avenue for the next several months. The house belonged to Herbert Sharpe, the musician, a friend of Bennett's from early London days.

140. Bennett lived and worked much of the time on his yacht. E. V. Lucas describes him in a moment of not working: 'Arnold never seemed to be quite so serene and complacent as in his scrupulous yachting attire. He was no navigator; he was a yacht-owner. To sit in a deck-chair surveying a calm ocean from his own

U. C. / MS. / 141
Private   14 St. Simon's Avenue
                                             24 Oct 1912

My dear Pinker,

I gather that Alice Perrin will be very dissatisfied—with you —if she doesn't get appreciably better terms in her new contract than in the previous one. I thought you might like to know. She wrote me for advice, but as her letter was not marked private I see no reason why I shouldn't acquaint you with her state of mind!!

                                             Yours, A. B.

U. C. / TS. / 142

                                             14 St. Simon's Avenue
                                             5th December, 1912
My dear Pinker,

Many thanks for your two letters of yesterday.

There are several reasons why I think it would be scarcely advisable to let Greenhough Smith have all the eight articles. First, it is a bad thing to let an editor have all he wants; second, I do not care to appear too frequently in *The Strand*; third, I ought to appear from time to time in a first-class review; fourth, the remaining four articles will be chiefly of a literary nature, and would probably prove rather a disappointment to the readers of *The Strand*.

As regards *The Metropolitan Magazine,* I do not mind treating the reminiscences as an extra article.

                              Yours sincerely, Arnold Bennett

------

vessel and approving it—not saying of it: "No good", his favourite term with which to dismiss a book, but "First-class"—"class" pronounced like "gas"—was joy enough, triumph enough.'

142. In an article on H. G. Wells in 1909, Bennett referred to *The Country of the Blind* as 'one of the radiant gems of contemporary literature, and printed in the *Strand Magazine*!' The *Strand*, which was edited for over forty years by Greenhough Smith (d. 1935), also published Jerome K. Jerome, E. Phillips Oppenheim, Conrad, and more Bennett. The remaining four articles of the present group were taken by the *English Review*.

The reminiscences appeared in the *Metropolitan* in January and the *Strand* in February 1913. The article was never republished in any of the collections of Bennett's essays.

U.C. / MS. / 143

> Hôtel Californie
> Cannes
> Xmas Day 1912

My dear Pinker,

Doran has a tentative arrangement, subject to our approval, for serialising 8 or 10 of my books by the Munsey Syndicate. The Syndicate is to have 40 per cent of the gross receipts (paying all expenses) & the remaining 60 per cent is, according to the project, to be divided equally between Doran & me. Doran has shown me the letters embodying the arrangement between him & Robert Davis, the manager of Munseys. It seems to me all right except the division between Doran & me, as to which I have not been consulted in any way. Although I leave the matter entirely to you, & do not wish you to consult me before settling the matter, it seems to me it may occur to you to ask Doran why he should take half of my share. He has never done it before in questions of serialising. I have not discussed it at all with him. I simply referred the whole thing to you. It seems to me if he had ten or (at most) 15%, that ought to suffice. We have given him no call on serial rights of the books. The first suggestion of Munseys taking up the books was made by Bob Davis himself to me, & the affair would never have matured at all if Davis & I had not at once conceived a strong mutual admiration. Davis is a first-class man, & he simply worships me. Apparently the only way in which you can earn your commission on Doran business is by standing up for my rights against me-as-a-friend-of-Doran's, if you understand! Though in this case I have agreed to nothing & made *no* comment. Of course if there is a valid reason why Doran should take half, all right. *Officially you know nothing of this matter till Doran shows you the papers.*

> Yours sincerely, Arnold Bennett

143. Bennett and his wife were in France briefly at the end of the year.

The Munsey Company, headed by Frank A. Munsey (1854–1925), published *Munseys' Magazine, Argosy, All-Story Magazine,* and *Railroad Man's Magazine.* Robert H. Davis (1869–1942) was in later years a columnist for the *New York Sun.* Bennett liked him well enough to write a brief article about him for the *American Magazine,* August 1913.

U.C. / TS. / 144

14 St. Simon's Avenue
20th January, 1913

My dear Pinker,

I enclose a copy of the final article for the *Strand*. The copy for the *Metropolitan Magazine* went by last Saturday's mail.

I have now definitely settled the affair of Lee Mathews and there has been no unpleasantness at all. He definitely ceases to be my agent—except in regard to contracts which already exist—on April 1st. I shall be glad, however, if you will say nothing at all to anybody about the future until I have seen you. You will easily understand the reasons for this discretion.

I think it will be best for you and me to tear up our present contract and enter into a new one on the basis of the descending scale of percentages which was arranged between you and me about twelve years ago in anticipation of the day when you should act for me both as literary and as dramatic agent. This contract ought of course to be drawn up with the greatest care. I have obtained from the Authors' Society a copy of its model agreement between agent and author, but I do not see that the ingenuity of Mr. Thring has evolved anything very useful except one clause which provides that after an agreement has been terminated the amount of fees to be received by an agent on any contract existing at the date of termination shall be limited to £500. This seems to me to be a fair arrangement. The only other things which I have to suggest are that the contract should be strictly personal between you and me, and terminable by six months' notice on either side, or by death, or by your bankruptcy or other failure to pay twenty shillings in the pound. I trust the last-named contingency is not immediate. As I told you the other day I propose in any case to except from the agreement theatrical agency in the United States, as I am in a fair way to be convinced that the best services are not to be obtained of American agents when they are forced to divide their commission with an English agent. What I am going to do as regards theatres in the United States I cannot yet decide. Before coming to any definite conclusion I must see both Edgar Selwyn and Alice Kauser.

I shall leave you to make a draft of the contract. For your

information I enclose copies of the Authors' Society's model agreement for both literary agency and dramatic agency.

Yours sincerely, Arnold Bennett

BUTLER / TS. / 145
(*From J. B. Pinker*)

Talbot House
21st January 1913

My dear Bennett,

Many thanks for your letter with its enclosures, including the final article for the *Strand*. I note that a copy for the *Metropolitan* went by Saturday's mail.

I am glad to hear about Lee Mathews, and I will, of course, say nothing at all to anybody about the future, until I have seen you. I shall be very glad if you will come and see me so that we may talk things over before I draft the agreement. Your suggestion was that when I negotiated the play I should have 10% commission on the first £2,000, 5% up to £4,000 and 2½% afterwards; if you negotiated the play, I was to have 5% commission up to £2,000 and 2½% afterwards. I want to talk over this and other things with you, as 2½% commission is impossible, even for mere mechanical collection of royalties. Your common rent collector is paid 5% to 7½%, and even after a play is placed an author wants better service from his agent than he could get from a rent collector. However, we can settle all these things when we meet, and if you will choose your time I will be in.

Sincerely yours, James B. Pinker

144. In September of 1912, G. Herbert Thring, Secretary of the Society of Authors, wrote to Bennett about recent efforts by the Society to protect playwrights from unreasonable claims by their agents. Bennett replied on 10 September: 'I quite agree with you that agents' fees are apt to work out much too exorbitantly. In 12 years, however, I have never had any trouble with agents, & I am now arranging that when receipts exceed a certain amount annually the percentage shall be reduced.' On Edgar Selwyn and Alice Kauser see pages 169–70 and 167.

145. For the terms of the contract see page 333n.

u.c. / ts. / 146

14 St. Simon's Avenue
12th February, 1913

My dear Pinker,

Very many thanks for yours of yesterday. 1.45 is an ungodly hour for a man who breakfasts at 7.30, but I shall only be too delighted to lunch at any hour with you and Henry James. Thursday the 20th would suit me best.

Yours sincerely, Arnold Bennett

u.c. / ts. / 147

Comarques
Thorpe-Le-Soken
March 21st, 1913

My dear Pinker,

I enclose copy of a letter which I have written to Methuen. I think that the last sentence is rather clever in giving him the idea that I take the matter more seriously than in fact I do.

I enclose the Agreement between us duly signed. I also enclose my own copy of it and I shall be much obliged if you will have it stamped for me.

Yours sincerely, Arnold Bennett

146. Bennett described a meeting with James earlier in the year in his journal: 'Henry James. At Pinker's. Very slow talker. Beautiful French. Expressed stupefaction when I said I knew nothing about the middle class, and said the next time he saw me he would have recovered from the stupefaction, and the discussion might proceed. Said there was too much to say about everything—and that was the thing most felt by one such as he, not entirely without—er—er —er—er—perceptions. When I said I lay awake at nights sometimes thinking of the things I had left out of my novels, he said that all my stuff was crammed, and that when the stuff was crammed nothing more could be put in, and so it was all right.'
James was less flattering in his remarks on Bennett in 'The New Novel' the following year. He saw 'a huge and in its way varied aggregation, without traceable lines, divinable direction, effect of composition'. He perhaps knew what Bennett had written of him in the *New Age*: 'But on the debit side:—He is tremendously lacking in emotional power. Also his sense of beauty is over-sophisticated and wants originality. Also his attitude towards the spectacle of life is at bottom conventional, timid, and undecided.'

147. Comarques, Thorpe-le-Soken, named after a Huguenot family, became the Bennetts' home on 24 February. Bennett wrote to an American friend the previous December: 'We now possess an early Queen Anne house near the Essex coast, and in February are going to remove ourselves there definitely for everlasting; our deaths will one day cause a sensation in the village we shall dominate, and the English villagers and landed gentry will wonder, as they stroll through the deserted house, why the madman had 3 bathrooms in a home so small; they will not know

NW. / T.C.C. / 148
(*From A. M. S. Methuen*)

[Methuen & Co Ltd.]
[36 Essex Street]
March 18, 1913

Dear Bennett,

I hear through Webster that you are a little vexed by my attitude in the matter of Sixpenny rights and I hope I may send you this letter to explain our point of view. I can assure you that I want to be reasonable and to treat you with all courtesy and consideration.

The difficulty arose in this way. When Pinker sent in the agreement for *The Great Adventure* and *How to be an Author* there was a clause which not only gave you the cheap editions in these two books but also gave you retrospectively the cheap editions of various other books which we had published by you. This clause might have prevented us from publishing Shilling, Sevenpenny, or any cheap editions of those older books and as the clause was revolutionary and unprecedented I protested. When I tell you that the older books which would be affected by this clause number eight with rights extending in some cases to 12 or 14 years you will see how revolutionary the proposal is. I told Pinker that as a general principle we thought it very unfair that an agreement for a new book should be so worded that certain valuable rights belonging to us in other agreements with the same author were taken away. . . .

Pinker is an excellent agent but I think that in this case he has been a little over earnest in watching over your interests. I have told him that I should like to put the matter before you and he has not objected.

I will only repeat that we should be very glad indeed to meet your views in any way that may seem reasonable to you and possible to us and I hope you will pardon my troubling you on a matter of business which as a rule would not be laid before you by me.

Yours sincerely, [A. M. S. Methuen]

---

that it was solely due to a visit to the U.S.A.' The home was abandoned after the marriage broke up in 1921.

Bennett's letter to Methuen (page 179) is in answer to the following letter from Methuen himself.

148. George Webster was on the Methuen staff.

u.c. / t.c.c. / 149
(*To A. M. S. Methuen*)

[Comarques]
March 20th, 1913

Dear Methuen,

Many thanks for your letter of the 18th. Please dismiss from your mind the idea that I am 'vexed' as it is absolutely incorrect. I believe myself to be capable of differing from my publishers on a matter of business without losing my good humour in the slightest degree. I am also quite sure that you wish to act in a perfectly reasonable manner. I can explain my point of view in quite a few words.

The sixpenny rights of my novels as distinguished from the two shilling, one shilling, or sevenpenny rights are worth a certain sum of money. If you are prepared to exploit the sixpenny market yourself I shall of course be only too pleased to leave the sixpenny rights in your hands. If not, I consider that I ought to be absolutely free to sell the sixpenny rights elsewhere, and that most decidedly I ought not to be called upon to pay over a portion of my percentage on them to you. I understand that as a fact your intention is to withdraw entirely from the sixpenny market for novels. You are of course perfectly justified in doing so, but I fail to see why your withdrawal from that market should take the sum of £50 out of my pocket on each novel. I do not conceive that in equity there can be any answer to this argument.

The purely legal aspect of the case remains. I do not pretend to be able to recall all the details of every contract I have signed, but if your legal position under any contract is such as to enable you to say to me that you will not allow me to dispose of the sixpenny rights on a given book elsewhere unless I hand over to you a percentage of the proceeds, and if you think proper to exercise the power vested in you by the contract, I shall assuredly not complain. But it is equally sure that I should be compelled to reconsider my whole position as regards the future, for the simple reason that I cannot see how you are justly entitled to participate in the profits of the sixpenny market without going into it. It is I admit a matter of opinion, but my own opinion is clear.

Whatever the outcome of the present difficulty may be I am

quite certain that our personal relations will remain undis-
turbed. You have been very kind to me and I have derived
nothing but pleasure from our encounters.

Yours sincerely, [Arnold Bennett]

U.C. / TS. / 150

Comarques
April 1st, 1913

My dear Pinker,
Many thanks for your letter and the enclosure. I enclose a
copy of the letter which I have sent to Methuen to-day. If he
shows signs of wishing to communicate with me further on the
point, you might gently indicate to him that I think I have
interfered enough.

Yours sincerely, Arnold Bennett

P.S. I assume that the *English Review* isn't getting in advance of
American publication with the new series of articles. A. B.

U.C. / T.C.C. / 151
(*To A. M. S. Methuen*)

[Comarques]
April 1st, 1913

Dear Methuen,
In further reference to your letter of the 27th ult., I have now
looked further into the question of the new agreement, and I
enclose a copy of Pinker's suggested clause for embodying the
arrangement to which at present you object. You said in your
letter that the proposed arrangement would take away your
rights in the cheap editions of the eight books provided for
under previous agreements. I think you will find that this is not
so. It only provides that I am to be free to publish cheap edi-

150. The series *The Story Teller's Craft* consisted of three essays. It began in the
English Review in April. In America it began in the *Metropolitan Magazine* in June,
and started with the second article, not the first (see pages 182-5). The series was
published in book form as *The Author's Craft*, in which was included a fourth essay,
'The Artist and the Public' (see page 192n.), which appeared in the two magazines
in October and September respectively.

tions with other houses in case you do not care to publish them yourselves, upon due notice being given. You have already withdrawn from the sixpenny market. It might conceivably suit you at some future time to withdraw from the sevenpenny or the shilling market.

The clause seems to me to be perfectly fair in intention, but if you consider that the wording of it is loose and that it ought to comprise more exact details of the possible procedure, I am sure that Pinker will be very happy to meet your wishes in any reasonable way.

Yours sincerely, [Arnold Bennett]

u.c. / ts. / 152

Comarques
April 2nd, 1913

My dear Pinker,

Many thanks for your letter of yesterday. With regard to the *Don Juan* play I am afraid that nothing can be done at present. In strict confidence, Vernon is preparing a scheme for the management of a West End theatre under conditions which, so far as I can judge, ought to lead to a certain amount of success, and I should much like you to discuss the affair with him. If there is any chance of it being matured about the end of the year he will have the play. If not, it will be offered to either the Royalty or the Haymarket. Whether he takes it or not I shall want the very best terms that are paid to any English dramatist at the present time. I consider that I shall be able to obtain even somewhat better terms than we had for the *Milestones* production at the Royalty.

Yours sincerely, Arnold Bennett

151. At this time and later the Amalgamated Press and Newnes issued some of Bennett's novels in sixpenny and sevenpenny editions. These do not, however, appear to have included the Methuen novels. Methuen issued several one and two shilling editions.

Methuen had lost an earlier battle with Bennett and Pinker. On 11 December 1911 he wrote to Pinker: 'I am afraid we cannot possibly pay 5d. on a two-shilling edition. We sell the greater part of our two-shilling books at 1s. 2d. and if you will subtract the cost from that sum and add 5d. you will see that there is *absolutely nothing* left for the publisher. I think you would like to give us at least a penny. . . .' On 18 December he wrote: 'we will give you fivepence on the 2s. edition though I can assure you that it leaves us practically nothing'.

152. Bennett's play *Don Juan de Marana*, which he always considered his best dramatic work, was conceived in 1909. He wrote a scenario of it at that time for Sir

u.c. / ts. / 153

Comarques
April 30th, 1913

My dear Pinker,
  Many thanks for your letter of the 29th and the enclosure.
I much regret to hear of the difficulty with the Metropolitan,
as it may complicate the question of the serial.

Yours sincerely, Arnold Bennett

P.S. I enclose copy of letter from Whigham which may throw
light on his attitude to you, & of my reply.

u.c. / t.c. / 154
(*From H. J. Whigham*)

[432 4th Avenue]
[New York City]
April 21st 1913

My dear Mr. Bennett:
  The first article of the series called *The Craft of the Story Teller*
was held in the office for a week or two before I had time to
read it, and the general impression in the office has been that
it is a great deal less popular in style and contents than the
other essays which we have all liked so much. I thought
seriously of publishing the second article first, and asking you
to read over the first article again in order to see if it might not
be improved from a popular point of view. But then I found
that the series had been placed in London and that the dates
had already been arranged. In the meantime, Reynolds has
cabled to London at my request to see whether the second
article could be run first.
  I imagine that this may create difficulties, and it may be
better to run the series as it is. In the meantime, perhaps it may

---

Herbert Tree. Nothing more than the scenario existed when he wrote this letter.
The play was written in its final form between 12 December 1913 and 25 January
1914.
  Frank Vernon (1875–1940), a friend of Bennett's, was an actor, author, manager,
and producer. He produced *Cupid and Commonsense* and was stage director for
Milestones.
  153. Henry James Whigham (1869–1954) was editor of the *Metropolitan Magazine*.

do no harm to point out just what I have said, that this first article could be made more interesting to the general reader by being lightened up a little, possibly by more complete illustration and also by simplifying the language. I am sure that when you read it over yourself you will recognise that there is a large preponderance of long Latin words which is quite unusual in your writing.

I know that you will not think that I am interfering unnecessarily in your business, for of course you know a great deal more about writing than I do. Only I have to edit a magazine for more than 300,000 readers, and the value of a manuscript depends a great deal on how far it will appeal to such a widespread circulation. It may be unjust but it is nevertheless a fact that an author who can appeal to a half million readers has a far higher commercial value than an author who can appeal to only 50,000. You have built up your success on the wider appeal and have made a large value thereby for yourself. If all the essays were like this first one of the new series, they would be appreciated by the 50,000 and not by the half million.

Possibly this will sound hypercritical as well as commercial to you. My excuse is that no harm is ever done by having a thorough understanding between the author and the editor of a magazine.

I hope you will come over again to see us soon.

With best regards, I am,

Yours sincerely, [H. J. Whigham]

U.C. / T.C.C. / 155
(*To H. J. Whigham*)

[Comarques]
April 30th, 1913

My dear Mr. Whigham,

Although I regret the cause of your letter to me, I am very glad that you have written and frankly stated your view.

I do not expect that the new series will have quite the popular appeal of the first series, but still I think it may be more appreciated than you anticipate. My experience has generally been that my articles have been printed with misgivings—and that in the result the public has 'asked for more' and the editor has handsomely admitted the fact.

My idea was that the larger public had never had any authoritative and honest account of the inner craft of writing and that such account would therefore be a novelty and would arouse interest. With the greatest respect for your opinion I still think so. Moreover I really *wanted* to write these articles: which is a good reason for writing them.

Your letter has caught me just as I am at work on articles three and four. I have always maintained that a writer who knows his business ought to be able to please his editor as well as his own conscience, and in putting these articles into final form I will bear carefully in mind your remarks, and I think you will not have reason to complain of their lack of lightness.

With reference to the third paragraph of your letter, you will not, I hope, forget a very important piece of the conversation that passed between us at Mr. Reynolds's lunch. When you suggested that I should contribute to your magazine, I asked: 'Do you want me to do my best and most serious work, or do you want me to adopt a popular standard?' Your reply did you credit, and you laid particular stress on your literary aims as an editor. I have not forgotten this, because I was extremely pleased with it. Now, the first series was certainly of a very wide appeal, and I am convinced that in the second series no harm will be done by assuming the willingness of your readers to move to a slightly higher plane.

Having been an editor myself in my time, I know something of the difficulties of the position, and I am always very sympathetic towards such difficulties. I shall try to lessen yours in regard to articles three and four, but it would be impossible for me to recast the first article, and I think that to change the order of the articles would be a grave mistake.

You will see me again in your city before I am much older.

Believe me, with kind regards,

Yours sincerely, [Arnold Bennett]

155. Bennett's letters of 21 October and 16 November 1911 indicate the sort of agreement he came to with the *Metropolitan* through Paul Reynolds, the American agent. The first essay of *The Story Teller's Craft* (*The Author's Craft*) is Bennett in his most lucid and engaging manner. He begins by describing a street accident:

'A young dog, inexperienced, sadly lacking in even primary education, ambles and frisks along the footpath of Fulham road, near the mysterious gates of a

BUTLER / TS. / 156
(*From J. B. Pinker*)
PRIVATE AND CONFIDENTIAL

Talbot House

1st May 1913

My dear Bennett,

I had a confidential talk this afternoon with Bruce Ingram, the editor of the *Illustrated London News*. He tells me that they are not satisfied with Chesterton's Notebook. No doubt you remember the page in the *Illustrated London News*. Chesterton has done it since L. F. Austin's death, and in a general way they never change, but Chesterton's political activities are a drawback to him, and while they do not mind any individual opinion they do not like a writer to be identified with any political party, so that they think of making a change. You are, of course, the ideal man for them, but I told Ingram that I had not the least idea whether you would do it or not, but I promised to sound you. They would not in any case want to make a change until they had given Chesterton three months' notice, but if you are disposed to do it I will discuss the question of terms with them. In any case, will you, please, treat this as strictly confidential, as they would not like Chesterton to hear that they had thought of making a change, since they will continue with him if they cannot get a first class man in his place.

Sincerely yours, James B Pinker

Marist convent. He is a large puppy, on the way to be a dog of much dignity, but at present he has little to recommend him but that gawky elegance, and that bounding gratitude for the gift of life, which distinguish the normal puppy. He is an ignorant fool. He might have entered the convent of nuns and had a fine time, but instead he steps off the pavement into the road, the road being a vast and interesting continent imperfectly explored. His confidence in his nose, in his agility, and in the goodness of God is touching, absolutely painful to witness. He glances casually at a huge, towering vermilion construction that is whizzing towards him on four wheels. . . .'
The *Metropolitan* began with the second essay and did not publish the first one at all. The first series of articles was *The Case of the Plain Man* (see page 163n.).
   156. Sir Bruce Ingram (1877–1963) had begun his long editorship of the *Illustrated London News* in 1900. G. K. Chesterton took over 'Our Note Book' from L. F. Austin (b. 1852) in 1905. In 1913 he was at the height of his popularity with the first series of Father Brown stories, but he had recently been supporting his brother in the sensational charges that Lloyd George and other government officials were using public office to make money in the Marconi Company.

   L.A.B.—O

u.c. / ts. / 157

Comarques
June 4th, 1913

My dear Pinker,

For your information I enclose copy of a letter which I have received from Granville Barker, who, with his wife, spent last week-end here, and also a copy of my reply. To-morrow Vedrenne and Eadie are coming up here on the same errand, and they will receive the same reply.

While I am anxious to help Frank Vernon as much as possible, I must of course insist upon the very best terms and conditions from him, and I think with you that some clear understanding ought to be arrived at pretty soon.

Yours sincerely, Arnold Bennett

P.S. In my reply to Granville Barker I have purposely made the reference to Lee Mathews. They are very intimate and Lee Mathews is almost certain to see the letter, which will please him.

A. B.

u.c. / t.c. / 158
(*From Harley Granville Barker*)

[No address]
June 3rd, 1913

Dear Bennett,

One shouldn't sully such pleasant week ends with business, and anyway perhaps it is to Lee Mathews I should be talking, but I will let him know I have written to you so that will be all right.

But as to the play which you think will be finished by the end of the year, why don't you let us pay you some more or less lordly sum for the first refusal of it and I daresay we shan't

157. Harley Granville Barker (1877–1946) produced *The Great Adventure* (the stage adaptation of *Buried Alive*). The play opened at the Kingsway Theatre on 25 March 1913, with Henry Ainley as Ilam Carve, and was a very considerable success. John E. Vedrenne (1867–1930) had been Granville Barker's partner at the Court Theatre, where from 1904 to 1907 many of George Bernard Shaw's plays were produced. In 1911 Vedrenne and Dennis Eadie (1875–1928) began a long tenure at the Royalty Theatre. They produced *Milestones* there, with Eadie playing John Rhead.

squeal over loud at your conditions and terms? We look towards you with some gratitude at this moment with regard to our Great Adventure. Even though an author is a mere literary gent to be kept chained in the back yard!!

Very sincerely yours, [H. Granville Barker]

U.C. / T.C. / 159
(*To Harley Granville Barker*)

[Comarques]
June 4th, 1913

My dear Barker,

The fact is, you are flattering me. I have not yet begun to write this play, and I therefore do not know yet what sort of a play it will actually turn out to be. My present intention is not to enter into a contract of any kind in regard to the play until it is finished. No sum that you or any other management could pay would compensate me for the lack of absolute freedom to deal with the play as I choose, according to the circumstances of the moment.

I am glad that you are informing Lee Mathews, as, although he is no longer my agent, he continues to be my chief friend in the theatrical world. My present agent is Mr. J. B. Pinker, Talbot House, Arundel Street, Strand, through whom all contracts will in future be made.

Yours ever, [Arnold Bennett]

BUTLER / TS. / 160
(*From J. B. Pinker*)

Talbot House
6th June 1913

My dear Bennett,

. . . I am very glad indeed that you are writing to the *Author* in reply to Wells' letters. I am glad to think that I have never written to him in the way he speaks of, but I do think he is most misleading for the ignorant authors in his spitefulness. As a

---

159. *Don Juan de Marana* was not taken by Granville Barker, or Vedrenne and Eadie, or Frank Vernon.

matter of fact, if any agent had muddled and mismanaged his business in the way that he has done himself, H. G. would have rent the air with his shrieks. I thought it was very reckless and thoughtless of him to say what he did in his previous letter. Those who know are aware that I am the only agent who ever had charge of the whole of his business, and I only wish that it were possible for me to make public the history of our connection, with Wells' letters to back me up.

Sincerely yours, J. B. Pinker

160. In letters printed in the *Author* on 1 May and 1 June, Wells said he was being plagued by agents who wanted to handle his business. He concluded, 'I know of no way of stopping this increasing nuisance of agents, except by proclaiming clearly that, like all sensible authors, I do not employ agents except for specific jobs.' Bennett's response was printed on 1 July:

'Sir,—

So long as my friend Wells is content to speak for himself about agents I am ready to listen in respectful silence, but when he begins to speak for "all sensible authors", I must protest. I maintain that I am a sensible author. If lampoonists and satirists are to be believed, I have a reputation for considerable business acumen. Bluntly, I think this reputation is deserved.

As one "sensible author", I wish to "proclaim clearly" that I should not dream of employing agents only "for specific jobs". On the contrary I am absolutely convinced that every author of large and varied output ought to put the whole of his affairs into the hands of a good agent, and that every such author who fails to do so loses money by his omission. I admit that some agents are bad. I know that some are good. A good agent will do a specific job better than an author, partly because he knows the markets better, and partly because he is an expert in the diplomacy of bargains. But a good agent is also very valuable in utilising opportunities as they arise—opportunities of whose very existence the author is ignorant. I reckon that in the latter activity alone a good agent recoups an author again and again for the whole of his commission.

In my experience it is precisely when agents are employed only for "specific jobs" that trouble comes.

Wells, my senior, once advised—nay, commanded—me to go to an agent. With my usual docility I did so. He told me to put the whole of my affairs into the hands of the agent. I did so. I have never regretted it. I have never had the slightest agency trouble as the result of following Wells' advice. I am quite sure that if I had not followed his advice I should be very decidedly worse off than I am. My gratitude to Wells is lasting. That happened some thirteen years ago. Experience has led Wells to change his views. Experience has only confirmed me in my views, formerly his. He may be right; I may be wrong. I will not dogmatise. But he must not speak for "all sensible authors".

Yours faithfully, Arnold Bennett'

Wells replied: 'I deplore my forgotten advice. . . . How are we to prove these things . . .? I must talk privately to E. A. B. in this connexion.' In a letter to his friend F. S. A. Lowndes of *The Times*, Bennett wrote: 'Wells on agents is a chump. I have often told him so. He is down on agents *because* he knows he has made a chump of himself and dropped a lot of money by trying to manage his affairs himself.'

Comarques
June 7th, 1913

My dear Pinker,

Thanks for your letters.

As to the *I.L.N.*, I repeat that I should much like to undertake this weekly article—and not for financial reasons. But I cannot do it for £300 a year, which works out at about £4 a thousand. As my earnings have averaged for some time past, and will certainly average for some time to come, over £300 a week, you will see that the price of the article, whatever it is, can only be of minor importance to me financially. But if I accepted £300 I should be doing the very thing I have always reproached Chesterton himself with—namely, selling work at a price which is unfair to the whole body of authors.

I should not dream of asking the *I.L.N.* to pay me my established price, which, as you know, is 1/- a word, or anything like that price. But some general considerations of value have to be taken into account. Though the writer of the *I.L.N.* article need not be a popular favourite, he must have a serious reputation among serious people; indeed he must be known among serious people as an exceptional man. He must be a highly skilled journalist. He must be full of commonsense. He must have a wide and continuous knowledge of current affairs. He must be capable of much diplomacy, in order to be sincere without offending a large heterogeneous body of readers. And he cannot take a holiday. Such a man is worth much more than £300 a year; a salary which an advertisement manager's assistant would refuse. In James Payn's time, and even in L. F. Austin's, he may not have been worth more. But times are changed. If any author of my acquaintance accepted one single penny less than £500 a year from the *I.L.N.* for the weekly article, I should charge him with underselling the market. And as a successful author I do not feel justified in underselling the market merely in order to find a good pulpit.

Please let me insist that I am not now arguing as a popular favourite, but simply as one of the few journalists who are able and free to do the weekly article in a manner which would satisfy the *I.L.N.* If I were arguing as a popular favourite I should naturally say that my name alone was worth etc., etc.

But in this matter I do not want to be paid for my name. I only want to be paid modestly and adequately for my stuff.

Yours sincerely, Arnold Bennett

U.C. / TS. / 162

Comarques
June 19th, 1913

My dear Pinker,
    I enclose copy of a letter from Lee Mathews, and copy of my reply, as to a proposed play from *Helen with the High Hand*.

Yours sincerely, Arnold Bennett

U.C. / T.C. / 163
(*From W. Lee Mathews*)

[No address]
18th, June 1913

Very dear A.B.,
    Are you prepared to dramatise *Helen with the High Hand*? If not, are you prepared to have it dramatised by anybody else, and, if so, by whom.
    Or would you give me the dramatic rights of *Helen with the High Hand*, and, if so, on what terms? Send me a line when you can.

Yours ever, [William]

U.C. / T.C.C. / 164
(*To W. Lee Mathews*)

[Comarques]
June 19th, 1913

Dearest William,
    Thanks for yours of yesterday.   I am not prepared to dramatise *Helen with the High Hand* myself. I am, however, pre-

---

161. Ingram subsequently raised his offer to £400, and Pinker thought that he might go to £500, but Bennett declined the one sum or both, and Chesterton continued to write 'Our Note Book' for another eighteen years. James Payn (1830–1898) had written the column before L. F. Austin.

pared to sell the dramatic rights of the book on the following terms:

1. The dramatist to be approved by me.
2. The dramatisation to be approved by me.
3. The play to be described everywhere as dramatised by So-and-So from the novel of Arnold Bennett. That is to say, I should want it to be made absolutely clear that whereas I am the author of the novel, I have no artistic responsibility for the play.
4. I am to be a party to all contracts for the production of the play, and for the publication of the play in book form.
5. The author's profits are to be shared equally between the dramatist and myself.

Of course, so far as I am concerned, the transaction will have to go through the hands of Pinker, who would settle the conditions in detail. This letter is only to give you a rough idea of what I should ask for.

Thine, [A. B.]

u.c. / ts. / 165

Comarques
June 23rd, 1913

My dear Pinker,

I enclose a letter from Vedrenne which speaks for itself. I am naturally not inclined to be difficult to please in the matter of terms for *What the Public Wants*, although it must be remembered that I have to pay 20% of my royalties to Davis. But I shall want you to insist on the following conditions. The play is to be produced in the evening bill for a run. I will not, under any circumstances, agree to a trial series of matinées. The term for which the licence is granted must not exceed seven years. If the option is not exercised within, say, twelve or eighteen months, it must lapse. I must have a full veto on the cast. Vernon must produce the play, or, in default of him, some other

---

164. The play was adapted by Richard Pryce, and was produced under the management of Norman McKinnel and Frederick Whelen at the Vaudeville Theatre on 17 February 1914, with McKinnel playing the male lead and Nancy Price playing Helen.

producer to be chosen by me. Unless Vedrenne will agree to all this, I prefer to do nothing at all.

Yours sincerely, Arnold Bennett

P.S. I shall be at the Berkeley tomorrow.   A. B.

BUTLER / TS. / 166
(*From J. B. Pinker*)

Talbot House
1st July 1913

My dear Bennett,

I received your fourth and last article for Austin Harrison, and I have read it with a great deal of enjoyment. That sounds like the conventional statement to make to an author, but that cannot be helped. You will have a regular gabble about your ears over it, but of course it is true, and the very best men will, I think, admit its truth. The second best men will know it is true, but they will think that it detracts from the glory and aroma of the artistic life to be frank about it. Of the writers I have known intimately, the three greatest (I am not now thinking of you or H. G.) have always in my experience felt and frankly discussed a desire to meet the public taste, and to win popularity, and all the best men of my acquaintance have been keenly anxious that their work should be made to produce as much money as possible. I am sure that the larger proportion of your readers will not have the least idea how exactly true your paper is, but one could produce ample evidence if they were not satisfied with your quotation of Meredith. You are a delight!

Sincerely yours, J. B. Pinker

165. Tom B. Davis (1867–1931) was a manager to whom Bennett sold part of his rights to *What the Public Wants* when it was produced at the Royalty Theatre in 1909.

166. 'The Artist and the Public', which followed the three essays on *The Story Teller's Craft* in Austin Harrison's *English Review*, discusses what is for Bennett the necessity and desirability of the artist's recognizing the existence of the public. He quotes Meredith's comment to a friend, 'I am engaged in extra potboiling work which enables me to do this [write poetry]', and adds: 'Oh, base compromise! . . .

u.c. / ts. / 167

Comarques
August 29th, 1913

My dear Pinker,

Many thanks for your various letters, including the last one received this morning. I see no objection now to anything in the contract with Vernon, and I return it signed.

As a matter of fact I should not object to the figure in Clause 10 being £900, but this point can be no doubt settled with Vernon afterwards. In the meantime we shall be quite safe with the figure at £800, and there is no need for us to alter it until Vernon has proved to us that it is impracticable. I also return the other two agreements executed. It seems to me that you are making a rather brilliant debut as my theatrical agent.

With regard to the Dutch rights of *The Great Adventure*, I am quite unable now to recall what the terms of the contract are, but I have not the slightest doubt that your terms for *The Honeymoon* are excellent.

I think that if Miss Horniman pays the same terms for *What the Public Wants* as she did before, it will be all right. What these terms were I have not the slightest idea.

I shall be glad for Iden Payne to do *Cupid and Commonsense* at the Fine Arts Theatre, Chicago, on condition that he guarantees a minimum number of performances during his Season. I should be content with a guarantee minimum of six performances. If the matter is arranged I will send him some cuts for the last act. These cuts were used in the original performance by the Stage Society, but I believe that they have never been used since. And when I saw the play at Hammersmith last year I thought that the last act dragged.

I should like you to treat Milton Rosmer with as much consideration as you can. He is not a strong man, but it seems to

Meredith subdued his muse, and Meredith wrote potboilers, because he was a first-class artist and a man of profound common sense. Being extremely creative, he had to arrive somehow, and he remembered that the earth is the earth, and the world the world, and men men, and he arrived as best he could.' Bennett's more important point in his essay is his belief that contempt for the public is self-destructive: 'The notion that art is first and the rest of the universe nowhere is bound to lead to preciosity and futility in art.'

Pinker must have had Henry James and Joseph Conrad in mind, and possibly George Gissing.

me that enterprises such as his ought to be encouraged by authors such as I.

I have received the author's copies of *The Regent* from Methuen, and I must say I strongly object to the jacket. It is the first time that Methuen has used a jacket of such a flaring description for the original edition of one of my books. In the first-place the design is extremely bad, and in the second-place, even if it were fairly good, it would still give a wrong impression of the book. It seems to me that the suggestion of playing down to the public is precisely the suggestion which ought to be most carefully avoided in my case, having regard to the delay in the publication of the third Clayhanger. I know very little of the cost of jackets, but I feel that it would be a good thing for everybody if the present jacket were suppressed as quickly as possible. If you do not agree with my view of the jacket please let me know.

Yours sincerely, Arnold Bennett

u.c. / ts. / 168

Comarques
September 16th, 1913

My dear Pinker,

I am having some little difficulty with the Income Tax people who, owing to the enormous discrepancy between my present income and my income three or four years ago, show an inclination to re-open the question of my previous assessments. They have asked me to give you an authority to disclose to them my transactions through you for the years 1906, 1907, 1908, 1909, 1910, 1911. I have declined to give such an authority, not because I think that I should have anything to

167. At the same time that Vedrenne and Vernon were preparing to produce *What the Public Wants* in London, Annie E. F. Horniman (1860–1937; supporter of the Abbey Theatre, Dublin, and founder of the Manchester Repertory Theatre) was planning to present it at Oxford, and Milton Rosmer (1882–), a member of Miss Horniman's company at Manchester, was making the same arrangements at the Theatre Royal, Leeds. Rosmer conducted a season of repertory in Leeds in 1913.

Iden Payne (1881–) organized Miss Horniman's company in Manchester, and produced for her from 1907 to 1911. In recent years he has been a visiting lecturer at various American universities.

fear from a full disclosure, but because, having looked at the Income Tax Act of 1842, I am convinced that they have no right whatever to demand such an authority from me. The mere fact that they asked for such an authority is proof that they are by no means sure of their own position. If they were sure of it, they would be able to deal direct with you without consulting me at all. The discussion between us is still proceeding. In the meantime will you please send me a list of the net sums, after deducting your commission, interest on borrowed money, and disbursements, which you received on my behalf from English sources during the years 1906, 1907, 1908, and 1909. What I received from foreign countries does not concern the Crown at all, as during this period I was not resident in England.

Yours sincerely, Arnold Bennett

P.S. You did not reply to my question as to when the money is due for the *Harper's* serial.   A. B.

U.C. / MS. / 169

Hôtel Du Rhin
4 & 6 Place Vendôme
[Paris]
2nd Nov 1913

My dear Pinker,

Many thanks for your various. I am *extremely pleased* the Nutt affair is so well settled. I don't like the form of agreement with Methuen. Please tell Lord Northcliffe that to my regret it is impossible for me to do the *Evening News* article. I haven't time, & my ideas would not perhaps rouse sympathy in his noble breast, & even at 1/- a word it would not pay me.

---

168. The figures Pinker sent for 1906 to 1909 were £712, £303, £532, and £276. Bennett's income in 1912 was £16,000, which, as he remarked in his journal, 'may be called success by any worldly-minded author. It is apparently about as much as I had earned during all the previous part of my life.'

The Harper serial, *The Price of Love*, began to appear in December 1913.

I will write as to the other things when I return home. We expect to reach Comarques on Wednesday night.

Yours sincerely, Arnold Bennett

P.S. I hope my refusal to do the *E. N.* article will not put you in an awkward position. Rather than this, I would do it.

u.c. / ts. / 170

Comarques
November 6th, 1913

My dear Pinker,

With regard to the use of some of my stuff by the Equitable Life Assurance Society in the United States, I should like you to inform the people concerned that although I have no wish to make a fuss, I strongly object to the whole thing, and consider that I have a grievance. In the first place, the *Metropolitan Magazine* had no right to grant the use of part of my article for the purposes of advertisement. In the second place, the Equitable Society ought certainly to have asked my permission. This permission would have been refused, as I most emphatically do not care to have my name employed in an advertisement. In the third place, the selection of the matter for the advertisement is grossly misleading as to my attitude towards insurance in general. A perusal of the whole article shows that I am by no means a partisan advocate of insurance.

I consider that the undistributed 10,000 copies of the booklet ought to be destroyed, and that, as some indication that they have been ill-advised, the Equitable Society ought to make a subscription to some charitable work in New York in our joint names.

If you do not agree with my attitude perhaps you will let me know. I am of course influenced to a certain extent by the fact

169. The Bennetts travelled on the Continent during part of October and November.

After Alfred Nutt died, Bennett desired to buy back his rights in *Whom God Hath Joined* (see pages 81–83). A long wrangle ensued with Mrs. Nutt, who had illegally printed 3,000 additional copies of the novel. Bennett obtained the novel, and Methuen published a new edition in 1915.

The *Evening News* wanted Bennett to inspect their plant and write an article on the future of newspapers. Bennett did not do the article.

that the officers of the Society are friends of Doran, but I do
not think that this fact ought to induce me to let the matter go
by without a clear protest.

Yours sincerely, Arnold Bennett

U.C. / TS. / 171

Comarques
November 26th, 1913

My dear Pinker,

Milton Rosmer writes me from the Theatre Royal, Leeds,
complaining that there is some risk of *What the Public Wants*
being taken from him. My opinion is that at all costs Rosmer
ought not to be put to this inconvenience. The right was given
to him quite a long time ago, and he has made all his preparations for beginning a difficult repertory enterprise at Leeds.
His programmes are out for the performance of *What the Public
Wants* on December 11th, 12th, and 13th. Whatever may be
argued about the performance of Miss Horniman's touring
company at Oxford, I do not see how it can possibly be argued
that Milton Rosmer's enterprise is not genuine repertory. At
any rate, it is the sort of thing that I am out to encourage, and
it must not be forgotten that had it not been for these repertory
movements *What the Public Wants* might have passed into limbo
long ago. I have not yet made any reply myself to Rosmer, but
I shall be very glad if you can send me a telegram in the
morning which will enable me to answer him personally in a
favourable sense. My opinion of Milton Rosmer himself is not
very high, but he is infinitely superior to the average manager,
and also I do not see how we can properly go back on our
engagements in an affair of this kind, merely because Vedrenne
chooses to put his own interpretation on a contract.

Yours sincerely, Arnold Bennett

170. The Equitable Life Assurance Society issued 15,000 copies of a leaflet
entitled *A Letter That Was Never Sent*. The letter, which comes from the essay 'The
Risks of Life' in *The Plain Man and His Wife*, describes a kindly and generous man
who is also a brutal scoundrel because he has in no way provided for his family
after his death. In the original essay, Bennett follows the account with a description
of another man who has insured himself to the hilt and whose cautiousness has
drained the joy out of his and his family's life.

U.C. / TS. / 172

Comarques
November 27th, 1913

My dear Pinker,

Many thanks for your express letter which arrived at 5.45 this evening. I enclose a copy of the letter which I have just sent to Milton Rosmer. I am entirely in favour of you saying to Vedrenne that if he chooses we will tear up the contract and return him his money. Quite apart from the fact that I totally disagree with his interpretation of the contract, his argument that the freshness of the play will be spoiled by performance in Oxford and Leeds is absurd. The play has been performed all over the place over and over again since its original production in London. I will not swear to it, but I am almost sure that it has been performed in Oxford itself, and for anything I know to the contrary it may also have been performed in Leeds. You can if necessary obtain a list of the places where it has been performed by telephoning to Lee Mathews. I have no doubt that provincial performances given by a company of Vedrenne's would be better in certain ways than the repertory performances, and that they would play to a great deal more money. But this is not the point. The point is that we wish to help the repertory theatre, and that in order to do so we inserted a special clause in the contract with Vedrenne, which clause we perfectly well knew could only result in a financial disadvantage to ourselves.

I refuse to give any quid pro quo to Vedrenne. I have every sympathy with Vedrenne as a manager, and I think that he has in the past tried to treat me fairly, but I cannot allow him to prevent me from doing the very thing which I reserved to myself the power to do in my contract with him. I have already told Vedrenne viva voce that he *will* have another play from me some time.

I see that in his letter to you of the 24th he refers to me. You are at liberty to tell him that in this matter my view is absolutely opposed to his. I have not written to him as I am very busy and do not wish to be drawn into a correspondence which can only be futile. I consider that both Casson and Milton Rosmer are entirely justified in the attitude which they have adopted. You will see that I have not given a final answer to

Rosmer, but this is only because I think it proper that the final answer should go through you. After all, engagements must be kept, and it seems to me monstrous that these two provincial managers should be treated as Vedrenne wishes us to treat them.

When you wire to Rosmer, will you please wire to me a copy of the telegram? I must leave you to settle with Casson or his solicitors as you think best.

Yours sincerely, Arnold Bennett

u.c. / ts. / 173

Comarques
November 29th, 1913

My dear Pinker,

I should be personally very much obliged to you if you could do a special favour to a young French friend of mine, Maurice Delage; he is in England and in a difficulty. He is a musical composer just beginning to make a name for himself, and he has had the idea of making a ballet out of a story of Kipling's called 'The Bridge-Builders'. He of course wanted to obtain Kipling's consent and approval, and he asked me what he ought to do. On his behalf I wrote to Kipling, whom I do not know personally, to ask what course should be taken, and suggested that perhaps Kipling would prefer him to see his agent first of all. Kipling replied very politely to me, and agreed that it would be better for Delage to communicate first with Watt. Watt asked Delage to come over from Paris to London and see him at three o'clock last Monday afternoon. He came. After four days of shouting into Watt's ear, Delage discovered that Watt did not grasp that there are no words in a ballet. He and Delage agreed as to the terms except on one small but not unimportant point, as to which Watt is, in my opinion, undoubtedly wrong. Nothing definite has been arranged. Delage asked whether he could have a short interview with Kipling as to the actual ballet itself, and pointed out that he had come over to England specially on the business. Watt answered that he must not think of seeing Kipling this time, and that in order to see Kipling he must come over again. In the end

172. Sir Lewis Casson (1875–), whose distinguished theatrical career has spanned six decades, was at this time director of Miss Horniman's company in Manchester.

Delage comes up to me in despair and asks me what he can do.

He is a friend of mine, a perfectly serious artist, and I am anxious to be of assistance to him if it is possible.

It occurs to me that there are two things which possibly you, out of sheer good-nature, can do. Are you on such terms with Watt that you could see him on behalf of Delage and settle the terms definitely? Are you sufficiently intimate with anybody close at hand who is sufficiently intimate with Kipling to give Delage a personal letter of introduction to him? Delage will call on you to-morrow morning (Monday) about 12 o'clock. If you can be of immediate service to him you will confer an obligation on me. The matter is somewhat pressing, as of course Delage cannot hang on in London indefinitely. There is no money in the thing for you at all. In the first place, from the financial point of view the matter is of the most trifling description, and in the second place I particularly do not want to suggest to Delage that you would be working as an agent. I prefer to tell him that I thought it probable that you would do anything that you reasonably could out of good-will.

Yours sincerely, Arnold Bennett

u.c. / ts. / 174

Comarques
December 1st, 1913

My dear Pinker,

Many thanks for your letter of the 28th. I have sent a little private note to Lewis Casson expressing my regret that he should have been caused any anxiety, and pointing out that there would have been much less trouble if he had not himself, by going direct to Vedrenne, given Vedrenne an entirely wrong idea of the situation. I have also written to Milton Rosmer.

Yours sincerely, Arnold Bennett

P.S. I felt rather strongly about this matter   A. B.

173. Maurice Delage's *Les Bâtisseurs de ponts* survives only as an overture. The war interrupted work on it. Delage (1879–) had been a student of Maurice Ravel, who was a friend of Bennett's. He probably spoke with A. S. Watt (d. 1948), one of the sons of the founder of the firm.

174. The provincial productions went on, that in London did not. Casson himself had objected to Rosmer's production. Possibly in connexion with the present difficulty, Casson resigned his Manchester post in November and became director of the Theatre Royal in Glasgow.

u.c. / ts. / 175

Comarques
December 27th, 1913

My dear Pinker,

Many thanks for your letter of the 24th.

As regards the *Cosmopolitan Magazine*, I will not cut down the first story at all. There was no word in the contract as to the length of the stories. I asked the man who came to see me in New York as to the question of length, and he said that they were not particular as to length. My suggestion that if they cared I would make some of the other stories rather shorter was offered out of pure good-nature. Nothing at all was ever said as to a maximum price. I shall complete the second story to-morrow. As you assume, I shall be only too glad to cancel the bargain with the *Cosmopolitan*. Hence, you are free to give them the alternative between accepting the stories I send as they stand and withdrawing entirely from the affair.

With regard to other short stories, I am afraid that I shall not have any scheme for a connected series of six. The fact is that I do not think that I ought to produce more than three short stories in a year. If you can obtain a commission for six stories to be supplied within a period of two years, I shall be most happy to accept it.

Doran said that the *American Magazine* would give me a commission for six short stories at thirty three cents a word if I would supply an outline of the stories for approval. This I need hardly say I absolutely declined to do.

With regard to the suggestion for *Munsey's Magazine*, I think it is a very good one indeed. I have discussed it in a general way with Doran, and I have told him that in principle it suits me, but at the same time that nothing I had said to him was to hamper you in any way in the negotiations. I should have said this in any case, but I felt all the more justified in saying it, having regard to the fact that Doran had no authority from Munseys to close the deal. Certainly, if Doran can guarantee me £3000 for serial rights, and at least £1000 on account of book rights, I should prefer to remain with him even if I had a somewhat better offer elsewhere. I have told him that there is no chance whatever of the third Clayhanger being ready for actual publication either in magazine or book form before the

L.A.B.—P

spring of 1915. Also that, assuming a deal was made with Munseys, I should not care to undertake to supply three serials in a less period than five years.

I approve of the scheme for cheap reprints.

Best wishes from both of us.

Yours sincerely, Arnold Bennett

u.c. / ts. / 176

Comarques
December 27th, 1913

My dear Pinker,

Many thanks for your letter and the cheque. I believe that with Doran's cheque and an instalment from Harpers I shall be all right. And even if I do want a little money it will only be for two or three weeks. I have been inconvenienced by two things. First, I have been compelled by family pressure to invest £500 instantly in a business, and secondly, I had entirely forgotten that I was liable to pay a call on some shares amounting to £550 early in January. And it is no part of my scheme to realise any of my securities at the present moment.

I have an idea that the monthly instalments due from Harpers are more than £168 each. It seems to me that each instalment ought to be an eighth part of £2250. Kindly let me know if this is not so.

With regard to theatres, I shall be glad if you will ask the member of your staff who is responsible, always to forward me particulars of returns immediately they are received. Perhaps you will let me have particulars of the Oxford performances referred to in the statement which I had the other day. I keep a personal record of all performances, and it may interest you to know that this year there have been between 2700 and 2800 performances of my various plays.

Yours sincerely, Arnold Bennett

175. The story for *Cosmopolitan* was 'The Life of Nash Nicklin'. *Cosmopolitan* withdrew from the bargain; it was paying $1,000 for the stories. The story was not subsequently published in any of Bennett's short story collections.

The Munsey Syndicate told Doran they would pay £3,000 for serial rights to a novel to be published in a single issue of *Munsey's Magazine*.

176. The family pressure possibly concerned the pottery business of his brother-in-law Frank Beardmore. The business failed a year or so later. Bennett's brother

U.C. / T S. / 177

Comarques
January 21st, 1914

My dear Pinker,

R. A. Scott James is starting a new paper. (Private, he says.) He seems to be extremely anxious that I should contribute at least one article if not more. I have told him that I have had offers of £50 per thousand in England, and that I am actually doing an article for the Boston *Youth's Companion* of 1500 words for £75. He says that he only wants to buy the English rights and that we are free to dispose of the American rights. To this I have replied that although the demand for my work in the United States is greater than I can supply, it is by no means easy to place odd short articles at a proper price, and that editors in the United States usually make their arrangements about twelve months in advance. You may take it that the length of the article will be about 1500 words. I enclose the last letter that I have received from Scott James. In my answer I have advised him to see you, but I have told him that £15 is absolutely out of the question. He is a friend of mine and I should like to oblige him as far as possible, as his ideas are excellent. Also I have a good scheme for an article which I am quite prepared to write. At the same time I have no doubt that his new paper is a commercial undertaking, and it is on part of my business to make a present to his backers.

Yours sincerely, Arnold Bennett

Frank, who was a solicitor, was also having, or was soon to have, financial difficulties. In later life, Bennett observed that he never returned to the Potteries 'except for funerals and the bankruptcies of relatives'.

177. R. A. Scott-James (1878–1959), then literary editor of the *Daily News*, was starting the *New Weekly*. Bennett noted a few days later in his journal: 'Scott-James came at 5 to beat me down in price of an article for his new paper'. The article, 'The Barber' (reprinted in *Things That Have Interested Me*—first series), appeared in the issue of 21 August. In describing the incident many years later, Scott-James depicted Bennett as quite willing to offer advice as well as to accept a high price for the article—in contrast to Hardy, who offered some poems free.

The *Youth's Companion* published 'School-days in the Five Towns' on 23 September 1915. The article, a reminiscence, has not been included in any of the essay collections.

u.c. / ts. / 178

Comarques
January 24th, 1914

My dear Pinker,

Many thanks for your two letters. As regards the play, I quite agree with you. Anything which you and Pryce decide will be satisfactory to me.

I have sent a letter to Davis care of you. He and his wife are to lunch with me on Thursday.

I will come and see you on Thursday morning next at eleven, if this is convenient.

As regards the Methuen Annual, I have received a request from Lucas; I may tell you that I talked to him straight. I pointed out to him that the astute Methuen was simply using him as a tool, and that I had no intention whatever of allowing Methuen to walk up and down his gardens chuckling over the idea that he had been clever enough to rope in the golden calves at a smaller expenditure than other people. In the end I made Lucas agree to pay me £20 for the right to reprint a few short extracts from my Journal, which had already been privately printed.

By the way, my Journal is now in its eighteenth volume, and almost the whole of it is yet in manuscript. Whenever I look at it it seems to me to be rather interesting, and some of my friends say that it is far more interesting than anything else I have written. Some day sooner or later it ought to be a valuable source of profit.

Yours sincerely, Arnold Bennett

P.S. Have you got two insurance policies on my life? If so, I should like to have them.   A. B.

178. Richard Pryce (d. 1942) was having difficulty in arranging the February production of *Helen with the High Hand*. See pages 190–1.

On Robert Davis see page 174.

E. V. Lucas edited *Methuen's Annual* of 1914 (the sole year it was published). In 1906 and 1907 Bennett printed extracts from his journal as Christmas gift-books. Only a few of the entries printed here and elsewhere in periodicals during Bennett's life were included in the three-volume *Journals of Arnold Bennett* published by Cassell in 1932–3.

u.c. / ms. / 179

[London]
17 Feby 1914

My dear Pinker,

My friend J. B. Atkins (assistant editor of the *Spectator*) is writing a holiday book about a pleasure-barge, & *I* am going to do the illustrations. He will hand the matter over to you as a whole if you care to handle it. He is to call on you. This is to warn you. I presume that my illustrations will help the commercial value of the book a little, & that this will assist you in making terms. I may tell you however, as between author & illustrator, that I shall hand over whatever is paid for the pictures to Atkins. Thus you could either make an inclusive bargain with the publisher, or two separate ones.

Yours sincerely, Arnold Bennett

u.c. / ms. / 180

Yacht Velsa
Genoa
1st April 1914

My dear Pinker,

Many thanks for your letter. It is extremely interesting. You were intensely right to refuse to submit synopses for approval. One might as well tear up the contract so far as the editor is concerned. I can imagine no letter of mine that bears such a construction. Davis never said a word to me as to synopses. I told him clearly that I could & would give no details beyond what I gave him viva voce, & even that I had no idea what the humorous book would be about.

The price for the short stories is fine in excelsis.

Certainly I had quite forgotten my promise to Edgar about the MS. There will be a hell of a row with Marguerite about it before Edgar gets it. In the first place I have given it to her, &

179. Bennett was in London for a few days in the middle of February.

A Floating Home, by Cyril Ionides and J. B. Atkins, was published by Chatto and Windus in 1918. The home was a barge that the Ionides family lived on for several years, travelling along English rivers. Bennett's eight water-colour illustrations are vivid, simple scenes; they display a competence gained from many years of work. He at one time thought of becoming a painter rather than a writer.

in the second place she hates me to give mss away. However, justice will prevail.

I have only seen Ames once. I thought him a polite & conscientious chump. But this view is provisional.

We are having a great time. We shall, I think, get to Rome in this craft, which was unexpected. But I doubt if we shall reach Corsica & Sardinia unless a wire from you as to articles stimulates me to prolong the cruise. I am daily getting the third Clayhanger into order. I am accumulating stuff for articles. I am enjoying myself enormously. We have both the car & the yacht. And the total cost is certainly under £45 a week, though we refuse ourselves nothing.

Marguerite sends her meilleurs souvenirs.

Yours sincerely, Arnold Bennett

U.C. / TS. / 181

Comarques
July 16th, 1914

My dear Pinker,

Many thanks for your letter of the 15th.

I have received the copy of the letter written by Ames.

As regards Tauchnitz, I do not mind *The Truth about an Author* and *Literary Taste* being printed together in one volume, provided that *The Truth about an Author* comes first, and that it is made perfectly clear on the cover that the volume contains two separate works.

I am glad to hear that Methuen is so enthusiastic as to *The Price of Love*. . . . If some very decided advantage as to terms can

---

180. Bennett was sailing off the coasts of France and Italy during the latter part of March and April.

Pinker, who was in America, closed with Robert Davis of the Munsey Syndicate for three serials, without providing synopses. The contract called for payment of $15,000 (£3,000) for serial rights to *These Twain* (the third Clayhanger novel) and $17,500 apiece for two subsequent serials.

Three short stories were contracted for with the *Metropolitan Magazine* at $1,500 apiece. See below, pages 219–26.

The manuscript for Edgar Selwyn may have been that of *The Great Adventure*, which opened in New York the previous October. Winthrop Ames (1871–1937), a playwright and theatrical figure, was associated with the production.

The stuff accumulated for articles is unknown. A few days earlier Bennett had finished a series of cruise articles, *From the Log of the 'Velsa'*. They were published from June to November 1914 in the *Century Magazine*, and were issued in book form by the Century Company before the end of the year.

be secured by entering into a new contract at once I shall be quite ready to enter into it. Otherwise I do not see the point of doing so. Everybody so far who has read this book seems to be very enthusiastic as to it, but no one has yet been able to inspire me with his enthusiasm.

Yours sincerely, Arnold Bennett

u.c. / ts. / 182

Comarques
July 30th, 1914

My dear Pinker,

Many thanks for your letter re *Nash's Magazine*. You will probably have foreseen that I should be obliged to decline such a commission. Left to myself, I might have produced something fairly agreeable under such a title as *How to Live on Sixty Minutes an Hour*. But when the exact lines of the essay are laid down for me in advance, I can only retire from the scene. Editors are astonishing. They always want you to do over again what you have done once for all; and they are always more concerned for the titles and notions of their stuff than for the actual stuff itself. Surely anybody with imagination ought to know that the surest way of making an essay second-rate is to dictate it in advance. And the more expensive an article the more violent is the editorial desire to spoil it. The whole attitude of *Nash's* is illogical. It is only because I am supposed to be able to find ideas of a striking nature that *Nash's* are ready to pay me 1/4d a word; and yet they begin by saying: 'I'll find your ideas for you'. The editor of *Nash's Magazine* may be a much abler man than I am, but the presumption is that if he could find the sort of ideas that constitute my attraction he would not be editing *Nash's Magazine*. By the way, you said 2,000 words in your previous letter, but 3,000 in this one.

Yours sincerely, Arnold Bennett

P.S. I am going to Cowes in the yacht till the end of next week.

A. B.

181. *The Price of Love* was published in the following autumn.
182. *Nash's Magazine* was a lively magazine published by J. Eveleigh Nash (1873–1956), who had been a literary agent briefly in the late nineties. It merged with the *Pall Mall Gazette* in 1914.

III

War Years and Later

1914–1922

*As a realist, Bennett had no illusions about the virtues of men. In 1911,
when Galsworthy and others were circulating a petition to outlaw the use
of aeroplanes in war, he was offering to the London public* The Honeymoon, *which plays upon the personal and national vanities of air-
power. He thought that Galsworthy's petition would achieve nothing.
Later he was approached by Norman Angell to support the Neutrality
League, which Angell headed. The League held that anti-Western
Russia was a greater threat than Germany to French and British civilization, and that going to war with Germany would insure Russian domination of the Continent. Bennett replied to Angell: 'I am in entire
agreement with your arguments, but in my opinion it is impossible, and
even wrong, to try to govern a country on a plane of commonsense which is
too high above its own plane of commonsense.' At the same time, common
sense told Bennett that there would be no war and, when war came, he
did not believe it could last. In October 1914, he predicted that human
and material losses would end the war within six months. The root of
such common sense was his own decency. Those friends who knew him
intimately agree that his brusque exterior cloaked the most kindly of
persons. He set himself, as person and artist, the ideal of 'a Christlike,
all-embracing compassion'. Frank Swinnerton, the closest of his friends,
is of the opinion that the war was a profound and damaging shock to
him.*

*His sympathies were clear: France and England were his homes.
German society he had long mistrusted. In the event, he gave much of his
time—without payment—to a variety of activities to support the war,
and he turned his journalism from books and persons to politics. The
completeness of his commitment occasionally resulted in rhetoric for the
government (as in* Over There, *which describes the Allied trenches in
1915 as 'the most cheerful, confident, high-spirited place I had seen in
France, or in England either'), and much more often in attacks upon
government leaders (as when he said of Lloyd George in the* Daily News:
*'his tendency towards chicane has gradually delivered him bound into the
hands of individuals whose characters offer the most dangerous of all
combinations—the combination of stupidity and ignorance with un-
scrupulousness'). In the* Daily News *and elsewhere, he published upwards of 400 articles and like material on the war.*

His creative life was of course affected. Between August 1914 and

November 1918 he wrote three and a half novels and two plays, no more than an ordinary writer might have produced in ordinary times. One of these works, The Pretty Lady, *is among his half-dozen or so best works. Two of the other novels,* These Twain *and* The Roll-Call, *rank high.*

U.C. / MS. / 183

Comarques
4th Augt 1914

My dear Pinker,

I was at Calais in my yacht on Sunday, & saw the first day of the mobilisation. I enclose an article (in duplicate) on my experiences—about 1600 words. It ought to be either in a daily, or in one of the big weeklies *this next Saturday*, if it is to retain whatever interest it has.

The *Nation* of course would be delighted to have it; but I thought you might find something of wider circulation.

Yours sincerely, Arnold Bennett

U.C. / MS. / 184

Comarques
8th Augt. 1914

My dear Pinker,

With reference to the 'absolute necessity' of certain authors, of which you speak; if later there should be any really bad cases within your knowledge you can use £100 of mine entirely according to your discretion in meeting distress. Of course in the form of loans. If they are never repaid, it won't be a life-and-death matter. I should not necessarily want to know the names of those helped.

Yours sincerely, Arnold Bennett

183. 'In Calais Harbour' appeared in the *Nation* on 8 August; it was republished in *Things That Have Interested Me* (first series). The article describes the sense of ordinary life going on and also the sense of doom in every detail of life.

184. Bennett's offer was not in response to a request from Pinker. Pinker wrote the day before to say that on account of the international crisis Methuen wanted to defer payments to authors unless the money was absolutely needed.

u.c. / ts. / 185

Comarques
August 17th, 1914

My dear Pinker,

I have received a rather urgent request from the *Daily News* for an article dealing with the war situation and its developments. Although I have certain ideas on the subject, like most of us, I am unable at present to produce such an article as they seem to want. I suppose the idea is to obtain something to balance the Wells articles in the *Chronicle*. Of course I have neither the ability nor the wish to compete with Wells at this game. There are, however, certain aspects of the case with which a novelist may perhaps be able to deal. I enclose an article which I wrote yesterday, and I could do some others which would gradually feel round the situation until I came to some general conclusion.

I should be glad if you would explain the matter to the *Daily News* personally. If they care to have this article, either alone or in conjunction with others, they can do so. The question of price I should leave entirely to you.

I also enclose a letter which I have received this morning from *Everybody's Magazine*. In answering it I have merely said that I have sent it on to you to deal with. The notion that I should sit down at once and compose a forecast to be published six weeks later is absurd. But assuming that something is arranged with the *Daily News* it is just conceivable that one of the later articles might do for *Harper's Weekly* or *Everybody's Magazine*.

Yours sincerely, Arnold Bennett

185. 'What the German Conscript Thinks', published in the *Daily News* on 24 August, began a series of articles by Bennett that ran until May 1916. With a few exceptions there was an article every week. The *News* paid £21 per article. Wells's articles were characteristically panoramic: he discussed the changing strategy of warfare that would make the aeroplane a decisive factor; he was knowledgeable about Balkan politics and history.

Everybody's Magazine did not publish anything by Bennett on the war. *Harper's Weekly* published two articles in September and two in November, but no prognostication.

u.c. / ts. / 186

Comarques
August 26th, 1914

Dear Mr. Wicken,

Many thanks for your letter of yesterday. I do not care to write an article on the subject suggested by the *Daily News*. I have, however, written another article called 'Let us realise', and I send you a copy of it herewith for possible issue in the States. The other copy I have sent direct to the *Daily News* with a short explanation of my views.

I am afraid it would be extremely difficult to do an article on the European situation at once, for publication in two months' time. Moreover, I doubt whether I shall be able to produce more than one article per week, the subject of which will have to decide itself each week according to the turn of events. In all probability my subjects will relate to the effect of the war on the average Englishman at home.

Your suggestion as to the Eclipse Cinema Company seems to me quite reasonable.

Yours faithfully, Arnold Bennett

u.c. / ts. / 187

Comarques
November 15th, 1914

My dear Pinker,

Many thanks for your letter of the 13th.

As regards the *New York Times*, I think that they ought to be invited to pay. If they decline to do anything at all I think that Reynolds might, on my behalf, place the matter before the Authors' League of America, of which I am a member. This

---

186. Frederick C. Wicken (d. 1930) was Pinker's managing clerk.

The *Daily News* suggested 'What the French Conscript Thinks'. 'Let Us Realise' was published in the *News* on 3 September. In America it appeared in McClure's *Harper's Weekly* on 29 September. The article is an excellent appraisal of the war as one of the last struggles between an old ideal of the nobility of war and a new humane ideal.

The Eclipse Cinema Company wanted to defer filming *The Grand Babylon Hotel* on account of the war. Bennett's film career apparently began with this intended production. No record of the film has been found. In 1917 the Hepworth Company filmed the novel.

would be more expeditious and perhaps more effective than placing it in the hands of the Authors' Society. In any case I do not want to bring an action.

I shall be sending you tomorrow a copy of an article dealing drastically with the bad parts of Shaw's manifesto on the war, published yesterday. About two-thirds of Shaw's statement is strictly first-class, and indeed quite unequalled. Most of the rest is absurd, and may do some harm. I should therefore particularly like my article to appear in some newspaper in the United States, preferably New York, whether I am paid for it or not. It will appear in the *Daily News* on Thursday. If the *New York Times* can cable over other things of mine, I do not see why their London representative should not cable this article, especially as Shaw's article appeared in the *New York Times*. In default of a New York paper, perhaps the *Chicago Tribune*—whose London correspondent Mr. F. W. Wile has recently been here to interview me as to the war—may care to have the article. I think that the London office of the *Chicago Tribune* is at Printing House Square. In any case, Mr. Wile is generally to be found at the offices of the *Daily Mail*.

Yours sincerely, Arnold Bennett

187. On 10 October the *New York Times* reprinted 'When the Truce Comes', one of the *Daily News* series, of 1 October, without permission. Other American papers were doing the same thing with articles that bore no copyright notice. H. G. Wells was encouraging the practice by giving his articles to the American press.

'Common Sense About the War', by Bernard Shaw (1856–1950), was published as a special supplement to the *New Statesman* on 14 November. It deals with several practical matters, such as the need for a modern conscription policy and adequate payments to soldiers' dependants; but its main point is that for many years England and Germany were equally guilty of militarism and that English militarists used the invasion of Belgium as their means to obtain war. Bennett's response, 'The Nonsense About Belgium According to Bernard Shaw', praises the minor points and then attacks Shaw for exaggerating the extent of British militarism: 'Mixed up with the tremendous common sense, however, is a considerable and unusual percentage of that perverseness, waywardness, and harlequinading which are apparently an essential element of Mr. Shaw's best work.' Shaw replied the following day, finding it amusing that Bennett should admire him wherever the two of them agreed and condemn him wherever they disagreed. The *Daily News* and the *New York Times* printed Bennett's article on the 18th. Bennett had published an article in the *Daily News* on 1 September on the inadequate wages paid to soldiers.

u.c. / ts. / 188

Comarques
December 1st, 1914

My dear Pinker,

Many thanks for your letter of yesterday and the enclosure, which latter I return. I see no reason why the play should not be sold at the price offered, unless you are able to obtain a better.

Special local work in connection with preparations for the raid is now occupying so much of my time that my own work is being seriously interfered with. The notion of a raid is to me entirely absurd. Nevertheless one cannot help feeling that the preparations ought to be done.

Yours sincerely, Arnold Bennett

188. The play was probably the one-act 'A Question of Sex', which a private club in America wanted to produce for a single night. The play was published in the collection *Polite Farces* in 1899.

Bennett was military representative on the Thorpe Division Emergency Committee for preparation against invasion. On 3 December the following letter from him appeared in *The Times* and the *East Anglia Daily Times*.

'Sir,—There is considerable talk in East Anglia and Essex of the martial spirit of the civilian inhabitants and of the deeds they mean to perform against invading Germans if they get the chance. This martial spirit is creditable, but it cannot be too clearly stated that at the present time a civilian's martial spirit can only be properly shown in one way.

That way is to enlist in the Regular Forces.

The Germans have not fought according to the rules of civilized warfare as laid down at the Hague. But in this regrettable fact we can find no excuse for imitating them. It is against the rules of civilized warfare for civilians to attempt to kill soldiers. Single snipers would expose their villages to reprisals whose nature we know; and, further, no bands of snipers formed suddenly in an emergency would have the slightest chance of being recognized by the enemy as combatants.

Moreover, the majority of potential snipers could only be armed with a shotgun, a weapon hopelessly outranged by, and practically useless against, the military rifle.

But there is a stronger reason against civilian fighting. As the military representative on the Emergency Committee which has charge of a large district as dangerously situated as any, I have received a personal positive instruction from the General Officer commanding the South Midland Division that the military authorities absolutely discountenance, and strongly object to, any form of civilian fighting. The arrangements to repel a raid are in their hands; the responsibility is theirs; and any man who acts contrary to their wishes must thereby confuse their plans, impede their operations, and endanger their success.

Any civilian who wants to help against a raid should go to the chairman of his parish council, and through him offer his services to the Emergency Committee of his district. The details of the very exhaustive and elaborate arrangements are now being completed, and there is, or will be, should the moment

BUTLER / TS. / 189
(*From J. B. Pinker*)

Talbot House
2nd December 1914

My dear Bennett,

. . . Do you remember when we were discussing *The Price of Love* you asked me what I thought Henry James and Conrad, for instance, would say of it? I can tell you exactly what Henry James says of it, as we discussed it yesterday. It and *Sinister Street* were, he told me, the only works of fiction he had read since the War broke out. 'I read it,' he said, 'with great interest, rather wondering all the time why I *was* so interested in it. It is an example of Bennett's amazing talent. I do not quite see why he should want to do it, but for what it sets out to be it is excellent. He has, it seems to me, rather declined in it on too easy a style, but it is wonderfully interesting to see how he can, after apparently squeezing his own particular orange so dry, come back to his original inspiration, and find us something fresh.'

I interrupted him to tell him what you had asked me, and he looked pleased and said: 'Oh, tell him if you will that I was greatly interested, and finished the book with great envy—envy of him and his possession of such material. The two young men in it are perfectly realised, so salient and altogether so presented. I have no material like that, and I envy him that.'

I asked James if he had read Shaw's Manifesto. He said, 'I have it here, and have made several attempts, but his horrible flippancy revolts me. To think of a man deliberately descending into the arena at the present crisis and playing the clown!'

Sincerely yours, J. B. Pinker

---

come, sufficient work to employ all male civilians with wit enough to understand the high value of hearty and obedient cooperation. It would perhaps be impolitic to publish particulars, but the chairman of every parish council has full information and is in a position to allocate duties.

Any civilian, whatever his motive, who tries to repel a raid on his own initiative and by his own devices will be guilty of an act essentially unpatriotic.

Arnold Bennett'

189. The accuracy of Pinker's report of James's words is suggested by the Jamesian metaphor of the orange. In his essay, 'The New Novel', written earlier in the year, James describes Bennett's art as 'the act of squeezing out to the utmost the plump and more or less juicy orange of a particular acquainted state'.

James's sympathies in the war were intense. When in consequence he became a British citizen, Pinker was one of his sponsors.

L.A.B.—Q

u.c. / ms. / 190

Comarques

3rd Dec. 1914

My dear Pinker,

Your letter is very interesting. Where is Eric? General Heath G.O.C. South Midland Division asked me to be his personal representative for this district which includes 30 parishes & the piece of coast where French landed 10 years ago. I told him of my public criticisms of the War Office. He said he didn't mind a bit. He said he wanted someone with commonsense. I said I had a lot of it. At present the work makes me lose 2 days a week. We have a jolly Territorial Engineers' subaltern staying with us. He is mining the district. His age is 18 & he has sole charge all alone here of 33 men, & does it well. I am rather pleased about H. J. Anyhow I agree with him as to the too easy style of the *P. of Love.* I infinitely regret to say that, having read the 2 vols of *Sinister Street,* I don't think it is permanent work; the beginning & the end are the best. I bet you anything Henry James would agree with me that the style is specious. The main character is not realised (but Stella is). I think the construction is very loose, but then people say that of my work. The invention is very poor: this is not a matter of argument, as its conventionality and facility can be demonstrated. The same is to be said of the episodical handling (as distinguished from the main construction). I could prove the weakness of this absolutely to you or anyone, with the book to refer to. All this is not much if Mackenzie has a fine mind. I wouldn't like to say, as I don't know his age. If he is under 30, what I object to may be mere youthfulness.

Yours sincerely, Arnold Bennett

190. Eric Pinker (1891–), elder son of J. B., joined the firm in 1908. He went into the army the previous August. Major-General Sir Charles Ernest Heath (1854–1936) was at this time Director of Quarterings, Headquarters of Army.

Henry James expressed admiration for Compton Mackenzie's developing style in his essay on 'The New Novel'. Mackenzie (1883–) was approaching his thirty-second birthday. He had published *Sinister Street* the year before.

u.c. / ts. / 191

Comarques
December 23rd, 1914

My dear Pinker,

You will see that I have phrased the enclosed letter so that you can show it to Whigham. But please do as you please as to that. There is a good deal about money in it, money being the one thing these people understand. What a monument of bad taste Whigham's letter is! I do not see how he refused the Velsa articles, as they were commissioned by the *Century*, and supplied by me article by article as they appeared. Perhaps you can put him right on this point.

Yours sincerely, Arnold Bennett

P.S. If Reynolds really did hawk the story about New York without letting you know, and if he is still your representative over there, perhaps some explanation ought to be invited from him.   A. B.

u.c. / ts. / 192

Comarques
December 23rd, 1914

My dear Pinker,

Thank you for your letter of yesterday and the enclosure from Mr. Whigham. I return the latter.

It is of course quite impossible for an author to argue with an editor about the quality of his stuff. If the editor does not like the stuff, there is no more to be said. All I have to remark is that I think 'The Life of Nash Nicklin' one of my best short stories, and decidedly superior to 'The Muscovy Ducks'. I should certainly not dream of holding Mr. Whigham to his contract as regards the third story. As regards 'The Life of Nash Nicklin', I am bound to say I regret that Mr. Whigham has allowed it to be offered to six other magazines, without consulting you. I entirely fail to understand such procedure. I should have thought that his obviously proper course was to have consulted you first. I also regret Mr. Whigham's veiled

191. Henry James Whigham, editor of the *Metropolitan Magazine* (see pages 182–5), was born in Scotland and educated at Oxford.

threat that he will do his best to spoil my market in America if I do not release him from his contract.

That six magazines for whom the story was assuredly not suited should have refused that story proves nothing. And quite apart from the suitability of the story, every author of any reputation knows that the first instinct of every editor is to refuse a story that is already written and in the market.

When Mr. Whigham originally asked me to contribute to his magazine, my first question to him was: 'Do you want me to do my best and most serious work, or do you want me to adopt a popular standard?' Because my answer depended on his. His answer was quite satisfactory, and he laid particular stress on the high literary aims of the *Metropolitan*. I cannot make it too clear that the size of the circulation of the magazine for which I write ought not to influence the character of my work.

In reference to Mr. Whigham's statement that his 'whole experience of my work has been unfortunate' and in particular that 'the original series of essays which we [he] published did not by any means come up to expectations', I should like to point out that I wrote two series of essays for him, and that in a letter to me dated 21st April, 1913, he refers very nicely to the first series, 'which we have all liked so much'. These two statements cannot be reconciled.

In the same letter Mr. Whigham very truly said: 'It may be unjust, but it is nevertheless a fact that an author who can appeal to a half million readers has a far higher commercial value than an author who can only appeal to 50,000.' He went on: 'You have built up your success on the wider appeal and have made a large value thereby for yourself.'

If I have done so it has been in the teeth of practically all the editors and publishers in America and in England. No editor and no publisher in America would have anything to do with *Buried Alive*, with the result that I did not even secure the American copyright. No American publisher would take *The Old Wives' Tale*, with the result that I did not even secure the American copyright. Even after the success of *The Old Wives' Tale* one of the most enterprising publishers in New York failed to acquire my *Clayhanger* series of novels because he could not see his way to pay a thousand dollars advance per volume. As you know, the right to publish those volumes has recently changed hands, after they have been on sale for years, at a price more than double that which was originally paid.

It is absolutely certain that if my best short stories, such as 'The Death of Simon Fuge' and 'The Matador of the Five Towns', which always have a steady sale, which are cited in text-books as examples, and which have been referred to in the highest terms by the most distinguished American critics,—if these stories were offered to the editors of big-circulation magazines, they would still be refused, as they were refused years ago, on the ground that they had 'no story value'.

Nevertheless I maintain that I am a better judge of what the public likes than the editors and publishers (and theatrical managers) with whom I have had dealings, and that the whole of my career proves it; for over and over again I have been right and they have been wrong. I am reminded that the editor of an English magazine took that first series of essays (which Mr. Whigham once liked so much) very reluctantly, and only because he had faith in your judgment. Before they were all published he was enthusiastic about them, and he asked for more. He did not get more.

Mr. Whigham says in his letter to you: 'There can be no doubt that the market for Bennett is not what it was two or three years ago, and I attribute that to the fact that Mr. Bennett has not been able to grasp the requirements of the big-circulation magazines.'

All I have to say is that, as you are aware, my prices in America (as in England) are today higher than ever they were; and that the demand by the very best magazines for my serials, my stories, and my essays is decidedly greater than I can supply. You are also aware that my last American contract, signed a few months ago, in full knowledge of all that has appeared from my pen, and in full knowledge of the inside of the literary market, was easily the best you have ever made for me. Mr. Whigham's supposition that the *Harper's Weekly* articles have been sold cheap is incorrect. They were supplied to fill a commission, and I believe the rate was two hundred dollars per thousand words. You will correct me if I am wrong.

Mr. Whigham says further, of his serial contract with me: 'I know perfectly well that if I wanted to resell the contract I could not begin to get the price which I have agreed to pay for it.' You and I, however, know perfectly well that we could place that serial instantly at a price higher by sixteen hundred dollars than Mr. Whigham has agreed to pay for it. I have not the slightest intention of suggesting, or consenting to, the cancellation of this contract; but if Mr. Whigham would care to have the documentary proof of what I say, I authorise you to put such proof confidentially before him. Mr. Whigham would then have to admit that he does not know the New York market as well as we do.

Again, Mr. Whigham says that my Holland articles 'have been of no real benefit to the *Century Magazine*'. By the same post as I received your letter I received a letter from the editor of the *Century* asking me for more stuff,—and not for the first time. I have written for very few American magazines. Besides the *Metropolitan*, I can only remember having accepted commissions from *Harper's*, the *Century*, the *American Magazine*, and the *Youth's Companion*. All these magazines have asked me more than once to contribute again.

I want Mr. Whigham to understand that I have no resentment against him. On the contrary, I sympathise with him. I fully realise that he must do his own business according to his own ideas. That I am convinced that 'The Life of Nash Nicklin' *would* please his readers, and therefore that I know his business better than he does, is beside the point. I leave you to deal with that particular story exactly according to your own judgment. I shall merely give my personal opinion that in causing the story to be hawked about New York without consulting you, Mr. Whigham has done something that rather puts him out of court, and which surely he must now regret. You could easily have placed the story; only the other day I forwarded to you a request for a story, from a magazine of at least as high a standing as the *Metropolitan*; but Mr. Whigham has probably lost the copyright.

I cannot help reminding you that the editor of *Pears' Annual*, who bought the story in England, and who should know by this time what a very large public wants, was somewhat enthusiastic about the tale.

Yours sincerely, Arnold Bennett

192. Bennett's facts appear to be accurate:
1. A letter from Whigham of 27 January 1913 and also the one of 21 April 1913

u.c. / ms. / 193

Comarques
5th Jan 1915

My dear Pinker,

Many thanks. I'm sorry I can't furnish a synopsis now. I have one but it is not definite. It will be definite by the end of February. All I care to say now is that the action will be largely in modern Paris (the first time I have written of it in fiction), & that the tale will be light & humorous in character, but with decidedly more sentiment, love, and advanced civilisation than there is in *The Card* and *The Regent*.

Yours sincerely, Arnold Bennett

---

printed above (pages 182–3) express entire satisfaction with the first series of essays, *The Case of the Plain Man* (*The Plain Man and His Wife*). The *Metropolitan* even issued one section of the series in pamphlet form at the end of 1912; and the Equitable Life Assurance Company used another section in an advertising scheme (see pages 196-7). On the difficulties over the second series, *The Story Teller's Craft* (*The Author's Craft*), see pages 182–5.

2. The enterprising publisher is unknown, but may have been Putnam, who had been interested in *The Old Wives' Tale* and *The Glimpse*. Bennett received $1,250 (£250) per novel from Dutton. The third Clayhanger novel was sold by Dutton to Doran for well above $5,000.

3. The last American contract, with Munsey, for $17,500 apiece for two serials, was decidedly Bennett's best contract. The price the *Metropolitan* was paying for its new serial (*The Lion's Share*) was $15,000.

4. The editor of *Pears' Annual* wrote to Pinker on 2 April 1914 to say of 'The Life of Nash Nicklin': 'The story is excellent & quite in the author's special vein.'

Nine months later, 'The Life of Nash Nicklin' was published in the *Metropolitan* itself, and Bennett commented in some private notes: 'The editor had absolutely declined to publish this story nearly a year ago, on the ground that it had no interest whatever.' The story was, though, the same one that *Cosmopolitan* had balked at earlier (see pages 201-2). Bennett never included it in any of his short story collections.

193. The new tale, *The Lion's Share*, deals in part with the suffragette movement. Although Bennett had treated of advanced civilization in his earliest sensational fiction, he was at this time preparing to give himself to it almost entirely. The third Clayhanger novel, *These Twain*, which he was now finishing (and which had been delayed on account of illness), was to be his last Five Towns novel. In *The Card* Denry Machin (who has the same birth date as Bennett) leaves the Five Towns briefly for his honeymoon in Switzerland; in *The Regent* he becomes a theatrical entrepreneur in London and visits America.

U.C. / TS. / 194

Comarques
January 26th, 1915

My dear Pinker,

Many thanks for your two letters. I return Whigham's letter to you, together with copy of my answer to his letter to me. He certainly ought to pay for the second story.

As regards the Melbourne Repertory Theatre, please do as you like.

Yours sincerely, Arnold Bennett

P.S. I will do an 8,000 word story for the *Century* for £300 with pleasure, and it would be a good one.   A.B.

U.C. / T.C.C. / 195
(*To H. Whigham*)

[Comarques]
January 26th, 1915

Dear Mr. Whigham,

Many thanks for your letter of the 15th. I quite appreciate and I reciprocate the friendliness of your attitude. At the same time I find nothing in your letter which answers any statement in my letter to Mr. Pinker. You still maintain that you know the New York market better than Mr. Pinker does, in spite of the indisputable proof to the contrary which is at your disposal, and in spite of the notorious fact that agents, for obvious reasons, always know the market better than editors.

You made your short-story contract with me entirely of your own free-will. Mr. Pinker did not stand over you with a revolver

194. The Melbourne (Australia) Repertory Theatre had proposed terms to Pinker for producing *What the Public Wants*.

Whigham's letter to Bennett does not survive. His letter to Pinker says in part:
   'I was simply appalled by the misconceptions which Mr. Bennett had fallen into as regards my desires or intentions.

   As I told you in my letter, I have no desire to cancel any contract which I ever made with you or Mr. Bennett. I have spoken to him very frankly about the pernicious habit which you and apparently all English agents have acquired of insisting on having stories commissioned. I must tell you just as frankly that I think the habit is just as bad for the author as it is for the editor, and it is one which I will never submit to in the future. . . .

   When I made this contract with you in New York for the Bennett stories, I knew I was doing wrong at the time and naturally I cannot blame you at all. . . .'
   The *Century Magazine* published no story of Bennett's until 1924.

and force you to accept his terms. If you had not previously read my volumes of short stories, you acted, if I may say so, rashly. If you had read them you surely must have known what to expect. The two short stories which I have supplied are fully characteristic of the bulk of my short stories. One of them, indeed, deals with two characters which have already figured in four previous stories, and these characters act quite consistently with their earlier appearances.

In May you said you could not publish 'Nash Nicklin' in your Christmas issue, but in December you say you cannot publish it at all. And, although you have apparently failed to secure the copyright, you ask that I should take the story back and give you another one instead. If you had asked this in May possibly something might have been done, as the story could undoubtedly have been sold elsewhere. But to ask it in December is strange. What is still more strange is your reiteration that you do not want to be released from your contract. If you do not want to be released from your contract, what do you want? If you want merely to make a general complaint against the practice of commissioning work in advance, I understand; and in reply I have only to say that this practice was invented by editors, and that the remedy is in the hands of editors. If on the other hand you want me to take back a story not at the eleventh but at the thirteenth hour, then I say that you do want to be released from your contract, and that moreover the proposition is utterly unreasonable. As regards the third story, undelivered, will you kindly inform Mr. Pinker at once definitely whether you want it or not. Please consider yourself absolutely free to cancel the short-story contract so far as the third story is concerned.

Your remarks about the relative values of English and American short-story writers are interesting as a disclosure of critical standards. I read a great deal of American literature, and I have also heard a great deal about the American short story. But I have never read any American short-story, except one or two by O. Henry and Ambrose Bierce, which in my opinion would rank with even the secondary short stories of Kipling, Wells, Hardy, Galsworthy, Conan Doyle, Phillpotts, George Moore, Frank Harris, Gilbert Chesterton, or Percival Gibbon, not to name sundry others. Nor do I know any American short-story writer (with the few exceptions aforesaid) who has made the slightest impression as a short-story writer outside his own country. Certainly I know of none who has aroused any interest whatever on the continent, where the works of most of the above-named English writers are much read both in the original and in translations. I wish you would send me a specimen of what you consider to be a first-class American short story. That I should try to imitate it is improbable, but I like to understand.

I hope, and I believe, that you will find the forthcoming novel not entirely unworthy of a modest corner in the livest magazine in America. I also hope that the next time you come to England you will let me know. I shall be delighted to see you, and I warn you that I have a great deal of plain talking to get through with you.

Yours sincerely, [Arnold Bennett]

U.C. / MS. / 196

The Berkeley Hotel
Piccadilly, W.
Wednesday 24th Feby 1915

My dear Pinker,

I am personally very much obliged to you for your help in the Wounded Allies affair, & Miss [?] Morrison is enchanted. I quite understand your wish not to be dragged to committee meetings. We shall, however, be very much obliged if you can attend *one* committee meeting on *Tuesday* next at 4 p.m. I don't know yet exactly where, but somewhere at Charing Cross, I think. You will receive final notice of it.

Yours sincerely, Arnold Bennett

P.S. Whigham has written me a letter of the boot-licking variety. These chaps must always go to extremes.   A.B.

195. The *Metropolitan Magazine* (self-advertised as 'the livest magazine in America') published 'The Life of Nash Nicklin' in September 1915 and the second story, 'The Muscovy Ducks', in July 1915. The latter story concerns Vera Cheswardine and her husband, a Five Towns couple about whom Bennett had written four stories that were collected in *The Grim Smile of the Five Towns* of 1907. The heroine appears to have been modelled upon the American girl, Eleanor Green, to whom Bennett was briefly engaged. The *Metropolitan* did not take the third story. It began publishing the novel, *The Lion's Share*, in October 1915.

196. Bennett's war work brought him up to London frequently. Among other activities, he was serving on the executive committee of the Wounded Allies' Relief

U.C. / MS. / 197

Comarques
20th Mch 1915

My dear Pinker,

There is a possibility of Knoblock turning one or two of my sensational novels into films. Only a possibility. Alice Kauser is his agent in U.S.A. She may call on you on Tuesday to discuss the relations of agents.

By the way I hear that, without a special clause to the contrary, kinema rights of plays belong to managers in U.S.A. Is this so? If so, have we sold the U.S.A. rights of the *Gt Ad*?

I shall be at the Berkeley *all* next week.

Yours sincerely, Arnold Bennett

U.C. / MS. / 198

Comarques
7–4–15

My dear Pinker,

I presume you received my letter at Newdigate enclosing a letter from Mair. If you didn't, the substance is that he thinks that if it gets about in newspaper offices (especially American) that I am going to the Front to write about it, the permission to go may be jeopardised, as there is a great deal of jealousy etc.

Yours sincerely, Arnold Bennett

U.C. / MS. / 199

The Berkeley Hotel
13 May 1915

My dear Pinker,

I have seen Mair. We expect to leave June 4th. There is no objection to you selling American rights of articles on *the French*

Committee. He wrote a pamphlet for the Committee in 1915, and satirized such committees in 1918 in *The Pretty Lady*. As 'Honourable Publicity Manager' of a 'War Fair' for the Committee in 1916 at the Caledonian Market, he produced a broadside that read in part: 'Note that the range of bargains will be enormous; it will indeed cover the entire field of human desire. Whatever your line may be, you will find matters to interest you at the greatest War Fair. As a simple illustration of the all-inclusiveness of these unique market days, be it noted that Lady Paget will sell live animals, while Lady Markham will sell five hundred tons of coal. And there will be everything in between these magnificent extremes.'

197. Knoblock does not appear to have done anything. An English film version of *The Great Adventure* had its first showing at the West End Cinema in Coventry Street on 3 December 1915. Henry Ainley starred in it, as he had in the play.

198. G. H. Mair (1887–1926) was in the Foreign Office. He was formerly on the editorial staff of the *Manchester Guardian* and the *Daily Chronicle*.

front at once. I shall see all of it, I expect. But it will be advisable not to include the English front at present; it seems the English are much more difficult to deal with as regards publication, but Mair assumes that it will ultimately be quite all right.

Don't deal with any English rights at present, please.

Yours sincerely, Arnold Bennett

u.c. / ts. / 200

Comarques
June 11th, 1915

My dear Pinker,

I do hope the *Strand* will not fight shy of my serial, as there is no reason whatever why they should do so.

The two principal characters are not both suffragettes. The two principal characters are Madame Piriac and Audrey. Madame Piriac, as may be seen from the scene between them in the fourth instalment, is a pronounced anti-suffragette. Audrey is a young girl finding her beliefs and her ways in life. She is certainly a suffragette for the time being, but before the end of the story she is powerfully influenced by Madame Piriac, who gradually grows more important in the tale. The title has reference to the question: which of these two women, with their different ideas, gets the lion's share of life?

The suffragette scenes start some time after the beginning of instalment four, and they end before the finish of instalment five, so that they cannot be said to occupy an undue space in the story. There are no more purely suffragette scenes. Most of the chief scenes in the latter part of the story pass on board Gilman's swagger new yacht, and in Paris in connection with Musa's great concert there. Audrey marries Musa and settles down.

The story is neither suffragette nor anti-suffragette. Suffragettism comes into it, and why not? Everyone was duly told that the story had to do with politics.

I repeat that there is nothing for the *Strand* to be afraid of. ~~And I am obliged to remind Mr. Greenhough Smith, in a very friendly manner, that on a previous occasion I had been shown to know the taste of his readers better than he did himself.~~

Although I should not be affected financially, I should feel bound to protest very strongly if the *Strand* really decided not to print my novel. If a novelist is to be barred from describing the livest and the most generally interesting scenes of modern public life in the pages of the *Strand* then he ought to be warned in advance. It is not as if there was the slightest bias, or attempt to proselytise, in my novel. There is not. It is not as if the novel was mainly occupied with politics. It is not. It is mainly occupied with the affections. It is not as if Suffragettism triumphed in my novel. It does not. The *Strand* knows quite well what kind of stuff I write. It knows that there is always something real, some vital question, behind my stories. If it forbids a serious writer even to touch a vital question, it sets him an impossible task.

Yours sincerely, Arnold Bennett

u.c. / ts. / 201

Comarques
July 25th, 1915

My dear Pinker,

Many thanks for your letter of the 23rd. I am extremely glad to hear what you say as to *The Lion's Share*. I have had a further letter from Greenhough Smith, to which I shall make a suitable reply in due course.

I do not expect to be out of bed until Tuesday, and I certainly do not expect to be able to let you have the third article on the Front, passed by the French Censor, earlier than Tuesday August 3rd. If the *Saturday Evening Post* is thinking of issuing the articles one after another without a break, perhaps you may think it advisable to cable to Lorimer advising him of the delay and its cause.

I am just getting over a rather severe attack of inflammation of the colon, due I am informed by my doctor to fatigue and nervous excitement at the Front.

As regards the setting up of *These Twain*, possibly the simplest plan would be for you to cable to the States for a copy showing

200. Greenhough Smith, editor of the *Strand Magazine*, had protested to Pinker about the suffragette material in *The Lion's Share*. He was reading the typescript of the novel. The crossed-out sentence in the fifth paragraph of Bennett's letter alludes to Smith's reservations about *The Plain Man and His Wife* that Bennett mentions in his letter to H. J. Whigham of 23 December 1914 (page 221).

all the cuts in red. Unless we are able to supply one of these copies to the printers, I am afraid that the only smooth course would be for the printers to begin the book again from a full copy which I have here.

Yours sincerely, Arnold Bennett

U.C. / MS. / 202

Comarques
12th Augt 1915

My dear Pinker,

Many thanks. I return the design. What I object to in it is the horrible ugliness of the whole thing—colouring & drawing. I will not agree to it in anything like its present form. Also it is utterly misleading. I draw in the book a man refined & artistic, especially with refined features, & the artist gives a man like a bookmaker or a moneylender. Edwin has plenty of hair & a beard. The artist makes him half bald & beardless. He is always very quietly dressed in blue with a black *bow* necktie & a stand-up collar. The artist gives him a grotesque waistcoat, a green suit, a low collar & a sailor's knot-necktie.

---

201. Pinker professed admiration for *The Lion's Share*, but Smith was still unappeased. The *Strand* refused to publish the novel, and it was taken over by the *Grand Magazine*.

Bennett was in France from 21 June to 15 July, visiting Rheims, Château-Thierry, Arras, and Ypres. His wife wrote that on his return 'the officers billetted with us were anxious to hear a full report of his impressions, but he refused to talk'. The refusal seems to have reflected the fact that what he saw distressed him greatly. For the public, though, he wrote a group of six articles, which began publication on 21 August in the *Illustrated London News* and the *Saturday Evening Post* (the latter magazine headed by George Horace Lorimer, 1868–1937). There is no doubt that the articles themselves suppress and distort much of what he saw. The trenches are spotless, the cannons are pretty affairs, the hospitals are incredibly efficient, and the German prisoners are brutalized. The rhetoric is more patriotic than felt. All the same, the basic contrast in the articles is true to Bennett's view of things:

'Nobody who knows Paris, and understands what Paris has meant and still means to humanity, can regard the [Parisian] scene without the most exquisite sentiments of humility, affection, and gratitude.'

'When you are walking through that which was Ypres, nothing arouses a stronger feeling—half contempt, half anger—than the thought of the mean, miserable, silly, childish, and grotesque excuses which the wit of Germany has invented for her deliberately planned crime.'

The articles were published in November in book form as *Over There*.

These Twain (the third novel of the Clayhanger trilogy) first appeared, with cuts, in *McClure's Magazine*, September and October 1915.

This man would have made Edwin sick. As regards the woman, the blouse is incredible. Also I particularly say that Hilda has *straight* & thick eyebrows, whereas the artist gives her eyebrows like a chinese. I am not going to give way to commercial travellers. What do they know about it? If one had asked their opinion of *Clayhanger* at the start, they would have said that God himself couldn't have forced it on the British public. They are nearly always wrong. I don't mind the *idea* of the present design; in fact I think it rather good. But it will have to be completely altered in detail before I approve of it.

Yours sincerely, Arnold Bennett

u.c. / ts. / 203

Comarques
October 28th, 1915

My dear Pinker,

Many thanks for yours of yesterday and the enclosures from Methuen. I return the latter. I enclose the slip proofs from America which I sent to Methuen for him to correct the English proofs from. You will see that there were practically no corrections at all except verbal slips in the typescript. I do not suppose that I altered 100 words in the whole book. As a fact I never alter a book after it is finished, and if Methuen is prepared to spend 6/- a sheet on author's corrections, he must have saved quite a lot on my previous books. It appears to me that the charge is excessive, and that a more economical scheme for undoing the original mistake might have been evolved.

I enclose one copy of the sixth instalment of *The Lion's Share* for the *Metropolitan*.

Yours sincerely, Arnold Bennett

u.c. / ts. / 204

Comarques
11th December, 1915

My dear Pinker,

I shall not be able to be present at the meeting of the Wounded Allies Relief Committee on Thursday next, and I

202. Bennett's objections were to a proposed dust-jacket for *These Twain*. The one used shows Edward bearded, bow-tied, blue-suited, looking rather refined and masculine. Hilda is seated playing a piano.

shall be obliged if you will take the chair in my absence.

I enclose a copy of a letter which I have received from Mr. Harry Preston, one of the leading spirits of the National Sporting Club.

I propose to arrange the concert at the Haymarket Theatre for Sunday the 20th February, as I am told by experts that this will be a good time. I have every expectation of being able to get together a first-class lot of artistes.

I also enclose copy of my letter to Mr. J. Moffat of the National Allies Relief Committee of New York together with copy of his reply dated November 26th. I presume that these ought to be discussed at the meeting. I do not see any advantage to us in the proposal, but perhaps I am mistaken.

Yours sincerely, Arnold Bennett

U.C. / MS. / 205

Central Hotel
Glasgow
till Thursday night
14th Dec 1915

My dear Pinker,

I shall write that play, but I shan't tell Doris so for about a week. As she will probably want both English & American rights the advance must be as much as on two separate contracts. I must be assured of a certain sum (substantial) in any case on delivery of the MS. I saw Vedrenne last night. He defined *Romance* as '*Milestones* & muck, and more muck than milestones'. By the way he said English rights of the *Great Adventure*

---

204. Harry Preston (1860–1936) was an acquaintance of Bennett's from the days when Bennett was writing *Clayhanger* in Brighton, at the Royal York Hotel, which Preston ran. It is not known what the present correspondence was about.

The concert was in aid of the Wounded Allies' Relief Committee. Bennett wrote in his journal on 21 February: 'This went off without a hitch, and I was very glad when it was over. I had no particular trouble, but I will never organise another. The theatrical element, [Henry] Ainley and Nelson Keys, had a much greater success than the musical element. The latter was naturally jealous, but could not help peeping and hugely enjoying the former.'

Nothing is known of the proposal from New York. John Moffat (1879–) was in charge of propaganda distribution in America.

film had been sold for £3,500. How do I stand in regard to this? Is the royalty on individual hirings or what?

Doris's ideas are all right.

Yours sincerely, Arnold Bennett

u.c. / ts. / 206

Comarques
27th December, 1915

My dear Pinker,

In reply to yours of the 24th, I will make the following observations as to the terms of the proposed contract.

If I am to receive £500 on account of the English rights on delivery of the MS of the play, and if Miss Keane is free to take up or leave the American rights after delivery of the MS as she pleases, this means that there will be considerable risk of me having on my hands a play written especially for a particular actress after having received only £500 for the work. As such a play as Miss Keane has in mind and as I contemplate writing would have only a small chance of being sold to any ordinary management, either here or in America, I do not think that the proposal is fair, and I am not prepared to agree to it.

Under no circumstances will I part with any share of the Stock rights or the Film rights. Rather than do so I would prefer to drop the contract altogether. The reasons for my attitude in this matter are perfectly clear, and I can rely on you to explain them to Mr. Nethersole. There can of course be no question at all as to the Film rights, and as to the Stock rights it was an American theatrical manager who strongly advised me never to part with them. The whole point is that a play after all belongs to its author, and that the theatrical manager can only properly claim a share in it in so far as he

205. Bennett was in the Midlands and Scotland for about two weeks in December.

A play to be based on the novel *Sacred and Profane Love* had been discussed with the American actress Doris Keane for two years. Miss Keane (1881–1945) was associated with Edward Sheldon (1886–1946), in whose highly successful play *Romance* she was now starring in London. Bennett saw the play twice, and on the second occasion reported in his journal: 'She played even better than before. She has a most powerful personality.' A few days later he had her to lunch, and wrote in his journal: 'I learnt a lot about her and got some general ideas as to how to write a play to suit her.'

L.A.B.—R

takes a risk and does actual work. In asking for a share in either Stock rights or Film rights the theatrical manager is merely asking for a gift.

The royalties are all right.

As regards performances in the colonies, it must be borne in mind that in many cases they are not continuous during the whole week. Hence the royalty should be arranged if necessary either on the basis of the returns for a single performance or on the returns for an agreed number of consecutive performances, without respect to time.

I am quite willing to let Miss Keane have the provincial rights on a royalty to be agreed.

With regard to Miss Keane's suggestion that she should be free to assign her rights for London and the English provinces, I am prepared to agree to this, but of course only on condition that whoever owns the rights she herself shall play the principal part in London. It must be of the essence of the contract that the principal part is played by Miss Keane herself both in London and in New York. I am only agreeing to write the play because I was very deeply impressed by Miss Keane's acting.

Yours sincerely, Arnold Bennett

U.C. / TS. / 207

Comarques
12th January, 1916

My dear Pinker,

I heard by telegram from the *Daily News* last night that they thought it inadvisable to publish the article which I had written for them this week. Of course I have no complaint to make on this score, provided that they pay for the article. I feel fairly sure, however, that of their own accord they will not offer to pay for the article, so that when the account comes in to you I shall be glad if you will see to the matter. If they do not pay for it I shall cease to write for them, as I have no intention of doing articles on approval. Twenty four hours before beginning to write the article I informed them—as a measure of precaution—what the trend of the article would be, but I heard nothing at all from them until twelve hours after

206. Louis Nethersole was Doris Keane's manager.

the article had been in their hands. I enclose a copy of it as it may interest you.

In the ordinary way I reckon as a journalist to be able to keep within the lines of the policy of the paper while expressing my own views, but as regards the particular question it has been impossible during the last week to divine what the policy of the paper actually was. I shall probably see Gardiner on Thursday, but I shall not mention the question of payment to him unless he mentions it to me. I had already warned him, apropos of an earlier article which they shied at but ultimately printed, that if there was to be any further difficulty of a similar kind I should have to ask them to pay me a salary instead of a price per article.

Yours sincerely, Arnold Bennett

P.S. I am at the Berkeley till Friday morning.   A. B.

u.c. / ts. / 208

Comarques
15th January 1916

My dear Pinker,

In reply to your letter of the 11th as to Miss Doris Keane, Miss Keane need be under no apprehension whatever as to the expensiveness of either cast or production. Miss Keane has already given me her idea of the scenario of the first three acts of the play, and so far as I can judge at present I shall adhere fairly closely to her suggestions, which I consider excellent. I have also given Miss Keane my rough idea as to the 4th act.

As matters stand, therefore, the first act will take place in a private room at a hotel, and it consists chiefly of a duet between the two principal characters. There will be a subordinate

---

207. The article for the *Daily News*, of which A. G. Gardiner (1865–1946) was editor, was probably one called 'The Rat-Trap', which appears not to have been published. It is a violent attack on the conscription bill, which was just being passed, as 'a police measure of the most Prussian kind'—stripping every unmarried male of all civilian security and leaving him at the mercy of hastily appointed tribunals set up by irresponsible people. The Prussianism of government leaders was a constant theme of Bennett's articles. If their ideals triumphed, the war would be lost at home.

Gardiner ended the series of articles in May, and then resumed it in January 1917.

character in the shape of a chambermaid who will have a few important lines. Perhaps there may also be another servant and a secretary.

The second act will take place in a drawing-room, and there will be in it three principal characters, namely, Carlotta, Ispenlove, and his wife. There will probably be one or two other people of quite minor importance, and perhaps two or three non-speaking rôles.

The third act will be in a room in a house in Paris. There will be three principal characters, namely, Carlotta, Diaz, and the cocotte.

I have not yet decided the exact setting of the fourth act, but the principal characters in it will be the same as the third act.

It is plain, therefore, that no special difficulty—scenic or otherwise—can occur in the play, and I may say that I prefer to obtain my effects with the dialogue and acting rather than out of crowds and scenery.

I return the draft contract. It seems to me that the alteration in clause 3 practically abolishes the stock rights, and I should like you to consider this further. As regards clause 7, I think that an undertaking to produce in any first-class theatre in the United States is too vague. It seems to me that a list of cities ought to be inserted, and that this list should only include at the most New York, Chicago and Boston.

Yours sincerely, Arnold Bennett

U.C. / TS. / 209

Comarques
17th March, 1916

My dear Pinker,

I enclose copy of a letter which I have today sent to Masterman.

Yours sincerely, Arnold Bennett

208. Bennett did not begin writing the play until April. It varies from the novel mainly in that it avoids an explicitly tragic ending. His description in the letter is accurate. The play concerns a passionate and talented woman of the Five Towns, Carlotta Peel. She gives herself one night to a famous pianist, Diaz (Act I, which takes place in a private home, not a hotel); subsequently as a famous novelist in London she is involved in an affair with her publisher, Ispenlove (II); she abandons her career to save Diaz, who has become a drug addict and who is living in Paris with a cocotte (III); she and Diaz enjoy an ambiguous triumph in London on his return to the concert stage (IV).

U.C. / T.C.C. / 210
(*To the Rt. Hon. C. F. G. Masterman*)

[Comarques]
17th March, 1916

My dear Masterman,

All my work and all the work of John Galsworthy which appears in the United States is handled by our agent, Mr. James B. Pinker, of Talbot House, Arundel Street, Strand. Mr. Pinker has placed for me considerably over £2,000 worth of stuff as to the war in the best journalistic mediums in the United States, and the greater part of this stuff has been written at the suggestion either of yourself or of G. H. Mair. I should in all probability be unable to place the stuff myself with anything like the same success, and I think I may say the same for Galsworthy, who has also, as you know, been writing under official suggestion. The placing of the stuff is in the hands of Mr. Pinker's managing clerk, Mr. Wicken, who is within a few months of 41 years of age and who has attested. The whole of Mr. Pinker's male staff, including his eldest son, is and has been for a long time in the army with the exception of Mr. Wicken. So far Mr. Pinker has been unable to obtain more than one month's exemption for Mr. Wicken. The case is one which naturally the Tribunal is quite incapable of understanding. It will shortly come up again for reconsideration. It has occurred to Mr. Pinker and myself, who are both seriously concerned, that if you could see your way to writing a letter to the effect that Mr. Pinker was rendering good service to an important Government department, such a letter might conceivably be of service with the Tribunal. I have not the least idea how this suggestion may strike you, but in any case I shall take it as a personal favour if you will give Mr. Pinker himself an interview. He would be very pleased to call on you at any time convenient to yourself. It would save time, which is rather precious, if you would be good enough to communicate with him direct.

Yours ever, [Arnold Bennett]

209. The Rt. Hon. Charles Frederick Gurney Masterman (1873–1927) was Director of Wellington House (Propaganda). He had been literary editor of the *Daily News* and was the author of books on literary and political subjects. He and Bennett became good friends. When he was dying in 1927, he said to his wife: 'If you're really in a hole, go to A. B. He's the one.'

210. It was arranged that Wicken would be called up and then put in a special class and left in civilian life.

U.C. / TS. / 211

Comarques
21st May, 1916

My dear Pinker,

Many thanks for your telegram and letter as to the Irish article. I enclose copy of a letter which I have written to Mr. Gowers, who, in the absence of Mr. Masterman, has officially asked me to do the article. I think it will be well for you to satisfy yourself personally as to the cable censorship.

I think that Masterman's department must have wanted a copy of my first Irish article for Mr. Raymond Needham, who looks after things in Dublin and who originally asked for the article to be done. I have therefore sent him a copy direct.

Yours sincerely, Arnold Bennett

P.S. I will send the article for the *New York Times* by train as the posts are so irregular; I will wire you by which train it is to arrive. Please see that the train is met.

U.C. / T.C.C. / 212
(*To Ernest A. Gowers*)

[Comarques]
21st May, 1916

Dear Sir,

I am obliged for your letter of the 19th. The best paper for the Irish article is the *New York Times*, and my agent Mr. James B. Pinker, of Talbot House, Arundel Street, London, W.C., who is known to Mr. Masterman, has arranged that the article shall be cabled over and shall appear in the *New York Times* on Sunday May 28th. I will see that the article is submitted for the formal approval of your department before it is delivered to the London representative of the *New York Times*. I shall be glad if the department will take the necessary pre-

---

211. Sir Ernest A. Gowers (1880–1966), reviser of Fowler's *Modern English Usage*, was in the Civil Service for many years. Sir Raymond Needham (1877–) was at this time serving in the War Office under the Lord-Lieutenant of Ireland. He had been a friend of Bennett's since early in the century. Bennett's article was a defence of Britain's conduct in the famous Easter uprising. It was given the front page of the magazine section of the *New York Times* on the 28th, and appeared in the *Daily News* on the 29th. The earlier article is unknown.

cautions to prevent any trouble or delay with the censorship. I mention this rather important point as I have recently had an annoying experience. I was specially requested by the French Government to write an article on a certain subject for a Paris daily paper. I wrote the article exactly on the lines laid down, and it was enthusiastically approved by the representative of the French Government. The Government, however, had so little control over its own Censor that the latter condemned the article in its entirety.

Yours sincerely, [Arnold Bennett]

BUTLER / T.C.C. / 213

[Comarques]
5th July, 1916

My dear Pinker,

Many thanks for your letter of yesterday. It is considered advisable that I should abstain from any more organising work for the immediate present, as I am suffering considerably from both neuralgia and dyspepsia. I shall therefore be very much obliged if you will preside at the meeting tomorrow afternoon.

Yours sincerely, [Arnold Bennett]

U.C. / TS. / 214

Comarques
17th July, 1916

My dear Pinker,

Would it be convenient to you if we were to lunch together on Thursday next?

Towards the middle of next week I am going to the North for a short holiday, and I should like to have a chat with you before I go. I have now completed the play for Miss Doris Keane, and I expect to send it to her direct within the next three or four days. This is for your information so that you may keep in touch with Mr. Louis Nethersole.

Yours sincerely, Arnold Bennett

213. The meeting was of the Wounded Allies' Relief Committee.

u.c. / ms. / 215

Comarques
30 Augt 1916

My dear Pinker,
    I enclose copies of 3 letters from Knoblock, Bright, & myself.
                                Yours sincerely, Arnold Bennett

u.c. / t.c. / 216
(*From Edward Knoblock*)

The Albany,
Piccadilly. W.
August 29th, 1916

My dear Arnold,
    I herewith enclose a letter from Bright which explains itself.
Will you kindly let me know what you mean to do in the
matter? I shall be quite frank. I think the whole trouble is due
to Pinker. He knows nothing about the theatre and its conditions. Every time I have seen him touch any theatrical matter
he has muddled it. He may be an excellent agent in his particular line, and no doubt is. But the two things are quite distinct.
    Personally I shall, of course, pay my share, though I think
it is Pinker that should have paid the whole amount out of his
own pocket.
    I know you won't mind my writing you like this. I daresay
you'll defend your own man, just as I'm defending mine.
                                Yours, [Edward Knoblock]

u.c. / t.c. / 217
(*From Golding Bright to Edward Knoblock*)

[no address]
August 28th, 1916

My dear Knoblock,
            re Milestones Film agreement
    When this was being negotiated by me, I sent the draft
agreement to Arnold Bennett, who kept it for some time and

215. Golding Bright (d. 1941) was the younger brother of Arthur Addison
Bright, a well-known dramatic agent. He took over part of his brother's agency
on his brother's death in 1906, and served Sir James Barrie and others. He was
known in later years as England's leading dramatic agent.

returned it through Pinker, saying that he thought it required some alterations, which he did not specify. I thought this was unsatisfactory and concluded there was no alternative but to submit it to Langton & Passmore which I did. The agreement went through, and I deducted from the advance payment made to both of you the lawyer's charges which amounted to £5. 5. 0.

Pinker on Bennett's behalf immediately objected to being charged half of these fees, and I have been in correspondence with him on the subject without arriving at any satisfactory conclusion. Bennett's contention now apparently is that the solicitor was not necessary, and that therefore he should not be asked to share this expense. I think it is a most unfair attitude to take up, and I shall be obliged if you will write to Bennett on the subject, as the whole matter was of course for your mutual benefit.

Yours sincerely, [Golding Bright]

U.C. / T.C. / 218
(*To Edward Knoblock*)

[Comarques]
30th August, 1916

My dear Edward,

Many thanks. In this instance the trouble is not due to Pinker. He gave me his view and I concurred in it and authorised him to act on it. Pinker's competence in the theatre does not arise in the present matter. As to his competence in film work my own experience leaves me in no doubt as to it.

I think the whole trouble is due to Bright. Bright's limitations are well known, and no one has defined them better than yourself. Pinker settles my film agreements without the aid of a solicitor, and if Bright cannot do as much he should at least have consulted Pinker before going to a solicitor on behalf of both of us. Courtesy demanded this, as he was acting exclusively for you. If Bright omits elementary business formalities he must accept the consequences. Had Bright suggested to Pinker that a solicitor was necessary in my interests, Pinker would at once have objected.

Thine, [A. B.]

218. A film version of *Milestones* was released by the Samuelson Film Company in December 1916 for a trade show, and in the following April for public showing.

u.c. / ms. / 219

Comarques
4th Sept 1916

My dear Pinker,

I enclose copy of letter received from Doris Keane yesterday & copy of my reply. You had better collect this money if it isn't paid this week. Miller has returned *Don Juan* to my secretary. I send it on to you in case you may need it.

Yours sincerely, Arnold Bennett

P.S. I have said nothing to Doris in reply to her suggestion about *her* selling the play, as this has to be thought over. In any case she must pay first. If she can get a good offer, we can always consider it. You might tell Nethersole this.   A. B.

u.c. / t.c.c. / 220
(*To Doris Keane*)

[Comarques]
4th September, 1916

Dear Miss Keane,

Thank you for your letter of the 1st. I am sorry that I am quite unable to agree with your suggestions as to the play. I may be wrong; but after all, just as you are an actress, I am a playwright. Throughout my connection with the stage expert theatrical managers and artistes have continually explained to me that they understood the business of playwriting better than I did. I have never written a play that expert theatrical managers and artistes have not condemned. I have never altered a play save to cut it. I have never got a play produced except after extreme difficulty and amid prophecies of disaster. With one exception, in which the circumstances were in my judgment so impossible that I left the country before the rehearsals began, I have not yet had a failure.

Esmé Hubbard, Owen Nares, and Hubert Harden, all of whom had appeared in the original production of the play, were among the cast.

219. Miss Keane wrote to express dissatisfaction with *Sacred and Profane Love*. She wanted Bennett either to make changes or to allow her to abandon the play at a cost of only half the contracted fee. She complained that he had not followed the scenario (though pages 235-6 indicate that he had).

Gilbert Miller (1884–) began his long career as a manager this year, when he produced *Daddy-Long-Legs* at the Duke of York's Theatre. He was interested now and later in producing *Don Juan de Marana*.

I think that what you object to in the play is the character, as you write that 'it is a part that many actresses could play'. Nevertheless the character remains the same in the play as in the book. In this connection it may interest you to know that while I was writing the play I was told again and again by theatrical and other people who knew the book and admired your acting, that the character would not suit you and that you could not possibly succeed in it.

Nor can I agree to your suggestion as to a modification of the contract. (I do not understand what you mean as to not following the scenario.) In saying that the contract is 'entirely in my favour', you are under a delusion which is very common among disappointed theatrical managers who have commissioned a play and don't like it. The contract is not entirely in my favour, and neither you nor any other experienced manager would be so foolish as to sign a contract entirely in favour of the other party. You were very anxious that I should write the play, as is shown by the fact that you persevered for over two years until I at length consented.

I told you at the time that I should have to put aside other contracts in order to accept your commission. In the period which I spent on the play I should have earned a minimum of £5,500, which is the smallest sum I receive in advance on a novel. I let this certainty go in exchange for a certainty of only £1,000. Why did I do it? Simply and solely because I was immensely impressed by your acting. Had I not been so impressed I should not have signed the contract. As a result at the present moment, whereas you will have lost only £1,000, I find myself definitely out of pocket by £4,500, and with the reversion of a play which owing to theatrical conditions it may be impossible to place for years. There was nothing unusual in the contract. Such contracts are constantly made. Both sides knowingly take risks, and neither side has the least right to complain when the risks materialise. If you could have been absolutely sure that the play would suit you you would have willingly paid £10,000 to get it. Because you were not sure you agreed to pay only £1,000. I need not remind you of the proverb about the cake. The balance of the £1,000 was due on delivery of the manuscript. It ought to have been paid then and it must now be paid.

While my attitude is absolutely firm as to both the play and the contract, I fully sympathise with your personal disappointment. And I hope that you sympathise with my personal disappointment. These disappointments have to be faced. They are the consequence of a deep and unchangeable difference of opinion which could not have been foreseen.

My wife joins me in kindest regards.

Yours sincerely, [Arnold Bennett]

U.C. / MS. / 221

Comarques
7th Sept 1916

My dear Pinker,

I enclose copies of letters from Doris to me & from me to her. You therefore credit yourself with commission on £750.

Yours sincerely, Arnold Bennett

U.C. / T.C. / 222
(*To Doris Keane*)

[Comarques]
7th September, 1916

Dear Miss Keane,

Many thanks for your letter of the 5th and cheque for £750. My Agent will send you a formal receipt. The typescript of the play has not yet arrived but it will doubtless be in the next post. Its delivery will definitely end the contract between us.

My account of the negotiations immediately preceding the contract would differ materially from yours, but the matter has no importance.

Yours sincerely, [Arnold Bennett]

220. Bennett's one failure was apparently the production of *What the Public Wants* at the Royalty Theatre at the end of May 1909. Charles Hawtrey put the play on after two weeks of rehearsals. It ran for a month. The Stage Society had produced the play at the beginning of May with a somewhat different cast. Bennett also had considerable difficulties over *The Honeymoon*, which ran for slightly under four months in 1911–12.

221. In her letter Miss Keane said that although she had originally been anxious for Bennett to write the play, she had given up the idea, and then Bennett and Pinker had pressed it. She enclosed the balance of the contracted fee.

u.c. / ms. / 223

[London]
11th Jan 1917

My dear Pinker,

Walpole spent all Sunday afternoon at my house in reading Jacob Tonson's *New Age* articles, which he had asked for. He said it would be ridiculous not to reissue a selection from them as a book. Swinnerton says the same. He was at Comarques also. I told him C. & W. could have the book if Spalding wished & could settle terms with you. I expect Doran would also like it. I enclose a letter from Swinnerton, which please return to Comarques. Perhaps you will see Spalding & Swinnerton & ascertain what their views as to terms are. I cannot call on you today. I return home this afternoon.

Yours sincerely, Arnold Bennett

u.c. / ms. / 224

Comarques
13th Jan 1917

My dear Pinker,

The Stage Society want to do Henry James's *Outcry*. As it was originally written for Repertory, is there any reason why you should not let them? Of course you know there are no fees attached to these performances. It seems to me it would be a great idea to let the S. S. do the thing. I am wrongly supposed to have vast influence with you, & have been asked to approach you. I do so, as I very fully share the views of the S. S. in this matter.

Yours sincerely, Arnold Bennett

223. Hugh Walpole (1884–1941) had recently returned to England from a sojourn in Leningrad as head of the Anglo-Russian propaganda bureau there. Bennett first met him in 1910, when he had published only *The Wooden Horse*, and helped him to obtain George Doran as his American publisher.

Frank Swinnerton (1884–), who met Bennett in 1911, became his best friend in later years. At this time he was on the staff of Chatto and Windus, which was headed by Percy Spalding (d. 1930) and the younger Chatto (d. 1942). The firm published the *New Age* articles as *Books and Persons* later in the year.

224. *The Outcry*, James's last play, was written in 1909–10 at the invitation of Charles Frohman, who was undertaking a repertory season at the Duke of York's Theatre. Its first production was that by the Stage Society, on 1 and 3 July 1917, when it had a success not much greater than *Guy Domville*. Bernard Shaw remarked apropos of it: 'there is a literary language which is perfectly intelligible to the eye, yet utterly unintelligible to the ear'.

u.c. / ms. / 225

> Comarques
> 7–3–17

My dear Pinker,

Many thanks for yours of the 5th & the enclosures.

I think you have done splendidly with the articles, and I hope that my work will be worthy of yours.

I should like to know what Harper's reply was.

With regard to Munseys, I see no reason why they should not keep their part of the contract strictly. If I did not keep my part they would immediately complain. The money is due on delivery of MS. and should be paid on delivery. They can be warned that the MS. will be delivered in May and they can arrange accordingly. After all this is an important contract, and the financial arrangements of the author who has entered into [it], no matter who he is, must largely be based on its fulfilment. What excuse have Munsey's to offer for not having paid the deposit? If, having paid the deposit, the author was in the slightest degree late in delivering the manuscript, indignant cablegrams would begin to pour out of New York. Perhaps you may think proper to set this aspect of the case before Davis.

I do not want the money now. My reason for wanting the main sum immediately after 30th June is that the second moiety of my income tax is due on 1st July.

> Yours sincerely, Arnold Bennett

P.S. As to cabling money, it would not be a bad plan anyhow to find out the cost. I agree as to American income tax. A. B.

225. *Cosmopolitan* contracted to pay $600 apiece for six essays; English rights went to *Nash's and Pall Mall Magazine* for £75 apiece. The series began in *Cosmopolitan* in November 1917 and in *Nash's* in January 1918.

Harper's was balking at paying extra for Bennett to do his own illustrations to a proposed series of yachting articles.

The Munsey delay had to do with Robert Davis's efforts to re-sell the serial contracts made with Bennett and other people (see page 258n.). The novel immediately involved was *The Roll-Call*.

The American income tax people were trying to collect on the American earnings of British authors. Pinker and Bennett thought they would have a hard time collecting.

u.c. / ts. / 226

Comarques
March 13th, 1917

My dear Pinker,

I enclose copy letter received from Swinnerton today, copy of my reply, and the original card from Orage. (I ignored this card.) I also enclose all Orage's letters to me in the past that have survived, simply for you to read. There was a most distinct verbal understanding between him and me that the copyright belonged to me. You will note that for about 18 months I wrote for nothing, and then at One Guinea a week. However, I believe the law is that in the absence of an arrangement to the contrary the copyright belongs to the author. If this is so, I would sooner do anything than ask him for formal permission.

I leave the matter to you.

I shall be at the Yacht Club Wednesday and Thursday, but I am engaged for lunches.

Yours sincerely, Arnold Bennett

The New Age Company is, or is shortly to be, in voluntary liquidation, & has, I believe, no resources in cash.   A. B.

u.c. / ts. / 227

Comarques
March 31st, 1917

My dear Pinker,

Many thanks for yours of the 27th. I enclose copy of a letter which I have received from Harpers and copy of my reply.

Yours sincerely, Arnold Bennett

226. A letter from Pinker says that Orage wrote to Chatto and Windus threatening action if they published the *New Age* articles without his permission. On 18 March Orage wrote to Pinker:

'It is true that Mr. Bennett was generous enough to contribute the articles for eighteen months without payment; but for the last year or so he received a guinea a week; and eventually a hundred £1 shares in the New Age Company were given to him. These amounts, while, of course, not payment in the market sense, were consideration in the technical sense; and they entitle me, in the absence of any agreement to the contrary, to be asked my consent to the republication of the articles. I may repeat my assurances to Messrs. Chatto and Windus that Mr. Bennett has only to ask my consent to receive it freely.'

See also Bennett's earlier comment to his sister and her husband regarding the *New Age*, quoted on page 122n.

U.C. / T.C. / 228
(*From* T. B. *Wells of Harper's*)

[Franklin Square]
[New York]
March 14th, 1917

Dear Bennett:

I am wondering now what ever came of my negotiations with Pinker about those articles on your yachting cruise up the Tiber. It was Pinker's own suggestion and not mine that we might get these articles for the same price as the American articles, with pictures included. He tells me you balked at that, but in these strenuous times, I am afraid we cannot make any better proposition. I wish, however, that we might have something from you during this year. Whenever you get an idea in your head for some short essay, won't you forward the suggestion to me? You can do that sort of thing better than anyone else and we ought to be able to use several of them during the year, which might result in a book.

With all good wishes to you both,

Very truly yours, [T. B. Wells]

U.C. / T.C.C. / 229
(*To* T. B. *Wells*)

[Comarques]
March 31st, 1917

Dear Wells,

Many thanks for yours of the 14th. All I have to say in reply is that if you really desire to have any articles from me it is easy to get them for next year. On the whole I think I would rather write for *Harper's* than for any other magazine in the world. But there will have to be some sort of relation between the market price and the price you offer. I may tell you that I have just arranged for a series of articles such as you suggest at the price of £95 for the serial rights in the States and in England, per thousand words. Also, I will not write any articles at all unless I have a definite commission in advance. It seems to me that perhaps you may care to reconsider your decision as to the articles on the journey to Rome.

Our kindest regards to you both,

Yours sincerely, [Arnold Bennett]

U.C. / MS. / 230

Comarques
5 May 1917

My dear Pinker,

The *Strand* article is called: 'Are We a Thrifty Race?'. It is about 3,000 words long. I have finished it, & shall have it typewritten & posted on Saturday direct to the *Strand*. I am exceedingly anxious that there should be no dissatisfaction on the part of Greenhough Smith. It is not the ordinary sort of article. And although it is, I think, very interesting it is not like my articles usually are. Hence he may feel disappointed. If so, you needn't worry him about the price, as I was of course quite prepared to do it for nothing, & I would have offered it for nothing, only it is bad for editors to get things for nothing. The article is a government article, & the *Strand* was chosen by the head of the department himself as being the best medium. He asked me if I could get the article into the *Strand* & I said I imagined I could. You can tell Greenhough Smith this if you like.

Yours sincerely, Arnold Bennett

Sisson has cabled me thanking me for article received, so I presume he likes it. A. B.

U.C. / MS. / 231
PRIVATE

Comarques
8th June 1917

My dear Pinker,

Many thanks for your letters. I return all the papers etc re *X*. I wrote a very pregnant paragraph about this case for the *New Statesman*, only to find that *X* & the editor are interviewing each other about a medical scheme which the *N.S.* has at

229. Bennett speaks less enthusiastically of *Harper's* in his letters of 12 January 1910 and 19 February 1920. Nothing was arranged with them.

230. Greenhough Smith rejected the article, and it was published in the *Fortnightly Review* in December. It is an appeal on behalf of the National War Savings Committee, and answers the question of the title by saying that the English have not been a thrifty race but that they are becoming one.

Edgar Grant Sisson (1875–1948) was editor of *Cosmopolitan* from 1914 to 1917.

heart & that *X* is very receptive. Squire told me that he would not hesitate to throw *X* over if the scandal was an obviously serious one, or if the events had occurred while *X* was a minister. But under the circumstances he did not care to do so. I agreed with him.

A paragraph about Mond will appear tomorrow.

Yours sincerely, Arnold Bennett

BUTLER / TS. / 232
(*From J. B. Pinker*)

Talbot House
8th June 1917

My dear Bennett,

Drinkwater would like to have *What the Public Wants*, and to enter into an arrangement to do it for a week in the autumn at 5% on the gross. It is a thin royalty, but he says this is the rate they pay all their authors.

I enclose a letter that I have just received from Davis, and I shall be glad if you will read it and return it to me with your instructions. Nothing was said in the course of the negotiations as to the character of the stories to be supplied under the contract, and it is absurd to suggest that the terms of a definite agreement are modified by any vague, personal talk that may have passed long afterwards between you and Davis. I am afraid we shall have to put the lawyers on to them, but I thought before we did that I might cable to Doran by deferred cable to say that you had instructed me to put the matter in the hands of the solicitors to collect the money, unless he thinks that can be avoided. If I cabled to Davis it might have on Munsey a contrary effect to the one we desired, but if I cable to Doran he will, of course, tell Davis our state of mind, without our having to threaten. I think this would be the better

231. The letter identifies a member of the Government.

Bennett became a director of the *New Statesman* in 1915, and on 28 October 1916 he began a weekly series of anonymous 'Observations' that continued until 1919. The immediate 'pregnant paragraph' was apparently not published. John Squire (1884–1958), poet and critic, and later editor of the *London Mercury*, was at this time acting editor of the *New Statesman*.

Lord Alfred Mond was attacked by Bennett for advertising the Mond Nickel Company as though it had the backing of the Government, in which Mond was a minister.

way, but if the result is unsatisfactory I suggest we should put the Authors' Society on to them.

Sincerely yours, J. B. Pinker

BUTLER / T.C. / 233
(*From R. H. Davis, of the Munsey*   [8 West 40th Street]
Syndicate, to J. B. Pinker)   [New York]
May 22nd, 1917

My dear Pinker,

We were somewhat surprised at the receipt of *The Roll-Call*, the fourth segment in the Clayhanger series.

It was understood between Arnold Bennett and myself that something in the vein of *Buried Alive* would follow *These Twain*.

We do not feel that *The Roll-Call* should have been offered the Munsey Company under the circumstances. A separate novel, complete in itself, not predicated upon previous work, was what we had every right to expect. You can hardly expect us to give any more space to the Clayhanger series, in view of the fact that it was specifically understood that we were to have something in a happier vein.

I quote from A.B.'s letter of April 22nd, 1915:

> Let us hope the next novel may contain an abundance of plot in the Frank A. Munsey sense of the word. You are magnanimous. I don't know another editor in the world who would not have said that *These Twain* was not in the least what he hoped for and expected. Take this as a testimonial and no mean one either.
>
> (signed) Arnold Bennett

Will you present my compliments to A.B. and lay all these matters before him. He will for a certainty recall our understanding.

With best wishes, believe me,

Very sincerely yours, [R. H. Davis]

P.S. Where do you wish the manuscript delivered?

232. John Drinkwater (1882–1937) produced *What the Public Wants* in repertory in Birmingham. He was soon to have his new play *Abraham Lincoln* produced in part under Bennett's auspices at the Lyric Theatre, Hammersmith.

See pages 174, 205-6, and 246 for the earlier stages of the Munsey negotiations. On Frank A. Munsey see page 174.

U.C. / TS. / 234

Comarques
June 9th, 1917

My dear Pinker,

Many thanks for yours of the 8th and the enclosure, which I return.

I shall not characterize Davis's letter.

After making it quite clear that, by reason of changes in their plans they did not really want any more novels from me, after even enquiring from you whether you could re-sell the next novel for them, and after playing a waiting game (which included a deliberate failure on their part to fulfil a clear financial condition of the contract), Munsey's now change their ground and object to the novel itself. I regret to say that this is just what I expected. It is, however, rather naive.

Private talk cannot possibly affect a most carefully drawn contract, but if Davis thinks proper to bring in private talk I also must give my version of the talk. I gave Davis an outline of the first of the three novels, but I absolutely declined to commit myself as to the nature of the other two. I did, nevertheless, distinctly state that I intended to write a London novel about Hilda's son, and he was very decidedly sympathetic to the idea. The fact that I was writing this novel for Munsey's has been well known for a long time, and Davis must have been aware of it, at any rate from Doran. I supplied you with a description of the novel last year.

The assertion that there is no plot in *The Roll Call* is ridiculous. It has plenty of plot—more plot than any other serious novel of mine of similar length. It has a strong suspended love interest, a strong suspended career interest, and it culminates in a powerful military interest based on the present war. Of course it is not a cinema drama. But it is a thoroughly topical novel, specially suited for the present time, and Munsey's would never have objected to it if they had really wanted my novels. In my opinion, whatever novel I had supplied, Munsey's would have taken exception to that novel, unless they felt sure of being able to resell it as a serial for publication *in instalments*— a purpose for which *The Roll Call* was not designed.

I told Davis that one of the three novels would in all probability be a light novel, and it will be. But Davis, just like

Harpers, was not a bit keen on a light novel at that time. I had made my success in long serious novels that publishers would not take seriously in a commercial sense until the public began to buy them; and, like all editors, Davis specially wanted the kind of thing in which I had made my success. This he has received, and my forecast about plot has been fulfilled.

The objection that *The Roll Call* is a Clayhanger novel is doubly absurd. When the contract was made Davis wanted Clayhanger. He couldn't have too much Clayhanger. The whole contract was founded on Clayhanger. It would never have been made had not Davis desired the kudos of publishing the third Clayhanger novel. Now he seems to imply that Clayhanger was rather forced on him. The fact, however, is that *The Roll Call* is not a Clayhanger novel. It is not a Five Towns novel. It is wholly a London and Paris novel. It is utterly complete in itself. And to argue that it is not so because the adult hero was a child, and of merely episodic interest, in the Clayhanger series, is, to say the least, disingenuous.

My letter from which Davis quotes was a private and informal letter, and I have no copy of it. I am sure, however, that, quoted in full, it will not bear the construction which he endeavours to put on it by the familiar device of separating some sentences from the context. If he objects to this statement let him produce the whole letter. I am sure that I did not fail to defend *These Twain* against his criticism of its plot. Further, after criticising the plot, Davis in his letter to me at the time (which I can produce) became warmly enthusiastic about the novel. This was why I called him 'magnanimous' and unique among editors. Which indeed he was, for he was practically the only editor I have ever known who, having contracted for an expensive contribution, did anything at all except complain that the contribution delivered was not in the least what he had expected. All authors are familiar with this experience. To imply that I used the word 'magnanimous' because Davis out of good-nature accepted something which he didn't want and which he had a moral excuse for refusing is—to use once more a mild word—incorrect.

All the above, of course, has no bearing on the main point, which is Munsey's legal obligations. I am sorry that legal proceedings are necessary to enforce these obligations. They must, however, be taken, and with the utmost promptitude and thoroughness. The third novel comes into the equation. I have written to the Authors' Society telling them to expect you.

Perhaps it would be well for you to send a copy of this letter to Doran. You can quote as much of it as you like to Davis.

Yours sincerely, Arnold Bennett

BUTLER / TS. / 235
(*From J. B. Pinker*)

Talbot House
11th June 1917

My dear Bennett,
I have this morning your two letters. I am sending a copy of your letter to Doran and one to Davis. I think you are most moderate. I cabled to Doran telling him that Davis was trying to avoid payment and my instructions from you were to fight, but asking if it were unavoidable. I shall await Doran's cable before seeing the Authors' Society. Doran will know whether they mean to make us fight or not. I expect Munsey has just thrown it at Davis and told him he must do the best he can. I never suspected Davis of honesty, but I thought he would have been more skilful than he appears in this.

Sincerely yours, J. B. Pinker

BUTLER / TS. / 236
(*From J. B. Pinker*)

Talbot House
2nd July 1917

My dear Bennett,
I have just received the following cable from Doran:—

Your letter June eleventh have had several interviews Davis and Munsey period Under date February nineteen fourteen Bennett wrote Davis definitely stating that London novel concerning Hilda's son was not for sale and stated clearly the three novels that were being discussed for con-

234. *Munsey's Magazine* published *These Twain* in two instalments in 1915. Such publication would not require of a novel the regular curtains that magazines would ordinarily demand of a novel to be issued in a half-dozen or more instalments. Bennett did not provide curtains in *The Roll-Call*, and he assumed that Munsey's would have difficulty selling it to another magazine.

tract period March eleven nineteen fourteen contract was executed upon this understanding so Munsey claims period I am authorised to offer Bennett ten thousand dollars spot cash for final release from contract for second and third novels period Otherwise Munsey will permit your litigation to proceed period My position is solely that of friendly intermediary period Cable decision

I propose now to ask the Author's Society to start proceedings, but before doing so I should like to know whether you have a copy of your letter. I should say that this letter does not really affect the contract, but the solicitors are sure to ask for a copy. . . .

Sincerely yours, J. B. Pinker

BUTLER / T.C.C. / 237

[Comarques]
July 3rd, 1917

My dear Pinker,
Many thanks for your two letters of the 2nd and the enclosures, including cheque for £426.10.8. I return the royalty accounts.

Re Munsey. I have no copy of my letter to Davis of February 1914, nor any recollection of it. I think I had better see you, and shall be glad if you can lunch with me at the Reform on Thursday next at 1.15. This is the only day I shall be in town. Please wire yes or no tomorrow.

Yours sincerely, [Arnold Bennett]

P.S. Please deal with the enclosed letter from Maurice Browne.

BUTLER / TS. / 238
(*From J. B. Pinker*)

Talbot House
16th July 1917

My dear Bennett,
I enclose copy of a letter that I received last week from Doran. I thought you would like to have this, as although it does not

237. Maurice Browne (1881–1955), an English actor and manager, founded the Chicago Little Theatre in 1912 and remained there until 1918. Bennett met him in America in 1911. His letter to Bennett does not survive.

give an actual copy of the letter you wanted to see, Doran has evidently seen it. . . .

Sincerely yours, J. B. Pinker

BUTLER / T.C. / 239
(*From G. H. Doran to J. B. Pinker*)

[38 West 32nd Street]
[New York]
29 June 1917

My dear Pinker,

I cabled you yesterday as attached. I am not going to elaborate upon that cable in this letter, for anything I might now say would be entirely superseded by a cable advice from you. Nor do I propose for a moment to become a part of a controversy in which I am not concerned except to the extent that I would not see disagreement between such dear friends of mine as those involved in the present difficulty, for you know the fellow who steps in to stop a fight usually comes off the worst used up of all concerned.

This much I should tell you: I have seen a letter written by A. B. on the Berkeley Hotel paper but dated from Comarques, February 1, 1914, in which he states about as follows: 'I am afraid I inadvertently misled you last evening. The London novel of Hilda's son is not for sale. The three novels which are available are the third volume of the Clayhanger, a humorous novel in the vein of *Buried Alive*, and a novel dealing with fashionable American and English hotel life on the Riviera and in other continental resorts, a novel which I have long had in mind to do in an ironic vein.' This is the substance of the letter an exact copy of which I am sure I could secure for you for the asking. On this letter Munsey and Davis claim they predicated the contract of March 11, 1914.

I have no comment to make upon the offer made by Munsey other than to tell you that I am unwilling to enter into the fight, still I am not willing to shirk the slightest part of the obligations and privileges of friendship; so command me in any way you choose.

Very sincerely, [George H. Doran]

239. On the novel in the vein of *Buried Alive*, see Bennett's letter of 23 February 1911, and the footnote. The hotel novel (*Imperial Palace*) was deferred another twelve years, and its subject was the Savoy Hotel in London.

BUTLER / MS. / 240

[? London]
[about 17 July 1917]

My dear Pinker,
    Many thanks for your two letters.

Cassells

I return the agreement signed and initialled.

Milestones

I enclose copy of letter from Thring. I doubt if this matter is
not Lee Mathews'. Anyhow he is ill just now.

Munsey

My letter to Davis seems rather categoric.

Yours sincerely, [Arnold Bennett]

BUTLER / TS. / 241
(*From J. B. Pinker*)

Talbot House
27th July 1917

My dear Bennett,
    I have this morning received by cable from New York the
money for the Munsey serial. It amounts to £3,668 : 15 :, and
I enclose, herewith, a cheque for the amount, less commission.
    I need not say that I am very glad this has come off. In face
of your warning of your dislike for litigation I did not like
running the risk, but I had either to accept Munsey's offer or

240. This letter is reproduced from a draft written by Bennett on a blank page of
Pinker's letter to him of 16 July.

Cassell published *The Lion's Share* in 1916, and Bennett was now arranging for
them to be his regular publisher. He went to Cassell through the urging of H. G.
Wells.

G. Herbert Thring was investigating a possibly unauthorized production of
Milestones in the United States. Lee Mathews was still acting as Bennett's dramatic
agent for old plays.

face that risk. It was obvious that Doran was not willing to stand up to Munsey, and meant to limit his part to the transmission of messages. I could not therefore test Munsey's temperature through Doran. The great difficulty in dealing with Munsey is that one never knows when he will bolt. When he does bolt he is a crazy creature, with an ungovernable temper. Your attitude is always of great help to me. There are few authors with courage enough to leave things to the agent and then abstain from fussing. You can understand that it tends to spoil one's nerve in a crisis like this if one's client fusses, and one requires all one's courage to get the good solution.

I have given Munsey leave to re-sell the story, but it is to be free for volume publication within twelve months.

Sincerely yours, J. B. Pinker

241. The original contract with Munsey called for a payment of $17,500 for each of two serials following *These Twain*, with an option on two more. The contract was ended with Munsey paying the sum for *The Roll-Call*. He published *The Roll-Call* in seven instalments beginning in April 1918. In *Chronicles of Barabbas* Doran describes Munsey as 'an intellectual mummy'; in contrast he praises Davis as a brilliant and trustworthy man who 'permitted himself to come under the Munsey blight'. At the beginning of the crisis, before the issue arose of the character of *The Roll-Call*, Davis had tried to arrange with Pinker the re-selling of the novels, and Pinker's response on this point elicited the following letter from Munsey on 29 March 1917.

'Dear Sir :—

I am writing you in response to your letter of February 9 to our Mr. Robert H. Davis, in which you say you will undertake the re-sale of the Arnold Bennett novels on the usual terms of a ten per cent commission. This letter from you is in answer to a letter Mr. Davis wrote you at my direction, asking if you could not place the Bennett novels elsewhere, as we now have no use for them, the plan of publishing complete novels having reached a point where we found it unwise to continue it further.

Under these circumstances, I assumed that as a matter of courtesy, particularly since we have done a good deal of business with you at one time and another, it would be your pleasure, as it would be my pleasure, and as it would be the pleasure of American business men generally, under similar circumstances, to make a strong effort to relieve us from taking these novels, and to do this without the exaction of a ten per cent commission, or any commission whatever, for an act of simple courtesy to a house that has been a good customer of yours.

From the foregoing you will doubtless get the impression that your attitude, as stated in your letter, is anything but pleasing to me. If, however, you still have any doubt about it, let me make it plainer. I wouldn't pay you ten per cent for what you ought to do if you have right ideas and right ideals, if it came to a matter of paying for the Bennett novels in full and then throwing them into the furnace. I hope this is amply clear.

You may therefore do whatever you please with regard to the Bennett novels, whatever is most representative of the type of man you are.

Yours very truly, Frank A. Munsey'

BUTLER / T.C.C. / 242

[Comarques]
December 3rd, 1917

My dear Pinker,

Many thanks for yours of the 30th and the enclosures including the cheque.

The novel has been considerably delayed through pressure
of other work, and illness. I am, however, sure to finish it before
the end of January. The mischief is that up to the present I have
searched for a title in vain. I enclose a paragraph.

Yours sincerely, [Arnold Bennett]

BUTLER / TS. / 243
(*From J. B. Pinker*)

Talbot House
5th February 1918

My dear Bennett,

I think I had better let you see a letter that I have just
received from Lawrence. He does not know that I am showing
it to you, and I shall not tell him you have seen it unless you
approve my doing so.

Sincerely yours, J. B. Pinker

COLLECTED LETTERS OF D. H. LAWRENCE / 244
(*From D. H. Lawrence to J. B. Pinker*)

Chapel Farm Cottage
nr Newbury
2 February 1918

My dear Pinker:

I am sorry to tell you that I am coming to the last end of all
my resources, as far as money goes. Do you think that Arnold
Bennett or somebody like that, who is quite rich out of literature, would give me something to get along with. It is no use
my trying to delude myself that I can make money in this world

242. The novel, whose working title and final title was *The Pretty Lady*, was
finished on 28 January. The paragraph was for an advertisement of it.

243. D. H. Lawrence (1885-1930) had Pinker for his agent from about 1912 to
1920. See page 26.

that is. But there is coming a big smash-up, after which my day will begin. And as the smash-up is not far off, so I am not very far off from a walk-in. . . .

Do try and tempt a little money out of some rich good-natured author for me, will you—or I don't know what I shall do. And really, you know, one can't begin taking one's hat off to money, at this late hour of the day. I'd rather play a tin whistle in the street. What a lively world! . . .

[D. H. Lawrence]

U.C. / MS. / 245

80, Picc. [Piccadilly]
[Royal Thames Yacht Club]
6th Feby 1918

My dear Pinker,

Lawrence

What a characteristic letter, and how unpromising for the future! I am not prepared to keep Lawrence, nor to give him a lump sum, as I doubt if the latter would help him very much. As to the vast fall in my income, I need only point out to you that it is about half what it was, & that I am keeping a number of people. I would willingly subscribe something towards a regular fund for Lawrence, say £1 a week for at least a year, if you think this would help and if you could get other subscriptions. So far as I am concerned there is no reason why he should know the names of the donors.

Pretty Lady

I want 3 sets of proofs. Please get Cassells to send me a third set of galleys 1-11, and to send three sets in future.

New Play

I was expecting an answer here to my letter to you of Friday. I hope you got the letter.

Samuelson

I have had no report for a long time as to this arbitration. I should like to know just how this, & any other pending matter, is going on.

Yours sincerely, Arnold Bennett

P.S. I return Lawrence's letter.   A. B.

u.c. / ms. / 246

80, Piccadilly
10-4-18

My dear Pinker,

Many thanks for yours of the 9th. I should prefer to start the column at the end of May, but if necessary I can begin it in the middle of May.

I return Cochran's letter.

As regards the boycott of the *P.L.* this is a matter for Cassells. I have asked them to send a review copy to the *Cambridge Magazine.* They have not yet sent a review copy to the *New Statesman*, or an advertisement! Nevertheless large numbers of people will look for a review in the *N.S.* Kindly see to this at once.

If Machen's onslaught is worse than Jimmy Douglas's in the *Star*, it will be a treat. I think Courtney's review in the *D.T.*

---

245. Bennett admired Lawrence mainly as an artist. In 1913 he recommended to the Stage Society that they should consider producing Lawrence's plays. In 1915 he and May Sinclair were the only two writers who publicly protested against the banning of *The Rainbow*. And during the present year he and Galsworthy were apparently ready to support a private edition of *Women in Love*, which had not yet found a publisher. Lawrence knew of Bennett's recommendation to the Stage Society. In 1915 he suggested to Pinker that Bennett and others might like to contribute money to him. And later in 1918, when Bennett held a government position, Lawrence wrote to him, 'I hear you think highly of me and my genius, give me some work.' Bennett replied, as quoted by Frieda Lawrence in *Not I, but the Wind* . . ., 'Yes, I do think highly of your genius, but that is no reason why I should give you work.' On the present occasion, support from other writers was not forthcoming, and Bennett contributed £25 on his own. He apparently contributed money on at least one other occasion. In the late twenties, in a letter to Aldous Huxley, who was a fairly close friend of Bennett's, Lawrence described Bennett as a 'sort of pig in clover'.

The new play was *The Title*, which Bennett began on 24 March.

The Samuelson Company arbitration possibly concerned the film version of *Milestones* that the firm had made (see page 241n.). A new version was made by the Goldwyn Pictures Corporation in 1920.

ought to be quoted. I have received numerous letters of congratulation as to the book. And yesterday Sir Alfred Hopkinson, late principal of Manchester University, and a strong mid-Victorian, stopped me in order to offer his laudations!

[Arnold Bennett]

u.c. / ts. / 247

Comarques
April 14th, 1918

My dear Pinker,

Many thanks for your letter of the 12th and the enclosure. As neither Swinnerton nor I seem to be satisfied with the proof pages of *Don Juan* and as there is apparently no probability of being able to get anything better just now, we have decided that it will be better to let the scheme stand over for the present. I return Doran's letter. He is evidently anxious to please, and I always appreciate that.

I enclose a letter just received from Hugo Vallentin, with which please deal. I have told him that you will do so.

I propose to call on you on Tuesday morning about 12 or 12.15 about a personal matter. I have been asked to take a rather important post in the Ministry of Information, and I do not see how I can refuse. It will, however, mean my living in

246. The new column began on 19 May in *Lloyd's Weekly Newspaper*, which was just on the verge of changing its name to *Lloyd's Sunday News*. In a letter to his friend F. S. A. Lowndes of *The Times*, Bennett wrote: '*Lloyd's Weekly News* have contracted to pay me £100 a week for a weekly 1,500-word article. I offered to bet Pinker he wouldn't get £100 a week. He wouldn't bet, but he said if he didn't get it he wouldn't agree to me taking the contract at all. Other people can say what they like, but I say: Give me Pinker.'

Charles Cochran (1873–1951), whose activities ranged from managing Sarah Bernhardt in England to introducing roller-skating in France, was interested in producing *Don Juan de Marana*.

The Pretty Lady was being boycotted by booksellers in Cambridge and Bath, and attacked by Arthur Machen (1863–1947) and James Douglas (1867–1940) in the *Evening News* and the *Star*. The review by W. L. Courtney (1850–1928) in the *Daily Telegraph* was very favourable. Bennett wrote to Hugh Walpole: 'Most of the reviews of the *P.L.* so far are specially footling. Astonishing the number of critics who daren't *mention* that the chief character is a whore!' The chief character was also a Catholic, and the Catholic Federation threatened Cassell with an action against the book. In May, W. H. Smith banned the book from their stalls. By September the book had sold 30,000 copies in England, a goodly number for a Bennett novel.

London, and transferring my secretary, Miss Nerney, to London. I expect that I shall be able to arrange for her to work in the Ministry of Information with me, but she will also have private work to do for me, and for this purpose, and for keeping all my office apparatus, I shall require a room. Now, the Ministry of Information is in Norfolk Street, and it has occurred to me that you may possibly have a room for which you have no particular use and that we might come to some arrangement by which you would sub-let it to me. Perhaps you will think over this beautiful scheme.

Yours sincerely, Arnold Bennett

U.C. / MS. / 248

80, Piccadilly
25th June 1918

My dear Pinker,

I do wish you had been in town yesterday. Vedrenne wanted to see me urgently about *The Title*, & I was obliged to see him, though I had no time or thoughts for my own business. He wants to produce *The Title at once* at the Royalty. He says *Marmaduke* at the Haymarket will probably be a success. (It is a most footling play.) He suggested Boucicault & Irene Vanbrugh for the chief parts. I ruled Boucicault absolutely out. His alternative was Aubrey Smith & Helen Haye, who would do. On reflection, I cannot understand his hurry. I wrote the play for Eadie. I told him several times that I was disgusted at Eadie not playing in it. Of course I *can* refuse anybody but Eadie. Then that may hold up the play indefinitely. On the other hand it may not. You must understand that yesterday I *provisionally agreed* to Aubrey Smith & Helen Haye if he could get them, though I told him flatly I didn't like the scheme at all. Today I

247. *Don Juan de Marana* was first published in 1923, in a private edition issued by T. Werner Laurie.

Hugo Vallentin was negotiating Swedish rights to Bennett's novels and plays.

Bennett became director of British propaganda in France. The Ministry of Information was headed by Lord Beaverbrook (1879–1964), of whom Bennett wrote in his journal: 'Beaverbrook asked me to accept the directorship. . . . He said no one could know French psychology better than I do—this conclusion he drew from reading *The Pretty Lady*!' He and Bennett became good friends. Bennett apparently used quarters at the Ministry for his private work. Miss Nerney (d. 1964) had been his secretary since 1912. See page 167n.

should like the matter to be reconsidered, & I want you to go & see him, & tell him I think he is being too precipitate, & that I don't understand his immense haste, & that anyhow a delay of a few months can't harm the play. Marguerite has some ideas about the affair & I have asked her to go & see you this morning at 10:45. She is always apt to be suspicious of others in all business affairs, but her ideas seem to me rather convincing, & she will tell you them. Perhaps you can see Vedrenne this morning, & report to me. I have to leave the office at 4:30 today. I write this before breakfast.

My objection to the scheme of Vedrenne is by no means confined to the absence of Eadie from the cast. I should much prefer the play to be done at the Haymarket. But of course we can't insist at all on that, & it would perhaps even be impolite to mention it. The Royalty is the theatre mentioned by name in the contract.

Yours sincerely, Arnold Bennett

BUTLER / T.C.C. / 249

[80, Piccadilly]
July 18th, 1918

My dear Pinker,

The contract with Lloyds is now drawing to a close, and although I have been satisfied with the quality of the articles, I do not think that it will be renewed. Some weeks ago Gardiner told me that the *Daily News* would like me to write once a week instead of once a fortnight. I said I would think it over, and I then told him that if I was free later on I would be glad to write once a week, but that the price of the articles would have to approximate more closely to the market price. I also said

248. On J. E. Vedrenne see page 186. He obtained an option on *The Title* in 1916, when the play had barely taken shape in Bennett's mind. Bennett wrote it in six weeks, finishing it on 18 May 1918. It opened at the Royalty on 20 July, with C. Aubrey Smith (1863–1948) as Mr. Culver, Eva Moore as Mrs. Culver, Leslie Howard as John Culver, and Nigel Playfair as Sampson Straight. It was well received. Helen Haye (b. 1874) had played Janet Cannot in *The Great Adventure* in 1913. Dion Boucicault (1859–1929) had produced and starred in *The Honeymoon* in 1911. He and Bennett quarrelled. Irene Vanbrugh (d. 1949), Boucicault's wife, starred in several Barrie plays.

Marmaduke, by Ernest Denny (1869–1943) and starring Eadie, ran at the Haymarket only until 27 July.

that it would be better for you and the manager of the *Daily News* to discuss the question of price. Since then I have heard nothing further.

I now leave the matter to you. No doubt you will first ascertain the notions of Donald.

Yours sincerely, [Arnold Bennett]

P.S. Danish-Norwegian rights of *The Pretty Lady*; yes.

U.C. / MS. / 250

Walton Park Hotel
Clevedon
Somerset
12–9–18

My dear Pinker,

Frank Rutter has been running for some little time a quarterly called *Art & Letters*. I have promised Captain Osbert Sitwell (5 Swan Walk, Chelsea), representing a group of young poets & artists, to acquire the same & stand the modest racket thereof. It is not a commercial proposition. I am ready to give Rutter enough to pay the debts on the thing, on the understanding that the sum does not exceed £100. I should be very grateful to you if, as a friendly act, you would see to the transfer of the ownership from Rutter to me, in proper form; and I will ask Sitwell to call on you anyhow. Secondly Chatto & Windus will publish the thing & look after it, on any terms agreed by Swinnerton & me. Do you think your good nature would carry you so far as to settle these terms with F. S.?

I shall be here till about the 23rd. I understand that on my return I am to be promoted at the Ministry to be the acting Director of *all* propaganda except propaganda in enemy countries. Some job! I absolutely deny that I have done anything as controller of French propaganda to deserve this dizzy elevation.

249. Lloyds renewed the contract. The *Daily News* articles were resumed in January 1917 after being discontinued in May of the previous year. A. G. Gardiner raised the price from 20 to 35 guineas per article.

Sir Robert Donald, editor of the *Daily Chronicle*, was serving as a Director in the Ministry of Information. At least a few of Bennett's articles for England as well as for America were written for the Government.

L.A.B.—T

You might on Monday send me details of this week's *Title* takings.

Yours sincerely, Arnold Bennett

TEXAS / MS. / 251

Comarques
29–9–18

My dear Pinker,
Please deal with the enclosed.
I am now not merely director of Propaganda at the M. of I., but *head* of the whole ministry, with authority over all departments, under the Minister himself. I cannot understand it, & don't like it. But I was not the man to refuse.

Yours, A. B.

250. The Bennetts were on a holiday in Clevedon from 10 to 26 September.
Art and Letters, edited by Frank Rutter (1876–1937), was a handsome *avant-garde* magazine. It survived until 1920, publishing Eliot, Pound, Wyndham Lewis, the Sitwells, and Huxley. In *Noble Essences* Osbert Sitwell (1892–) describes meeting Bennett for the first time and speaking vehemently to him about the need of younger poets for an outlet for their work. Bennett seemed unimpressed. The next morning Sitwell received a letter from him saying he would back such a venture. For various reasons, the proposal could not be carried through. Up to this time, Sitwell had published only a single volume of verse, in collaboration with his sister.
251. In an article, 'The Greatest Moment', Bennett describes his elevation:
'Imagine a wayward novelist, with no experience of bureaucratic methods, having dominion over hundreds of exalted persons, including Bank directors, railway directors, historians, K.C.'s, heads of trusts, poets, and generals! You cannot. At least I could not. I told a Minister that I could not sleep for responsibility. He said:
"You will get used to it."
The strange thing is that I did.
Great and awful days! What tales I could tell of rival Ministries fighting one another quite as tenaciously as the Allied armies fought the German armies— and with far more bitterness. A friend of mine in the War Office told me that an order had been issued forbidding any member of his section, under any pretext whatever, to enter my Ministry.
Still, when I visited the War Office, even the mightiest swells had to see me. Which was something.
I had a few Generals of my own. I remember the first time I rang the bell and said to one of my secretaries:
"Ask General X if he will be good enough to come and see me at once."
And General X came and was received in audience. A great moment for a novelist! . . . I felt that I was doing something to redress the balance on behalf of all privates, and all officers from Colonels downwards, in all the British armies.'

U.C. / MS. / 252

> 80, Piccadilly
> 27–10–18

My dear Pinker,

I will write a 40,000 word book (roughly divided into 10 equal chapters) on women provided you can place the serial rights at a good figure in U.S.A. I ought to make more out of the book there than here, so that the total received at date of volume publication ought not to be less than £2,500. I repeat my warning to you that there will necessarily be some plain speaking in the book, & subjects must be dealt with that are not often dealt with. Of course the phrasing will be as ingeniously decent as I know how to make it.

Nor will there be any sentimentality in the book about women. In fact, controversy will assuredly be aroused!

> Yours sincerely, Arnold Bennett

BUTLER / TS. / 253
(*From J. B. Pinker*)
PRIVATE

> Talbot House
> 8th November 1918

My dear Bennett,

As soon as the armistice is signed, Eric and I are most anxious to get him out of the Army. Can you help us? He is as anxious as I am that he should get back to work. I have had no holiday for five years, and you know what difficulties I have had to keep going for the last four years. I do not see that there can be any serious reason against his release once the fighting is finished, but unless one does something he will probably be kept loitering about month after month to his disgust and disadvantage.

> Sincerely yours, J. B. Pinker

252. *Our Women* was issued serially in *Cassell's Magazine* and *Cosmopolitan* beginning in December 1919. The plain and decent language included the opinions 'that women have a tendency to general negligence when the eye of none but a husband can thereby be afflicted', 'that in the region of creative intellect there are things which men almost habitually do but which women have not done and give practically no sign of ever being able to do', and that 'a husband should . . . be compelled by legislation to disclose fully his financial situation to his wife and to allot to her a percentage of his net income for her private and uncontrolled use'.

u.c. / ts. / 254

80, Piccadilly
November 8th, 1918

My dear Pinker,

I have consulted M.S.2—which is the department at the War Office concerned with these matters—and I am told that there is nothing whatever to be done at this end. If application were made here it would simply be referred to France and the usual stereotyped answer given. I am advised that the best course is for Eric to put in—through his C.O.— an application for permission to relinquish his commission, and that there is a good chance of it being favourably considered, as a scheme of partial demobilisation is already on the carpet. I do not think it would be any use my appealing to Reginald Brade; and I do not care to approach Milner, first because the matter is not important enough (from his point of view), and second because I had a great public scrap with him in the *Daily News* in which I reckon that he did not come off best.

Yours sincerely, Arnold Bennett

u.c. / ts. / 255

80, Piccadilly
December 10th, 1918

My dear Pinker,

Many thanks for your letter of the 9th. I do not think it would be proper to let Harpers have the book about the Modern Woman, unless Doran had previously refused to pay the same terms as they offered. I know that nothing binds me to Doran. Nevertheless, he is my regular publisher, and I should not be easy in my mind if anything was done behind his back.

Yours sincerely, Arnold Bennett

254. Bennett once described Alfred Viscount Milner (1854–1925) as a person 'with the imagination and elasticity of Portland Stone'. He attacked him on several occasions for his German background, his record in South Africa, and his current policies as a member of the War Cabinet, particularly his advocacy of the conscription bill. Bennett discussed the conscription issue in an article 'Clatter and Racket', which appeared in the *Daily News* on 24 September 1915. Milner replied on 29 September. Bennett made a rejoinder with 'Last Words on Conscription' on 5 October. See Bennett's comments on the issue on page 235n.

Reginald Brade (1864–1933) was Secretary at the War Office from 1914 to 1920.

255. Doran published the book. Pinker was proposing a £500 advance and a royalty of 20 per cent. to Harper's.

80, PICCADILLY,

W. 1.

27 - 10 - 18

dear Pinker

I will write a 40,000 word book
(roughly divided into 10 equal chapters) on women
provided you can place the serial rights at a good
figure in U. S. A. I ought to make more out of
the book there than here, so that the total received
at date of volume publication ought not to be less
than £2,500. I repeat my warning to you
that there will necessarily be some plain speaking in
the book, & subjects must be dealt with that are
not often dealt with. Of course the phrasing will
be as ingeniously decent as I knew how to
make it.

Nor will there be any sentimentality
in the book about women. In fact, controversy
will assuredly be aroused!

Yours sincerely
Arnold Bennett

u.c. / ts. / 256

Comarques
January 9th, 1919

My dear Pinker,

Many thanks for your letter of the 7th. I telegraphed you as follows this morning:—

> *Don Juan.* Please conclude contract with McCarthy at once. Returns not enclosed with your letter.

I have not the slightest intention of altering my terms with Dean. He wrote to me asking for another appointment, and I enclose copy of my reply. I do not know when I can deliver a new play to Dean. We can discuss that when the terms of the contract are settled.

As to Doran's project for cheap books, I leave that entirely to you. It seems to me a device for advertising his *Bookman*. I do not think that any of the later books ought to be included.

Yours sincerely, Arnold Bennett

u.c. / t.c.c. / 257
(*To Basil Dean*)

[Comarques]
January 9th, 1919

Dear Captain Dean,

Many thanks for your letter of the 7th. It will be impossible for me to give myself the pleasure of seeing you until next month, as I am very busy here and shall not come to London.

I hear from Mr. Pinker that you want my terms modified. This cannot be done. To ask that the royalty should be lowered until the receipts reach the paying level and should then be

256. Lillah McCarthy (1875–1960) the actress—formerly Mrs. Granville Barker and soon to be Lady Keeble—was interested in producing *Don Juan de Marana.* Bennett was now writing his play *Judith* that she had persuaded him to write. The returns were for *The Title.*

Basil Dean (1888–), who several years earlier had organized the Liverpool Repertory Theatre, was now undertaking the management of the Aldwych. He produced there the play abandoned by Doris Keane, *Sacred and Profane Love.* The play opened on 10 November 1919, with Iris Hoey and Franklin Dyall in the leading roles. In 1920 Dean rejected Bennett's new play, *The Bright Island.*

Doran was contemplating a $1.00 reprint series. He had bought the *Bookman* from Dodd, Mead a few months earlier.

increased, means that the author is to share the risks of the manager in addition to taking his own risks. I have no intention of doing this. Even if the royalty were increased to 20% beyond the paying level, 5% being paid up to that level, I doubt whether the result would be as good for the author as 10% all through. And I need not say that neither you nor any other manager would give 20% above the paying level. I know something about the question of royalties, and I am quite sure that with any sort of a success the manager makes far more than the author. I know that the managerial profits from *Milestones* were more than five times the profits of the authors. And I also know that at the present time the managerial profits of *The Title* are twice those of the author.

I do not make these observations as a basis for discussion between you and me. The negotiations for my contracts are exclusively in the hands of Mr. Pinker.

Yours sincerely, [Arnold Bennett]

u.c. / ts. / 258

Comarques
January 15th, 1919

My dear Pinker,

I have received some copies of *The Roll Call*. They are odious in a very high degree. I do not complain of the quality of the paper, but I object to there being two half-titles, one before the title and the other after it! I object more strongly to the illustrated cover being passed without reference to the author and still more strongly to the descriptive matter not being submitted to the author. The description of the book inside the jacket: 'Can a man love two women is the theme of this book,' is perfectly ridiculous and extremely misleading. Really Hutchinsons ought to have more sense than to make fools of themselves and of me in this style.

The cover is merely painful.

Yours sincerely, Arnold Bennett

258. *The Roll-Call* was the only one of Bennett's books that Hutchinsons published.

U.C. / TS. / 259

Comarques
January 16th, 1919

My dear Pinker,

As you know, Doran wants me to write some articles for his *Bookman*, and he does not want to pay too much for them. I should like to oblige him, if this is possible, and I have decided that I will write six articles for him of 1,500 words each, chiefly about the theatre. The only question is the price. I have discussed this with him, and I think that I shall be prepared to accept £200 for the six. He quite understands that this is a special price for him, and that it is not to form a precedent. It is understood that he is to talk the matter over with you tomorrow and to settle it, and that you are not absolutely bound by what I have said to him.

Yours sincerely, Arnold Bennett

P.S. I have shown this to Doran.

BUTLER / TS. / 260
(*From J. B. Pinker*)

Talbot House
30th January 1919

My dear Bennett,

I enclose a cutting from the *Westminster Gazette* that I thought might interest Sardonyx. Sir Albert Stanley omits to say that the reason there is more tonnage available than they have cargoes for is because the Government will not allow cargoes to be shipped. I expect you know, but the general public does not know, that the Government has throughout the War been the biggest profiteer in the country, and it is persisting in this policy now. It will not allow stuffs to be shipped here until it has sold all its stocks of feed and raw material. It is trying to sell them at top War prices, and of course buyers refuse to buy, fearing they will be left to unload them on to a falling market. The Government is of course trying to force buyers to take the stock simply by prohibiting imports. If the subject interests you, I will get you some further details.

Sincerely yours, J. B. Pinker

U.C. / TS. / 261

Comarques

March 1st, 1919

My dear Pinker,

Leonard Rees, editor of the *Sunday Times*, called on me on Thursday and asked me for the serial rights of my next novel. I referred him to you, and as he put himself to the trouble of calling on me perhaps you will be good enough to call on him. I said I did not know whether the serial rights of my next novel were sold or not, that nothing could be done for over a year, and that in any case the price was high.

I do not suppose that anything can be done, but it will possibly be worth while to keep the *Sunday Times* on the end of

259. The *Bookman* did not publish the theatre articles. They were published in England in the *Daily Express*, beginning 26 January 1921.

260. 'Sardonyx' was Bennett's signature for his weekly column of anonymous 'Observations' in the *New Statesman*. Pinker offered him likely material on several occasions. On 8 February the following paragraphs appeared.

'Considering the experience of shippers, the statement of Sir Albert Stanley [1874–1948; at that time head of the Board of Trade] at Huddersfield—"There is more tonnage available than we have cargoes for"—sounded exceedingly odd. In fact, it gave away the whole Government show. For, be it known that of all war profiteers the Government is the greatest. When the Government started to control, it consulted brokers and merchants as to the proper percentage to be added to cost price to cover warehousing, insurance during warehousing, and a fair profit. The answer was that ten per cent on cost was a bit more than merchants were accustomed to get. Well, Dora forbids the enterprising journalist to disclose the prices at which the Government buys or sells controlled commodities. Therefore, although I have taken pains to gather some exact information, I cannot publish it in really attractive form. But I can get half-way round Dora by calling six commodities, chosen at random from scores, A, B, C, D, E and F. I am in a position to state positively that on commodity A the Government makes a profit of 28 per cent, on B a profit of 45 per cent, on C a profit of 30 per cent, on D a profit of 21 per cent, on E a profit of 60 per cent, and on F a profit of 16 per cent. I guarantee these figures.

'What has all this to do with shipping? First, it must be pointed out that the alleged lifting of control from certain commodities by a magnanimous Government is a farce. For the importer still cannot import without a license to do so, and the importer is not in the least likely to obtain a license so long as the Government has any stocks to dispose of. Shipping facilities, therefore, are doled out, not in accordance with cargo space available, but in inverse ratio to the Government's desire to make profits. Now, the Government consists of Departments, and each Department is anxious for profit, and for much profit; and the entire affair has degenerated into a grand departmental game. The game is departmentally so delightful that in order to continue playing it, Departments are willing to stand the horrid abuse which they receive *viva voce* from Colonial shippers in particular.'

a string. I see no prospect of even beginning a novel for at least a year, as I am full up with plays.

Yours sincerely, Arnold Bennett

BUTLER / TS. / 262
(*From J. B. Pinker*)

Talbot House
25th April 1919

My dear Bennett,

Methuen proposed to do a 2/- edition of *Whom God Hath Joined* and offered a royalty of 2d. per copy on this. I protested against this, and told Methuen that I felt sure you would not be willing to accept less than 3d. a copy. Methuen says that in these circumstances he will have to abandon the idea. The cost of paper has gone down very considerably, the cost of binding has gone down to some extent—though not to a very large extent—but against this the printers have increased their charges. What happens is that the workmen ask for a rise of wages, and the printers add a very big profit and pass it on to the publisher. The publisher is passing it on to the author, and it seems to me that so long as the author will bear the load he will be left to bear it. Even with the increase in the printing, I think Methuen should be able to pay a better royalty than they propose. It is, of course, a matter for your decision, and I shall be glad to have your instructions as soon as you have considered it.

Sincerely yours, J. B. Pinker

U.C. / TS. / 263
(*To Eric Pinker*)

Comarques
June 14th 1919

My dear Eric,

I am writing to you officially on behalf of the Lyric, Hammersmith, about St. John Ervine's play *John Ferguson*.

261. Leonard Rees (1856–1932) edited the *Sunday Times* from 1901 until his death. Bennett wrote four plays in 1919 and 1920: *Judith*, *Body and Soul*, *The Bright Island*, and *The Love Match*. He also did an adaptation of *The Beggar's Opera*. His next novel was *Mr. Prohack*, begun in October 1920.

262. Bennett declined the 2d. royalty.

We all think it is a very fine play, and although we are by no means sure of its drawing powers, we should like to produce it if terms can be arranged.

The financial terms you will of course discuss with our business manager. But there are two other points of great importance. The play is an Irish play and would have to be played throughout with an Irish accent. This is never satisfactory, and it would certainly militate against the success of the play in London. I venture to suggest to the author the possibility of transferring the scene to England and the changing of some of the Irish idioms. I fully realise the artistic difficulties of this process and I do no more than suggest it for his consideration, in his interest as well as in ours.

I strongly urge a change in the title. After *Abraham Lincoln*, the public would very probably think that this play was another history of a man, which it is not. Moreover, there is no attractiveness or descriptive value in the present title.

I should consider it an honour for our theatre to produce this play.

I am exceedingly busy next week. Can you possibly call and see me at the Yacht Club on Tuesday at 3 p.m. I cannot come along to you just then, and if we cannot meet then I see no opportunity of us meeting next week. Please send a line to the Club.

Yours sincerely, Arnold Bennett

263. The Lyric Theatre, Hammersmith, was bought in 1918 by Nigel Playfair (1874–1934), who was then acting in *The Title*. He had been on the stage since 1902, and with this venture became a manager. Bennett learned of the enterprise and raised capital for it; and he and Playfair and Alistair Tayler (d. 1935) became the Directors. Their first production was A. A. Milne's *Make Believe*, which opened on 24 December 1918. The following February they had their first success, John Drinkwater's *Abraham Lincoln*; and in 1920 and 1924 they had extraordinary successes with *The Beggar's Opera* (adapted by Bennett) and *The Way of the World*. They also produced *As You Like It*, *The Merry Wives of Windsor*, *The Rivals*, *The Cherry Orchard*, and (at the Regent Theatre) Capek's *The Insect Play*. *John Ferguson*, by St. John Ervine (1888–), produced on 3 February 1920 with its County Down setting, was coolly received. In America at the same time it had a considerable success.

In his Introduction to Playfair's *The Story of the Lyric Theatre Hammersmith*, Bennett observes:

' . . . no play or piece has been given which the Directors . . . did not unanimously believe to have considerable artistic merit. There is no exception to this. West End managers are fond of referring to the Lyric Board as amateurs. Nevertheless the Lyric Board, in face of some unique difficulties, has successfully

u.c. / ts. / 264

> 12B George Street
> Hanover Square W.1.
> June 25th 1919

My dear Eric,

You flatter me. I have to deliver a play to Edyth Goodall on August 21st; a play to Basil Dean at the end of the year; and a play to Vedrenne and Eadie at the end of March. You may be perfectly certain that after this debauch of work I shall be compelled to take three months holiday. The terms you are likely to obtain for my next novel are very good indeed; but, seeing that I have already contracted to deliver six short stories, beginning December 1920, I do not see how I can possibly hope to deliver any part of the novel until the early months of 1921. I can easily divide the novel into instalments, each ending with a curtain; but I cannot agree to submit any portion of the actual novel to the *Cosmopolitan* in advance. I imagine that the senior partner will agree with me in this attitude.

> Yours sincerely, Arnold Bennett

P.S. Please note address.   A. B.

---

remained in management for seven years, and the Lyric Theatre has made handsome profits, on the policy of trusting the intelligence of the public.'
Playfair later notes of his fellow directors: 'they have . . . had their full share of worry and responsibility; and, by the terms on which they entered the concern, they have given themselves no opportunity of any material profit, and very little of any of the rewards of fame.'

264. 12B George Street, opposite St. George's Church, became the Bennetts' London flat. Bennett kept it until the end of 1922.

Edyth Goodall, the actress (1886–1929), had an option on *Body and Soul*, Dean on *The Bright Island*, and Vedrenne and Eadie on *The Love Match*. All the options lapsed.

Eric Pinker elicited an offer of £1,500 from Hutchinsons for serial rights to *Mr. Prohack*. In America the novel was serialized by *Delineator*, not *Cosmopolitan*, beginning July 1921. In England the *Westminster Gazette* began publishing it on 7 November 1921.

The six stories were possibly 'The Fish', 'Nine O'Clock Tomorrow' (also called 'The Lost Girl'), 'Mr. Jack Hollins and Destiny' (also called 'Entirely Reasonable'), 'Last Love', 'The Mysterious Destruction of Mr. Lewis Ipple', and 'The Yacht'. Available magazine files are incomplete, and a full account of serial publication cannot be given. The stories appeared in England in *Nash's and Pall Mall Magazine* in April 1922, May 1922, August 1922, April 1923 (uncertain; the story also appeared through mischance in the *Storyteller* of the same date), December 1921, and December 1922. The first three stories also appeared in America in *Cosmopolitan*

u.c. / ts. / 265

Comarques
6th October 1919

My dear Pinker,

Many thanks for your two letters of the 3rd. I return all the enclosures except your account.

With reference to Professor Ganguli's letter to Messrs. Chatto & Windus, my answer is that I will not entertain the proposal. It is obvious that a man who is capable of calling the book *The Best of Bennett* is not capable of making a proper selection. Moreover I do not care for the idea to be executed in India.

Yours sincerely, Arnold Bennett

u.c. / ts. / 266

12B George Street
January 8th 1920

My dear Pinker,

I felt all the time you were here yesterday that I had forgotten something. I had. I particularly wanted to ask you whether you had any intention of going to the U.S.A. soon. It seems to me that some useful work might be done there in the way of enquiring into the whole film situation. Both the Selwyns are in big companies, and each is in a different company. My belief is that American authors who are on the spot get higher prices than English authors. Anyhow I am convinced that the film business, so far as I am concerned, has a bigger future than I thought a year or two ago.

Yours sincerely, Arnold Bennett

P.S. I have asked John Wright, the author of that Venetian etching that I showed you, to send a good proof of it to you. The price, I think, will be about 3 guineas.   A. B.

---

in December 1921, January 1922, and April 1922; the fourth appeared in America in *Hearst's International* in March 1923. Two other stories that Bennett may have been referring to are 'The Paper Cap' (serial publication unknown) and 'The Perfect Girl' (*Nash's*, February 1923). All the stories were republished in *Elsie and the Child* in 1924, a few of them with slightly modified titles.

266. Edgar Selwyn, Bennett's dramatic agent in America, became Vice-President of the Goldwyn Pictures Corporation. His brother Archibald was associated with another firm.

John Wright (1857–1933), the painter, was a friend of Bennett's. In his journal in 1916 Bennett records visiting Wright for 'half a week of water-colouring'.

u.c. / ms. / 267

Hotel d'Italien
Mont Estoril
Portugal
19–2–20

My dear Pinker,

It has occurred to me that I have been wasting quantities of impressions that people might care to read. Many years ago at Xmas I used to issue a small annual privately printed volume to my friends called *Things that have interested me.* I dropped it after 3 years. I enclose some items from a sort of journal, of various lengths. I also enclose a copy of a description of a prize fight, also from a journal, which I gave to the *New Statesman*; & which you will probably like. These impressions deal with both life and the arts. They are of all lengths up to 2,000 words. They are certainly as interesting as *Books & Persons.* But in the main they are not popular, nor intended so to be; they are *my* lark. I am wondering whether you could arrange for a series of them to run in some monthly in U.S.A. I should like the *Atlantic Monthly*, because I like Sedgwick; he has a sound mind & has given much distinction to the *A.M.* In default, possibly *Harper's*, or some weekly, such as the *New Republic.* I could furnish 60 or 70,000 words in a year, & keep on for ever. I do not expect the price I get for my 'popular' articles; I only expect the best price that can be got for this [sort] of work. Also I must not forget that Doran wants something for the *Bookman.* I should not want publication to begin before the autumn. The enclosed pieces have not been corrected by me. There wouldn't be much serialising in England, but we could get a bit. All this has nothing to do with the Portugal article, if you arrange it. By the way I am doing some pictures which Swinnerton thinks well of for publication purposes (colour). He also thinks well of the journal scheme. We are having a great time.   Yours, A. B.

267. From 29 January to 3 March, Bennett was on a holiday in Portugal with Frank Swinnerton. An article on his visit, 'Some Impressions of Portugal', appeared in *Harper's* in January 1922.

'The Prize Fight' appeared in the *New Statesman* on 13 December 1919.

Ellery Sedgwick (d. 1960) did not take the new series of impressions. A few such impressions appeared in the new *London Mercury* in 1920, and a brief series began in the *New Statesman* on 18 November 1922. The *Bookman* published nothing of Bennett's for another two years.

u.c. / ts. / 268

12B George Street
March 6th 1920

My dear Eric,

Many thanks for your letter of yesterday and the enclosure. I think you might possibly write to your father and suggest that he should look into this question thoroughly.

I have seen *John Ferguson*. It is very fine, but its chances will be very seriously jeopardised if it is not drastically cut. It is 15 or 20 minutes too long. There can be no doubt about this in the mind of any impartial person. It seems to me that you might, on behalf of your client, go into this matter with Playfair, who alone decides such matters. It is urgent.

Yours sincerely, Arnold Bennett

u.c. / ts. / 269

Comarques
April 1st 1920

My dear Eric,

Many thanks for your three letters.

I assume that it is quite in order that Lanoire should receive half of the monies paid by Grasset; but I am absolutely against making 25 francs into a £. In any other class of business the proposal would be laughed at. This matter is commercial and must be treated as such.

As regards the Portuguese article, I had better get it done and let you have it. I ought to be able to deliver it to you before the end of the month. I have four water-colour drawings, rather good (and six that are not so good). Any of them would reproduce excellently. Perhaps you had better find out what *Harper's* would pay for one or more of them if the work happened to please them, which I think it would, as it is certainly far better than the one that Scribnres used as a coloured frontispiece. The price having been settled, one or more drawings could be sent over.

As regards my next novel, I am thinking about it very seriously indeed, and I am anxious to get on to it as soon as I

268. Eric Pinker's letter concerned American income tax on British authors. On Nigel Playfair, see page 275n.

can clear off my various plays. I do not, however, think for a moment that the idea of the book would appeal to *Harper's Bazaar* at all. The thing is not yet sufficiently advanced for me to write a synopsis. You may take it from me that it is the best idea I have had for a novel for years and years. I mentioned this to Flower the other day, and added that it belonged to Methuen. He at once said that he would do everything he could to get it off Methuen, and he means to see either you or J.B. about the best method of doing so. I fancy he would be quite ready to buy the serial rights in the dark if he could get the book rights. In any case this novel cannot possibly be delivered before the autumn of next year.

Yours sincerely, Arnold Bennett

P.S. Many thanks for account and cheque for £1564.1.6. I enclose formal receipt herewith and return the royalty accounts. A. B.

U.C. / TS. / 270

Comarques
April 9th 1920

My dear Eric,

Many thanks for your two letters of yesterday.

I had certainly forgotten that Hutchinsons had bought the British serial rights of my next novel. I should be glad if you would send me exact particulars of the contract. I ought to tell you that the novel will be the story of an old Nonconformist minister with a millionaire son. The father retires and gradually

269. Maurice Lanoire translated everals of Bennett's works into French. He was now proposing to do a collection of short stories, to be published by Bernard Grasset. With the post-war decline of the franc, the rate of 25 francs to the pound would have brought Bennett little more than half his customary French royalty.

The Portuguese article in *Harper's*, January 1922, has conventional tinted illustrations by Vernon Howe Bailey. The reference to Scribner's is a mistake: the Century Company book, *From the Log of the 'Velsa'*, has as a frontispiece a handsome water-colour of Bennett's.

The new novel, whose germination is reported in the journal on 15 August 1919 and 9 March and 5 May 1920, was to be about Lord Beaverbrook's father. It was never written, but the death-bed scene that Bennett was contemplating for it was used in the last chapters of *Lord Raingo* of five years later.

Sir Newman Flower (1879–1964) entered the Cassell firm in 1906; he rose to become its head. and in 1927 its owner. He took *Lord Raingo* for Cassell's.

becomes very worldly under the influence of the son. There is
a love interest, but it is of minor importance, and has nothing
to do with the old man. The book ends with the death of the
old man, done on a magnificent scale. You are now warned as
to the nature of what you are selling the serial rights of! All I
can say to reassure you is that there will be nothing in the book
to offend from the sexual aspect.

Yours sincerely, Arnold Bennett

u.c. / ts. / 271

April 28th 1920

My dear Pinker,
Will you come and lunch at the Reform on Thursday next
the 6th instant. I want you to meet Clutton Brock, the art critic
of *The Times* and general philosophical writer. He seldom sells
any of his stuff in America, except to Sedgwick, and he certainly
ought to do so. He is a first-rate writer with a big reputation in
literary circles. I have told him that he ought to come to you
and he is quite prepared to do so. I do not suppose that there
is much money in him, but there is certainly kudos in him.
Moreover for the sake of literature he ought not to be selling
first-rate articles at Six Guineas to the *Manchester Guardian*, as
he does. I should very much like you to take him up. Swinnerton
will be at the lunch.
I am sending you the music which I mentioned to you today.
The name of the composer is van Dieren.

Yours sincerely, Arnold Bennett

u.c. / ts. / 272

12B George Street
May 17th 1920

My dear Pinker,
About a year ago Marguerite began to give recitals of
French poetry at the Anglo-French Society's rooms. Since then

270. The contract with Hutchinson was abandoned.
271. Arthur Clutton-Brock (1868–1924) had been a friend of Bennett's for
several years. Pinker did not take him on.
Bernard van Dieren (1884–1936), the Dutch composer and critic, lived in
London for a good many years. Bennett liked his music.

L.A.B.—U

she has enlarged her borders and given recitals at Bedford College, London, Glasgow, Leicester, and Nottingham University, besides private recitals. In her later recitals she has undoubtedly had very great success. Of her recent recitals I have only heard the private ones; I have been very much impressed by them—and so have other people. In particular she wants to visit all the principal universities. What I tell her is that she ought to give a matinée recital at some West End theatre— and I think it would be better if she gave it for a charity. If Vedrenne and Vernon were not perfect idiots they would have asked her to recite before now at the Little Theatre. But they are perfect idiots and incapable of seeing a thing until it has hit them in the chest. I believe that they have an idea that Marguerite is an amateur. She is not. She is a fully trained professional with professional stage experience. If Basil Dean were not a perfect idiot perhaps he also might have thought of asking her to recite at the St. Martin's theatre. I should like you to have a talk with Marguerite and see what can be done. It is not a question of money at all, at the beginning. The praise which she gets from good judges who have heard her is tremendous, and naturally she desires to exploit her talent. Hearing about America, she has dreams of going to America. I insist that the first thing to be done is to get a hearing at a West End theatre at a special performance arranged for her. I cannot help thinking that she would draw enough money to cover expenses and a bit over.

Yours sincerely, Arnold Bennett

u.c. / ts. / 273

12B George Street
May 21st 1920

My dear Pinker,

Many thanks for your letter of yesterday. I am very glad that there is some chance of Le Bas's scheme going through. You were certainly quite right in vetoing the proposal for introductions. With regard to the selection of the twelve by Wells, if the fact that he has selected them is to be publicly and prominently stated, I am agreeable. But if not, I do not see where the advantage lies. I probably have no more sincere admirer than

H. G., but I should be extremely surprised to learn that he has read twelve of my books right through. He very seldom reads a book through. His taste is often good and he rarely likes anything that is bad, but he is capable of the most extraordinary caprices. I think that Swinnerton would be a much better selector.

I have seen Swinnerton about the publication of my journal of impressions. I have decided, subject to anything that you may have to say, to publish the first volume in January next, and to deliver the copy in September. This first volume will not be serialised, except as to small parts of it, but it ought to serve as an advertisement to help serialisation of future stuff. Swinnerton suggests a book of from 50,000 to 60,000 words, price 7/6d, and he will mention the matter to Spalding. The remainder of the affair is, of course, in your domain. I suppose that Doran will see to it in U.S.A.

Swinnerton feels sure that C & W would be willing to publish a new edition of *How to Become an Author*. I gave him the book to read and he is enthusiastic about it. The chapter giving detailed information about papers would be cut out. As I am constantly getting enquiries for this book I think that it would sell.

I should like to know as soon as possible how many instalments the *Cosmopolitan* will want to make of my novel. It would be advantageous to them to decide the point and let me know quickly.

Yours sincerely, Arnold Bennett

BUTLER / T.C.C. / 274

[12B George Street]
May 27th 1920

My dear Pinker,

Do you know who owns the copyright of *How to Become an Author*? This point has a certain importance if Chatto is to republish it.

Yours sincerely, [Arnold Bennett]

---

273. Sir Hedley Le Bas (1868–1926), a publisher friend of Bennett's, proposed to issue twelve of Bennett's novels, each with an introduction by a well-known

BUTLER / TS. / 275
(*From J. B. Pinker*)

Talbot House
May 28th 1920

My dear Bennett,
    In reply to your letter of yesterday, I may say that I own the copyright of *How to Become an Author* and if you would accept it from me as a token of affection I should be very pleased.

Sincerely yours, J. B. Pinker

U.C. / MS. / 276

12B George Street
June 8th 1920

My dear Pinker,
    Many thanks for Joseph Conrad's play *The Secret Agent*. I am sending it to Playfair at once. I ought to tell you that, being a dramatic author, my position as chairman of the theatre is rather a delicate one, and that therefore I never read a play until it has been read and approved by the other two Directors. You will understand the reasons for this.
    There will be no delay in this matter.

Yours sincerely, Arnold Bennett

U.C. / TS. / 277

Comarques
June 19th 1920

My dear Pinker,
    The Lyric will take *The Bright Island*. I have told the other directors that I shall want the same terms as I have from West

---

person. Pinker thought 'it would be absurd to have men of lesser calibre writing Introductions to your books'.
    The first of three series of *Things That Have Interested Me* was published by Chatto and Windus (headed by Percy Spalding) in 1921. It consisted of previously-published articles as well as journal extracts.
    The *Cosmopolitan* serial, *Mr. Prohack*, went ultimately to *Delineator*.
    275. Chatto and Windus did not issue a new edition of *How to Become an Author* at this time.
    276. Conrad was inspired to dramatize *The Secret Agent* by the modest success of a dramatization of *Victory* the year before. The Lyric Theatre did not take the play.

End theatres, except that I shall not ask for any advance at all. They are to have the right to produce up to the end of 1921. They are very pleased indeed with the play, which rather re-assures me.

I am going on with Lasky, and something will come of it. I have also brought him into touch with Wells, who was much impressed with the new film which Lasky showed us in his private theatre on Friday afternoon. I expect I shall fix the main points of the contract with him personally, but of course I shall tell him that the contract must be settled between you and his representatives in London. In the meantime I should like to know from you what is the lowest advance and the lowest total figure which I ought to accept. Lasky said that I could have either a lump sum or a royalty as I chose. Selwyn assures me that he is all right. He is rather dull, very ignorant of everything outside his own line, and very clever. Beaverbrook tells me that the 'live man' of the firm is Zukor.

It is just possible that I might be able to call on you on Thursday morning next, some time.

Yours sincerely, Arnold Bennett

u.c. / ts. / 278

Comarques
August 12th 1920

My dear Pinker,

Many thanks for your letter of the 11th. As regards the Hodder & Stoughton reprints, this is a matter which I must leave entirely to you, but I may as well put my general view

277. The Lyric Theatre did not produce *The Bright Island*, presumably because *The Beggar's Opera*, which had opened on 5 June, was to occupy the theatre for three years. A comic satire done in the vein of *commedia dell' arte*, *The Bright Island* is one of Bennett's best plays. It was not produced until 1925, when the Stage Society gave two performances of it.

Jesse Lasky (1880–1956) and the Hungarian-born Adolph Zukor (1873–) were two of the men responsible for the American domination of the film world in these and later years. They had recently united their independent firms to form Famous Players Lasky, which later became Paramount Pictures. Lasky was soon expounding the doctrine of an internationalized cinema, and was hoping to engage the interest of Galsworthy and Kipling as well as Bennett.

On Lord Beaverbrook, see page 263n.

before you. In my opinion if the books cannot be sold at a profit at their present price, the price ought to be raised. The fall in the value of money has got to be resolutely faced, and I regard it as bad economics for a publisher and an author to be content with a decreased remuneration in money, and a very much decreased remuneration in actual values, for the sake of keeping a book before the public. If the price were raised, the sale might diminish somewhat, but the proposition would nevertheless remain commercial.

I am well satisfied with Hodder & Stoughton's publishing, and I do not want to change.

Yours sincerely, Arnold Bennett

U.C. / TS. / 279

Comarques
August 28th 1920

My dear Pinker,

Many thanks. I return the second copy of the Lasky agreement signed. I have sketched out the beginning of a film, and have an appointment with Ford to lunch with him on Wednesday. My arrangements may, however, be entirely upset by the probable death of Rickards, who has tuberculous meningitis and is not expected to recover. I should certainly have to go to Bournemouth for his funeral.

Yours sincerely, Arnold Bennett

278. Hodder and Stoughton wanted to keep the price of *The Author's Craft* and *Married Life* (*The Plain Man and His Wife*) at 2s. 6d. but reduce Bennett's royalty from 15 to 10 per cent. They were losing money on the books. Bennett agreed to the reduction.

279. Hugh Ford was an editor for Famous Players. Bennett's film story was called *The Wedding Dress*.

Of E. A. Rickards Bennett said on one occasion that he 'influenced my view of life more than any other person I have ever met'. He had been a close friend from Bennett's early London days. Earlier in 1920, Bennett recorded in his journal after one of his visits to Rickards in the hospital: 'Glimpses, through Rickards, into a vast world of sickness and tragedy—a whole world complete in itself and looking on angrily and resentfully and longingly at our world.' This experience, much more than Beaverbrook's account of his father (pages 279-81), must have provided the basis of the death-bed scene that occupies one-third of *Lord Raingo*. Rickards died on 29 August. Later in the year Bennett wrote an introduction for and saw through the press the memorial volume *The Art of E. A. Rickards*.

u.c. / ts. / 280

> Comarques
> August 30th 1920

My dear Pinker,

I have had Gilbert Miller here for the week-end. As a matter of fact I invited him in order to find out more about how things stand in the West End, and also to become more intimate with him for my own purposes. He is still keen on *Don Juan*, and he thinks that Jack Barrymore ought to and would do it in the U.S.A. or even here. Has Barrymore got a copy of the play? If he has not, will you send a copy to Miller and Miller would talk to him about it. Miller leaves for New York on September 8th. He says that the only thing that prevents him from doing the play in London is the absence of an actor equal to the rôle of Don Juan. I certainly think that Miller is a man to cultivate. He appears to me to be more cultivated and to have more initiative and a better conception of business than any other manager. But of course he has a very clear notion of his own ~~importance.~~ advantage.

> Yours sincerely, Arnold Bennett

u.c. / ts. / 281

> 12B George Street
> 11th October 1920

My dear Pinker,

I want to get a job for a man whom I have known for a number of years, and whom I can thoroughly recommend for a minor position of trust. He was at one time cashier to the Garrick Club, but left there because he could not stand the long hours. Then for a number of years he was employed as a sort of factotum and general clerk by Lanchester and Rickards. He is nearing 50 years of age and can do almost anything, from acting as watch-dog in an office and writing letters to meeting people at railway stations and taking children out for a walk. He is very intelligent and has excellent manners and style, but his chief point is that he can be trusted. The various people

280. John Barrymore (1882–1942), of the Anglo-American acting family, was soon to make a film *Don Juan* that apparently precluded his doing Bennett's play.

who have employed him would all give him the highest testi-
monials. I thought that you might know or hear of something
that would be suitable. I am extremely anxious to do something
for him. He would not want a high salary.

Yours sincerely, Arnold Bennett

u.c. / ts. / 282

12B George Street
30th November 1920

My dear Pinker,

Paris Nights

Many thanks. I return the Agreement duly initialled.

Short stories

Three of these are complete and ready for delivery, but on
reflection I will deliver them one at a time. I do not want the
Cosmopolitan to receive too much at once. I enclose the first one,
entitled 'The Lost Girl'. No connection with Lawrence's new
novel! I have just read the latter. It is very remarkable indeed,
and would be great if it had a real theme and some construction.
This man is a genius, and is far and away the best of the younger
school.

Yours sincerely, Arnold Bennett

BUTLER / T.C.C. / 283

[12B George Street]
16th December 1920

My dear Pinker,

I think that, without any special effort, I made rather a
favourable impression on Everett and Frank Newnes today. I
gave them the idea of a series of articles under some such general

282. Hodder and Stoughton were preparing a new edition of *Paris Nights*.
    'The Lost Girl' was published in *Cosmopolitan* in January 1922 under the title
'Nine O'Clock Tomorrow'. It appears in the collection of stories *Elsie and the
Child* of 1924. Lawrence's novel of the same name was begun in 1912 in reaction
against *Anna of the Five Towns*. He wrote then: 'I hate Bennett's resignation.
Tragedy ought really to be a great kick at misery. But *Anna of the Five Towns* seems
like an acceptance—so does all the modern stuff since Flaubert. I hate it.' He said
the same of Conrad: 'I can't forgive Conrad for being so sad and for giving in.'

title as *How to Make the Best of Life*, dealing with the various aspects of activity. I said that the series must be at least 40,000 in all, so as to make a book, and that the number of subjects would be about ten. Everett asked me if I could give a list of the subjects. I said that if I did give a list it would be a mere suggestion, and that I should not be bound by it. He agreed. In any case I do not propose to do anything towards giving a list until terms have been provisionally settled. I referred him to you as to terms. I suggest that it might be convenient for him to buy the world's rights. I said that I could not furnish any copy at all until September, 1921. I also made it quite clear that the subjects would be treated truthfully and not sentimentally. I mentioned as to enquiries for series of articles from both the *Strand* and *Cassell's*. He smiled, and said that he knew what that was leading up to!

Yours sincerely, [Arnold Bennett]

BUTLER / MS. / 284
(*From J. B. Pinker*)

Talbot House
11 Jan 1921

My dear Arnold,

I am going for my holiday at the end of the month (it is just 7 years since I had one) and as we have to stay twenty-four hours in Paris on our way to Corsica can you recommend an hotel? My wife and daughter will be with me, and I want to take them to a nice place that won't be depressing if the weather be bad.

Have you any news of Dunlops?

Yours ever, J. B. P.

283. The series was published by the Newnes-Pearson *Strand Magazine*, beginning in May 1922. They apparently paid £3,000 for it. P. W. Everett (d. 1952) was editor and director at Pearson's; Frank Newnes (1876–1955) now headed his father's firm and was a director at Pearson's.

284. Bennett recommended the Continental. He and Pinker also traded information on industrial shares, Dunlop and others, that they were both buying.

Pinker visited the Conrads, who were in Corsica for two months. In her memoir *Joseph Conrad and His Circle* Jessie Conrad describes the visit.

'J. B. Pinker was a very delightful companion, and his wife always ready to fall in with any plans we made for an outing. . . . Mr. Pinker had a knack of soothing my husband in difficult moods, who needed either sympathetic indulgence or

U.C. / TS. / 285

12B George Street
1st March 1921

My dear Eric,

Many thanks for your letter of yesterday. I suppose that I shall also get copies of the book in due course.

I enclose a letter received from the Secretary of the Altrincham Y.M.C.A., A.D.C. and copy of my reply. If he writes to you you can deal with the matter as you like. Please return me the original letter.

Here is another matter which you can discuss with J. B. on his return. I have recently earned £180 from the *Express* and £25 from the *Observer*, and some time ago I collected £100 from the *Evening News* for two short articles. This work was due entirely to me and my personal relations. It cost you nothing whatever. I am aware that according to my contract you are entitled to take commission on it all; but I suggest that you should reflect upon the point in a spirit not of law but of equity.

Yours sincerely, Arnold Bennett

---

tolerant disregard. Mr. Pinker's wonderful voice was a joy and a delight to us all, and his daughter was a very able accompanist. . . .

'One night my husband retired early from the dining-room, displeased with something on the menu, and we five sat laughing and talking over the rest of the meal. . . . At last no reasonable pretence remained for lingering where we were, and we prepared to return to the sitting-room at the very end of the long passage. . . . J. B. Pinker walked first, the flickering light from his candle falling on his white head. His wonderful voice rose in a sacred chant and the waiters—all Swiss—fell into line with clasped hands or making the sign of the cross. Very profane, no doubt, but inexpressibly funny because it was a sudden impulse. . . .

'Mr. Pinker, deadly serious and filling the place with his voice, proceeded right to the door of our private sitting-room. Suddenly my husband flung it open and said icily: "Yes, and I'm a Catholic, aren't I?"

'. . . I passed on to my room without facing my lord and master, and left J. B. Pinker to weather the storm. For some time no sound broke the silence in the next room, then I heard the singer's voice murmuring insinuatingly, I could not catch what was said, but the effect was a peal of amused laughter from the "Catholic" and I knew the storm was over.'

285. The *Daily Express* articles, on the theatre, began on 26 January 1921. Articles appeared in the *Observer* on 14 July 1918 and 13 February 1921, and in the *Evening News* on 19 December 1918. The second article for the *Evening News* could not be found.

The letter from the Secretary of the Amateur Dramatic Company of the Y.M.C.A. (W. Eric Landon) does not survive.

u.c. / t.c.c. / 286
(*To the Secretary of the Y.M.C.A. Amateur Dramatic Company*)

[12B George Street]
1st March 1921

Dear Sir,

In reply to your letter, I have every sympathy with your desire to produce good plays, but there is another side to this question. It is certainly the business of the Secretary of an A.D.C. to know that modern plays cannot be performed without fees, and if he has any doubts about the point it is his business to find out before rehearsals of a modern play are commenced.

If your Society chooses to run itself upon an economic basis which will not bear examination it is perfectly entitled to do so, but it should not ask outsiders to make pecuniary sacrifices in order to hide the absurdity of the economic basis. If it wants funds it should ask for funds as subscriptions. How do you suppose playwrights are to live? Can you give me any reason why I, who am an agnostic, should contribute to the support of the Y.M.C.A.? It is true that I have often supported Y.M.C.A. organisations for other than religious reasons, but I have done so directly by means of a subscription.

You cannot do any performances of my play without any fee at all. Assuming that you have a doctor among your members, what do you think he would say if you invited him to give you six consultations at the price of two consultations?

It is possible that some arrangement might be made for a reduced fee on the extra performances of which you speak, but if you wish to negotiate perhaps you will be good enough to communicate direct with my agent, Mr. J. B. Pinker, Talbot House, Arundel Street, London, W.C.2.

Yours faithfully, [Arnold Bennett]

butler / ts. / 287
(*From J. B. Pinker*)

Talbot House
21st March 1921

My dear Bennett,

I find here on my return your letter of the 1st raising the question as to the commission on the amounts received from the *Express, Observer* and *Evening News*. The amount involved is so small that one is tempted not to argue about it. I should therefore leave it to you to decide as you please but for the principle involved, which is, of course, what interests you too. You would, I know, be the first to admit that you were able to sell those articles on those terms because of my work in building up your market. If when the market is worked up an author is going to take pieces of business into his own hands he will naturally take all the easy pieces and leave the agent the difficult ones. That would be most unfair to the agent, and it would end in changing the whole relationship. As you know, it frequently happens that there is work to do for an author which involves no commission for the agent, or a commission so insignificant as to be negligible, but at the same time it is work that the author particularly wishes done. One does it with the good will and energy that one applies to the more profitable business, but only because one has towards the author the feeling of complete service. If the author is to take isolated items of his business and withhold commission, the agent is bound to react and withhold his services where they would yield no immediate commission.

I shall take up the Collected Edition with Pawling and Doran.

Sincerely yours, J. B. Pinker

BUTLER / T.C.C. / 288

[12B George Street]
25th April 1921

My dear Pinker,

I enclose the fourth instalment of *Mr. Prohack*. After leaving it for a month (in order to do the film which was delivered last week) I have read this novel all through as far as it's done, and I am rather pleased with it. I think that Mr. Prohack is a fairly original character.

287. Sydney S. Pawling (d. 1921), of Heinemann, and George Doran were proposing to do a collected edition of Bennett's works. Their plan, and other similar plans, came to nothing. Although Bennett was faithful to Pinker, he changed publishers so often that he made a collected edition a difficult enterprise. In 1926 the Library Press issued seven of the lesser novels in a uniform edition.

I hope that you will be getting some money for me soon, as I shall have serious need of it. I have been making the most fantastic payments lately and have already borrowed money from the bank as it would be suicidal to sell securities.

Yours sincerely, [Arnold Bennett]

U.C. / TS. / 289

12B George Street
27th April 1921

My dear Pinker,

How to Make the Best of Life

Many thanks for your letter of yesterday. Each of the articles will be complete in itself, and they can be divided how the purchasers like, but they will certainly all deal with the subject indicated in the title. I cannot possibly change the form of the book as a whole, making the book too short and leaving myself with four odd articles! The length and number of the articles was definitely agreed. Please note, it was also definitely agreed with Frank Newnes personally that the first article should not be delivered until September.

Mr. Prohack

I return the proofs. The cuts which have been made are most ruthless. They certainly impair the interest and atmosphere of the story, and I do not understand why they have been made. The length of the serial, 100,000 words, was suggested by the *Delineator,* and the number of instalments was also fixed by them; and I arranged the details of the narrative specially to suit serial publication. It is somewhat discouraging to have the thing spoilt by cutting after I have taken all this trouble. I always thought that 14,000 words was a stiff dose for one instalment, but I assumed that they knew just what they wanted. It is difficult to estimate the amount of the cuts, but at a rough guess I should put them at over 40% of the whole. Perhaps you can throw some light on the mystery.

There is no need for me to see any more proofs. The copy delivered was very carefully corrected, and they have only to reproduce it accurately.

With regard to publication in the *Sunday Times,* perhaps you will tell the editor that to keep pace with the *Delineator* it will be necessary for him to average about 3,200 words a week. This, I imagine, he will easily be able to do, without making any cuts at all.

As the final instalment of the serial will be out before Christmas, I assume that book publication can take place in the autumn.

I am sending you today the copy for the *Sunday Times*. Will you kindly let me know whether it will be more convenient to have it set for book publication in England first and send English proofs to America for the American printers, or vice versa.

Yours sincerely, Arnold Bennett

U.C. / TS. / 290

Comarques
22nd July 1921

My dear Pinker,

Many thanks for your letter of the 21st. No, I will not agree to the new proposal. Not because of the decrease in the advance, but because I do not want those six trifling short stories to appear as a volume. It would be quite all right for them to appear in the form of a monthly publication, which has no real importance, but as a volume they would look merely absurd. How stupid publishers are! They are always attracted by the very latest possibilities.

Yours sincerely, Arnold Bennett

P.S. Thanks for your telegram re *Sunday Pictorial*. I have sent the second article to Buhrer today, and the third will be sent in about a fortnight's time. They are only due to be delivered once a fortnight. A. B.

289. *How to Make the Best of Life* began appearing in the *Strand Magazine* in May 1922.

The *Sunday Times* apparently bought the serial rights to *Mr. Prohack* from Hutchinson, and then resold them to the *Westminster Gazette*, in which paper the novel began appearing on 7 November 1921.

290. The new proposal was apparently to publish the six stories referred to on pages 276–7 in book form. The stories have no relation to one another.

Albert Buhrer of the *Sunday Pictorial* took a series of miscellaneous articles that ran fortnightly from 24 July to 13 November. Bennett had been writing occasionally for the *Pictorial* since 1915. Payment per article had risen from £100 to £150 in these six years.

u.c. / ms. / 291

> Yacht Marie Marguerite
> St. Malo
> 22–8–21

My dear Pinker,

Many thanks for your letter. I am glad Ray Long likes 'The Fish', but it certainly is not a bit better than the one you liked so much. Of the six, I think there is only one that falls below the general level.

I was talking to Beaverbrook the other day about income tax. He pointed out to me that I was earning money out of England, and that income tax was not payable on money received for work done abroad but not received in England. The last 2 articles for the *Sunday Pictorial* were done at Deauville & the first of the *Strand* articles is being done at St. Malo. The payment for these amounts to £700, and the lessening of my taxable income by £700 would make a difference of at least £250 in the tax. Please see that the payments for these items are made direct (not through you) to my current account at Cooks, Paris. Beaverbrook told me that he had put Kipling on to a firm of accountants who had 'cut Kipling's income tax all to ribbons'. I have not the name of the firm, but I can of course get it, & perhaps you could see them on my behalf. Also I could see Needham, who is supposed to be one of the leading authorities on this great and distressing subject. It seems to me that the time has arrived when income tax must be treated seriously & every advantage taken of the strict letter of the law. So far as I can see, my difficulty would arise on the point: How long must money remain abroad before it becomes 'capital' and ceases to be liable to tax if brought over to England?

By the way, Beaverbrook told me that he paid £40,000 a year in income tax.

> Yours sincerely, Arnold Bennett

291. The yacht *Marie Marguerite* was bought the previous year, 'just to show these rich chaps that a writer can make money too'. It had a crew of eight. Bennett was sailing off the English coast and the Continent during much of 1921.

Ray Long (1878–1935) was editor-in-chief of the International Magazine Company, which published *Cosmopolitan*, *Good Housekeeping*, and *Hearst's International*. He was dissatisfied with some of the stories that Bennett was writing for *Cosmopolitan*. A letter of 18 May 1921 from him to H. G. Wells remarks upon his

U.C. / MS. / 292

Yacht Marie Marguerite
[Fowey]
4-9-21

My dear Pinker,

Many thanks for your letter of the 1st & the enclosures. I return Doran's statements, & Taylor Platt's & Hodder-Stoughton's. There are several books out of print. It seems to me that *The Roll Call* and *The Old Wives' Tale* ought not to be o.p. But of course I don't want him to reprint books that won't sell.

Why have not Hutchinsons paid that £1,250?

Yours sincerely, Arnold Bennett

P.S. Apparently Hodder & Stoughton have not realised their ambition in regard to the pocket-philosophies. It is characteristic of that negligence which I have always noticed in their methods that they persist in calling my best known book *Old Wives Tales*. It is really remarkable that they don't know the titles of their own publications. Ernest apologised to me for this long ago!

BUTLER / T.C.C. / 293

[Yacht Marie Marguerite]
[Brightlingsea]
29th September 1921

My dear Eric,

Many thanks for your letter of the 28th. I read the scenario of *The Old Wives' Tale*. It is impossible for me to say anything

---

dissatisfaction. According to him, Bennett confessed that writing for *Cosmopolitan*'s million and a quarter circulation gave him stage fright! See pages 276–7 for the stories involved.

On Sir Raymond Needham see page 238n. From 1916 to 1919 Bennett's income was £8,319, £6,552, £8,960, and £9,228. In 1920 it rose to £15,783, approximately the sum he earned in 1912, his first very successful year.

292. Taylor Platt was touring with a production of *Milestones*. He is otherwise unknown.

The Hutchinson reference apparently concerns the proposed novel on Beaverbrook's father (pages 279–81).

Sir Ernest Hodder-Williams was in 1921 beginning to relinquish control of his firm to his younger brothers. After his death in 1927, Bennett briefly considered writing a novel about him.

about this. Doubtless they have done their best, and it is no
worse than the best of its kind and better than most things.
But read the captions! I need not say that the spirit of the book
is wholly and absurdly falsified.

You can tell them anything you like.

Yours sincerely, [Arnold Bennett]

BUTLER / T.C.C. / 294

[12B George Street]
7th October 1921

My dear Pinker,

Spender has asked me to go to Washington for the disarma-
ment conference for the new *Westminster*. At first I refused, but
he is a man of great and authoritative persuasiveness. The
enclosed letter explains itself, and has only just been delivered
by hand.

When Spender asked me about terms I said that I would
accept the same terms as Wells was getting, whatever they
were, and that I should find out what they were. The unnamed
gent referred to in my letter to Spender is of course Wells.

Yours sincerely, [Arnold Bennett]

U.C. / MS. / 295

12B George Street
22–10–21

My dear Pinker,

Many thanks for yours about income-tax. I want to see you
about a still more important matter at once & I propose to
call upon you at 11.30 on Monday unless you 'phone me that

293. The Ideal Film Company produced *The Old Wives' Tale*, with Fay
Compton as Sophia and Florence Turner as Constance. The film had its first public
showing towards the end of January 1922.

294. J. A. Spender (1862–1942) was editor of the *Westminster Gazette* for most of
its thirty years as an evening paper. It was now to become a morning paper and to
lose Spender as its editor. Bennett had resolved after the war to give up politics,
but Spender, Wells, and Mrs. Bennett persuaded him that he had a duty to go to
Washington. Wells was paid $16,000 for 30,000 words, a sum that neither he nor
Bennett regarded as attractive, in view of the special work involved. In the event,
Bennett did not make the trip, and Spender went himself.

L.A.B.——X

this won't do. The matter is of the greatest urgency & I shall want at least an hour of your valuable time.

Yours sincerely, Arnold Bennett

BUTLER / T.C.C. / 296

[London]
26th October 1921

My dear Eric,

Donald Calthrop is prepared to produce *The Love Match* fairly soon if terms can be arranged, and he proposes to come to see you tomorrow. I have definitely told him that I will not be too hard in the matter of terms, as he is a young manager, and that I will instruct you to this effect. Provided I get 10% all through if the receipts reach a certain amount, I shall be quite content, and as I have always told you I do not mind at all about the advance, assuming that an early production is guaranteed. I will not have McKinnel in the principal part.

Yours sincerely, [Arnold Bennett]

U.C. / MS. / 297

Yacht Amaryllis
Cannes
17–1–22

My dear Pinker,

I am sorry that it is impossible for me to reach London before you leave for New York, as I wanted to talk to you fully about the Lasky film. I must be content to write to you at length. You will doubtless be seeing Mr. Lasky, and I should like you to explain to him that in my opinion the transaction between us did not at all develop along the lines which he & I

295. Bennett and his wife had agreed to separate two days before. Technically Bennett was the wronged party. A characteristic sense of responsibility to his wife made him settle three-quarters of his estate upon her and give her £2,000 yearly. Later she would not accede to a divorce to enable him to make legal his marriage to Dorothy Cheston, whom he met in March 1922.

296. Donald Calthrop (1888–1940) was an actor-manager. He had recently assumed the management of the Aldwych Theatre. Norman McKinnel (1870–1932), who was associated with him, had managed and played the male lead in *Helen with the High Hand* in 1914. Calthrop and McKinnel presently sold their option on *The Love Match* to Frank Vernon.

were agreed upon, and that in the result I consider that I have some sort of a grievance against his corporation. I do not in the least blame him, for I am quite sure that he meant all that he said. Nor do I blame his London lieutenants, who treated me with the greatest courtesy. My view is that Mr. Lasky and his staff were working at cross-purposes. I will put down the circumstances.

Mr. Hugh Ford came to lunch with me, & before he came I sent him a brief scheme for a story. He liked the scheme; his only objection to it was that it might prove to be too long and too complicated, but we agreed that it could easily be simplified. He liked it so much that he said he would have the opening of it scenario-ized within a week, so that I might judge better the question of length. We parted with this quite definite arrangement. I heard nothing whatever for quite a number of weeks. In the meantime, as Mr. Hugh Ford had approved the general idea without reserve, my mind continued to work on it. At last I wrote to enquire the reason of the delay. In reply Mr. MacAlarney informed me that Mr. Hugh Ford had quitted London long before and that in his, Mr. MacAlarney's opinion the story was not at all suitable for film purposes. Upon this I wrote to Mr. MacAlarney formally protesting against the great waste of time which had been imposed upon me. Mr. Mac-Alarney very courteously admitted the justice of my protest, and indeed our relations were throughout of the most friendly nature. As I was very anxious to demonstrate my good faith and my desire to meet the company to the utmost possible extent, I started again with an entirely fresh scheme, and submitted it to Mr. MacAlarney. He came to see me about it, and he discussed it [at] great length and with remarkable cleverness, but always with a bias—natural enough—towards the conventional film psychology. As there was nothing in his suggestions to which I could fundamentally object—though as a whole they modified somewhat my own conception of the story—I accepted practically all of them. I wrote the story out at length in full detail, and I divided it, as I should think any workmanlike author would, into scenes. After I had sent it in another considerable delay occurred, and either Mr. Mac-Alarney or his staff evidently did not realise that an author of my sort does not and cannot switch off at will from one subject to another, that a subject occupies him until it is finished, and that therefore they were wasting my time and costing me money. At length I heard from Mr. MacAlarney that he was disappointed with my film, and that in particular, I had attempted to scenario-ize the story and had failed to do so properly. Now I had made no attempt to scenario-ize it. I had merely divided it into scenes for the sake of his convenience and mine. I should not have dreamed of trying to do work which is obviously that of a film-expert. So far as I could gather, Mr. MacAlarney's objections to the story as I told it were twofold; first, to the whole complexion and psychology of the story as worked out (though he had approved it in outline) and second to the lack of what he called 'plot' or 'incident'. Mr. MacAlarney sent Miss Turnbull to see me. Miss Turnbull told me that she had been in the film business for five years, but as I had been in the story-telling business for thirty-five years, I did not take too seriously her remarks to me about story-telling. She struck me, however, as being an extraordinarily able woman, and she seemed to know far more about the film as a popular medium of narration than either Mr. Hugh Ford or Mr. MacAlarney. Her point of view, nevertheless, was the conventional film point of view. I accepted many of her suggestions for remodelling the story; for instance I agreed that the principal heroine should be a lady of title, and I agreed to give more importance to the fashionable and luxurious country house scenes in the story. I further agreed that the second heroine, whom I had made of humble birth, should be of good birth. On the other hand, I declined her suggestion for a motor-car race between the two heroines to London in quest of the hero. When Miss Turnbull had finished her very clever exposition of her notion of what my film ought to be, I pointed out to her that she had entirely omitted from it my central idea—namely, the repeated dramatic use of a certain costume. She admitted that she had forgotten it, but said that it had not particularly appealed to her. Now I am convinced that this is a first-rate idea for the film, and sooner or later it is bound to be used. As an example of the lack of co-ordination which existed in the London offices of the company I ought to mention the following detail. The important scenes in my story pass in a nursing-home or private hospital, and in the rooms of a fashionable dressmaker.

Miss Turnbull objected broadly to both these classes of scene, on the ground that the public did not like hospital scenes and that the mannequin business had been much overdone on the films. I was unaware of the existence of either of these objections, and it struck me as astonishing that Mr. MacAlarney, who had been familiar with the substance of the story from the start, and had minutely criticized it, should never have breathed a word to me about them. Finally Miss Turnbull urged me to re-write the story as nearly as possible *in the form of a novel*. She said that the staff would understand it better if I did so. I admit frankly that I thought this exceedingly queer.

I re-wrote the story, embodying as many of Miss Turnbull's suggestions as I honestly could, in the form of a novel of about 30,000 words in length. I delivered it, and, after further delay, I was informed that it was not approved; also that Mr. Mac-Alarney could not get any director to interest himself in it. No reasons for the decision have ever been given to me.

Let me now go back to my original negotiations with Mr. Lasky. I told Mr. Lasky that I had no technical experience whatever of film work, that I strongly objected to most of the films I had seen, and that to my mind the most important quality of any story was that it should strike the observer as being *true*. He heartily agreed. He said he knew the sort of story that I wrote, and that he wanted me to write that sort of story specially for the film, and that he was coming to me and to people like me because he wanted something different from everything that he had hitherto been getting. He wanted to break away. He wanted in particular to break away from the star-system and to give more importance to the author. Nothing could have been clearer than the understanding between us.

And nothing can be clearer than the fact that Mr. Lasky's staff in London did not want to break away from the old style of film and to get something different. Their tendency throughout the dealings with me was to conventionalise my subject and treatment, though I had certainly not shown any lack of the spirit of compromise in the conception of my story.

I was told that the film-trade had a system by which it knew infallibly what the public would like. Neither the film trade nor any other amusement trade has any means of knowing what the public will like. It can only know what the public *has* liked. And it is notorious that films which the trade condemned absolutely in advance have proved to be enormous successes. There can be no technical objection to my story. In reply to the objection that it does not interest directors I give my opinion that it will interest the public. Both in novels and in plays, I have backed my opinion against the opinion of 'experts' and over and over again I have been right. You yourself have good reason to know that in both novels and plays my greatest successes were hawked in vain all over the place and turned down everywhere by experts before they actually reached the public. And I have no doubt that the same thing would happen in regard to films if I were given the relatively free hand which I understood Mr. Lasky to promise. That risks would have to be faced I do not deny, but all changes are attended by risks. I maintain that it is utterly illogical to invite me to write a film and then to let the film be turned down by experts who have been brought up on the very class of film which I am asked to replace. I do not question the ability of these experts in their own field. On the contrary I have great respect for them. But I refuse to take seriously their general and sweeping objection to the work that I do. If Mr. Lasky had not considered me to be among the foremost experts in story-telling, with a following throughout the world, I take it that he would not have come to me. Having come to me, I think that he should have the courage of his original gesture.

Undoubtedly the transaction has been unsatisfactory for the company, but it has been far more unsatisfactory for me. The company has lost 5,000 dollars. I have lost three months time. You can tell Mr. Lasky how much three months of my time is worth.

Yours sincerely, Arnold Bennett

P.S. I think you had better have the above typewritten! And please do not forget to see the Author's League secretary about the cutting of *Mr. Prohack* by the *Delineator*.   A. B.

297. The yacht *Amaryllis* belonged to Herbert Sullivan, nephew and biographer (with Sir Newman Flower) of Sir Arthur Sullivan. Bennett was sailing with him during December and January.

Hugh Ford, Robert E. MacAlarney, and Miss Turnbull are otherwise unidentified. Bennett had begun working on *The Wedding Dress* in November 1920.

On 28 January J. B. Pinker sailed on a business trip to America, and on 8 February he died of pneumonia in New York. He admitted to his son Eric before he left England that he was seriously unwell; but he was the sort of man who never consulted a doctor, and he insisted on going. Jessie Conrad records the sense of premonition with which he parted from her and Conrad a few days before he sailed, and the unbelief with which Conrad heard of his death. In a letter to the writer Bruno Winawer, Conrad said: 'I have suffered a most painful loss in my old friend J. B. Pinker who died five days ago. . . . Our friendship lasted for 22 years. He was 6 years younger than myself and I feel quite overpowered by this blow of fate.' Bennett's relationship with Pinker was more formal, and his stoicism in the face of death a long-cultivated attitude, but his shock at the news was remembered many years afterwards by his secretary, Miss Nerney. His journal, as published, ends abruptly for the year 1922 with the day prior to Pinker's death. And he undertook no serious writing for the next several months. In a letter to his nephew Richard, written as he came home from his yachting cruise, he remarked: 'I had quite enough worries and harassments on coming home, but the worst by far of all this morning: my agent, J. B. Pinker, died suddenly in New York last night. Apart from the fact that he was a very old friend of mine, he had the whole of my affairs in his hands. There is no other really good agent in England. The difference between a good and a bad agent might mean a difference of thousands a year to me.'

IV

After J. B. Pinker's Death

1922–1931

J. B. Pinker's indifference towards doctors, says Eric Pinker, reflected a refusal to consider the fact of death. In consequence, his business rested solely in his hands. He did not take his sons into partnership, and his contracts with his authors were terminable upon his death. William Heinemann noted in the nineties that a man could establish himself as a literary agent by renting an office; and it was almost as easy for an elaborate agency to vanish. In the present situation, Eric Pinker took over the business and succeeded in maintaining it. During the next several years the office staff enlarged considerably from the seven people who earlier ran it, and the volume of business expanded. By 1926 the firm was ready to set up a second office in New York and extend its connexions to the Californian film world. Bennett was invited to invest in the American enterprise but declined.

For Bennett, the next few years saw the writing of two of the most important of his later novels, Riceyman Steps *and* Lord Raingo. *He also wrote further film stories. The abundance of letters on the latter subject in 1929 obscures the fact that Bennett was then engaged in writing his last play (unmentioned in these letters) and also beginning work on his longest and most complex novel,* Imperial Palace. *Nevertheless, the attention to films is characteristic: he was interested in every form of art, and his literary career was an unceasing quest for means of expression.*

U.C. / MS. / 298
PRIVATE

12B George Street
21-2-22

My dear Eric,

I have seen both Walpole & Mrs. Lowndes. Walpole has every intention of sticking to you for England, but I doubt if he will for America, as he is convinced that he can get better results by directly employing an American agent. I don't think he will suggest any change immediately. Mrs. Lowndes has every intention of sticking to you, but she objects to paying commission on work which she obtains through her own connections & which you would not obtain for her yourself in any event. This is a feeling generally held by authors. I share it

myself & have more than once discussed it with J. B., who had
his way but did not convince me. I am aware that the exclusion
of certain work from commission might lead to abuses on the
part of the author, & I agree that no exception should be made
to authors who are only beginning. But I think that authors of
really established position are justified in demanding exceptions & I have always thought so. In my own case the amount
of work I get direct is negligible, but such as it is no agent
would ever have got it for me. I should agree that a whole book
or play or film should never be an exception, through whatever channel it may be arranged; but a great deal of journalism
& oddments might very properly be excepted from commission
when the author gets it all alone. I shall not at present suggest
any alteration of my contract with the firm, so that you can say
to everyone that I am continuing with you exactly as before;
but later on I might suggest certain modifications to you. Mrs.
Lowndes is going to ask you to see her at her home.

Yours ever, A. B.

U.C. / TS. / 299

12B George Street
4th March 1922

My dear Eric,

Many thanks for your letter. I enclose copy of my reply to
Playfair.

I am quite willing to accept the terms which you suggest, but
if you can get better terms, do. I think the advance should be
£300. The most important point for me is that the play should
be produced by Playfair.

It is a good idea to plant the play on Calthrop. He is very
hard up for a play, and also for capital, and he could play the
principal male part all right.

Yours sincerely, Arnold Bennett

298. Hugh Walpole withdrew from Eric Pinker for America; Mrs. Belloc
Lowndes withdrew for both England and America. They were the only important
losses to the firm.

299. The terms Eric Pinker suggested for Nigel Playfair's production of *Body and
Soul* apparently included an advance of £150. Playfair produced the play on 11
September 1922, at the Euston Palace of Varieties (renamed the Regent), with
Nan Marriott Watson, Viola Tree, and Martin Walker in the leading roles.

The play for Calthrop was possibly *The Bright Island*, as yet unproduced.

U.C. / T.C.C. / 300
(*To Nigel Playfair*)

[12B George Street]
4th March 1922

My dear Playfair,

Many thanks for your letter of the 3rd. It contains one gross inaccuracy, namely a statement to the effect that my work is in great demand. This is entirely contrary to the facts. My plays have never been in great demand, except by the public.

I have written to Pinker about the terms, and I think that you (or Horne) and he would be able to come to an agreement. I do not, however, share your ideas about my duties as chairman of the Company. The suggestion that the Company should take up this play did not come from me, nor should I ever have dreamt of putting forward such a suggestion. My first impulse was to refuse to let the Syndicate handle the play; but if I had done so the shareholders would have been entitled to say: 'Here is a nice chairman—refusing his own plays to his own syndicate!' Whichever course I took my position would have been somewhat delicate. I should consider myself fortunate to have the play produced by you in London, but on the other hand I should consider the Syndicate extremely fortunate to get hold of such a play—the playing qualities of which have already been amply proved.

Yours sincerely, [Arnold Bennett]

U.C. / TS. / 301

12B George Street
21st March 1922

My dear Eric,

The Great Adventure

Many thanks for your letter of yesterday. It goes a long way, but not the whole way, to answer my criticisms, and I will leave the matter at that.

The dress rehearsal yesterday was awful, and I enclose copy of a letter which I am delivering to Bourchier this morning and which explains the greater part of the fiasco. The question is, if Bourchier cannot be taught a lesson, whether it is worth while

300. A. B. Horne was one of Playfair's backers. The play, *Body and Soul*, had its first performance at the Playhouse, Liverpool, on 15 February 1922.

going on with the contract for *The Great Adventure*, seeing that Bourchier would have to play the principal part. He would simply kill it. I am seeing Vernon tomorrow afternoon.

Yours sincerely, Arnold Bennett

U.C. / T.C.C. / 302
(*To Arthur Bourchier*)

[12B George Street]
21st March 1922

My dear Bourchier,

They say that a bad dress rehearsal means a good first night, and I hope it may be so in this case. But I am quite sure that if you continue to play in the key you adopted yesterday you will very shortly be playing in a dead failure.

Until yesterday you played on the lines laid down by the author and producer, and you were most admirable. Then suddenly, in defiance of all your promises and undertakings, you switch round and adopt the key of low comedy—even of farce. I say nothing of the gags with which you have peppered the piece, because I am simply not going to permit them. I cannot prevent you from ruining the play by turning it into a farce, but I can prevent you from introducing gags and I shall certainly do so.

I credit you with the best motives. I know that you think you are helping the play along. The mischief is that instead of helping the play along you are killing it. The play will fall between two stools. The farcicalities will offend the kind of audience for whom the play is written, but they will not be sufficient to delight the kind of audience that giggles. You get laughs from gigglers, but these laughs are worthless. You would get far louder laughs if you sat down on your hat twice in every scene.

I have explained again and again—what ought to be obvious—

301. *The Great Adventure* was being revived. Bennett's criticisms were of the proposed contract.

The dress rehearsal was of *The Love Match*, which opened on the 21st at the Strand Theatre, of which Arthur Bourchier (1863–1927) was lessee, manager, and principal male actor. Frank Vernon was the producer of the play. Bourchier was near the end of a long and distinguished theatrical career, which began with his founding the University Dramatic Society at Oxford when he was an undergraduate. The arrangement for him to play Ilam Carve in the revival of *The Great Adventure* was abandoned.

that Russ is an extremely able man of the world. He is not a
low comedian; and he is not the sort of clown that would
stumble three times over the same pouf or the sort of abject fool
who in a grave crisis would make the mistake of offering an
incriminating trinket to an injured husband instead of cigar-
ettes, or the sort of callous joker who, just after a harrowing
scene with the husband and desirous of helping the husband,
would transform a serious telephone conversation into an
extract from a rollicking farce.

I could continue this catalogue, but I need not.

None of the other artistes gave a new and forbidden rendering
at the dress rehearsal; none of them either clowned or gagged;
and I see no reason why you should. I regard your tactics as a
serious breach of faith with Vernon and myself, they cannot be
described otherwise; and hence I will not pass them over in
silence. They upset the balance of the play, damaged scene
after scene, did much injustice to some of the other artistes, and
spoilt your own serious scenes.

You have said that the play wants a new fifth act. The play
is a coherent whole, and it is inconceivable that an audience
which has been continually *dérouté* by farcicalities should remain
in a condition to appreciate the closing scenes. The play does
not need a new fifth act. It merely needs the splendid interpretation which hitherto you have given it. You can still give that
interpretation. On the other hand, by utterly changing the key,
by deliberately acting contrary to reiterated advice, and by
breaking faith with the author and producer, you can ruin the
entire affair. It is for you to choose.

I must add that my impressions are not in the least based
upon the attitude of the audience yesterday. The audience was
a special one and could not of course appreciate either the
spirit or the points of the play. In fact the effect was just as if
the theatre had been one vast gallery.

I have shown this letter to our friend Duff Tayler, and I have
sent a copy to Vernon who gave me permission to write to you
direct.

Yours sincerely, [Arnold Bennett]

302. *The Love Match* lasted for one month. Bourchier himself pleased the critic
of *The Times*; the play did not.

On Alistair (Duff) Tayler, see page 275n.

U.C. / TS. / 303

12B George Street
25th April 1922

My dear Eric,

I enclose copy of a letter from Methuen and copy of my reply, for your information.

Yours sincerely, Arnold Bennett

U.C. / T.C. / 304
(*From Sir Algernon Methuen*)

[36 Essex Street]
April 22nd 1922

Dear Bennett,

I congratulate you on *Prohack*. It is brilliant and I have read it with intense admiration. Supple and shrewd also.

By the way are you going to desert me altogether? I hope not. Please believe I want more books from your wonderful pen.

Yours sincerely, [A. Methuen]

P.S. Owing to the great demand the first edition is etc. etc.

U.C. / T.C.C. / 305
(*To Sir Algernon Methuen*)

[12B George Street]
25th April 1922

My dear Methuen,

Many thanks for your kind letter. I am very glad that you like the book. It is rather hard on a publisher when he is expected to do well with a piece of merchandise which he does not really believe in.

As regards the future, I know that I am bound for several books. I should of course be delighted to continue our relations, but it will not have escaped you that you are at a disadvantage as compared with certain other firms in that you do not buy serial rights.

With kind regards.

Yours sincerely, [Arnold Bennett]

305. *Mr. Prohack*, issued in May, was the last of Bennett's novels published by Methuen. There had been unpleasantness between Bennett and Methuen over a

u.c. / ts. / 306

12B George Street
25th April 1922

My dear Eric,

There ought to be a public in the United States for the enclosed article on James Joyce's *Ulysses*. It is to be published here by the *Outlook*, which asked me to write it. Doran might like it for his magazine. The price is not very important.

Yours sincerely, Arnold Bennett

u.c. / ts. / 307

12B George Street
20th May 1922

My dear Eric,

I ordered three copies of *The Old Wives' Tale* the other day from Hodders and received three copies of the American edition in English jackets. Is it right that there should be no available complete English edition of this book? I know that it has not a large sale, but it surely has a steady sale.

Yours sincerely, Arnold Bennett

u.c. / ms. / 308

12B George Street
28–5–22

My dear Eric,

Having regard to what has passed, I don't see why Lasky should have announced in the papers that he had come over to see me among others, unless he had some definite offer in his

---

possible delay in the publication of the novel and also over the fact that in advertising the book Methuen had relied upon an out-of-date list of Bennett's other novels.

306. Bennett says of James Joyce (1882–1941) in the review:

'Anyhow, with his wilfulness, he has made novel reading into a fair imitation of penal servitude. It is not as if his rendering of life was exhaustive, or had the slightest pretension to be exhaustive. The rendering is extremely and ostentatiously partial. . . . His vision of the world and its inhabitants is mean, hostile, and uncharitable. . . . Withal, James Joyce is a very astonishing phenomenon in letters. . . . He has a prodigious humour. He is afraid of naught. . . . The best portions of the novel (unfortunately they constitute only a fraction of the whole) are immortal. I single out the long orgiastic scene, and the long unspoken monologue of Mrs. Bloom which closes the novel.'

Outlook published the review on 29 April, and Doran in the *Bookman* in August.

mind. I haven't heard from him, and I don't think I ought to make the first move. I am engaged for lunch & dinner both Monday & Tuesday, & for tea on Monday, & I leave on Wednesday afternoon for the yacht. I think it would be better if I saw him, but I don't propose to approach him.

Yours, Arnold Bennett

U.C. / MS. / 309

12B George Street
30-5-22

My dear Eric,

Many thanks for your letter about Marston. I quite appreciate all the difficulties. But I was not thinking of a star of the first magnitude; only a reasonably good selling star.

You are under a most grave misapprehension. You think I am going away for a holiday. I am not going away for a holiday. I am going away to work, & shall in all probability come back with one play written by Knoblock & me, & one written by me alone: besides a lot of other stuff.

My address will be as able.

Yours sincerely, Arnold Bennett

U.C. / TS. / 310

12B George Street
30th May 1922

My dear Eric,

Many thanks for your letter of the 29th, as to *Mr. Prohack* and Lasky.

As regards Lasky, I should like to see him unless of course

308. Lasky was shown Bennett's letter of 17 January, and late in February he wrote to Eric Pinker's New York associate (who was now the agent Carl Brandt, 1889–1957), saying that the letter was accurate and that he was now trying to arrange for a screen production of the story.

309. Maurice Marston (1897–) was a partner in the publishing firm of Leonard Parsons Ltd. Bennett was trying to find a good writer for their list.

Knoblock and Bennett wrote *London Life* in June. The other play was not written. Instead, Bennett began thinking about *Riceyman Steps*. On a visit with Knoblock to Southampton the previous summer, Bennett stepped into a bookshop owned by T. James of 34 Bernard Street, and conceived there the notion of writing a story about two misers. He returned this summer with Knoblock and 'had the idea that my projected short story ... would make a fine novel; and within about an hour I had decided to make it a novel, and was much excited'.

everything goes smoothly between him and you. I would come to London to see him if the yacht was not too far away; or he could come to the yacht, where he would have the advantage of seeing both Knoblock and myself together.

My view is that although his firm has fulfilled the letter of the contract with me, the spirit has not been observed. Had I known what to expect I would never have entered into the contract. I do not blame Mr. Lasky, but I do blame his subordinates. I am under the impression that he realises that his subordinates have not been altogether favourable to his schemes, and that it behoves him as the man who personally made the contract with me, to see that something is done. If I had made the contract through a subordinate I should have nothing to say; but I did not. Mr. Lasky admits that he gave me a certain impression at our interviews, and that this impression has not been justified by events. I am convinced that the story which I supplied would make a very good film, and I think that it ought to be done. In any case I consider that I have been very imperfectly remunerated for the three months hard work which I put into the thing. I should not care to undertake anything else for Mr. Lasky's firm on the same terms unless this first affair is satisfactorily cleared up.

I do not believe very much in the judgments of these experts. How long had you been trying to sell *The Card*? Years and years. And yet now when it is produced—and not very adequately produced (I could have done it much better myself)—it is a most striking success. It has no slapstick stuff in it, or very little, and yet it keeps the audiences laughing the whole time.

Yours sincerely, Arnold Bennett

u.c. / ms. / 311

Yacht Marie Marguerite
7-7-22

My dear Eric,

The play is done & at the typewriter's, & Knoblock has returned to the Albany. A copy is to be delivered to you on Monday. If it doesn't come, please telephone to Knoblock.

310. *The Card* was produced by the Ideal Film Company, with Laddie Cliff, an actor in variety, making his film début as Denry. It was reviewed enthusiastically in *The Times* on 1 May. In 1952, J. Arthur Rank produced another successful version, in which Alec Guinness starred.

London Life is the title; 3 acts and 9 scenes; the history of a Cabinet minister, some big sets, including a political reception & dance, an evening open-air fête in the gardens of a millionaire's palace, and an afternoon on the Terrace of the House of Commons. It is intended primarily for Drury Lane, & Alfred Butt is (in theory) greatly interested in it. If that fails, then Grossmith & Malone, & then Cochran & the New Oxford.

Yours sincerely, Arnold Bennett

u.c. / ms. / 312

Yacht Marie Marguerite
15–7–22

My dear Eric,

Lilian

I'll write 1000 words, if the price is reasonable. But it must be understood that the end simply is that Lilian has the baby, looks after it, & runs the business. She may marry again—probably will marry the doctor. But she can't possibly *marry* him in this book. She may perceive how comfortable and loving & useful he is.

I haven't wired as I only got your letter here today.

Yours sincerely, Arnold Bennett

P.S. Under no circumstances will I write anything until a definite contract has been made.

311. Bennett was sailing off the English coast during June, July, and August. The Albany was Knoblock's London club.

Drury Lane, of which Sir Alfred Butt (1878–1962) was co-manager, was the home of spectacular entertainment. George Grossmith (1874–1935) and J. A. E. Malone (d. 1929) controlled the Winter Garden and other theatres; Grossmith, who introduced the revue to England, took over the management of Drury Lane in 1931. Charles Cochran (famous later for his revues and his Young Ladies) was then running the New Oxford Theatre.

312. Apparently George Doran objected to both the brevity and the morality of *Lilian*, a very light novel that Bennett wrote between 4 December and 24 January. It concerns a vain and pretty typist who loses her job and then saves herself by becoming the mistress of her former employer. When she becomes pregnant, he marries her. He dies before the child is born, and the doctor who has tended him turns his attention upon her. The novel ends at this point. Bennett implies that Lilian, who is a frivolous cousin of Sophia Baines of *The Old Wives' Tale*, may make a virtuous mother and an energetic proprietress of the typewriting business she has inherited. The novel began appearing in *Cassell's Magazine* in July, and was published in book form later in the year.

U.C. / TS. / 313

12B George Street
8th November 1922

My dear Eric,

I very much differ from the general verdict on *The Secret Agent*. I think that Act I and the first two scenes of Act II are superb. To my mind the third scene of Act II is comparatively weak, and the author has not been well served by his interpreters here. Act III is not equal to Act I, but it is very good, except that the last scene is a great deal too long. The scene between husband and wife before she kills him is simply magnificent. The play is extremely interesting, dramatically, as well as in all the details of psychology. It holds you completely. If it holds you completely the construction must be fundamentally good. Here and there—especially in the last act—I think the construction is a bit clumsy, but the occasional clumsiness is a trifle. The entire newspaper press has talked mere bosh about the construction. It would. The play is certainly the best I have seen for a very, very long time, and by a long way the best. It is highly distinguished. Twenty years will pass before such a play can possibly hope to have a success in London. London is fed on pap, and dishonest pap at that. I should think that on the continent the thing ought to have a very considerable success. It is, artistically, a most disturbing play, for the reason that it shows up, in a way that nothing but a first-rate work of art can do, the superlative fatuity, futility, infantility, and falsity of even the respectable better-than-average English plays that we talk seriously about in this here city.

Yours sincerely, Arnold Bennett

313. Conrad's play opened at the Ambassadors Theatre on 3 November. Conrad wrote to a friend: 'My play has failed. It was put to death by the press with all imaginable reverence and respect but with a ruthlessness that was really like Ancient Rome.' Eric Pinker forwarded a copy of Bennett's letter to Conrad, and Conrad replied in part to Bennett: 'One can't very well thank a man for his native generosity (and yours shines in every page you have written in all these years); one can only be deeply moved by it.' He agreed with Bennett's comments, and noted that he had written the third scene in Act II three times.

u.c. / ts. / 314

12B George Street
13th November 1922

My dear Eric,

I see that the advertising of *Lilian* has at last begun. On Saturday I saw for the first time an advertisement of this book, which I suppose has been out for quite a month. I do not know why the advertisements have been postponed. The other big firms seem to have kept up their advertisements as usual.

Such advertisements as I have seen do not strike me as satisfactory. I was told long ago that the first edition of *Lilian* was exhausted on publication, but I see no reference to this fact in the advertisements, although the number of editions of other books, mentioned in the same advertisement, are given.

Further, I object to a new book being put under an old book, as mine is put under *Tell England*. It is quite possible that *Tell England* is selling even now far better than *Lilian*, but the custom of all good publishing houses is to put new books first.

It may be argued that Cassells advertising is Cassells business and not mine. But I shall not agree. I know you will support me when I say that I am not a grumbler about advertising. Indeed I cannot remember having raised a complaint on this subject for many years.

Yours sincerely, Arnold Bennett

P.S. It seems to me that it should be part of your business to keep a critical eye on the advertising of the books of your clients.   A. B.

u.c. / ts. / 315

12B George Street
14th November 1922

My dear Eric,

I enclose, in duplicate, the typescript of the first part of my new novel, about 20,000 words. I have not yet thought of a title. The only one that has occurred to me is *Resist not Evil*, but I do not know whether this will quite do. I should like you to

314. *Tell England*, an inspirational novel by Ernest Raymond (1888–), was published in February.

read it yourself before sending it out. It is a rather serious work. Elsie is the real heroine. As I told you on the telephone, I do not see it in the *Cosmopolitan*, but I certainly think that there ought to be a place for it serially in the United States. I feel pretty sure that it will hold the reader. I was very disappointed that *Lilian* could not be serialised in America. It was not everybody's meat, but it was in my opinion somebody's meat. I have no doubt that Brandt did his best. Nevertheless his best was not good enough, and the loss to me was considerable. What happened to *Lilian* in the way of refusals I have no idea, as you did not send me any report of any kind. I do hope that the same fate will not occur with the new book.

I estimate that the total length will be between 80,000 and 100,000 words.

Yours sincerely, Arnold Bennett

u.c. / ts. / 316

12B George Street
24th November 1922

My dear Eric,

Laurie

I quite agree with you. I did not think there was very much in the scheme, but I felt that you ought to know about it. I should be pleased to let Laurie have my play *Don Juan*, which I have decided to get published by someone or other in a limited edition. It is the best play I ever wrote, and will certainly one day be produced. At the present moment Faber is rather keen on it.

Serial novel

The whole movement of this book is slow, and must be slow. It is in the same mood as *The Old Wives' Tale*. I have just finished

315. *Resist not Evil* became *Riceyman Steps*, a title that Bennett took from the name 'Plum Pudding Steps' that local inhabitants applied to the steps leading to Granville Square in Clerkenwell. (The steps are so dark that if a girl goes down them often with a young man she will soon be as fat as a plum pudding.) Bennett spoke of the transfer of his setting from Southampton to Clerkenwell as 'a feat of transport surpassing anything ever done in that line in the U.S.A.—the moving of an entire bookseller's shop with all its books and dust from a South Coast port'. He began writing the novel on 10 October.

The firm of Brandt and Brandt, which replaced Paul Reynolds as the Pinkers' New York connexion, was headed by Carl Brandt (see page 314n.).

the second part, making 32,000 words in all, and I will send it to you shortly. I still think that something ought to be done with it.

Yours sincerely, Arnold Bennett

u.c. / ts. / 317

12B George Street
25th November 1922

My dear Eric,
Many thanks for your two letters.

How to Make the Best of Life

I enclose this agreement signed. I notice that the subject matter of clause 5 has been altered in form and expanded. I have struck out the words 'obscene, indecent'. I do not like these words. Who is to decide what is obscene or indecent? Many Catholics considered that *The Pretty Lady* was obscene, and Sir Ernest might well think it indecent. But I do not. I object to these words on principle, and not because there is anything whatever in *How to Make the Best of Life* to which anybody could possibly take exception. On the whole I think that the clause has been improved, but I scarcely see myself in the position of having allowed my publishers to decide what is or is not obscene or indecent. If there are any arguments on the other side I am very willing to hear them.

Laurie

I think you should try him first with *Don Juan*. But later on I see the possibility of letting him have a selection of extracts from my journal, which has now been going on for over thirty years. Please do not, however, allow him to get away with a false idea of what this journal is. It is mainly a journal of impressions, and it contains scarcely any reminiscences of well-known people. Nevertheless all the people who have read it seem to find it rather enthralling. I would not agree to him

---

316. T. Werner Laurie (d. 1944) wanted to publish a limited edition of some reminiscences. Leslie Faber (1879–1929) directed and starred in a revival of *The Great Adventure* in 1924, but neither he nor anyone else ever produced *Don Juan de Marana*.

having any say as to the periodical in which the stuff should appear first, supposing that it was used serially.

Yours sincerely, Arnold Bennett

u.c. / ts. / 318

75, Cadogan Square
S.W.1
12th January 1923

My dear Eric,

It must be quite two months since I heard a word as to the progress of *London Life*, and quite three months since I heard a word about the Lasky affair. Both these matters are very important to me and I do not enjoy my complete ignorance of their progress or lack of progress. I know that in making no disclosure until something is actually done you are merely following the tradition of your office. But I always objected to this method, and more than once I complained to J. B. about it. J. B., however, was very set in his ways. I begin this year well by solemnly announcing my opinion that an author should receive about once a month a full and exact account of what has been done or not done in regard to any really important matter. I feel sure that if you had important matters in the hands of another person you would insist on knowing all about them at pretty short intervals.

Yours sincerely, Arnold Bennett

317. Hodder and Stoughton issued *How to Make the Best of Life* ('a subject as to which I know ½ nothing,' Bennett wrote to his nephew Richard, 'but a good subject') in 1923. Eric Pinker explained that the intention of clause 5—a new one recommended by the Society of Authors—was to 'indemnify the publisher in case of an action being taken by a third party after the book is published'. Bennett yielded.

Laurie published *Don Juan de Marana* in 1923. He did not do anything with the journal extracts.

318. 75, Cadogan Square, described by Bennett as 'my rather noble thing in houses', was his home from December 1922 to October 1930. In *Noble Essences*, Sir Osbert Sitwell tells of a visit there by a friend just after Bennett moved in. The removal was accompanied by a severe attack of influenza, and the friend found Bennett in bed, looking at himself reflected in several mirrors that hung on the walls. 'The friend remarked: "I couldn't lie there looking at myself reflected on and on into infinity like that!"

'To which Arnold replied, in a tone of complacency:

'"I . . . t suits me down to the ground!"'

BUTLER / TS. / 319
(*From Eric Pinker*)

Talbot House
26th [16th] January 1923

My dear Bennett,

I sincerely hope all my clients have not made the same New Year's resolution as you, or at least that if they have they are not so good at keeping their resolutions as I expect you are. If I had to report to every client even monthly I should have to employ extra staff for work which seems to me would serve no practical purpose. As you will doubtless have assumed, I am keeping up this tradition of the office because I think it is a good one, but naturally I am always ready to change any tradition in accordance with my clients' wishes, particularly your wishes, if it is possible for me to do so, and I will see that my end of your resolution is looked after in future. There are other considerations in addition to the above with which I will not trouble you now, but which I should like to put before you some time when we meet.

I regret to say that I have no progress to report in either of the two matters which you mention and which are to the fore at the moment. Golding Bright tells me that Dean is still favourably considering *London Life*, but he fell ill again and had to go back to his Nursing Home, in consequence of which his decision is again delayed. Bright seems to think that Dean is the most hopeful possibility at present, so that it would not be wise to press him too hard.

I have tried all available means to influence Lasky—with the suggestion that he should take some [of] the old books to make up for *The Wedding Dress* and so on, without success. As you know, things in the film world have been pretty bad for the last year or more, and are only just beginning to look up again. I shall go and see Lasky when I go to America in April, and shall do my utmost to make him feel the weight of the moral obligation which undoubtedly he has towards you.

The portion of the new novel you sent me is now in America under consideration with Ray Long.

Sincerely yours, Eric S. Pinker

319. Basil Dean was currently managing director of the St. Martin's Theatre. He was noted for his productions of spectacular plays, one of the most famous being

U.C. / TS. / 320

[75, Cadogan Square]
17th January 1923

My dear Eric,

Many thanks for your letter of the 16th, (dated 26th). I am only asking you to report on *important* matters. When matters involving thousands of pounds are in progress (or not in progress) the client naturally and properly wants to have exact information about them. Such information may well influence him in his plans. All agents keep their clients informed, and I see no reason why literary agents should be different from other agents. If your solicitor had something important of yours in hand, and told you nothing about it for three months, I guarantee you would be getting restive under the silence.

I shall be pleased to hear your further arguments when we meet. I meant to have seen you at the Reform Club today, but as my chest is still weak I did not venture out in the fog.

Yours sincerely, Arnold Bennett

P.S. Perhaps you will make a point in future of seeing that all copies of plays, including the prompt book and the actors' parts, are returned to you on the expiration of the contract. For example, *The Title*. Is this contract expired, and have you had all the scripts returned? Also *Sacred and Profane Love* and *Judith*. A. B.

U.C. / TS. / 321

75, Cadogan Square
17th January 1923

My dear Eric,

Many thanks for your letter of the 15th. I enclose one set of proofs of *How to Make the Best of Life*. This is for Doran. The

---

James Elroy Flecker's *Hassan*, which he produced at His Majesty's Theatre this year. During 1924 he was co-manager with Alfred Butt of Drury Lane, where *London Life* finally appeared. On Golding Bright, see page 240.

The Wedding Dress was never produced. In an article 'In the Film World', published in *The Savour of Life* in 1928, Bennett recounts his experience with Lasky. He notes therein his total earnings of his books and plays from the films up through about 1923: *The Great Adventure* and *Buried Alive*, first sale, £200, second sale, £1,250; *The Grand Babylon Hotel*, £150; *The Card*, £500; *Milestones*, first sale, £200, second sale, £2,000.

Ray Long (see page 295) was considering *Riceyman Steps*. As Bennett foresaw (in his letter of 14 November 1922), Long did not take it.

other is all ready, but I am still wondering about the title. I do not care for your title *The Best of Life*, and I have not got rid of my fancy for *Experience has taught*. The literary life is very difficult.

I will see Everett before the end of the month.

Yours sincerely, Arnold Bennett

U.C. / TS. / 322

75, Cadogan Square
29th January 1923

My dear Eric,

Sir Hedley Le Bas, who is a friend of mine, has a scheme for publishing 'The Twelve Best Novels of Arnold Bennett, selected by H. G. Wells', and he is to see you about it. Wells has already consented to do the selection. I think that by means of canvassers he accomplishes very large sales. He says that he feels sure he can get the consent of the various publishers concerned. He is a thoroughly straight and decent fellow, and if the project goes any further I should advise you not to be too rigid in the matter of terms.

Yours sincerely, Arnold Bennett

U.C. / TS. / 323

75, Cadogan Square
2nd February 1923

My dear Eric,

No one will give me a good title for my book, so, with regret, I shall have to call it *How to Make the Best of Life*. I am sending the proofs by this post. I wish you would reason with the publishers about the 'rules' above and below the running title. The rules are against all the traditions of good typography, and very ugly.

Yours sincerely, Arnold Bennett

321. On Everett, see pages 288–9.
322. On the beginning of this proposal, see pages 282–3.

BUTLER / T.C.C. / 324

[75, Cadogan Square]
9th March 1923

My dear Eric,

Many thanks for your letter. I expect to finish my novel on Tuesday next, and one morning within the next few days after that I will call and see you.

I have been so busy getting over influenza, and settling into my new home and writing my novel, that I have not really had an opportunity of asking you and Mrs. Eric to come here. Could you possibly lunch on either Saturday or Sunday, the 17th or 18th?

Yours sincerely, [Arnold Bennett]

BUTLER / TS. / 325
(*From Eric Pinker*)

Talbot House
19th July 1923

My dear Bennett,

The contract for *London Life* is not through yet. Golding Bright is still arguing about details with Dean. I am doing my best to keep them both up to scratch, and hope to get the thing settled quite soon now.

I am afraid that after all there is going to be some trouble with Cassells about *Riceyman Steps*. Cassells decided they could not serialise the story, and the payment for the serial rights apparently stuck in the Board's throat. . . .

Cassells wanted me to ask you whether you would consider giving them the serial rights of the next novel for nothing, because they were unable to use this one. I told them, however, that I was sure it would be quite useless making any such proposals to you, whereupon they said that they would not proceed with the setting up of the book, as it had been previously arranged they should. With your approval, I propose to be absolutely unyielding in this matter. Publishers are getting too fond of doing this kind of thing, and in this case I do not think there is anything either in ethics or law to be said for Cassells.

Sincerely yours, Eric S. Pinker

324. Bennett finished *Riceyman Steps* the following Saturday, the 17th.

u.c. / ms. / 326

Yacht Marie Marguerite
[Ostende]
23–7–23

My dear Eric,

Thanks for your letter of the 19th.

Years ago Flower, talking about *The Old Wives' Tale*, told me that had he had the chance he would gladly have used it as a serial, & that he wanted from me absolutely the best realistic stuff I could do.

Otherwise I should not have dreamed of writing a book like *Riceyman Steps* for a serial.

I know that Flower thinks highly of the book, and as regards its particular tone & quality he has himself said in a recent article:—

'*When I read the manuscript* [*of R. S.*] *it reminded me more of The Old Wives' Tale than any other romance he has given us.*'

You know that when I have made a contract I am always exceedingly anxious to give satisfaction to others, quite apart from satisfying myself. I regret that there should be any trouble about *Riceyman Steps*, but my conscience is absolutely clear in the matter.

I don't quite know what you mean by the Board saying 'they would not proceed with the setting up of the Book'. When last I saw (or heard from) Flower he was *exceedingly* anxious to get the book out in the autumn, & expressed anxiety lest possible serialisation in the States might prevent this.

You have my instructions to act according to your own judgment; but under no circumstances will I give them another novel for nothing.

Yours sincerely, Arnold Bennett

P.S. Kindly send a copy of the above letter to Miss Nerney for my archives. A. B.

326. Bennett was sailing off the English coast during most of June, July, and August.

U.C. / MS. / 327

> Yacht Marie Marguerite
> 13–8–23

My dear Eric,

Many thanks for yours of the 8th. I enclose a letter I have received from Flower with a copy of my reply. (Please return these to Miss Nerney.)

I think your suggestion is an excellent one. Please do as you like.

> Yours sincerely, Arnold Bennett

U.C. / T.C. / 328
(*From Newman Flower*)

> 8 August, 1923

My dear Arnold,

Pinker and I had a conference yesterday about *Riceyman Steps*. You probably know the difficulty we are in with regard to the serial. Let me say at once that I think this is one of the best books you have written for years, but I think that as a serial it is quite impossible. I think you recognise this, because you said when we discussed it in January that it was peculiar.

The trouble is, of course, that there is no movement much in the first half of the book. Pinker has, I believe, submitted this serial everywhere, and has not had an offer for it, so I have asked him to suggest to you whether you would agree to the following: We have another agreement for two books and one serial from you. Can we not pass the serial of *Riceyman Steps* and take the serials of both the two books in the next agreement?

You once reminded me that I said I would run *The Old Wives' Tale* as a serial. If I had the right to abridge it I think it would make a fine serial, but I don't think *Riceyman Steps* comes into the same category, from the serial point of view, as *The Old Wives' Tale*. . . .

I hope you will see your way to agree to my suggestion if you can.

> With all good wishes,
> Yours sincerely, [Newman]

327. Eric Pinker suggested as a compromise solution that Cassell's payment of £1,000 for the serial rights be halved.

U.C. / T.C. / 329
(*To Newman Flower*)

[Yacht Marie Marguerite]
13 August 1923

My dear Newman,

Many thanks for your letter of the 8th which has just reached me.

I do not conceive it possible that any grave trouble can arise between you and me. Pinker understands the situation, and as the negotiations are in his hands I will not butt in.

Nothing could surprise me less than that Pinker failed to sell the novel elsewhere. Of course he failed. The novel was written at your most startling instigation for *you*, and you are the only man in the world who would have given me such encouragement. Had you not expressed a strong desire for my best realistic work I should not have dreamed of delivering *Riceyman Steps* for serial purposes.

I have no doubt that you and Pinker will be able to come to some satisfactory agreement. (I expect to be in London soonish —in September—and we must then foregather.)

Ever yours, [A. B.]

BUTLER / T.C.C. / 330

[75, Cadogan Square]
5th September 1923

My dear Eric,

Many thanks for your letter of yesterday.

The *Riceyman Steps* affair seems deplorable. It seems to me that there is something very gravely wrong with the contract if it does not contain a clause fixing the outside date for the publication of the book. In the absence of such a clause the publisher is practically in a position to refuse any serial he likes. I think that we had better not have any more of these contracts. The present one amounts to a farce. I am perfectly innocent in the matter. I wrote the book at the special instigation of Flower, and I shall be involved in a very severe loss.

I am not mistaken about what Doran said. He mentioned the matter himself. He mentioned the sum and he jokingly reminded me that I had said to him at Christmas that it was exactly the sum which I should need to 'get into' this house.

I shall be very much obliged if you can manage to send me my monthly cheque not later than the 3rd of the month, in accordance with the ancient custom of your esteemed firm.

Yesterday F. S. and I were discussing the question of agents' percentages, and we agreed that we should both suggest to you the propriety of not paying you a commission on journalistic work not obtained through you. This payment of commission on such work has stuck in my throat for many years past, and as a fact I have not mentioned to you (as an honest man would) various articles upon which you are under our contract entitled to demand a commission. The system seems to me to be inexcusably unfair, especially having regard to the fact that the bulk of my journalistic work sprang from the publication in volume form of my *Evening News* articles, to which publication J. B. was strongly opposed but which I insisted on. J. B. thought that they would injure my reputation. I did not. He afterwards admitted several times that he had been quite wrong.

The chief argument J. B. brought against any change in our arrangement was that unless an agent had *all* the author's business he would not take the same interest in the author's business. This argument annoys me acutely and always did. Why should he not take the same interest?

I do not propose any very drastic changes in our contract, but nevertheless in my opinion while unestablished authors pay too little commission established authors pay too much. My obligations to your father were very considerable, and I have always said so openly and have always done my best to get new clients for the firm. At the same time the firm has been very well rewarded for J. B.'s faith in me, and I call that account square.

Of course you will not breathe a word to F. S. that I have mentioned his name here. You will shortly be hearing from him.

Yours sincerely, [Arnold Bennett]

330. Doran's royalty payment was overdue.

F. S. is Frank Swinnerton.

In *Just as It Happened* Sir Newman Flower tells of the outcome of the quarrel over *Riceyman Steps*. He had paid Bennett £1,000 for the serial rights to the novel.

'This [sum] had been insisted upon by his agent. I could not get an offer of fourpence for these serial rights in England. . . .

'We [Bennett and Flower] were sitting at the luncheon table. He put down his

L.A.B.—Z

BUTLER / TS. / 331
(*From Eric Pinker*)

Talbot House
7th December 1923

My dear Bennett,

Flower tells me that he has an idea for a long complete story, which he is very keen for you to write, as he thinks for one thing that the volume of stories would be greatly strengthened by having a long story as the backbone. I understand that Flower is going to see you early next week, when he will put this idea before you, so I am not proceeding with the contract until I hear further.

Sincerely yours, Eric S. Pinker

U.C. / TS. / 332

75, Cadogan Square
12th December 1923

My dear Eric,

Many thanks for your letter of yesterday and the enclosure from the *Royal*. This is very deplorable, and I think that it is a pity that nothing should have been said until after the delivery of seven articles out of ten. I also think it is a pity that I was not told that the *Royal* catered specially for the young.

---

knife and fork quietly. He ceased to chew. He looked at me in his queer, mysterious fashion; one did not know what he was going to say. Then he raised his right hand—as he so often did when his terrible stammer and loss of words would not permit his lips to loose those words that waited on them. He held his hand in the air. . . . searching . . . trying to speak. . . .

'Presently he said:

'"This is a . . . great novel. . . . Those editors who-who don't . . . who don't w-want the . . . the s-serial rights . . . are fools. My dear Newman, they . . . they are bloody fools. . . . But they are all God's creatures. . . ." His hand came down to the table. "They are all . . . God's creatures . . . we m-must pity them. T-tell them. . . ." The hand began to go up again, then waved up and down like a semaphore signal, "Tell them . . . to g-go to Hell. . . . And I will repay you . . . will repay you a thousand pounds. . . . Kipper on toast. . . ." (He was studying the menu which a waiter was holding like an order for execution before his face.) "Kipper . . . kipper on toast . . . I-I will repay you . . . repay you a thousand pounds. . . ."'

331. Flower suggested a story involving the servant Elsie in *Riceyman Steps* and the daughter of Dr. Raste in the same novel. Bennett wrote the story as 'Elsie and the Child', and Flower published it as the title story of a collection in 1924.

At the same time I am not surprised that the articles are a disappointment. My experience now extends over some thirty years, and I have nearly always found that commissioned articles are a disappointment to the people who have commissioned them. I remember that *T.P.'s Weekly* was so disappointed with my articles that it declined to pay more than seven guineas each for them, whereupon I left the paper. These disappointing articles, like all my disappointing articles, when collected in book form, have had a continuous sale, year after year, and still have. I think that what has saved me is the fact that editors generally like my articles when they read them in magazines which they do not edit. It is only when they get them in their own magazines that they do not like them. I have often noticed this. I recollect *Harper's* not very long since printed with much reluctance and regret an article of mine which it had commissioned, and the editor told me that he wondered I could write such stuff. Immediately afterwards the *Century* came eagerly along and expressed a strong desire to have from me articles as good as the condemned article in *Harper's*.

All which is calculated to make authors sardonic and calm under reproof. I can remember only one instance of an editor admitting that my articles had given satisfaction. When I had finished a series for the *Sunday Pictorial* the editor wrote to me to say that the articles had done his paper good. I have never fully recovered from this shock. No doubt the said editor is a large-minded lunatic and a traitor to his class.

As for the present series, my opinion on them is of course worthless, but it cannot be denied that some of the articles, such as those on small-talk and friend-making, are of an absolutely original nature. Nobody has ever, so far as my knowledge goes, treated such subjects in such a way, or treated them at all, in a magazine before. I think that the articles before-mentioned, and the one on books, are as good and as jolly as the *Royal* would be likely to get from anybody. I have received many unsolicited compliments on the first of the series, and my most candid critic told me that the one on books was the best she had ever read on the subject.

I will see what can be done with the remaining three *Royal* articles, but of course you will understand that I cannot completely alter my tone towards the end of the series.

Yours sincerely, Arnold Bennett

U.C. / TS. / 333
PRIVATE

75, Cadogan Square
27th December 1923

My dear Eric,

Referring to our conversation some weeks ago about a new contract between us:—

Please take this letter as formal notice to terminate the old contract with your father under Clause VI.

Roughly I suggest the following variations of the old contract. 5% commission on books.

Films to be kept out of the contract entirely. I see no prospect of doing any film work at present, but if I do any I think it will come through my personal relations with the film kings. Of course if you achieve any film contract entirely off your own bat, I shall be very willing for you to take 10% of the proceeds. I want to except films from the contract so as to be free to employ another agent, particularly American, if I wish to do so. I have, however, no such other agent in mind at all.

I am willing for you to have 10% on all serials and short

332. C. Arthur Pearson paid £300 apiece for the rather long articles that began appearing in the *Royal Magazine* in November 1923. The first article was on friend-making. On 1 February Bennett had written to Pearson's:

'You have no doubt read all or some of my recent articles in the *Strand* [*How to Make the Best of Life*]. They dealt with the more serious side of life,—effort, education, ideals, economics, family rearing, etc. I now want to write something of a lighter nature,—rather lighter in texture and much lighter in subject, the general subject which I propose being the pleasures, diversions, and distractions of life. I hope I am not deceiving myself in thinking that I could deal with this matter in a way which your readers would find (a) amusing (b) informative (c) helpful in the business of making their lives fuller and more interesting. I should suggest such subjects as travel, friendships, collecting, hobbies, games, reading, the arts (including music), scientific lore, the lore of the town one lives in, the lore of the countryside or village one lives in, etc. etc. . . .'

In November Pearson's wrote Eric Pinker to say they were delighted with the sixth article, 'Games and Pastimes'. In December they wrote to say that the articles did not have much life to them and that Bennett did not seem to be interested in writing them. The series was never published in book form.

After *Harper's* published 'Some Impressions of Portugal' in January 1922, the *Century* took three stories and an article. They had not published anything by Bennett since 1914. On the *Sunday Pictorial* see pages 294 and 349.

stories, and on all articles for which you obtain a commission; but articles which come to me direct I wish to exclude from the contract as already agreed between us.

With regard to clause VII of the old contract, I think that £500 ought to be altered to £100 in the case of contracts which are over two years old.

The new contract is of course to be personal to yourself, and shall be voidable at once in case of your death (which I desire not), or your retirement from business. This is much more important now than it was in your father's time. When he was alive I had you to look forward to in case of accident, but whom have I to look forward to now?

Yours sincerely, Arnold Bennett

BUTLER / TS. / 334
(*From Eric Pinker*)
PRIVATE
Talbot House
3rd January 1924

My dear Bennett:

I write to acknowledge receipt of your letter of December 27th containing formal notice to terminate as from this date your contract with my father, which has been carried on with me. Any new contract we make will, I take it, come into force on the 27th December 1924, at the end of the 12 months mentioned in Clause 6 of the present contract.

I have very carefully considered the variations you suggest in the new contract, and propose that instead of different rates of commission we should have a uniform rate of $7\frac{1}{2}\%$.

In regard to film rights of books already written, if you do not intend immediately to deal with these yourself or through another agent, I suggest that they should remain in the contract until you decide to make other arrangements to accord with which their exclusion would be necessary. If you agree to

---

333. The old contract with Pinker, dated 19 March 1913, stipulated in Clause I that Pinker was to be sole agent except for plays in the United States and Canada, in Clause II that the commission on all literary work was to be 10 per cent., except for $7\frac{1}{2}$ per cent. for plays, in Clause VI that upon Pinker's death the contract was terminable immediately upon notice and that the contract was otherwise terminable on either side after twelve months' notice, and in Clause VII that when the contract was terminated Pinker should have no claim except on previously contracted material and then only to the amount of £500 on each contract.

this, I propose that I should be allowed to deduct 10% commission on the film sales where I have to employ another agent and split the commission with him. In cases where I make the deal direct, the commission to be 7½% as I have proposed for other things. I don't think I can do more than I am doing in the film market. I am employing two agents in New York and one in Los Angeles, besides my own energies.

I don't think I quite understand the inwardness of your proposal with regard to Clause 7, and in any case it would seem to me fair that this clause should be the same in the new contract. The legal position is that the heirs of an agent who dies are entitled to any commission earned under contracts the agent made for his author before his death, as long as the agency business is carried on, so as to be able to collect the payments due under the contracts, and the major part of the work having been done, this would seem to me fair in ethics also. I propose, therefore, that Clause 6 and 7 in the new contract should be identical with the same clauses in the old. The eventuality mentioned in the last paragraph of your letter would thus be met. I do not think you can say I am not doing my best to provide for the 'succession'. I have my young brother with me now, and I hope in a few years he will have trained on into an able assistant. Looking further forward, I have three step-children, and I shall be very disappointed if I cannot make at least one respectable Literary Agent out of them, and it was not for lack of wishes that my wife presented me on Christmas Day with a daughter instead of another potential occupier of my chair.

I shall be glad to hear from you as soon as you have considered my counter proposal, and if you would like to see me to discuss them I am, of course, as always entirely at your service.

Sincerely yours, Eric S. Pinker

U.C. / TS. / 335
PRIVATE

75, Cadogan Square
7th January 1924

My dear Eric,

Many thanks for your letter of the 3rd.

My intention certainly was not that the present contract

---

334. Ralph Pinker (1900–) joined the firm in 1923. He began to take charge of the London office in 1926, when Eric went to America to establish a New York branch.

should terminate twelve months hence. My intention was that it should terminate at the end of last year. On your father's death I told you that I would give you twelve months before making any alteration, so that you should be able to say to your other clients that I had continued with you exactly as with your father. You know I gave you considerably more than a year. Had I not been anxious to help you in every way I should have terminated the contract at once under Clause VI. It is quite true that I have not given you formal notice in writing, and if you insist on formalities I am of course in your hands.

I think it will be better for you to have 10% on commissions for serials and stories, and 5% on books. If you get commissions for the former you will have well earned your 10%. You cannot possibly earn 10% on the books. There is no trouble whatever in negotiating for a book. I suppose that I never make less than £2,000 out of a novel, and I consider that £200 on this is decidedly excessive, and that £100 is richly sufficient. Moreover I do not conceive that anybody on earth would disagree with me.

Film rights are not in the present contract and I see no reason why they should be in the new contract. You will be perfectly free to deal with any cinema rights off your own bat, provided that I have not forestalled you by my personal efforts.

I agree to clause VII remaining as it is.

I do not agree to Clause VI remaining as it is. I think that the period of notice should be six months.

I am sure that you are doing everything possible to provide yourself with an adequate successor, but you cannot have one for a number of years. This of course is not your fault, nor do I suggest that it is.

If I acted on the advice which I have taken I should do as has been done in other cases, namely, give myself freedom to withhold any business from you if I thought I could do it as well myself. I should not, however, for purely sentimental reasons touching our friendship, like to make such a suggestion.

Yours sincerely, Arnold Bennett

TEXAS / MS. / 336

75, Cadogan Square
13–1–24

My dear Eric,

In writing to you on Friday I did not express myself well about the old rate of commission on book contracts made previous to the 1st inst. I meant that I thought the old commission should continue on contracts which were actually working,—that is on books actually published. I think that the new commission should apply to books not yet published. Otherwise I should be bound to the old commission for years to come in respect to, for instance, the Cassell books: which in my opinion would be quite contrary to the spirit of the new arrangement.

Yours sincerely, Arnold Bennett

U.C. / TS. / 337

75, Cadogan Square
16th January 1924

My dear Eric,

A number of self-important people of whom I am one, think that Tomlinson is one of the greatest writers of the age. He will probably become popular in another ten years time, but in my opinion he will never become very popular because he is not likely to write fiction. His particular stunt ought to be to write series of descriptive articles for high-class American magazines. There is very little scope for him in English magazines.

His best book is *Sea and Jungle* or some such title.

There is no question of him being 'able to go on doing work like this'. He has been doing it for 15 years, and he is in the very prime of life.

I certainly consider that if you get the chance you ought to try him. At the worst you will have a great writer on your string.

Yours sincerely, Arnold Bennett

336. The contract was settled on the terms indicated in the letters of the 7th and 13th.
337. H. M. Tomlinson (1875–1958) published *The Sea and the Jungle* in 1912. He did not come to Pinker.

u.c. / ts. / 338

75, Cadogan Square
5th February 1924

My dear Eric,

London Life

Many thanks for your letter. I enclose copy of a letter which I have written to Bright. As he wrote to me I thought I might as well write to him, but you will see that at the end I have put the matter in your hands.

Yours sincerely, Arnold Bennett

u.c. / t.c.c. / 339
(*To R. Golding Bright*)

[75, Cadogan Square]
5th February 1924

My dear Golding,

London Life

Many thanks for your letter of the 1st. So far as I am concerned the answer is easy. I do not very much care either way.

I agree with you that a production at Drury Lane would have certain scenic advantages. I do not, however, attach a great deal of importance to these advantages, though I attach some. On the other hand it is just possible that Drury Lane may not be quite the best place for the play, seeing that the regular 'patrons' of Drury Lane of this generation have certainly never seen anything like it, and it would strike the great majority of them as rather thin stuff.

Financially I see nothing to choose between the two theatres. If a play gets a fair start a certain number of people will go to see that play, and a smaller theatre, to my mind, means simply a longer run. This applies particularly to plays whose appeal is not of the very crudest kind.

The terms suggested seem to me to be fairly reasonable.

Despite the fact that I see no great material advantage in Drury Lane, a production there has attractions for me as being in the nature of a jolly lark.

I will cheerfully agree to the Drury Lane project only on one condition, namely, the play is the next play produced there, and that it inaugurates Basil Dean's management. There would be some kudos for the authors if Dean began with this play, and there would be some kudos also for Dean himself. Dean is a very remarkable man.

I am sending a duplicate of this letter to Pinker. You will therefore no doubt discuss the matter with him.

Yours, [Arnold Bennett]

u.c. / ts. / 340

75, Cadogan Square
15th February 1924

My dear Eric,

Many thanks for your letter of yesterday and the enclosure. You were of course quite right to submit the proposal to me. There is my play *The Bright Island*. I suppose it is about 20,000 words in length. How would this do? Should I make more out of it by ordinary publication? What rights does the *Bookman's Journal* want for its £100? What about copyright in America, and so on. All this is very complicated.

I enclose two copies of the story, 'Elsie and the Child'. I regard this story as entirely unsuitable for serial publication, unless it is printed in one instalment as Flower will print it. I doubt whether any American editor will see anything in it. Nevertheless I must give my opinion that it is rather good, and far better than I expected it to be under the circumstances. I arranged with Flower that it should be between 15,000 and 20,000 words in length. It is 18,500 words.

Yours sincerely, Arnold Bennett

P.S. I leave the matter to your judgment, but I fancy it *may* be a mistake to conceal from Flower the fact that I have delivered the story.   A. B.

339. *London Life* opened at *Drury Lane* on 4 June, inaugurating Basil Dean's very brief reign there, and starring Henry Ainley, Lilian Braithwaite, and Mary Jerrold. The play was not well received. One of the patrons of the theatre, the critic for *The Times*, thought he had seen other things like it: '*London Life* differs very little in plan from the old agoramaniac Drury Lane dramas. We miss the old catastrophes, convulsions of nature and fatal accidents . . .; but the hall mark of the type is there: the transaction of domestic and sentimental and other private affairs in the presence of the largest possible crowds in the most public places.'

340. The editors of *Bookman's Journal* wanted something from Bennett for their Vine Book series of editions de luxe. They issued *The Bright Island* in 1924 in an edition of two hundred copies printed by the Golden Cockerel Press.

u.c. / ms. / 341

PRIVATE

75, Cadogan Square
20th May 1924

My dear Eric,

With reference to McClure, I think that your proper course was to send McClure on to me, seeing that journalism is now excepted from our contract. McClure could only have come to you about this in the false assumption that you were my agent for such work. It is not as if *you* had gone to *him* & suggested it. However, I do not mind your handling the matter, provided you exceed what I should do myself, by the amount of your commission. If you carry the thing through, but not in a superlative manner, I think I shall be justified in asking you to accept half commission.

Yours sincerely, Arnold Bennett

BUTLER / ms. / 342
(*From Eric Pinker*)

Talbot House
21st May 1924

My dear Bennett,

Frankly the course you suggest I should have followed in regard to the McClure matter never occurred to me. I regard and always have regarded such things as perfectly legitimate business and naturally I don't turn good business away. It is true that McClure's approached me which may be regarded from one point of view as just luck, but luck which I submit the firm may be considered to have earned by virtue of the position which it has attained. McClures would very likely have approached me or some other Agent about you if you had no Agent at all: these people nearly always do go to the Agents first when they want anything: and had such been the case the

---

Flower published 'Elsie and the Child' in Cassell's *Storyteller* in September. *Century* published it in three instalments beginning in September. Bennett's expectations about the story perhaps had to do with the fact that the sentimental feelings Elsie had aroused in readers of *Riceyman Steps* had annoyed him; he may have approached with reluctance a somewhat sentimental sequel. The concealment from Flower is unexplained.

341. The McClure Newspaper Syndicate, to which the letter refers, was no longer associated with S. S. McClure, whose empire had collapsed during the war.

Agent would have put up the offer to you in the ordinary course of business.

In your letter of 27th Dec. last you say—: 'I am willing for you to have 10%—on all articles for which you obtain commissions' and in a p.s. to your letter of 22nd Jan.—: 'Of course as regards journalism there is nothing to prevent you from getting commissions for me on a 10% basis'—and I take these 2 sentences to apply without modification to a case like the present. I cannot *go out* to get you commissions for journalism because I don't handle your journalism, any more than I can try to get commissions for work by Authors who are not my clients. On the other hand, if I receive an enquiry for the work of an Author who has no Agent, I put it forward and the Author, if he accepts the proposal, does not suggest that he should only pay one half commission because the enquiry was unsolicited because he might have been able to do as well or better by himself. This parallel must not be pushed too far because in your case I do of course keep my eyes open for anything which may be turned to your advantage, but surely the cases are analogous? They seem to me to involve the whole principles of agency.

I don't want you to take this letter as implying a refusal to accept your suggestion as to commission—a thing which needless to say I should never do—but I should like you to consider what I have said.

My feeling at the moment is rather that I am entitled to 10% or nothing, but I am content to leave it to you.

Yours sincerely, Eric S. Pinker

U.C. / MS. / 343

PRIVATE
75, Cadogan Square
22–5–24

My dear Eric,

Many thanks for your letter. You have been my agent for everything for many years, & now that you are not my agent for everything people are naturally still coming to you on the assumption that you are. It seems to me that your proper course, when you are approached in this way, is to explain that you are *not*, and to refer the applicants to me. I do not conceive that any other course can be right.

It is perfectly open to you to '*go out* to get me commissions'. Of course you can. I have expressly told you that you are at liberty to do so, on a 10% commission basis. And in so doing you are entitled to call yourself my agent. But the case is different when an applicant comes to you on a false assumption.

However, we will leave this matter open for the present. I am like you—I only want the fair thing.

Yours sincerely, Arnold Bennett

U.C. / TS. / 344

75, Cadogan Square
7th August 1924

Dear Mr. Wicken,

Many thanks for your letter of the 6th and the enclosures from Messrs. Cassells. I return the proofs duly corrected, and also their letter.

As regards Messrs. Cassells' suggestion that I should alter the names of newspapers unless the newspapers which I name happen to be in the Cassells Combine, this most singular suggestion has been made to me before—in connection with *Riceyman Steps* and of course I declined it.

'In spite of what Messrs. Cassells say in their letter, I certainly do regard the suggestion as an "unwarranted interference with my discretion as an author". Upon what possible grounds am I

---

343. The McClure negotiations continued for several months. In September Bennett wrote to his nephew Richard:

'I am having a great argument and negotiation with the McClure syndicate about a weekly article for a year. Their present star turn, Wells, is just closing his contract. They want another star, and of course there is only me. These articles are published all over the world and are largely political. They gave Wells 30,000 dols. for a weekly article of 1,000 words. I told them I was worth less than Wells in the market and that I would do the job for 26,000 dols. a year. They offered me 18,000, 20,000, and 21,000. In vain! Then they said could I do 2 sample articles at 500 dollars each, my price, for them to judge? So I am doing them at once. But I don't think they will rise to my price for the series, and if they don't I certainly shan't descend one dollar towards theirs.'

The Wells series ran in England in the *Westminster Gazette*, and was published in book form as *A Year of Prophesying*. Bennett's two articles appeared on 24 and 30 October 1924, in the *Birmingham Gazette*, and presumably appeared elsewhere. One was on education, the other on socialism. Bennett later did a series of about nine articles for the Syndicate.

to alter the names of newspapers mentioned in my book (always chosen with the greatest care by me) in order to aid the publicity of Messrs. Cassells? If Messrs. Cassells want to enforce such a "routine" they ought to insert a clause about it in their contracts. Then we should know where we stood. Only my close friendship with Mr. Newman Flower prevents me from bringing this matter officially to the notice of the Society of Authors and the Authors' League of America. Kindly send a copy of these remarks to Messrs. Cassells.'

Yours sincerely, Arnold Bennett

U.C. / TS. / 345

75, Cadogan Square
11th September 1924

My dear Eric,

With reference to our conversation yesterday about a new edition of *The Old Wives' Tale*, I think on reflection that the suggested scheme does not wholly appeal to me. In the first place I can see no point in the second preface. The second one could not take the place of the first one, which contains some really interesting stuff about the origin of the book and which could not be merely re-written. The only object of a second preface would be to persuade the public that they were getting something new worth having which in fact would not be worth having. In the second place I think the new edition ought definitely to be a cheap edition—at 5/- from the start. Personally I would sooner have a smaller profit on a 5/- edition than a larger one on a 7/6d edition.

I have not been at all satisfied with the marketing of this book through the last few years. I do not expect a large sale of any novel more than a year old; but we have here a book that is continually being referred to in the press and elsewhere as the finest novel of the century. It may well be in fact one of the worst novels of the century, but it certainly has the reputation

344. Wicken was managing clerk of the firm. See page 214.

One of the Cassell editors wrote to Eric Pinker to suggest the changes in the stories in *Elsie and the Child*, of which Bennett had just read proofs. He hoped that Bennett would not regard the suggestion 'as an unwarranted interference with his discretion as an author'. In *Riceyman Steps* Henry Earlforward sends Elsie out to buy the *Evening Standard*, but she can find only the *Star*. Violet Arb advertises the sale of her shop in the *News of the World*. Cassell published no comparable papers.

of being the finest. It is constantly being asked for at booksellers
—in vain. This I know because I myself had numerous complaints about the impossibility of getting the book—I frequently
receive such complaints and have done for years and there must
be many disappointed bookbuyers who do not take the trouble
to complain to me. If you will refer to your correspondence
files you will see that again and again for years past I have
worried you about this matter. Financially the matter is quite
a small one, and I should perfectly understand if H & S said
that they could not really take much trouble over it, as the
return would be inconsiderable. But in that case I should ask
them to relinquish the book. There are a number of smaller
and active firms who would be very glad indeed to have the
book in their lists and who would go to some trouble over a new
edition if only for the sake of the prestige which they would
imagine would come to them.

I am open to argument, but my opinion at present is that a
5/- edition would be best, that it should be produced in a
distinctive format (which need not cost any more than the
ordinary format), and that it should be specially advertised.
I can see no other way of demonstrating properly to the public
that the book is not out of print.

Yours sincerely, Arnold Bennett

u.c. / ts. / 346

75, Cadogan Square
18th September 1924

My dear Eric,

Be it known unto you that I have put up my price for ordinary
commissioned journalism to 2/- a word. I have demanded it
from the *Sunday Pictorial*, and they agreed without a murmur—
for a series of articles. This is for your information in case you
have any schemes in your head in my behalf.

Yours sincerely, Arnold Bennett

345. Eric Pinker had proposed a new edition of *The Old Wives' Tale*, to be issued
by Cassell. Hodder and Stoughton's edition, costing 8s. 6d., was out of stock. It was
arranged that Hodder and Stoughton should issue a new edition at 5s.

346. The series, approximately one article a month, began in the *Pictorial* on
19 October.

u.c. / ts. / 347
PRIVATE

75, Cadogan Square
18th November 1924

My dear Eric,

I was talking to Le Bas and Walter Roch today about authors, and they held the view that authors of reputation did not make half as much as they would do if they were properly handled; the fault being partly that of the agents and partly that of the publishers. I said to Le Bas: 'But you are a publisher and you turned me down.' He said: 'I did not turn you down. I could not do anything with Pinker, who is not what I call businesslike. I asked him for information easy to obtain and he never did obtain it, and I have not had it to this day. Further, I called on him several times, but he never called on me, though it was I who was trying to put business into his hands. Some men with the same chance would have lived on my doorstep till they had done the job.' I said: 'Shall I tell Pinker this?' He said: 'Do, by all means. Tell him I said so.'

Yours sincerely, Arnold Bennett

u.c. / ts. / 348
PRIVATE

75, Cadogan Square
21st November 1924

My dear Eric,

I am delighted to have your letter of the 19th and the enclosure. You may rely upon me to deal with Le Bas faithfully. You will have noted that I personally made no comment to you on his remarks. I merely suggested that I should pass on his remarks to you. He accepted the suggestion that I should do so, and I did so. We are now clear. I had an idea that Le Bas was not talking strictly by the book, and I am glad that you have made out such a perfect case, because it gives me the opportunity of showing him that neither you nor I have such a great deal to learn from him in the way of business. His attitude was that neither authors nor their agents knew their job in a

347. Sir Hedley Le Bas was persisting in his scheme to publish twelve of Bennett's earlier novels (letters of 21 May 1920 and 29 January 1923). Walter Roch (1880–), a former Member of Parliament, was one of Bennett's intimate friends at the Reform Club.

commercial sense. I maintained to him that I was a pretty good business man. He said: 'Arnold, you are a rotten business man. Your books ought to have three times the circulation they do have, and if you were a good business man they would have.'

I heard this morning from Le Bas that he means to approach you again about the matter. So you had better act as though you completely ignored his remarks. This will be the truest wisdom.

Yours sincerely, Arnold Bennett

u.c. / ts. / 349

75, Cadogan Square
8th December 1924

My dear Eric,

As you may know, E. V. Lucas is a close friend of mine. He wants to do a one-volume edition of the Clayhanger Trilogy (*Clayhanger*, *Hilda Lessways* and *These Twain*). We have had two interviews about the enterprise, and some correspondence has been exchanged. I enclose a copy of the last letter from Lucas. His printers and other advisers have not convinced me that the Trilogy cannot be done in less than 1200 pages or at a less price than 10/6d. But they have convinced him. Personally I cannot see why if immensely long books like *The Brothers Karamazov* & *War & Peace* can be sold at a low price, the Clayhanger Trilogy cannot be sold at a low price.

However, there it is. I have accepted his conclusion. I have also agreed definitely with him about the royalty mentioned in his letter, and you cannot go back on this. It will be well for you now to go to Lucas about the contract. I want you to understand that Lucas has already put a new spirit into Methuens; he is full of ideas and he is anxious to be fair and very ready to compromise in the execution of those ideas. Therefore I suggest that you should meet him in the same mood, always remembering that he and I have been intimate for many years and that I should like to oblige him.

As you will see from his letter, he has also suggested a cheap

348. Bennett was yet to write a best-selling novel. *Riceyman Steps*, with which he did unusually well, sold somewhat above 30,000 copies in the first three months of publication.

L.A.B.—2 A

edition of my books (the set to be sold at One Guinea, or 3/6d each separately). This is simply a question of binding, as the old plates will be used. He says that they have had an extraordinary success in this way with six books of Milne's, and 6 books of somebody else's whose name I have forgotten. A contract will be needed for this.

I do not know how this latter proposal will affect Le Bas's proposal. I do not see why it should affect it as the markets will be quite different in the two cases; but if the two proposals do clash, it must be Le Bas's proposal which will give way.

I need not tell you, while dealing with Lucas in the spirit which I have indicated, to safeguard my interests as much as is reasonably possible.

I shall be leaving England at the end of the week for about a month, and I hope to God that I shall have no address. I need a holiday. I have just finished one play of my own, and, with Knoblock, I am just finishing a dramatisation of *Mr. Prohack*. Although both these plays will be finished this week, they will not be available for the market until after my return, when they will be re-read with care, and finally passed.

Yours sincerely, Arnold Bennett

U.C. / TS. / 350

75, Cadogan Square
20th January 1925

My dear Eric,

A long short story of mine called 'The Death of Simon Fuge' is often mentioned by connoisseurs, and I see it is mentioned in Johnson's recent book on me. The other night Rebecca West

---

349. Methuen, of which Lucas became chairman, published *The Clayhanger Family* in 1925. The royalty was a straight 10 per cent. The cheap edition to parallel that of A. A. Milne (1882–1956) did not go through. Neither did Le Bas's scheme.

Bennett's vacation is described in a journal entry upon his return from it: 'I got home on Thursday night in a thick fog after a calendar month of almost continuous sunshine in Genoa, Naples, and Pisa. Owing partly to the soft influences of the climate and to a self-determination to do absolutely nothing for a month, I did not keep a journal. This was a great mistake. And the self-determination was not kept, for I did begin to write an article for Tom Eliot's *Criterion* and failed to finish it.' He did not write the article.

Bennett wrote his play *Flora* (*The Dance Club*) in the autumn; he rewrote it in March 1925. He and Knoblock wrote *Mr. Prohack* in December and January.

mentioned it, and George suggested that it should be issued in an Edition de Luxe. I have often had this idea myself, and I think the story is about as good as anything I ever wrote. It is 20,000 words long. I now wish to suggest to you that it should be done as a Christmas Gift Book for next autumn. I do not know who owns the publishing rights. The edition would have to be a first class specimen of bookmaking—and I should attend to all the details myself. It would have to be very limited in regard to number, it would have to be signed, and it would have to be dear.

Kindly reflect upon this small matter.

Yours sincerely, Arnold Bennett

u.c. / ts. / 351

75, Cadogan Square
11th February 1925

My dear Eric,

I hear that you have had 'flu. I also read in the papers that *I* have had 'flu. However, I have not, and I hope that you have not. If you have, I hope that you are better.

I enclose the article for *Home Chat*. I think you might properly tell the editor, from me, that he set me a very difficult task when he asked me to deal with this vast subject in 1000 words. I have done the best I could in the space.

I saw Swinnerton yesterday, and he told me that Chattos had been very carefully into the 'Death of Simon Fuge' idea, and had come to the conclusion that it was not a commercial proposition, though they would much have liked to do it. Perhaps you can consider how it could be made a commercial proposition and then approach some other firm.

Yours sincerely, Arnold Bennett

350. L. G. Johnson (1894–) published a slender book on Bennett in 1924 ('not bad' said Bennett). Rebecca West (1892–) was soon to write *The Strange Necessity* and later to write a pamphlet on Bennett ('as a man he was great, he was grand; he was Coquelin's Cyrano de Bergerac, but tenderer, more lovable'). And George Doran was in London admiring the grace and wit of Bennett's friends ('you can't get this in New York, George,' said Bennett).

351. *Home Chat* published 'Thirty Years On' on 21 March as part of a celebration of their thirtieth birthday. The article described women and marriage thirty years in the past and in the future.

No limited edition of 'The Death of Simon Fuge' was ever published.

u.c. / ts. / 352

75, Cadogan Square
26th February 1925

My dear Eric,

I enclose a letter from Clunie, a bookseller, with yet another complaint about the impossibility of getting *The Old Wives' Tale*. For years I have been receiving complaints about this book, and for years I have been forwarding them to your firm, and for years I have been assured by Hodder & Stoughton that the book is in print and can be obtained without difficulty. Clunie specifically says that he has failed to get a copy from Hodder & Stoughton themselves. I consider that this state of affairs is simply monstrous, and I am sure that you share my opinion. It seems to me that the book ought after all to be taken away from Hodder & Stoughton. I shall be glad if you will take measures to see that Clunie receives a copy at once from Hodder & Stoughton, and let me know that they have done so. You can also tell Hodder & Stoughton that I am extremely annoyed and that I should esteem an explanation or some apology direct from themselves.

Yours sincerely, Arnold Bennett

P.S. Please return Clunie's letter.

u.c. / ts. / 353

75, Cadogan Square
23rd June 1925

My dear Eric,

Many thanks for your letter of the 22nd about the serial. I doubt whether this novel will do for a serial in U.S.A., as there is a 'mistress' in it. I explained this in the synopsis, and there will be nothing at all crude in the novel itself on this part of the story, but it is a different thing reading about a mistress in a synopsis and reading the actual tale in full. However, you will see. The title of the novel will be *Lord Raingo*, which I think is rather good.

Yours sincerely, Arnold Bennett

353. Bennett began writing *Lord Raingo* on 13 May.

U.C. / TS. / 354

75, Cadogan Square
1st July 1925

My dear Eric,

I have just made a new contract with Mr. W. A. MacWhirter of the *Sunday Pictorial*. I thought originally that I was selling him the world rights of my articles, but he himself offered to try to sell the American rights for me some time ago, so it is clear that I am only selling him the British serial rights. He failed to sell the American rights, as the offers he received were ridiculous.

Yesterday he again offered to try to sell American rights for me. I have no idea whether he will be able to do anything. I told him that you only acted for me in regard to books and plays. I see no reason, however, why, if you care to do so, you should not try to handle the American rights of these S.P. articles. Perhaps you would see MacWhirter. He is an exceedingly nice fellow, and he has the merit of being extremely pleased with *all* my articles. The articles will be done at intervals of about a month during the next 6 or 9 months.

Yours sincerely, Arnold Bennett

U.C. / TS. / 355

75, Cadogan Square
12th September 1925

My dear Eric,

Many thanks for your letter of yesterday about *Lord Raingo*. I have written about 45,000 words of this novel, but I do not want to send you any of it yet. I think that this is only about a third of it. I hope to finish it in April at the latest. I doubt rather whether it would do as it stands for a serial, but of course, in order to oblige Flower, I should have no objection to it being cut for serial purposes.

Yours sincerely, Arnold Bennett

354. The *Sunday Pictorial* series began on 19 October 1924 and continued at irregular intervals through 1929. The subjects ranged from 'Is Love-Making a Lost Art?' and 'Are Scotsmen Really Mean?' to 'Our Greatest Blunder of the War' and 'Can the Doctors be Cured?' (the last an attack on the medical profession). Many of these articles are uncollected. W. A. MacWhirter (d. 1955) is presumably the 'large-minded lunatic' referred to on page 331.

u.c. / ts. / 356

75, Cadogan Square
14th October 1925

My dear Eric,

Many thanks for your letter of the 14th and the enclosure. Doran refers to the 'distinction which would accrue to A. B.'. My first observation is 'Distinction be damned'.

My second observation is that unless the affair presents itself to me as a sound commercial proposition I have not the slightest interest in it. I do not see myself writing 25 introductions for a total payment, which includes all royalties, of £1000. No. Decidedly not. I should have an enormous amount of trouble and the royalty would be 40 cents, or about 2/-, a copy, being very little more than my ordinary royalty.

I fully appreciate the excellence of Doran's motive in trying to launch the edition de luxe, but I can see no point in it whatever if I do not make a reasonable amount out of the transaction.

I enclose a copy of the list which I sent to Doran.

Yours sincerely, Arnold Bennett

u.c. / ts. / 357

75, Cadogan Square
17th October 1925

My dear Eric,

By the end of this month I shall be sending you half or perhaps a little more than half of my novel *Lord Raingo*. For your private ear I may say that I see no hope whatever for it as a serial. The book will be finished in February. Assuming that it is not serialised, could it be published in June—about? I should think that this would be a good time.

I want *Things that Have Interested Me* to be published in January, if this is considered suitable.

Please remember that there are also 13 short stories—some of them very good, whatever the editor of the *Strand* may think of them—which are the material of a volume. These stories are all done, and the last one (and the best) will be delivered to you shortly.

Yours sincerely, Arnold Bennett

356. Doran's proposal came to nothing.

357. Twelve stories appeared in the *Strand Magazine* from 1924 to 1927. The *Strand* editor, Greenhough Smith, refused to publish the thirteenth story, 'The

U.C. / TS. / 358

75, Cadogan Square
17th October 1925

My dear Eric,

Thanks for your letter about Harper's suggestion. The answer to this proposal is, I regret to say, an absolute negative.

In the first place some of the stuff I do not want to be reprinted at all.

In the second place, other parts of the stuff will be published in the third series of *Things*.

In the third place I intend to continue to be able to look George in the face.

Yours sincerely, Arnold Bennett

U.C. / TS. / 359

75, Cadogan Square
11th November 1925

My dear Eric,

I enclose a short story 'The Cornet Player', which completes my contract with the *Strand*. I should like you to read it and tell me whether you think or do not think that it is more than usually original.

As regards short stories generally, I find that I am in the vein for them and can produce them when you feel inclined to make contracts for them.

Yours sincerely, Arnold Bennett

Great Huntress' (which came midway in the series), and published an article by Bennett in its place. All the stories except 'The Great Huntress' appear in Bennett's last two short story collections, *The Woman Who Stole Everything* and *The Night Visitor*.

358. Harper's proposed to publish in book form the series 'Getting Level with Life' that Bennett wrote for the McClure Syndicate. Where these articles originally appeared is unknown. Two or three of them may be included in the collection of *Things That Have Interested Me, Third Series*, published in April 1926.

359. 'The most original story I have ever written', Bennett noted of 'The Cornet Player' in his journal. He appears in the story as the original narrator, meeting a man in a teashop and listening to the man describe a life that has been devoted to cornet-playing. The story has at once an objectivity and an intimacy that differs from the detached ironical compassion of most of Bennett's work. It appears in the collection *The Night Visitor*. Eric Pinker tried without success to sell the story to at least thirteen magazines in America.

U.C. / TS. / 360

75, Cadogan Square
18th November 1925

My dear Eric,

I enclose two copies of the concluding chapter of Part I of *Lord Raingo*.

Flower asked me to lunch on Monday. He seems to be positively ecstatic about this book, and says that he will certainly use it as a serial—uncut, if possible. I have authorised him to cut it if necessary.

Part I contains 83,000 words. I think that the whole book will contain about 135,000 words. It will be finished in February. (D.V.)

Yours sincerely, Arnold Bennett

U.C. / TS. / 361

75, Cadogan Square
26th November 1925

My dear Eric,

Eden Phillpotts and I have written the libretto of a comic opera, provisionally entitled *Vallombrosa*. Frederic Austin is writing the music. I want a draft contract between the authors and composer. The arrangement is that the authors and composer shall share the profit in equal thirds. I think that Austin will have to have some special rights for the printed music. But what? Also gramophone records, in which swag of course the authors must have their share. Further, I think that some date should be fixed by which Austin should deliver the music. Again the making of a contract with a manager must be a matter in which all three of us have a voice.

You will be acting only for myself.

Yours sincerely, Arnold Bennett

361. Frederic Austin (1872–1952) was well known as both composer and singer. He wrote the music for Bennett's adaptation of *The Beggar's Opera* in 1920, and took the part of Peachum. The writing of *Vallombrosa* marked a renewal of friendship and collaboration between Bennett and Eden Phillpotts.

u.c. / ts. / 362

> 75, Cadogan Square
> 12th December 1925

My dear Eric,

Thank you for your letter of yesterday. I return the contract with Cassells, signed.

I shall be sending you the comic opera contract signed shortly. This contract was not properly drawn. Happily I am a good agent myself. You had given Austin exclusive rights over the music printed alone, but you had not given Phillpotts and me exclusive rights over the words printed alone. I have set this right.

I leave on Monday morning. Address as above.

> Yours sincerely, Arnold Bennett

u.c. / ts. / 363

> 75, Cadogan Square
> 17th April 1926

My dear Eric,

Many thanks for your letter. I am glad you are back. I hope that you will be able to come and lunch with me one day soon.

Of course my fixed rate of 2/- a word only applies to *commissioned work*. I do not expect to get it for work which *I* want to sell. You may, however, manage to collect 2/- from U.S.A. and Britain combined.

> Yours sincerely, Arnold Bennett

u.c. / ts. / 364

> 75, Cadogan Square
> 28th April 1926

My dear Eric,

How shall I answer the enclosed letter from Greenhough Smith? (I wrote to him myself about 'The Great Huntress'.)

---

362. The opera, re-entitled *The Bandits*, was never produced.

Bennett left England on the 14th to go to Rome for two months, and to travel in Italy and France for a third month.

'The Epidemic' seemed to me to be quite a good story, and I could not possibly admit that it is below my form, because I am sure that it is not. Perhaps the title put people off.

If the *Strand* has sold the American rights of 'The Great Huntress' I assume that the American rights of the story which I am to write will belong to me.

Yours sincerely, Arnold Bennett

BUTLER / TS. / 365
(*From Eric Pinker*)

Talbot House
17th June, 1926

My dear Bennett,

The *Daily News* are proposing to run a series of articles by well known authors on the subject of 'What Marriage will be like one hundred years hence'. I suggested your name to them and they are willing to commission one article from you of seven hundred words in length, for which they will pay at the rate of 2/6 per word for the British Serial Rights.

Will you please let me know whether you will write this article for them? They are anxious to have the copy as early as possible.

The extra 6d per word may perhaps mitigate your objection to yet another encroachment on my part, but I am afraid that as regards the principle of the matter we are fundamentally in disagreement. I am quite ready to come and argue the case with you sometime, if you like. I think you would find very few authors in agreement with your view.

Sincerely yours, Eric S. Pinker

U.C. / MS. / 366

Amberley
Sussex
18–6–26

My dear Eric,

Thanks for yours of yesterday. I wired you today that I would do the article.

364. The *Strand* published 'The Epidemic' in January 1927. They published no more stories of Bennett's besides those already contracted for.

No serial publication of 'The Great Huntress' in America is known. The story is not included in any of the collections.

I shall be very glad to have your arguments. In the meantime, I argue thus:—

(1) If you can get a higher price than I get for myself, you are certainly entitled to your commission, no matter how the transaction has begun.

(2) If a buyer comes to you, knowing that you are my agent (as they all know, probably), and says, 'I want an article by Bennett',—then I maintain that your proper course is to refer him to me, stating that you are not my agent for journalism.

(3) If a buyer comes to you and says, 'I want such and such an article. Whom do you advise me to go to?' And you reply, 'Bennett'; then I think that you are entitled to your commission.

This seems to me to be fair. I'll give you every chance to argue me out of the position.

Yours sincerely, Arnold Bennett

P.S. No doubt you received my letter in reply to yours about the proposed article on American women.   A. B.

u.c. / ts. / 367

75, Cadogan Square
16th July 1926

My dear Eric,

Many thanks for your letter of yesterday and the Pugh share certificate. I return this in case he may be able to cancel it, and issue 900 shares to me and 100 to you (if this is the proper proportion). I think that this would be the simplest way. I meant to suggest this before, but I forgot.

Flower lunched with me yesterday. He suggested a new contract, and I did not demur. I do not see that we can obtain any advantage by leaving him, and I do not wish to leave him. He is undoubtedly very pleased with *Lord Raingo*, from beginning to end. He has only recently read part II, which is very tragic, and I feared that it might not make a very favourable

366. Bennett was in Amberley on a working holiday from late May until the middle of July.

Of the *Daily News* article, Bennett wrote in his journal, 'This is my highest price for journalism up to now. What footling subjects these editors choose!' The article was published on 28 July. The *American Magazine* wanted to pay $1,200 for an article of 4,000 words on 'Why I Would Never Marry an American Woman'.

impression on him. My fear was groundless. No publisher could be more enthusiastic or more frank in stating his enthusiasm.

I told him that I was about to write a long short story (18,000 or 20,000 words), designed to be the opening story in my volume of short stories, which I hope will be published next spring. He at once asked if he could have the serial rights. You can sell these to him if you like (guaranteeing a minimum of 18,000 words). The story, however, is not yet written.

Yours sincerely, Arnold Bennett

P.S. I have signed the receipt for the shares and enclose it herewith, in case the present certificate cannot be cancelled. If the certificate is cancelled you can tear up the receipt. A. B.

u.c. / ts. / 368

75, Cadogan Square
6th August 1926

My dear Eric,

Thanks for your letter of yesterday and the enclosure. I think you have done very well indeed with this new Cassells contract, and I congratulate you. I do not want a royalty of 30%, as I think it is excessive. I was under the impression that Cassells paid £600 for the last long-short story. The new long-short story will be finished and delivered in about a fortnight.

Yours sincerely, Arnold Bennett

P.S. Is Flower bound to serialise *The Vanguard*? If so, you may as well deliver it & get some money out of them.   A. B.

367. Ralph Pugh was head of a new film organization, British Authors Productions, in which authors were to be shareholders. He received from Bennett a sketch for a scenario, but apparently nothing further was done.

Bennett's fears for *Lord Raingo* were not entirely groundless. In America the *Saturday Evening Post* had agreed to buy it if they liked the last part, but they did not like the last part: '£3–4,000 gone to pot through my damnable artistic integrity', Bennett noted ruefully to Frank Swinnerton. In England the novel was serialized by Max Beaverbrook's *Evening Standard*, not by Cassell. It began appearing on 20 September.

The new story was 'The Woman Who Stole Everything', one of Bennett's best portraits of a modern girl. It was published in Cassell's *Storyteller* in May 1927, and was the title story of the collection published in June 1927.

368. Eric Pinker contracted for three novels after *The Vanguard*. He obtained an increase in advance on book rights from £1,000 to £1,250, and an increase from £900 to £1,000 on serial rights for two of the novels. The price on a long short

u.c. / ts. / 369

75, Cadogan Square
12th August 1926

My dear Eric,

Unless one of your letters has miscarried you have not reported to me lately about the definite offer to buy a film scenario from me by some person whom you did not name. You first mentioned the matter in your letter of May 27th. I am beginning to assume that this affair is dead, owing to you not being satisfied with the financial showing of the gentleman in question.

Nor have you replied to the argument which I put before you when I was in the country some six weeks ago about the cases in which you should and the cases in which you should not refer a possible buyer of articles to me.

Yours sincerely, Arnold Bennett

u.c. / ts. / 370

75, Cadogan Square
4th October, 1926

My dear Eric,

I have agreed with Wardour Films Limited (173 Wardour Street; telephone Regent 2533-4; General manager Mr. Thorne) to write the English titles for the English production of the German 'Ufa' film, *Faust*. I offered to do the work for £300. They said they could not pay more than £200. I would not budge. They gave in. I have already begun the work. The film is not as good as they think it is, but I can make it better. I have told Thorne that you will communicate with him at

---

story was to remain at £500 (Bennett was mistaken about the amount). Flower had balked at paying 30 per cent. royalty after sales reached a certain figure.

The Vanguard, a return to the early fantasias such as *The Grand Babylon Hotel*, was largely written during the holiday in Amberley in the previous months. Bennett noted in his journal when he finished it: 'I have never worked more easily than during the last six weeks.' No serial publication is known. It was published in America in the autumn of 1927, and as *The Strange Vanguard* in England in January 1928.

369. Eric Pinker had reported an offer of £2,000 for a scenario of two to three thousand words.

once as to the contract, which can be either a formal contract or an exchange of letters. He of course did not want an agent, but I said there must be an agent.

There is nothing particular to say about the conditions. Nothing has been said as to the payment. It must at any rate be made as soon as *I* have said that my work is complete.

I said that if there should be any fundamental difference of opinion between us as to the titling, Thorne's decision must of course carry, but my name must disappear from the film. He said there was no chance of this occurring. I merely mention the point to you.

I shall be glad if you will communicate with Thorne immediately. I am seeing him again tomorrow afternoon.

Yours sincerely, Arnold Bennett

U.C. / TS. / 371

75, Cadogan Square
5th October 1926

My dear Eric,

I was explaining some things to the Wardour people this afternoon, when the London representative of 'Ufa' came in, and heard what I had to say. He at once said that, in addition to communicating with Berlin to get the necessary work done, he would inform America, as the suggestion would be even more valuable there (where the story of *Faust* is not so well known as here) than in England.

It then occurred to me that at any rate my titles ought not to be used in America without payment if I am selling to the Wardour people only the English rights (as I presumably am). I said nothing about the point to the people present, but perhaps you may think well to deal with it tomorrow morning. In that case you need not say that you have had the tip from me.

Yours sincerely, Arnold Bennett

370. J. C. A. Thorpe (not Thorne) managed Wardour Films. Bennett finished doing the titles by about 1 November. The film had its first English showing, with credit to Bennett, on 2 January 1927. The following year Bennett wrote his Faustian play, *The Return Journey*.

U.C. / TS. / 372

75, Cadogan Square
20th November 1926

My dear Eric,

I enclose a letter which I have received from Brandt. The relevant part is marked. Doubtless Brandt has spoken to you about this scheme for a series to be called 'One Hour Series' (I think), on various subjects, at the price of one dollar. He asked me to do a book on the English novel. I replied that I would not look at it unless I was assured of at least £1,000 on or before book publication. He said that he thought this could be done.

I forget now how long the book was to be, but I think that the length he named was from 30,000 to 40,000 words.

T. B. Wells came to see me yesterday afternoon. Wells said that he would like the American serial rights, and that he would pay $3,000 provided the stuff was 40,000 words long and he could use it in four instalments of 10,000 words each. I made no reply to this, and I told him that I should consult you. He is to see you about it.

I may tell you at once that I will not accept $3,000 for the American serial rights. Indeed I think I should insist on the top figure mentioned by Brandt. Further, it is quite possible that Brandt said only 30,000 words. I cannot remember. Whatever the length, I will not do it unless I can be assured of £1000 on or before publication of the book.

Wells said that I ought to get $2,000 advance on the book. He also said that Lippincotts were not good publishers nowadays and that Jefferson Jones would not in his opinion be equal to the job. I know nothing about this aspect of the matter.

Lastly I told Brandt with the utmost clearness that I would not touch the thing unless Doran consented. I have told Wells the same. You will notice that Brandt says nothing on this point.

Would the British serial rights be worth anything? I doubt it.

I should rather like to do the book, and I think I could make it interesting.

The matter is now in your hands. I am leaving the serial rights to you in this case because it is Brandt who got busy on them. I should never have thought of Wells for myself. Therefore it seems to me that, if anything comes of the proposition, you and he ought to benefit on the serial rights as well as on the book.

Please return Brandt's letter. I have not replied to it, and shall not do so unless you wish me to do so.

Yours sincerely, Arnold Bennett

U.C. / TS. / 373

75, Cadogan Square
29th November 1926

My dear Eric,

I understand that the wife of the British Minister at Frankfort is to write to you about a German translation of *Lord Raingo*. The matter is of course entirely in your hands. In any case the lady would have to furnish proof that she could write good literary German. So many of these aspirants cannot write any language.

Yours sincerely, Arnold Bennett

P.S. Will you please deal with the enclosed letter?   A. B.

U.C. / TS. / 374
(*To Messrs. J. B. Pinker and Sons*)

75, Cadogan Square
19th January 1927

Gentlemen,

With reference to my *Evening Standard* articles, I understand that they are being largely cabled to U.S.A. and used there, either in whole or in part, in several newspapers. I have had another enquiry for them today from the Herald-Tribune Syndicate. I have given no definite reply. I think it might be worth your while to go into the matter with expedition. The only snag is that the *Evening Standard* might be saying that they had had enough of them, because of the price. I have no doubt that these are easily the highest paid *book* articles in the world.

---

372. Carl Brandt had the previous year offered Bennett $11,500 (£2,300) and expenses to give thirty to fifty lectures in America. Neither that proposal nor the present one came to anything. T. B. Wells was still at Harper's. Jefferson Jones (1880–1941) was head of the General Literature Division at Lippincott.

I get £300 a month for them from the *Evening Standard*, and the length runs from 800 to 1000 words each.

I am going away tomorrow morning for five or six weeks, and shall not have a fixed address. But all communications can be made to Miss Nerney, who will have a certain amount of power to act on her own responsibility.

Yours sincerely, Arnold Bennett

P.S. I enclose three articles, the first of which marked No. 1, will appear in London on the 27th instant. A. B.

U.C. / TS. / 375

75, Cadogan Square
11th March 1927

Dear Ralph Pinker,

Victor Gollancz, of Ernest Benn Limited, saw the original MS of *The Old Wives' Tale* about two months ago, and he had the idea of issuing a facsimile of it in a limited edition. Doran interested himself in the enterprise and was ready to take 250 copies out of the 500. They both said that there would not be any money in it for anyone, and I agreed to this theory.

The matter has now taken definite shape, and Benn and Doran between them will do a limited edition of 500 copies at about Five Guineas each. I have seen specimens of the reproduction and have approved them.

I have asked Gollancz to communicate with you, as of course you will have to obtain the permission of Hodder & Stoughton. Gollancz estimates the cost of production at about £600. If the price is to be Five Guineas and 400 copies out of the 500 are sold, the publishers between them would apparently receive about £1400 from the trade. Assuming that this calculation is fairly correct, I am inclined to think that there ought to be something for the author. I do not, however, insist on this.

374. The *Evening Standard* articles, a weekly series that began in the preceding November and continued until early in 1931, bore the title 'Books and Persons' of the earlier *New Age* articles. They had a startling success, and established Bennett once again as the liveliest and now as the most influential reviewer of books in England. Most of them remain uncollected. American serial publication of them is unknown.

L.A.B.—2 B

I think that the mere publication would be a fine piece of kudos for me, and that it would also stimulate to a certain extent the sale of the ordinary edition of the book.

If you do not hear soon from Gollancz, perhaps you will write to him. The matter is in your hands.

Yours sincerely, Arnold Bennett

u.c. / ts. / 376

75, Cadogan Square
19th March 1927

Dear Ralph Pinker,

Thank you for your letter of the 18th. I need not go into details.

When I said originally that I should expect nothing from the issue, I had been told, or I had understood, that there would be no profit in the affair for anybody. But when I saw Mr. Gollancz the other day the figures which he roughly gave seemed to imply that quite a substantial profit *might* be made.

All I ask is that if there is a profit I should share in it. Why not? The fact that the whole thing is 'exceptional' appears to me to be beside the point. As regards 'taking the risk', publishers nearly always take a risk.

I do not ask for a royalty. If a percentage can be agreed between you and Mr. Gollancz for overhead charges, I should be perfectly content to accept a proportion of the net profits, if any. If Mr. Gollancz prefers his own offer, well and good.

It should be borne in mind that the suggestion for the facsimile did not come from me, but from Mr. Gollancz. True, I was very pleased with the suggestion. But I assume that Mr. Gollancz did not make a suggestion in which he saw no possibility of profit.

I do not desire to make anything if Benns make nothing. If Benns make something I want to make something.

375. Ralph Pinker (see page 334) took over the management of the London office from Eric, who early in 1926 established an American branch for dramatic and film work and returned to America at the end of 1926 to extend the agency to literary work.

Sir Victor Gollancz (1893–) was managing director of Benn's from 1920 to 1928. Chairman of the firm was Sir Ernest Benn (1875–1954).

Please settle the matter. You have a free hand from me.
Doran will be dealt with separately.

Yours sincerely, Arnold Bennett

u.c. / ts. / 377

75, Cadogan Square
30th March 1927

Dear Mr. Wicken,

With reference to my proposed articles on my cruise in the
Eastern Mediterranean, I cannot very well give any sort of a
scheme of them as I do not know the kind of thing that will
strike me as interesting. All I know is that I shall visit Greece,
the Aegean islands, Athens, Crete, the Dalmatian coast, and
probably Smyrna. I do not know what else. I shall be at sea
about a month, so that I ought to get plenty of material.

When I was in Spain some years ago I wrote a series of
articles for the *Daily Express*. These will give an idea of the sort
of thing that I do on these excursions. My book, *The Log of
Velsa* would also give an idea.

Yours sincerely, Arnold Bennett

P.S. I enclose a *Standard* and a *Pictorial* article.

376. The facsimile edition was published later in the year. It is an extraordinary
display of a fine calligraphic hand and an orderly mind. Bennett remarks in his
prefatory note:
   'The manuscript here reproduced . . . is . . . the first and last writing of *The
Old Wives' Tale*. Plays must be rewritten, once, twice, several times; for there is
always a lot of mere artifice in the disposition of details of the dialogue. But I
have never, except on one minor occasion [actually with both *A Man from the
North* and *Anna of the Five Towns*], had the courage to write a novel, or any part
of a novel, twice over. I say to myself: "What you have written you have written,
and there it is, for better or worse. . . ."
   'Of course if your manuscript is to have even the most modest pretensions to
calligraphic decency, you must know all the time exactly what you are about to
do; otherwise a regular mess will ensue. It will be noticed that now and then
in the writing of *The Old Wives' Tale* something rather like a regular mess did
ensue, consequence of not having absolutely decided in advance just what I
wanted to write, and in what order, and how. The reader, however, sees the
worst of these messes; no page, so far as I remember, was destroyed and re-
written. . . .'
377. Bennett left England on 15 April to go to Sicily. There he joined Otto
Kahn, the American banker, and others for a cruise that lasted until late in May.
The party included Jo Davidson, the sculptor, and Rudolph Kommer, the theatrical

U.C. / TS. / 378

75, Cadogan Square
31st March 1927

Dear Mr. Wicken,

I ought to have said yesterday, but I forgot to do so as I was pressed for time, that I do not think it is a good policy to offer my journalism to the Beaverbrook papers. If my journalism is to be sold there I can sell it myself as well as anybody else can. This, however, is not the point. The point is that I do not want Lord Beaverbrook and the editor to suppose that I am taking any advantage, through you, of my close intimacy with him. If I were you, therefore, I should not press the matter at all with the *Sunday Express*, especially as there seems to be some chance of them buying the serial rights of my next novel.

Assuming that I send any journalism to you in the future to handle, it ought never to be offered to the Beaverbrook papers unless I give instructions to the contrary.

I am not blaming your firm in the least. I ought to have warned you when I first mentioned the articles to you.

Yours sincerely, Arnold Bennett

U.C. / TS. / 379

75, Cadogan Square
31st March 1927

Dear Ralph Pinker,

With reference to the British serial rights of *Accident*, I have had a talk this afternoon on the telephone with Lord Beaverbrook, and I have definitely agreed to sell them to him for £2,250. Will you kindly therefore put the matter on a formal basis? It will of course be necessary, if the serial should be sold in America, to make the dates coincide.

I had intended to finish this book before Easter, but on second thoughts I decided that I should be able to make the

director, who was then associated with Max Reinhardt. These two men became good friends of Bennett's.

The articles on Spain began to appear in the *Daily Express* on 23 April 1924, while Bennett was there.

378. Bennett's next novel, *Accident*, was already half written. He had begun it the previous November.

last third much better if I left it until my return from the Mediterranean. The book will therefore be finished on or before the end of June.

Yours sincerely, Arnold Bennett

P.S. I gather from Lord Beaverbrook that he wants the serial for the *Daily Express* (and especially for the Manchester edition). If this is so, I should think that the Mediterranean articles would be quite off.

I suppose you will let him know about the sale at once. A. B.

U.C. / TS. / 380

75, Cadogan Square
14th April 1927

Dear Ralph Pinker,

Lord Beaverbrook telephoned me today saying that you had offered him the ten articles on the cruise for £25 each. I said there must be some mistake, and he admitted himself that the price was too low. I assume of course that there has been some mistake. You or your firm know that my price for articles is 2/- a word. The only exception to this is the Beaverbrook papers, which have my stuff at 1/6d a word under an old-standing arrangement.

I have written to Lord Beaverbrook tonight to say definitely that there has been some mistake, and that the matter cannot go through as it stands.

He is quite willing to buy all the ten articles, and I should think he was—at that price.

Yours sincerely, Arnold Bennett

379. Bennett left off writing *Accident* on 24 March. He resumed work on it on about 8 June, and finished it on 19 July. It began appearing in the *Daily Express* on 16 July 1928 under the title *Train de Luxe*. Cassell issued it in book form the following January.

380. The cruise articles, 'Mediterranean Scenes', began appearing in the *Sunday Express* on 24 July. They were issued in book form in 1928 by Cassell.

U.C. / TS. / 381
(*To Messrs. J. B. Pinker and Sons*)   [Sicily]
                                                  20th April 1927

Gentlemen,

I enclose a short story 'The Hat'. This is for the Newman
Flower contract and for America. May God help you to sell it
there at a good price.

                                    Yours sincerely, Arnold Bennett

P.S. Will you please deal with the enclosed letter?

U.C. / TS. / 382   75, Cadogan Square
                                          July 28th 1927

My dear Eric,

                       Florentine Journal.

This is an old volume of my journal. I have given it to T. S.
Eliot to publish in three instalments in his *Criterion*. I want you
to see to it in U.S.A. I think Harpers might like it. Anyhow
copyright must be preserved. I have left instructions for Miss
Nerney (who returns on Tuesday) to send you a typescript of
the stuff.

Eliot wants to begin publishing in October, but I have told
him I fear this may be too early for America. I am going away
to-day.

                                    Yours sincerely, Arnold Bennett

BUTLER / T.C.C. / 383
                                        [75, Cadogan Square]
                                        6th September 1927

My dear Eric,

A company called the Sloane Productions Company (in
which I am a shareholder) is about to start an international

---

381. Eric Pinker sold 'The Hat' for $1,500 to *Liberty Magazine* in America, where
it appeared on 11 February 1928. English publication is unknown. It was republished in *The Night Visitor and Other Stories* in 1931.

382. Bennett went on a holiday to St. Leonard's-on-Sea until 4 September.

In 1918 Bennett wrote of T. S. Eliot (1888–1965) to an American friend: 'You
have an American poet, T. S. Eliot. I was so struck by his work that I made his
acquaintance.'

season at the Court Theatre, in early October. The second play
to be done ought to be *Mr. Prohack*. Golding Bright agrees, but
he has cabled to Knoblock for confirmation. I only write to tell
you that the contract should be just the ordinary contract, not
too stiff. I think it is important to bear in mind the possibility
of the play being moved to another theatre if it is a success.
That is all.

Komisarjevsky is the manager and producer. No one better.
The suggestion that *Mr. Prohack* should be done did not come
from me at all. In fact at first I was against it.

With regard to the Florentine Journal for the *Criterion*, cannot this thing be hurried up? Is there any real chance of the
rights being disposed of in the U.S.A.? You see, the point is that
Eliot does not run the *Criterion* for money, and I am anxious to
help him as quickly as possible.

I am going to Germany for a week or ten days on Friday.

Yours sincerely, [Arnold Bennett]

383. Theodore Komisarjevsky (1882–1954), the distinguished producer, came to
see Bennett with a project for producing at least two plays in a three-month season
at the Court Theatre. He had obtained the option on the lease of the theatre for
that period (with no possibility of getting an extension), but he lacked the greater
part of the necessary backing. The plays he proposed to do were Merezhkovsky's
Paul I and *Mr. Prohack*. The initial adverse view of the project that Bennett mentions in the letter was evidently quite transient and was superseded by one that
was decidedly favourable, as his letter also indicates. And in fact, before the
discussion with Komisarjevsky ended, Bennett had virtually decided to furnish
the needed backing.

The history of Sloane Productions, which was created at Bennett's instigation,
merits a note. It introduced Charles Laughton, who was then unknown, to the
public, and launched his career as a major actor. He had played a small part in
Komisarjevsky's production of *The Three Sisters*, in which Bennett had seen and
noted him, the consequence being that he was engaged to play the major roles,
viz., Count Pahlen in *Paul I* and the title role in *Mr. Prohack*. In the former he was
acclaimed by the critics, and the production itself was accounted a *succès d'estime*;
but *Mr. Prohack* gave evidence of being a solid success and Laughton was a sensation. The play, nevertheless, had to close at the expiration of the short lease, on
31 December. But Bennett, who had much confidence in the success of the play,
had banked on its continuing at another theatre; and this had decided him to go
into the enterprise; for, to quote his own words about the project, 'A play that is a
success is bound to find a theatre—and if not at once, very soon.' And this belief
was not unjustified but was precisely what would have happened in normal circumstances. Dennis Eadie, proprietor of the Royalty Theatre, wanted to have
Mr. Prohack there, and offered the theatre as soon as it would be free. As the house
was let for the run of the play currently showing, he could not give the exact date
immediately, but was able to say that it must be very soon, as the play there was
not a success.

Laughton, meanwhile, upon the forced closing of *Mr. Prohack*, took a holiday in

U.C. / TS. / 384

75 Cadogan Square,
17th November 1927

Dear Mr. Wicken,

I enclose a letter just received from Godal Films. (Please return it to me.) I do not know anything about the Company.

I am quite ready to do a film story, but there must be no 'approval' clause in it. You will notice that of the £500 offered, £450 would be dependent on 'approval'. This is ridiculous.

I will not touch anything unless I am guaranteed £500 certain, and there must be a further sum if the story is approved. You can be quite firm about this. Personally I do not think that £500 is enough.

If you can sell him the rights in one of my novels, all right. But only on the condition that I do not have to do any work on the same.

Yours sincerely, Arnold Bennett

U.C. / TS. / 385
(*To Evelyn Dagnall*)

75, Cadogan Square
12th December 1927

Dear Mrs. Dagnall,

Flora

Mrs Patrick Campbell has a scheme for doing this play.

I have agreed with her that she shall do it on the following conditions.

Switzerland, having put his affairs into the hands of an agent. The agent issued an ultimatum to the Chairman of Sloane Productions (Bennett) in the first week of January to say Laughton could not wait more than four weeks for *Mr. Prohack* to continue, as he had been offered the name part in the forthcoming production of *A Man with Red Hair*, Ben Levy's adaptation of Hugh Walpole's novel. Laughton himself could not be contacted, and the four weeks expired the day before Eadie telephoned to say that the Royalty would be free at the end of the coming week. And thus the enterprise came to an end, to the cost of its backers, and with the burial of a delightful comedy.

The *Criterion* published extracts from Bennett's journal, from the year 1910, in the following December, January, and February. In New York, Doran's *Bookman* published them in November and December. Bennett noted later in his journal that the *Criterion* 'is a dull production and always will be'.

Bennett went to Germany with Max Beaverbrook.

384. Edward Godal (1889–) was organizing British Amalgamated Films Ltd.

1. No contract can be signed until she has satisfied you that she has the capital.

2. I will have nothing to do, myself, with the discussion of terms. All this must be done between you and her.

3. I only want my ordinary terms; but there must be no talk of her wanting specially low terms because she has not got much capital, etc., etc.

4. She can have an option on the American rights, but of course she must pay for it.

5. I must have an absolute veto on the cast.

You need not communicate with her, I think, until you hear from me again. I am only telling you this so that you may know how things stand. She is expecting to get into association with Gilbert Miller, through Sidney Howard, who is writing a play for her. She has also a third play.

Yours sincerely, Arnold Bennett

u.c. / ts. / 386

75, Cadogan Square
29th December 1927

Dear Mrs Dagnall,

I enclose copy of a cable received from Estelle Winwood this morning and copy of my cabled reply. I enclose also copy of a letter which I have written to Mrs Patrick Campbell.

Yours sincerely, Arnold Bennett

385. Evelyn Dagnall, widow of T. C. Dagnall, the theatrical manager, joined the Pinker firm in 1926. She left at the end of 1928.

Bennett first mentioned Mrs. Patrick Campbell (1865–1946) in his journal in 1896, when, as theatre critic for *Woman*, he saw her in *Romeo and Juliet*. In 1923 he wrote in his yachting journal:

'Mrs. Patrick Campbell came for lunch and stayed till 4:30. She made a sensational entrance both into the lunch and into the ship—the *cabotine's* entrance. But she gave a magnificent conversational display. In fact it was dazzling. Only she is incapable of listening. She gave me the impression of a tremendous personality, a considerable genius, and a woman without scruple when she really wants anything.'

His play *Flora* (see page 346) had been rejected by several West End managements before Mrs. Campbell took an interest in it.

Sidney Howard (1891–1939) had recently written his most famous play, *The Silver Cord*.

386. Estelle Winwood (1883–), formerly a member of the Liverpool Repertory Theatre, established herself as an actress in America in 1916. The copies of the cables do not survive.

U.C. / T.C.C. / 387
(*To Mrs. Patrick Campbell*)

[75, Cadogan Square]
29th December 1927

Dear Mrs Campbell,

With reference to *Flora* I have sadly to tell you that I have had a very serious enquiry about the American rights of *Flora* from a star. You will I think understand that it would be impossible for me to refuse this offer if terms can be satisfactorily arranged. I should of course much prefer the play to be done in America by you, but there seems to me to be no assurance that you will be able to do it in America within a reasonable time. I shall naturally keep the English rights for you until you have had time to discover whether or not you will be able to take them up.

I know you will hate this letter, mais que voulez-vous.

Ever your devoted, [Arnold Bennett]

U.C. / MS. / 388
(*From Mrs. Patrick Campbell*)

64, Pont Street
S.W.1
Dec 29th/27

Dear Mr. Bennett,

You must be joking! If this play was produced by me in London tomorrow, it couldn't be played by me in America before *September* 1928 as this season ends in New York in *March* —therefore you cannot mean:—'there seems no assurance that you will be able to do it in America within a reasonable time'—

I told you to your good stoney face that I could only consider doing this play myself, if you let me have the American rights & you agreed to do this—but you said you made a condition too:—'I must know the money is in the Bank.'

I am waiting now to let you know when the money is in the Bank.—It was understood that I must discuss with your agents a stipulated date after production in London to pay a sum on a/c of fees for the American rights—also the scale of terms for American and London rights—

Please write & tell me that my memory is correct & I'll hurry up things as quickly as I can. My love to you both.

Beatrice Stella CW
(Mrs. P. C.)

u.c. / ts. / 389

75, Cadogan Square
6th January 1928

Dear Mrs Dagnall,

Many thanks for your letter of yesterday.

I enclose the correspondence which has just passed between Mrs Campbell and myself. (Please return this correspondence to me when you have done with it.) It shows exactly how things stand. I think that I cannot do anything further myself, and I will therefore leave the matter to you.

A month has now passed since Mrs Campbell first approached me, and so far as I know she has not yet obtained any capital. She is still extremely vague on this crucial point.

As no contract has been signed or even agreed in draft I must of course be free to make a contract with Winwood. I should much prefer Winwood not to have the English rights, but if she absolutely refuses to take the American rights unless she gets the English rights, she must have the English rights.

On the other hand, if the Winwood scheme falls through, I should like to do what is possible for Mrs Campbell.

Will you therefore kindly get into touch with Mrs Campbell. I give you a free hand to act as you think best.

Yours sincerely, Arnold Bennett

u.c. / t.c.c. / 390
(*To Mrs. Patrick Campbell*)

[75, Cadogan Square]
30th December 1927

Dear Mrs Campbell,

Thank you for your letter of yesterday. I was not in the least joking. If your backers will at once give me an absolute guarantee of production in U.S.A. at any time during 1928, under

388. Mrs. Campbell (born Beatrice Stella Tanner) was, in her second marriage, Mrs. G. F. M. Cornwallis-West. 'You both' at the close of her letter refers to Bennett and Dorothy (see page 298).

a money penalty, I will call off my negotiations in New York.

I see the matter like this. You and I have made no contract. (Moreover any contract would have to be made between me and your backers.) All you and I have done is to agree that certain clauses shall form part of any contract.

You are perfectly free to come to me and say: 'I am not in a position to make a contract.' I should have no grievance against you if you did this. Similarly, I am free. If I can get a guarantee of a suitable production in U.S.A. do you mean to argue that I must give it up on the chance of you at some future time making a contract to produce there? I think that you do not.

You are perfectly correct in stating that you said that if you could not have the American rights you would not take the English rights; and I shall have no grievance against you if you drop them.

My experience of the theatrical world is nearly as long as yours, and I have learnt the advisability of taking a certainty when I can get it.

Nothing has yet been settled in U.S.A. and perhaps nothing will be settled. I wanted to let you know at the earliest possible moment how things stood.

All good wishes for the N.Y.

Always yours sincerely,

[Arnold Bennett]

u.c. / ms. / 391
(*From Mrs. Patrick Campbell*)

64 Pont Street
Dec. 31st/27

Dear Mr. Bennett,

Please don't think I would be anything but very unhappy if you missed a certainty on my account.

In your letter you say:—'The backers must at once give me an absolute guarantee of production in U.S.A. during 1928, under money penalty. . . . Moreover any contract would have to be made between me & them'. I am willing you should bind *me* in any way you, & your agents, & my lawyer think fit &

proper—but I wouldn't like to bind my friends quite as you say, & in any case it is impossible it could be done '*at once*'.

My arrangements with bankers were going forward on their understanding that I held first option on the American rights— Mr. Gilbert Miller is not to be in London until the end of January. Would you like me to send the play out to him, he might take both the English & American rights?—I would like to be of some use to you, & I would like to play *Flora* but I couldn't myself go into *management* unless I held the option on the American rights.

A happy New Year to you both.

Beatrice Stella CW
(Mrs. P. C.)

U.C. / T.C.C. / 392
(*To Mrs. Patrick Campbell*)

[75, Cadogan Square]
4th January 1928

Dear Mrs Campbell,

Many thanks for your letter of the 31st.

I felt sure that you would see my point of view.

As regards contracts, I hope that you will not think that I was casting any reflection upon your business methods. Not in the least. But except in the case of a regular and established management contracts are generally made with the people who find the money. I personally would not make a contract with anybody else in these circumstances. The backers may of course form themselves into a limited company for the special purpose of their enterprise. The contracts at the Court Theatre have all been made with the backers, not with the Director of the Season. You yourself told me some months ago that you had then recently made a mistake in not having a contract with the right people. And you were quite right.

If my contract were made direct with you, you might with the best will in the world find yourself unable to fulfil the terms of the American side of the contract if the English production were a failure, and the backers might and in all probability would say that as they were not parties to the contract they had no liability.

As regards my suggestion that production in the U.S.A. must be absolutely guaranteed, with a money penalty in case of failure to produce, I say this only in view of the probability of my getting a certainty of production under another management. If *Flora* is produced and succeeds in the U.S.A. I might well, at a moderate computation, make £5,000 out of the affair. I have before now received over £500 in U.S.A. in royalties for a single week. You will not argue that I ought to throw £5,000 in one quarter on the chance of getting £5,000 in another.

I fully admit the hardship to yourself. But my experience of the stage is that it is a long succession of hardships, especially for an author. I am not accusing you of dilatoriness. I have not forgotten that I said that I would not make a contract until the money was in the bank for the production. I know that the process of getting money is usually a long one. But these things are beyond my control and beyond yours, and they are, also, rather beside the point. So far, you are free and I am free. You have not bound yourself and I have not bound myself. The arrangement between us was provisional. You are possibly suffering damage, and I greatly regret it. But if you failed to get your capital and the whole thing fell into the sea, would you say that I had a moral claim for damages against you? I think not.

Yours sincerely, [Arnold Bennett]

392. The letter is misdated 1927.
Sacred and Profane Love drew £500 a week for Bennett in New York in 1920.
Flora was never produced in either New York or London. The affair spilled over into the Campbell-Shaw correspondence. Shaw wrote to Mrs. Campbell on 18 January: 'I do not see any room for hesitation about *Flora*. Either you are in business as an actress or you are not. It is now, I take it, a case of "Mrs. Patrick Campbell at liberty. Matrons, heavies, comedy, character: 64 Pont Street." Well, here you are offered a leading part in a play by an eminent author. Of course, you take it without any fuss. . . .' Mrs. Campbell replied: 'I haven't been asked to play *Flora*. I have been asked whether I would get the necessary backing and do the play myself. . . . It is stupid of me that I cannot as you do realise I am an old lady who has arrived at "Heavies, Matrons etc." I see myself an unwanted child just as I see you, not as an old gentleman, but as a brilliant adorable Irish lad whom I love with ardour.' Mrs. Campbell's career on the London stage ended a year later.

U.C. / TS. / 393

75, Cadogan Square
31st January 1928

Dear Ralph Pinker,

Thanks for yours of yesterday. I too have frequently heard the rumour that I was leaving the *Evening Standard*. I heard it so often that I told the editor about it. His reply was that he had heard nothing of it himself. When I suggested to Beaverbrook some months ago that they must be getting a bit tired of me, he would not hear of such a thing. My own opinion is that they must sooner or later get tired of paying me £3,750 a year for such a short article on such a subject. I believe, however, that they are very pleased with it.

I have been approached (by Newman Flower) about transferring the article to another paper at the same price, but I have of course told him that there is nothing doing. If I leave the *Evening Standard* of my own accord it will not be to go to another paper, even at twice the price.

Yours sincerely, Arnold Bennett

U.C. / TS. / 394

75, Cadogan Square
22nd February 1928

Dear Mr Wicken,

Many thanks for your letter about Godal and the draft agreement.

I return the contract.

I will only sign it, before the flotation of the company, on the understanding that my name is not used in the prospectus of the Company.

Clause 2 seems to me to give the Company rather too ample opportunity for turning down the completed thing.

The phrase 'said synopsis' is used in this clause, but it is not used earlier.

I am quite prepared to discuss an idea for a story with Godal, but I am not prepared to ask whether any given idea will do. I must be free to choose my own idea. And I will only 'consider' his suggestions as to the working out of the idea. I will not be bound by them.

Clause 7 is utterly impossible. I would not on any account agree to it, or agree to anything like it. It simply gives the producer the right to use my name on anything he cares to present to the public.

You might make it clear to Godal that he is not offering to pay me in any generous fashion. Quite the reverse. I can always get £100 per 1000 words for short stories, without counting the book rights. And I have no trouble beyond writing them, and nobody to consult.

Yours sincerely, Arnold Bennett

P.S. I hope your broken bone is now cured completely. I was sorry to hear of the accident.   A. B.

U.C. / TS. / 395

75, Cadogan Square
23rd February 1928

My dear Eric,

Thank you for your letter of yesterday.

I do not want Mrs. P. C. to play the part, but I do not agree with you that a bad performance is worse than no performance at all.

What about Friday next week for lunch? I am going to Manchester on Sunday until Wednesday.

Yours sincerely, Arnold Bennett

U.C. / TS. / 396

75, Cadogan Square
17th March 1928

My dear Eric,

I enclose copy of a letter received from Mr. C. L. Harrison [Hanson], of my reply, and of his answer to my reply. Will you please deal with the matter direct. I think that a moderate fee will meet the case.

Yours sincerely, Arnold Bennett

394. The negotiations with Godal seem ultimately to have come to nothing.
395. Negotiations with Estelle Winwood having collapsed, Eric Pinker suggested not producing the play as preferable to returning it to Mrs. Campbell.

u.c. / t.c. / 397
(*From Charles L. Hanson*)

28, Linnaean Street
Cambridge
Massachusetts
February 4th, 1928

Dear Sir,

Among the selections I should like to include in a volume of travel sketches to be published by Ginn and Company for use in high schools is an extract from *Your United States*, pages 49–69. Your publishers, who have been most helpful in cooperating with me, have referred me to you. If you can see your way clear to allow me to reprint these pages, you may be assured of complete and appreciative recognition of your courtesy in the volume under consideration.

Yours very truly, [Charles L. Hanson]
(Mechanic Arts High School, Boston)

P.S. What follows is 'pure innocence', not designed to influence your decision, doubtless already made, but to give me the pleasure of saying that as a reader I have enjoyed your writings ever since they began to appear and as a teacher it has been an added pleasure to recommend such writings of yours as from time to time have seemed likely to prove stimulating and otherwise helpful to my pupils. [C. L. H.]

n.c. / t.c. / 398
(*To Charles L. Hanson*)

[75, Cadogan Square]
20th February 1928

Dear Sir,

I am obliged for your letter of the 4th. I want to ask you this: Do you make a profit out of the proposed book? Do the publishers make a profit? Is the book made up exclusively of extracts from the works of authors to whom you don't intend to offer remuneration?

If the answers to these three questions are in the affirmative, I must ask another: Where do the quoted authors come in?

L.A.B.——2 C

The financial aspect of the affair may be trifling; but the principle of the affair is important. If a magazine reprints extracts from my old work, it pays for the use of the extracts.

If, because your book is meant for the high service of education, you are working for nothing and the publishers are working for nothing, then I will give you free permission to use the long extract which you mention. Not otherwise. You may reply that you have to live and the publishers have to live. But so have I.

All of which does not impair in the least my appreciation of your enjoyment of my books.

Yours sincerely, [A. Bennett]

u.c. / ts. / 399

75, Cadogan Square
11th April 1928

Dear Mr. Wicken,

Thank you for your letter of the 5th. I agree.

I hear that Thorpe (formerly of Wardour Films) has now joined another company and suggests that I should do a scenario for Dupont. He wanted to discuss the story with me. I have told him that the first thing to do is to settle terms, and have referred him to your firm.

Yours sincerely, Arnold Bennett

u.c. / ts. / 400

75, Cadogan Square
14th April 1928

Dear Mr. Wicken,

Thank you for your letter of yesterday and the contract with B.I.P. Ltd. The contract seems to be in order, except that the story is certainly not entirely 'original', inasmuch as Thorpe and Dupont gave me the idea for it.

I think I can get on very well with these two men. Dupont

398. In his reply, Charles Hanson asked Bennett to suggest a fee.

399. Thorpe was now with British International Pictures (referred to by Bennett in subsequent letters as B.I.P.), for which A. E. Dupont (1891–1956) was a producer. Dupont, of German-French birth, produced two early films of some consequence, *Vaudeville* and *Moulin Rouge*. The scenario proposed to Bennett became *Piccadilly*.

is obviously an artist. I am dining with them tonight, and I may hand to them then the first rough sketch of the entire thing.

Yours sincerely, Arnold Bennett

P.S. I return the contract signed.   A. B.

U.C. / TS. / 401

75, Cadogan Square
22nd May 1928

Dear Mr. Wicken,

Crosby Gaige

Thank you for your letter of yesterday. I absolutely refuse to give Mr. Gaige an option on all the remaining volumes of my Journal. This decision is final. It is not in the least because I distrust Mr. Gaige, who is a great friend of mine. It is because I might for various reasons wish not to continue publication of my Journal. I have as yet no idea how it will be received, especially by my friends. The whole Journal runs at present to about 800,000 words at least—probably more. I am not going to give any publisher the first rights on all this mass of stuff. The serial value of it, or of some of it, might in the future be worth quite a lot, and Mr. Gaige wants only unpublished material.

I will give him the option on two more volumes similar in length to the first one. This is my limit, so far as the contract goes. I fully anticipate that if the first volume succeeds my business relations with Mr. Gaige will extend far beyond three volumes. But I will not bind myself. It seems to me that all the binding is to be on my side.

As regards the other conditions:

(1) I agree.

(2) If the 40 copies are to be part of the 500, 750, or 1,000 copies printed, I will not agree. My royalty must be on the total number of the edition as mentioned in the volume itself. If the 40 copies are to be extra copies I agree, but only on the understanding that none of them is to be sold.

(3) Partly dealt with above. I agree to extension of the option to four months.

(4) I agree.

I know from Mr. Gaige's intimate friends that when it comes down to business he is a very hard man. We shall soon see whether he or I can be the harder.

Grand Babylon Hotel

I note your P.S. I do not suppose that Jackson will take up the option, but if he does the payment must be in cash.

Yours sincerely, Arnold Bennett

u.c. / ts. / 402

75, Cadogan Square
31st May 1928

Dear Mr Wicken,

Mr Thorpe and Mr Dupont are both very enthusiastic about the story which I have written for them, and of which they fully approve. Indeed I cannot remember any occasion on which people who have bought my work (of any kind) have shown such enthusiasm as these two did last night.

They at once asked me to write another story. I am considering the matter.

Yours sincerely, Arnold Bennett

u.c. / ts. / 403

75, Cadogan Square
23rd June 1928

Dear Mr Wicken,

Many thanks. To my mind there is a great deal in Thorpe's argument. Still, if *Piccadilly* is a success, we shall see what we

---

401. Crosby Gaige (1872–1949) was an American producer who was making an apparently short-lived venture into publishing. Earlier he was associated with Bennett's dramatic agent in America, Edgar Selwyn, and he met Bennett in 1911. He was now arranging to issue a limited edition of thirty to forty thousand words of the first year of Bennett's journal. The price would be two guineas (ten dollars), and Bennett's royalty would be 15 per cent. Negotiations fell through. The three-volume *Journals of Arnold Bennett*, published by Cassell after Bennett's death, reproduces about one-third of the regular journal he kept. There were other miscellaneous journals that sometimes ran concurrently with the regular one.

Jackson was an American connected with a German film company, the Ludwig Blattner Corporation, that was interested in producing *The Grand Babylon Hotel*.

shall see. It is quite true that he, or rather Maxwell, gave me the idea for *Piccadilly*, as also for the next film; but as I was specially called in to execute what they could not execute themselves this seems to me to be beside the point. They gave me two ideas for *Piccadilly*. I worked out the first one in full and then they did not like it, while admitting that the fault lay in the very essence of the plot. I thus wrote two films for one price.

Yours sincerely, Arnold Bennett

P.S. I return the contract signed.

U.C. / TS. / 404

75, Cadogan Square
28th June 1928

Dear Mrs Dagnall,

I have written a play (for which I have not yet found a title). I promised the first refusal of it to Sir Gerald du Maurier. I delivered it to him on Tuesday night, and today I had an interview with him and he said he would put it into rehearsal in July.

He is certainly very hard up for a play, and he will pay the right terms, whatever they are. I do not want to demand excessive terms in any way, but I think I ought to have what you consider to be good terms, and you are in a strong position in the matter of negotiation. I understand that on his side the negotiations are conducted by Miss Butler.

It is most clearly understood between him and me that he makes a contract for the English rights only. I prefer that the English and the American rights should not be in one contract. If Gilbert Miller wants the American rights he can of course have them, on the proper terms.

I leave everything to you.

I am going away early on Saturday morning for a month,

403. *Piccadilly* was written, and rewritten, in little more than two weeks during April and May ('the most strenuous fortnight I've had for years', Bennett noted in his journal) at a price of £2,000. In its published form, issued by the Readers Library in 1929, it is 18,000 words long. Thorpe apparently had reservations about the new contract. John Maxwell (d. 1941) was the chairman of British International Pictures.

though of course if the rehearsals do in fact begin in July I suppose I shall have to come over to London for a bit.

My French address is 'Ma Coquille', Le Touquet-Paris-Plage, Pas de Calais, France.

Yours sincerely, Arnold Bennett

U.C. / TS. / 405

75, Cadogan Square
7th July 1928

Dear Mrs Dagnall,

1. Royalties are all right.

2. But the fact that du Maurier is an expensive star is no reason why the author should accept smaller royalties than usual. He is an expensive star because he draws people.

3. I think the advance is rather small.

4. An advance should certainly be paid if the American rights are taken up.

5. No period for the option is mentioned. It should be as short as possible.

6. Indeed, I am going to alter the end of the second act to please du Maurier and Miller. If I do this I think I shall insist that the play is the next production at the St. James's theatre.

The above are simply my general observations, and Mrs Dagnall has full powers to act on my behalf.

Yours sincerely, Arnold Bennett

404. The play presently had a title, *The Return Journey*, and Sir Gerald du Maurier (1873–1934) took it. After fifteen years as manager of the Wyndham Theatre, du Maurier joined Gilbert Miller at the St. James's in 1925. His last success had been in *The Last of Mrs. Cheyney* at the St. James's in 1925.

405. Bennett interrupted his French vacation to return to London briefly to consult with du Maurier and Miller.

Mrs. Dagnall had proposed a royalty of 5 per cent. on the first £600, rising to 12½ on everything above £1,500. The suggested advance was £200.

The play opened at the St. James's Theatre on 1 September, with Sir Gerald du Maurier in the leading role of Dr. Henry Fausting, a Cambridge don, who undergoes rejuvenation by science, and education through woman. W. J. Turner, whom Bennett had befriended a decade before, wrote of the play in Bennett's own *New Statesman*: 'It reveals him as a man who if he ever did think has now ceased to think.' Bennett had no hope that the play would please London: 'Career as a dramatist closing!' he noted in his journal while writing the play. The play was a failure. In 1929 Bennett wrote his last play, one that remains untitled, unproduced, and unpublished.

u.c. / ts. / 406

75, Cadogan Square
12th October 1928

Dear Mr. Wicken,

I ought to have been a literary agent. I sold the serial rights of the *Piccadilly* scenario yesterday afternoon to the new *Film Weekly* for £300 cash. And I am convinced that I could have got £400 if I had been more courageous. I said 'I will name a figure and it is the lowest I will take.' The other side closed immediately. You will now have to credit the firm with the percentage.

Yours sincerely, Arnold Bennett

u.c. / ts. / 407

75, Cadogan Square
19th October 1928

Dear Mr Wicken,

Thank you for your letter of yesterday and the enclosure. If I ever gave you any instructions about arranging for the publication of *The Return Journey* I have completely forgotten the fact.

I think that the terms which Chatto & Windus offer are reasonable enough, but I do not want this play to be published at present.

Several times during the last few years I have asked the firm (through Swinnerton) whether they wished to continue the publication of my plays, and the reply was always in the affirmative. For myself, although I know that some publishers attach value to the appearance of my name in their catalogues and are prepared to pay indirectly for that value, I strongly object to any of my books being published at a loss to the publishers. Nor do I wish to publish any book on any terms unless I think that it has a good chance of a fair sale.

I shall probably sooner or later suggest to you the publication of a volume of my collected plays.

Please communicate to Chatto & Windus as much of this letter as you properly can.

Yours sincerely, Arnold Bennett

406. *Piccadilly* began appearing in the *Film Weekly* on 22 October.
407. *The Return Journey* was never published.

U.C. / TS. / 408

75, Cadogan Square
22nd October 1928

Dear Mr Wicken,

Thank you for your letter of the 19th. The point is that I want to be free to accept commissions to write original films. For instance, if *Piccadilly* is a success, British International will probably ask me to write a third film. It is obvious that, having received the offer of a commission for a film on a given subject, I cannot go to Authors Productions and say: 'Will you give me a commission on this subject?' While I would like to oblige Mr Pugh, for whom I have the friendliest feelings, I do not want to agree to a transfer of the contract with him which would tie me up to a new Company not yet in existence, and which might also prevent me from doing profitable work which I should enjoy doing. In my opinion British International is likely to become the biggest English film company. I have great faith in the chairman and the managing director.

Yours sincerely, Arnold Bennett

U.C. / TS. / 409

75, Cadogan Square
26th October 1928

Dear Ralph Pinker,

At the request of the Bishop of Liverpool, I have written a volume for the 'Affirmations' series of booklets published by Benn (1/-). It is about religion. I do not expect to make anything out of it, and I did not mention the question of finance to the Bishop, who called on me for the purpose of getting me to help. Still, I suppose that some contract is made, and perhaps it will be well for you to fix the matter with Benns. From detailed information which has been given to me by authors of

408. John Maxwell was chairman of British International, which in the 1930s was one of the major English film companies. He left British International to become head of Gaumont British Films, and was described in 1937 as 'the most prominent personality, perhaps, in the British film world today'. Bennett was now writing his second scenario, *Punch and Judy*, for him and Thorpe. Ralph Pugh (see pages 355–6) was organizing a subsidiary company of British Authors Productions.

booklets in other series of Benn's, I should say that he always expects to get something for half nothing.

Yours sincerely, Arnold Bennett

u.c. / ts. / 410

75, Cadogan Square
5th December 1928

Dear Ralph Pinker,

Many thanks for your letter of yesterday. I have the scheme for the next novel in my head; but I certainly cannot begin to write it until I have cleared off some of the arrears of short stories. It is just possible that I might begin the thing in April or May. It will be a serious novel, and probably about 120,000 words long. I doubt its possibilities as a serial, but you never know.

I hope that you are now absolutely clear of your influenza. I had a small dose of the same myself.

Yours sincerely, Arnold Bennett

u.c. / ts. / 411

75, Cadogan Square
6th December 1928

My dear Eric,

I should be much obliged if you would let me know privately in some detail, what are the relations now between George and

409. On 14 September 1925, Bennett initiated a series of articles in the *Daily Express* entitled 'My Religion'. He was followed by Hugh Walpole, Rebecca West, and others. The series drew a remarkable response from readers, including Dr. Albert David (1867–1950), Bishop of Liverpool. Most of the correspondence was directed at Bennett's article, the substance of which was expressed by one reader as follows: 'I *think* there must be a God, as I do not see how the universe could have made itself; but this does not interest me. I *know* there is an Arnold Bennett.' The present invitation from Dr. David was presumably a consequence. Bennett's booklet, *The Religious Interregnum*, published by Benn in 1929, speculates upon the sort of religion that will replace what Bennett considers to be a dying Christianity. Admitting that he himself lacks a religious instinct, he nevertheless expresses regret for the growth of irreligion: 'it means the cutting-off of an ever-growing mass of people from regular communion with the infinite, or, if you prefer the word, God. . . . Grandeur is forgotten. . . .'

On Sir Ernest Benn see page 362n.

410. Bennett decided to write his new novel, *Imperial Palace*, in March 1927. The idea for it is mentioned in his letter of 1 February 1914, quoted in G. H. Doran's of 29 June 1917 (see page 256), as having been long in his mind. The root of it is in *The Grand Babylon Hotel* of 1900. On the day he began writing it, he noted in his journal: 'I have been fighting for years against the instinct to write this particular novel.'

the Doubledays. I hear all sorts of stories here, chiefly to the effect that he has no real power.

I should also like to know for how many books I am still bound to the firm.

I was not at all pleased at their objection to publishing *Mediterranean Scenes*. In fact I cannot understand it. I think that this is a pretty good book, and such is general informed opinion of it here. I have always been supposed to be rather good at travel stuff. At the worst the book is very readable. It makes a volume pleasing to the eye, and Flower told me today that he fully expects to sell the edition out. Swinnerton told me that they had refused to publish his *London Bookman*, though he had not asked them to publish it.

I hope that all is going well with you.

Kindest regards to Mrs Eric.

Always yours sincerely, Arnold Bennett

U.C. / TS. / 412

75, Cadogan Square
6th December 1928

Dear Ralph Pinker,

I hope that Doran's accounts have been and will be examined with the greatest care, and compared with the contracts. I am told, and have had various details to prove, that his accounts are very unreliable

Yours sincerely, Arnold Bennett

U.C. / TS. / 413

75, Cadogan Square
3rd January 1929

My dear Eric,

Thanks for your letter of yesterday and the copy of the letter from Chesters. I have written to Chesters direct, and I enclose copy of my letter.

Yours sincerely, Arnold Bennett

411. George Doran merged with Doubleday, Page in 1927 to form Doubleday, Doran. The order of names was the order of power.

Swinnerton's *A London Bookman* was published in England by Secker in 1928.

413. J. & W. Chester published the one-act opera *Judith*, the libretto of which Bennett wrote for Eugene Goossens (d. 1962) in 1924. It had its first performance at Covent Garden on 25 June 1929.

u.c. / t.c.c. / 414
(*To Messrs. J. & W. Chester and Co.*)

[75, Cadogan Square]
3rd January 1929

Gentlemen,

Messrs. Pinker & Sons have sent me a copy of your letter to them of the 2nd instant, and I am replying direct.

Mr. Goossens' idea was that Mr. Charles Ricketts should be asked to design a setting and the costumes for *Judith*. I fully agree with this. Mr. Ricketts did the sets and the costumes for my play *Judith*, and they were very satisfactory.

In my opinion the set should be simple, except as regards the large tent in the centre, which should be elaborate. The more the attention is concentrated on the tent the better. The text of the opera gives all necessary indications. I think that the costumes, especially Judith's, Holofernes' and Bagoas', are more important than the set. The first and the last ought to be very rich. In the play Miss Lillah McCarthy (Lady Keeble) wore as little as propriety and the censor would allow—that is, after she had removed her travelling garment. It is to be remembered that she came prepared to fascinate Holofernes.

Lady Keeble has the designs for the sets and for the costumes, and I should not be surprised if she still has the actual costumes. Her London address is 65 Curzon Street, W.1. and her country address is Hammells, Boar's Hill, Oxford.

If you need any further information, kindly let me know.

Yours sincerely, [Arnold Bennett]

414. Eugene Goossens remarks in *Overtures and Beginners* that 'except for Shaw, I doubt whether any writer of this period had read or acquired more knowledge about the subject of music than A.B.'.

Bennett describes Lillah McCarthy's original costume in his journal:

'Her tent costume frightened one of the lessees of the theatre. Above a line drawn about ½ inch or 1 inch above the *mont de Vénus* she wore nothing except a 4-in. band of black velvet round the body hiding the breasts and a similar perpendicular band of velvet starting from between the breasts and going down to the skirt and so hiding the navel. Two thin shoulder straps held this contrivance in position. Bracelets and rings, of course. The skirt was slit everywhere and showed the legs up to the top of the thigh when she laid down there at Holofernes's feet. She looked a magnificent picture thus, but a police prosecution would not have surprised me at all.'

Six months after writing the above letter about the operatic costumes, Bennett wrote to his nephew Richard: 'I have . . . succeeded in getting some changes in Judith's costume. As . . . designed the poor thing had to vamp Holofernes in a

U.C. / TS. / 415

75, Cadogan Square
25th January 1929

Dear Mr Wicken,

I had a long interview with Thorpe and Hitchcock last night about the new film *Punch and Judy*. Hitchcock is to be the producer. He talked a good deal about wanting more 'colour'— a great film word—and had various absurd suggestions for changing the general environment of the film (which I have made chiefly financial). I argued with him for three hours, and defeated him on every point. Thorpe openly argued on my side and against his own man. Towards the end Hitchcock's principal phrase was 'I agree. I agree.' He finished by saying that he would prepare a few leading ideas for the actual scenario. Thorpe is certainly very pleased with the film, and I assume that he definitely intends to take it substantially as it is. Anyhow I shall alter it, if I alter it, only in small details.

Yours sincerely, Arnold Bennett

U.C. / TS. / 416

75, Cadogan Square
29th January 1929

My dear Eric,

Thank you for your letters of yesterday.

The novel

If I were you I should not count on this before the end of the year. I have got the main ideas for it, but that is all. I think it will be too long for a serial.

Doran

Why did he not mention the cheap edition earlier? I do not feel very much inclined to accept his suggestion. £800 in 5

---

nightie which might have been bought at Harrods. She will now at least look a bit indecent—at least I hope so.' It is not known whether Charles Ricketts (1866– 1931) did the designing.

415. Alfred Hitchcock (1899–) began his film career as a technician for Famous Players Lasky in 1920. By 1925 he was a director. His first notable film, *The 39 Steps*, came in 1935.

years for ten books seems to me to be not enough—especially
as a cheap edition would in all probability damage the sale of
the ordinary editions. It seems to me that George had better
be asked to think again.

Yours sincerely, Arnold Bennett

U.C. / TS. / 417

75, Cadogan Square
29th January 1929

Dear Mr. Wicken,

Many thanks for your letter of yesterday.

Piccadilly

I only saved this film from disastrous titles by sheer accident.
If I had not happened to be dining with Thorpe on Thursday
night about *Punch and Judy* I should not have had a chance on
the titles unless I had held up the production tomorrow night
by legal process. I had received about half the draft titles six
or seven weeks ago and had put them into order in my own
phrasing. These I delivered immediately after receipt of them,
and I heard nothing whatever further about titles until last
Thursday night. I had the full list sent down to me last
Friday morning and I spent the whole of Friday at home on
them. I spent the whole of Saturday at Elstree finally settling
the titles in conference with Thorpe, Dupont, Durell, Mycroft
and (in the afternoon) Maxwell himself. I must say that both
Thorpe and Maxwell are very good on the subject of titles, once
they have grasped my rule that the characters must speak
exactly as people do speak in real life. I am glad to be able to
report that every title was at last settled to my entire satisfaction.

The film itself is very good indeed so far as it goes. Its defects
are that Dupont has very little sense of humour and has failed to
convey a lot of my comedy and that the end of the film is not
properly rounded off. In fact the story is not really ended at all.
Wong, and an unknown girl in the East End, are marvellous.
Gray is bad at the beginning and better at the end. Thomas is
just what you would expect him to be. The Chinese boy is
excellent. The inquest is not well done, but on the whole

Dupont has stuck honestly to the story—except at the end. I could have obtained a much better film if I had *lived* at Elstree during the shooting; but this of course is impossible.

By the way I will never (unless I am very hard up) write another film for £2,000. The price is very insufficient. I must have spent a good two months in all on the work. And I have spent a good three months on *Punch and Judy*.

Talking Film

£1000 is the very lowest I will take for even the shortest talking film, and if the I.V.T.A. (I wish you would tell me what these initials stand for) will not pay this you can close the negotiations immediately. There would be a lot more work in connection with the talking film, as I should have to be at the shooting.

I doubt whether I should be prepared to do a long talking film for £4,000. Here again I should have to be at the shooting, which would probably take about a couple of months at least. I could earn more money more easily in the time at other work. I consider that £4,000 would be inadequate. I am quite ready to make experiments, but only at a fair price.

City of Pleasure

I saw this film last night. It begins very well, with the fun-fair scenes, etc; but the actual story, as screened, has absolutely no connection with *The City of Pleasure*, whereas I had bound up the story with the environment of the City of Pleasure. Also every shred of comedy has been carefully removed from the film. Why, I cannot imagine; unless the director failed to see any comedy in the book. To witness this film made me very gloomy.

Yours sincerely, Arnold Bennett

417. Durell is otherwise unknown. Walter C. Mycroft had been a film critic for the *Evening Standard*, and he later became a producer at Elstree.

Jameson Thomas and Gilda Gray starred in *Piccadilly*. The film made a name for Anna May Wong (b. 1907). It had its first showing on 30 January 1929.

I.V.T.A. was the International Variety and Theatrical Agency. *The City of Pleasure* was produced by a German company.

u.c. / ts. / 418

75, Cadogan Square
4th March 1929

Dear Mr Wicken,

Punch and Judy

Referring to your conversation with Miss Nerney today on the telephone, I certainly think that the £1000 ought to be paid at once. As I have previously told you, I think, Hitchcock's arguments made no impression upon me at all, and as the discussion proceeded Thorpe took more and more my side, until he definitely ranged himself on my side. There remained nothing to argue about. Hitchcock, when they left me, said that he would put his ideas for a scenario down on paper within the next ensuing few days. Since then about six weeks have elapsed and I have heard nothing at all from either Hitchcock or Thorpe. In no circumstances shall I accept any of the ideas which Hitchcock suggested and which I rejected with Thorpe's full sympathy. I finished the interview with the clear impression that the story was to be accepted as it stood. Thorpe of course did not actually say so. For one thing he is always very cautious, and for another he could not well give an acceptance in the presence of Hitchcock, after Hitchcock had elaborated his general notion that I should entirely change the milieu of the story and make all the characters characters in a circus.

Rather more than a month ago, when I was seeing Thorpe about *Piccadilly*, I said to him (textually): 'Hitchcock was absolutely defeated the other night.' Thorpe agreed.

Yours sincerely, Arnold Bennett

u.c. / ts. / 419

75, Cadogan Square
12th March 1929

Dear Mr Wicken,

Many thanks for your letter of yesterday about *Punch and Judy*. Certainly I regard Thorpe's answer as unsatisfactory. What it apparently means is that Hitchcock apparently does

---

418. The £1,000 was the second half of the payment to Bennett for *Punch and Judy*, to be paid on satisfactory completion of the story.

not like the story and probably will refuse to do it. (I see from
the papers that at present he is engaged on a sound film.) Of
course I would much prefer Dupont to do it; but I see no reason
whatever why I should wait for my money while the B.I.
settles which of its producers is to do the film. In any case I am
not going to alter the story except in trifling details. If there is
to be any giving-way, the giving-way will not be done by me.
If the B.I. prefers the stories of its producers to my stories, it
ought to commission stories from its producers and not from
me. You are at liberty to make all this quite clear to Thorpe.
You can also make it quite clear that rather than alter the story
in any essentials I would lose my second £1,000, in which case
the B.I. would lose its first £1,000.

I now leave the matter to you.

Yours sincerely, Arnold Bennett

P.S. I enclose a letter from B. A. Woolf & Co about *The Grand
Babylon Hotel*, which please answer. I am not familiar with the
facts.   A. B.

TEXAS / TS. / 420

75, Cadogan Square
19th March 1929

Dear Mr. Wicken,

Thank you for your letter of yesterday. *Punch and Judy* would
have been written rather differently if I had known that it was
to be a 'talkie'. There is one great difficulty, namely that
Dupont's knowledge of the English language is not sufficient to
enable him satisfactorily to take charge of the production of
English dialogue.

Another difficulty is that I do not very much care to have
my name associated with a talkie unless I write the dialogue
myself. This would be a big job, and would take a great deal of
time. It would also necessitate my frequent presence at the
studios—especially as I have a lot to learn about the mere
technique of the job.

I had heard from Thorpe to say that Dupont would produce

419. Woolf was a German company apparently interested in filming *The Grand
Babylon Hotel*.

the film, but no word was said as to it being produced 'Talkie'.
I have an appointment to lunch with Thorpe and Dupont at
the Savoy on Thursday. It seems to me that the matter will need
a considerable amount of adjustment.

Do you think it would be a good plan for me to write to
Thorpe at once and state the difficulties, so that he will not be
surprised on Thursday when he hears my view of the case? Or
will you communicate with him or see him in the meantime?
He appears to be in a great hurry to get the work started—
probably because Dupont is on a very high salary. This fact
would doubtless help you to enforce our views.

I am going away on Tuesday next to the South of France for
at least three weeks, and cannot alter this arrangement.

Yours sincerely, Arnold Bennett [signed by Miss Nerney]

TEXAS / TS. / 421

75, Cadogan Square
19th March 1929

Dear Mr. Wicken,
Further to my letter of this morning, you can give all or any
of the following information:—

Last year I made nearly £22,000 after deducting all commissions. Considering that I did not work at all during at least
six weeks, this means that I earned at the rate of £2,000 a
month. I spent over two months on the story of *Punch and Judy*
and thereby lost over £2,000 on it, as I receive only £2,000
from B.I.P. If I am to work further on *Punch and Judy* with a
view to making it into a 'talkie', I will not accept less than
£2,000 extra. I have already told you that I would not do a
talkie for less than £4,000. It will be more trouble to write
Punch and Judy for a silent film and then turn it into a talkie
film, and will involve more work than to have written it direct
for a talkie.

I must repeat that I cannot have my name associated with a
talkie unless I control the whole of the dialogue. Sooner than
agree to this I would scrap the whole thing and be content with
the £1,000 which I have already received.

Yours sincerely, Arnold Bennett [signed by Miss Nerney]

L.A.B.—2 D

U.C. / TS. / 422

75, Cadogan Square
21st March 1929

Dear Mr Wicken,

I had lunch with Thorpe and Dupont today. They have satisfied me that the thing can be arranged on satisfactory lines. The affair will mean a considerable amount of extra work for me, as it has been decided between us that I shall write all the dialogue, on a detailed scenario now being prepared by Dupont, who will if necessary come to see me on the Riviera in about a fortnight's time. (I am going there on Tuesday morning.)

I did not say a word about finance at the lunch, preferring to leave the money question entirely to you. Nor did Thorpe say anything. I leave you a perfectly free hand, except that I will now say that I think I ought not to receive less than £1000 extra—as the absolute minimum. Perhaps you will get into touch with Thorpe at once.

Yours sincerely, Arnold Bennett

U.C. / TS. / 423

75, Cadogan Square
25th March 1929

Dear Mr Wicken,

Thorpe spent three hours here today, with Dupont. He said he would pay £500. I refused. He said there would be plenty of work for me to do for B.I.P. later on, in fact more than I could do. I then said I would accept £600 if he would give me a definite contract for £4,000 worth of work during the next 12 months at the rate of £100 a day. He said he could not do this. He then offered £750 without any future contract. I stuck to my point: no reduction on £1,000 unless I had a contract. He said he could not give me a definite contract, but he could assure me that I should have plenty of work, for which work I should fix the price. I laughed at this idea, seeing that he was all the time refusing to allow me to fix my own price for the matter in dispute. In the end he could not answer my arguments and he went away saying that he would get into touch with you. He begged me to think it over. I said it was no use me thinking it over any further, as I had already thought it over, and that I would not accept less than £1000 unless I had a contract for future work on my own terms.

You now know where we stand.

The atmosphere throughout the long interview was of the most friendly description.

Yours sincerely, Arnold Bennett

U.C. / TS. / 424

75, Cadogan Square
2nd May 1929

Dear Mr Wicken,

Thank you for your letter of yesterday. There is something going on behind the scenes which I do not understand. It may be that Dupont is causing trouble in some way. I am fairly sure that I shall not be expected to approve the dialogue. In any case the chances of my approving it are exceedingly small. Five and a half weeks have now passed since Thorpe and Dupont and I had a very friendly and very long lunch here (indeed it lasted till after tea), when it was decided that Dupont should finish his scenario and let me have it for approval. He was to have come to Antibes with the scenario; but afterwards Thorpe wrote that this would be unnecessary and there would be time for me to approve it afterwards. The original time-schedule was that Dupont should go with all his performers to America about the third week in April!

I shall have nothing to do with the dialogue. B.I.P. are perfectly entitled to turn the picture into a 'talkie'. What is more I cannot see how in the present circumstances of the film world they can do otherwise; but they are not entitled to ask me to have anything to do with the dialogue. I contracted to supply a story, which story I have supplied.

I should not be surprised if some effort is made by the B.I.P. to get free of this contract; but I fail to see how they can honestly do so.

Yours sincerely, Arnold Bennett

424. Bennett was apparently now being asked only to review the dialogue written by Dupont. He and Dorothy were spending a holiday in Antibes during April.

u.c. / ts. / 425

75, Cadogan Square
27th May 1929

Dear Ralph Pinker,

This is journalism. I do not know whether you will care to handle it in America, but if you do. . . .

On the strength of the enclosed two articles in *Life and Letters* the *Daily Telegraph* has bought from me, blind, 40,000 words of my *Journal* for £1,000.

I have promised to deliver the copy by the end of the year; but it will almost certainly be ready by the end of September. T. B. Wells of Harper's has been asking me for years for some extracts from my *Journal*, and I have been wondering whether this might suit him, and whether concurrent publication could in some way be arranged—if not with him, then with some American daily, weekly, or monthly. I think that the price need not frighten anybody, as I shall be fairly well satisfied with the price of the English rights even if I do not get anything from America. On the other hand the thing must not be sold for almost nothing.

The stuff will be in the same vein and of the same quality as the enclosed; but I do not guarantee that all or any of it will be French stuff.

Please see that the enclosed extracts are returned to me in due course.

Yours sincerely, Arnold Bennett

u.c. / ms. / 426

[Italy]
11–7–29

Dear Ralph Pinker,

I am going to Russia about August 10th till August 31st. I shall write articles thereon. I have already sold the British rights of these—whatever they are—to the *Daily Express*. Can you sell them in U.S.A.? If so, please do. They will be daily paper articles of about 1200 words each, I think. But I don't

---

425. *Life and Letters*, which Sir Desmond MacCarthy had begun in 1928, published extracts from Bennett's journal in January and February 1929. *Harper's* published nothing more of Bennett's.

yet know how many. I don't suppose I shall be able to write them till my return, on account of examination of baggage on leaving Russia. I am now on Lake Garda for about a week. 75 C. Square is my only sure address.

Yours sincerely, Arnold Bennett

u.c. / ms. / 427

Italy
12 July 1929

Dear Mr. Wicken,

Thank you for yours of the 3rd. What is meant by a 'dramatisation'? A play, or a film? There are mysteries in this affair. When last I saw Thorpe I could have closed with him for £2,750 in all. Dupont was enthusiastic. Now it is said that neither Dupont nor Hitchcock will produce! In any case I would *in no circumstances* agree to Hitchcock, as I am quite sure he would spoil the thing. I would agree only to Dupont. I would sooner lose the second £1,000, unless my position is made absolutely sure. I am not at all keen on doing a 'dramatisation' of any kind; & I certainly would not do it on the off chance of it being accepted. Anyhow there is no hurry. If nothing is done, then I have received £1,000 & the story remains mine.

Yours sincerely, Arnold Bennett

P.S. Will you kindly send a copy of this letter to Miss Nerney for filing? A.B.

426. The Bennetts had gone to France and Italy for six weeks at the end of June. The Russian trip was made with Max Beaverbrook. Four articles on the trip were published in the *Daily Express*, beginning on 4 September. American publication is unknown. Bennett concluded the articles with the following observation.

'I sympathise with the original democratic ideals of the autocrats and their terrific exertions to abolish the scandalous social injustice of Czarism. But my brief glimpse of the Soviet régime has disappointed and disturbed me. As for its ultimate success, one can say no more than that the régime is still holding together. It may succeed, but I very much doubt. Nor do I in the least desire its success. It presents itself to me as an extremely sinister business, based on a great ideal, but vitiated by prodigious lying and by blindness to the finer needs of ordinary human nature, conducted without scruple, and inevitably slipping back into the very evil which it was designed to cure. I departed from Russia with relief.

Russia had got on my nerves.'

He had written to Dorothy at the beginning of the trip: 'I doubt if I have ever seen anything as thrilling as Russia.'

u.c. / ts. / 428

75, Cadogan Square
9th September 1929

Dear Ralph Pinker,

Thanks for your letter of the 5th, which reached me on the 7th. I always told Gollancz that a reproduction of the MS of *The Old Wives' Tale* would not sell. My suggestion to you is that, with a firm like Benns, you are justified in sticking absolutely to the terms of the contract, whatever they may be. Before deciding anything I should like to know how many copies are to be sold.

Yours sincerely, Arnold Bennett

u.c. / ts. / 429

75, Cadogan Square
16th October 1929

Dear Ralph Pinker,

I had lunch with Newman Flower yesterday. I told him about my new novel. This book will be 150,000 words long, and ought to be finished about the end of March next. I had quite forgotten that the serial rights were sold to Flower. He has resold them to the *Woman's Journal*, which cannot possibly use the story as it will stand when completed. Flower is very anxious to publish the book next autumn, and he will see the *Woman's Journal* about an early serial publication. To help him I have promised that a very substantial part of the novel, probably one half, can be delivered about the 15th January.

I have also arranged with Flower that he shall publish in an edition de luxe my story *Venus Rising from the Sea*, similar to the forthcoming edition of *Elsie and the Child*. As regards the latter book, I agreed with him some time ago, as the expenses of production were decidedly heavier than we had anticipated, to go in with him on the half-profit system, especially as I had not looked on the edition as a financial proposition for me at all. I think, however, that *Venus Rising from the Sea* should be the subject of a more ordinary contract. Perhaps you will see to this.

428. Benn wanted to sell off the remaining copies at a reduced price with a reduced royalty.

I have also told Flower that he can publish the 40,000 word slab of my *Journal* which I have sold to the *Daily Telegraph* in Britain, and which your New York office is to handle for America. A contract should be made for this book too. 20,000 words of it can be sent to America pretty soon if you wish.

Yours sincerely, Arnold Bennett

U.C. / TS. / 430

75, Cadogan Square
25th October 1929

Dear Ralph Pinker,

Thank you for your letter of yesterday. With regard to the limited edition of *Venus*, I do not want Flower to be too hard pushed. Still I expect that he is well capable of looking after himself, if it comes to the point.

It seems to me that the *Journal* is unlikely to earn a £400 advance.

I should like Hodder & Stoughton to be told that I must approve of the 'making' of the limited edition of *The Old Wives' Tale*. They are certainly not a firm to be trusted to do this kind of thing on their own.

Yours sincerely, Arnold Bennett

U.C. / TS. / 431

75, Cadogan Square
5th December 1929

Dear Ralph Pinker,

Many thanks for your letter of the 4th and the sketches. I return the latter. I will not tell you what I think about them. All I will say is that they simply will not do, and that I would

---

429. *Imperial Palace* did not appear in *Woman's Journal*. The limited editions of *Venus Rising from the Sea* (written in April and May 1929) and *Elsie and the Child* had drawings by E. McKnight Kauffer and were printed at the Curwen Press. Cassell issued them in 1931 and 1929 respectively.

Cassell issued *Journal, 1929* in 1930. Doubleday, Doran issued it as *Journal of Things New and Old*.

430. Newman Flower was reluctant to pay more than a 15 per cent. royalty on *Venus Rising from the Sea*, since he was paying £200 to the artist. He agreed to pay a £400 advance on the journal, with a royalty of 20 per cent., rising to 25 after the sale of 3,500 copies.

never under any circumstances agree to any drawings based on such sketches or of any drawings of a similar school.

Further, I had no idea that it was intended to illustrate the book. If this idea had been suggested to me I should at once have stipulated for an artist approved by myself; probably suggested by myself. The result of the combined labours of several men upon the illustrated edition of *Elsie and the Child* is a book of which one can be proud, and which will certainly be sought for by collectors of taste. An illustrated *Old Wives' Tale* on the lines suggested by Hodder & Stoughton would simply be laughed at. The illustrated limited edition, indeed, is a branch of publishing which Hodder & Stoughton do not understand. They are incredibly behind the times, at any rate behind *my* times. I do not want any illustrations in the proposed edition. I want only a title-page in black and red. But I do want the book to be printed by a good firm, such as the Curwen Press. The ordinary commercial printer cannot satisfactorily succeed in this affair.

I should like you to comprehend with clearness that my feelings on the whole subject are very strong. I would far sooner have no limited edition at all than have one which people of taste in book production would ridicule.

Yours sincerely, Arnold Bennett

U.C. / TS. / 432

75, Cadogan Square
21st January 1930

Dear Mr. Wicken,

Thank you for your letter of the 20th. Lanoire cannot have the French rights of *The Old Wives' Tale*. I was under the impression that I told you or someone in the office about the O.W.T. proposition. It has been under translation for some time by His Excellency M. Coppet, Governor of the Tchad. The translation is now nearly finished. It has been personally revised by two of the finest novelists in France, André Gide and Roger Martin du Gard. André Gide will write an introduction for it. Of course I have not made any contract yet, so that the translator is entirely in my hands. I shall not, however, be very

431. The edition was abandoned.

stiff about the contract, as the opportunity of getting a first-class presentation to the lettered French public is almost unique. There are dozens of writers who would give their heads to have an introduction by Gide. Also both Gide and du Gard have spent an immense amount of time on the work, gratis. The book will almost certainly be published by *La Nouvelle Revue Française* (which published *The Ghost*). I would sooner have my books published by this firm than by any other in France.

Yours sincerely, Arnold Bennett

P.S. I think that Lanoire abandoned definitely his project of translating my books some years ago.   A. B.

u.c. / ts. / 433

75, Cadogan Square
23rd January, 1930

Dear Mr. Wicken,

Thank you for your letter of yesterday. Yes, this complication is a great pity. But I must say that in my opinion (1) I ought to have been told that Lanoire was taking up my translations again, and (2) Lanoire took his own risks when he translated *The Old Wives' Tale* before making a contract. I personally cannot possibly agree to a man playing fast and loose like this.

432. Bennett apparently did not know Roger Martin du Gard (1881–1958), but he and André Gide (1869–1951) had been friends for many years. A correspondence between them of eighty-five letters, edited by Linette F. Brugmans, was published in 1964 (*Correspondance André Gide-Arnold Bennett*, Genève, Librairie Droz, Paris, Librairie Minard). Gide, who first read *The Old Wives' Tale* in 1920, wrote after Bennett's death:

'Avant d'avoir lu *Old Wives' Tale*, mon admiration pour l'œuvre de Bennett comportait encore bien des réserves. Nos relations n'en étaient pourtant pas gênées, tant était grand notre plaisir à parler des œuvres d'autrui, sur lesquelles nous nous entendions toujours à merveille. Devant le *Conte de bonnes femmes*, toutes mes réserves tombèrent. Ce livre mérite de prendre place à côté des plus importants. Rien de plus simple que son intrigue; rien que de banal, que d'ordinaire dans la relation de la vie de deux sœurs d'abord très unies, qu'une médiocre aventure sépare, qui se rejoignent enfin dans la petite ville où s'était écoulée leur enfance, où il ne reste plus qu'à mourir. Mais quelles profondeurs d'émotion la sympathie de l'auteur sait éclairer sous la peinture minutieuse et patiente des événements mesquins de ces humbles existences! Quelle subtile convenance dans le choix! Quelle exactitude dans le ton des dialogues!'

The Ghost (*Le Spectre*) was published in 1926.

On Maurice Lanoire see pages 279–80.

As soon as he abandoned his claim for translating my works I began to look about for another translator, and I had not the slightest idea that Lanoire was beginning again. The news comes as a complete surprise to me. I regret that Lanoire should be upset, but the fault is entirely his own, unless of course you came to a definite understanding with him without informing me. You will understand that I have personal relations with men of letters in France. . . . Coppet's translation of *The Old Wives' Tale* has been going on for years—three at least. I positively do not expect to be told that anyone proposes to translate one of my books after he has translated it!

The following is rather beside the real point:—Lanoire is not a good translator. He is a Bordeaux man, and I have been told again and again that his French is inclined to be provincial in style.

Yours sincerely, Arnold Bennett

U.C. / TS. / 434

75, Cadogan Square
13th February 1930

Dear Ralph Pinker,

Thank you for your letter of yesterday about Benns. Quite right.

With regard to the American serial rights of my *Journal of 1929*, the *Daily Telegraph* have re-sold the British rights to the *Daily Mail*, and I hear that publication is supposed to begin about the end of this month. I do not, and never did, anticipate that you would be able to dispose of this item in U.S.A., but I thought I would give you the chance to do so. You may be interested to know that I have received £1000 for the British serial rights. 40,000 words. And I had merely to choose passages from my daily diary and put them into shape. Easy work. I think you will agree that the price is not a bad one.

Flower says that he proposes to publish the book in April. Of course it will be necessary for you to arrange with Doran as to this.

Yours sincerely, Arnold Bennett

434. Benn still wanted Bennett to accept a reduced royalty. Ralph Pinker refused for him.

The journal began appearing in the *Daily Mail* on 29 March.

u.c. / ts. / 435

75, Cadogan Square
26th February 1930

Dear Ralph Pinker,

I have now heard definitely from André Gide that *La Nouvelle Revue Française* is very anxious to publish the French translation of *The Old Wives' Tale*. I have told him in reply that I have requested you to arrange the contract with the *N.R.F.* Please therefore write to them and keep them alive. They are a very unbusinesslike firm, but they have a cachet for high-class stuff unequalled in France.

Yours sincerely, Arnold Bennett

u.c. / ts. / 436

75, Cadogan Square
2nd April 1930

Dear Ralph Pinker,

Thank you for your letter of the 1st. The Society of Authors is not a money-making concern, but it needs all the funds it can obtain, and I am in favour of the Society asking for a commission where it does an effective work of *introduction* between an author and an agent. I cannot, however, see that the Society has a right to claim commission for forwarding an application to an author's recognised agent, and I should certainly support you in resisting such a claim. It seems to me that to forward letters or applications is a part of the ordinary business of the Society. I am sending a copy of this letter to the secretary of the Society.

Yours sincerely, Arnold Bennett

butler / t.c.c. / 437

[75, Cadogan Square]
2nd June 1930

Dear Ralph Pinker,

Re the serial of *Imperial Palace*. I pointed out to Eric that Flower originally bought the serial rights of this novel for his

435. *Un Conte de bonnes femmes*, translated by Marcel de Coppet (1881–), appeared the following year.

436. The Society of Authors passed a resolution that agents should pay a commission of 2½ per cent. on any earnings that came to them through the Society.

own magazines. If he sells the magazines, without selling the commitments, that is his own affair. If he had kept the magazines he would certainly have printed the serial in one of them, as he was always ready to print my work.

Further, we resold the serial of *Accident* for him for £2,250. I forget whether the price he paid me was £900 or £1,000, but even at the higher figure the profit on the deal was £1,250. He and I divided this sum between us equally. So that he has not got very much to complain of.

Doran, who had been talking to Flower in New York, advises me to accept £500 from Flower, if Flower offered it, as a release from his obligation to take the serial rights. I am quite willing to do this because Flower is a great friend of mine and has always done his best for me and has always been very enthusiastic.

Doran told me that if I delivered the copy about the middle of July, that would be in plenty of time for autumn publication. If it is in time for autumn publication in America it will be in time for publication here. Doran is exceedingly anxious to publish in the autumn. So am I. By the end of the year I shall probably have another novel ready—a much shorter one, with a much better chance of serialisation.

You now have all the relevant facts as they appear to me.

Yours sincerely, [Arnold Bennett]

BUTLER / T.C.C. / 438

[75, Cadogan Square]
7th July 1930

Dear Ralph Pinker,

I have finished *Imperial Palace*. It is 243,000 words in length. The complete typescript will be delivered to Flower during this week, and I have definitely arranged with him that I shall have the slip proofs complete not later than the 15th August, so that they can reach Doran not later than the end of August. Doran has assured me that this date will give him plenty of time. As

---

437. Cassell had begun to dispose of its magazines a few years before, under the pressure of internal difficulties and the changing magazine market. No serial publication of *Imperial Palace* is known.

he will get a duplicate of my corrected slips, it will not be necessary for him to send proofs to me.

I think I shall send the duplicate to you to be forwarded to Doran, as you will be able to forward them in the proper manner. Both my secretary and myself will be out of London.

Yours sincerely, [Arnold Bennett]

NW. / T.C. / 439
(*From Eric Pinker*)

[9 East 46th Street]
[New York]
September 10, 1930

My dear Bennett,

I thought you might like to have a report from me on the situation in Garden City and points east following Doran's change of allegiance. The 'low-down' as I have gathered it appears to be that George's exit from Garden City was quite sudden and unexpected, except in so far that we have all thought that his stay there was of uncertain duration. About the only part of the tale that seems, for fairly certain, to be a fact is that George has a five year contract with Hearst at $75000.00 a year and that his main duties will be those of an Ambassador, to fulfil which he will spend the greater part of his time in Europe. The Doubleday story is that George's reasons for leaving were that he could not bear to refuse so much money and that the various domestic upheavals in his

438. The timetable for the composition of *Imperial Palace* is interesting to recapitulate:

5 December 1928: Bennett expects to begin the novel in May; it will be 120,000 words long.

29 January 1929: he has all his ideas for it and can perhaps deliver the manuscript by the end of the year.

25 September 1929: he begins writing, and estimates that the novel will be 150,000 words long.

16 October 1929: he expects to finish in March; the novel will be 150,000 words long.

5 July 1930: he finishes the novel; its 243,000 words make it one-fifth again as long as *The Old Wives' Tale*; its rate of composition has been faster than that of any of the other serious novels except *Clayhanger* (whose 160,000 words were written in five months); from a structural standpoint—mastery of new material, complexity of action, multiplicity of characters—it has required more effort than any of the other novels.

The novel was published in October.

family had unsettled him. You know of course of Stanley Rinehart's divorce from George's daughter and I understand that Mrs. D. has now insisted on her separation from George being made permanent and put into legal form.

Other sources of information all say that there was some kind of an explosion and one story of this, which rather appeals to me, is to the effect that George when last in England allowed himself to be persuaded by Mitchell Kennerley and others that no high class publishing house could afford to be without reproductions of its leading authors made by Jo Davidson. George on finally accepting this view ordered five heads from Davidson including those of H. G. and Hugh, at $5,000.00 apiece and it is the receipt of the bill for $25000.00 that caused all the fleurs de Doran in Garden City to wither on the spot.

Nelson Doubleday told me that he had a definite agreement with George that George was not to steal any of the Doubleday authors with which to build up the Cosmopolitan Book Corporation's list and George told Nelson that Hearst was cognizant of this agreement. Where we go from here I don't quite know. They say that Doubleday's passed up the dividend on the Common Stock last year and this may be true as it seems to be generally agreed that they have not been doing so well lately. . . .

Yours ever, [Eric Pinker]

BUTLER / T.C.C. / 449

[75, Cadogan Square]
19th September 1930

My dear Eric,

Many thanks for your most informing letter. I had a long talk with Ralph last night.

439. 9 East 46th Street was the New York address of the Pinker firm.

The upheaval at Doubleday followed one in the previous year in which Stanley Rinehart (1897–) and others left to found their own firm. Mitchell Kennerley (d. 1950), brother of W. W. Kennerley (Bennett's brother-in-law), had been in the publishing business for many years, mainly in America, where he issued works by Lawrence, Conrad, and others. Nelson Doubleday (d. 1949) was the son of the founder of the firm. Bennett had now to decide whether to continue with Doubleday as his American publisher.

The busts by Jo Davidson (1883–1952) of Wells, Walpole, and others were not all completed. From October to January he did one of Bennett.

The Cosmopolitan Book Corporation apparently had a short life.

George told me the following things:

(1) His salary was £10,000 and £3,000 for expenses. But he would be likely to underestimate the figures.

(2) That he was absolutely boss of the book department at Hearsts. The latter statement, I may say, I received with a certain amount of reserve, and I hear that he told quite a different story to Ralph.

I do not think that George's relations with his family are as bad as some people say. I am absolutely sure that he is devoted to his daughter . . ., and he appears to have provided for mother and daughter quite adequately.

Nelson was obviously very keen to see me when he was over, and it was arranged that he should come down to Cornwall to have a talk; but this project was stopped by his father's illness. He has written to me twice since. . . .

I should like, out of pure, absurd friendship to oblige George if I possibly could. I am fairly familiar with George's defects as a man of business, but I like him very much. Still, unless he can guarantee a good sale for a book, and can back his guarantee by an advance to cover it, I shall restrain my friendly feelings. I will have another talk to him next week. . . .

I have been thinking of some more short stories, but I doubt if you have arranged the American sale of some of those already written. I am inclined to write some exciting short stories for a change. I should enjoy doing this, and I do not see why I should not write them as well as anybody else.

I am already very keen on my next novel, and the scheme of it is complete. I shall begin it in December and it will be finished—I think—about May. It is based on the plot of the story 'The Dream' which you sold to some newspaper in Chicago. If I had seen the possibilities of that plot earlier I should never have squandered it on a short story. However I have turned a short story into a novel before, in *The Glimpse*. As regards the serial rights, I do not see that these will be prejudicially affected by the bones of the plot having been previously used as a short story. Anyhow, if they are I cannot help it.

Further as to future work I have not decided anything beyond the next novel.

I hope you and yours are all right. I must say again, at the risk of being monotonous, that I am very favourably impressed by Ralph.

> Ever yours, [Arnold Bennett]

U.C. / TS. / 441

> 75, Cadogan Square
> 25th September 1930

Dear Ralph Pinker,

Doran has been to see me again. Nothing fresh happened. I told him frankly that the chief thing he was up against was the reputation of the Hearst organisation here, chiefly due to the methods of one man. He said that he fully realised this, and that he would make no attempt to get authors into the Hearst fold until he was in a position to prove that he had complete command of the book publishing section of Hearsts and could assure a proper selling organisation. He assured me, with various corroborative detail, that Hearst was heartily behind him.

> Yours sincerely, Arnold Bennett

U.C. / TS. / 442

> 75, Cadogan Square
> 8th October 1930

Dear Ralph Pinker,

Punch and Judy

Thank you for your letter of yesterday and the enclosures. The only comment I have to make is that Thorpe accepted the story, subject to the arrangement of price for the turning of the film into a talkie. I asked for an extra £1,000 for the extra work. He began with £250 and I screwed him up to £750, but he would go no higher, and I would not come down.

> Yours sincerely, Arnold Bennett

440. The new novel, *Dream of Destiny*, was begun on 25 November. 'The Dream' and a few other Bennett stories were published in the *Chicago Tribune*. 'The Dream' is collected in *The Night Visitor*.

442. Ralph Pinker's letter reported that British International had informed him that Bennett's original story was unsatisfactory and that they were awaiting a new story from him. Negotiations ended there, and Bennett received no more than the first £1,000. 'It is a great and fearful world, the film-world,' Bennett wrote in his journal on one occasion. See pages 380–1 and 384 for the beginning of the negotiations.

BUTLER / T.C.C. / 443

[75, Cadogan Square]
13th October 1930

Dear Ralph Pinker,

I assume that a formal contract was made between Goossens and me for *Judith*. The libretto of *Don Juan* is almost, but not quite, finished, and Goossens is already composing the music. As soon as the libretto is completed I will let you know, so that you can fix up the contract on the same terms as for *Judith*.

Yours sincerely, [Arnold Bennett]

U.C. / TS. / 444

75, Cadogan Square
30th October 1930

Dear Ralph Pinker,

Some weeks ago Eric asked me what I was going to do next. I told him that I should do a novel, 100,000 words at the most, and some short stories. I enclose, in duplicate, the first of the short stories, 'The Flight'. It is rather more than the usual length—somewhat under 7,000 words.

Yours sincerely, Arnold Bennett

BUTLER / T.C.C. / 445

[97, Chiltern Court]
12th December 1930

My dear Eric,

Many thanks for your letter of the 5th. I thought it very probable that 'The Flight' would sell easily. It seemed to me to be the sort of story which does sell easily. I am very glad that it is disposed of.

And what about the talkie rights of *Imperial Palace*? Ralph

443. *Don Juan de Marana*, a full-length opera, was first produced on 24 June 1937 at Covent Garden, with Eugene Goossens conducting and Lawrence Tibbett singing the title role. The opera was received coolly, and much of the blame was put upon the librettist for creating an unsympathetic hero (a criticism Bennett anticipated and rejected in the preface he wrote in 1923 for the play).

L.A.B.—2 E

came to ask me if I would accept £4,000 for them. I said I would.

I have written one fifth of my new novel.

All good wishes to you both.

Yours sincerely, [Arnold Bennett]

BUTLER / T.C.C. / 446

[97, Chiltern Court]
28th January 1931

My dear Eric,

Many thanks for your letter of the 20th and all its news. The arrangement about the free distribution of *Imperial Palace* is satisfactory to me, provided it does not harm the ordinary sale of the book. I should say that the Book-of-the-Month Club must be in difficulties. This year they have only sent me half of the annual amount which they pay me for advising them (£262. 10. 0), and they say that this is to the 30th June! I should not be surprised to hear on the 30th June that the affair is 'off'.

Nelson wrote or cabled me before Christmas that he had up to then sold within a few hundred of 20,000 copies, so that in the following 3½ weeks he has not been doing a terrible amount of business. However I never believed George's unofficial figures, and I do not believe Nelson's.

George has been here several times. He makes a pathetic spectacle. . . .

All good wishes,

Ever yours, [Arnold Bennett]

445. The lease at Cadogan Square ran out, and the Bennetts moved on 9 November into a new flat at Chiltern Court, above Baker Street Station. E. McKnight Kauffer decorated the flat. Bennett reported to his nephew Richard that there were 660 feet of bookshelves.

'The Flight' was sold to *Woman's Home Companion* for $1500. It appeared in April 1932. It is not included in any collection.

446. *Imperial Palace*, whose preoccupation with a luxury hotel in the face of the Depression offended many socially conscious critics, was perhaps Bennett's greatest commercial success among his novels—and that despite competition from Vicki Baum's *Grand Hotel*. It was briefly near the top of the best-seller list in America, running second to the Baum novel. The Book of the Month Club, which Bennett had been advising since 1929, arranged to distribute seventy to eighty thousand copies of the novel in America after normal sales had passed their peak. Their payment to Bennett was six cents per copy.

By 28 January 1931 Bennett was a mortally sick man. He had drunk unsafe water on a visit to Jo Davidson's country home in France earlier in January, and had returned to England with what was diagnosed as a case of influenza. He made a recovery that lasted from 26 January to 3 February, writing on the 2nd what proved to be the last of his 'Books and Persons' articles for the Express, *an article about an old friend of his and J. B. Pinker's, Mrs. C. N. Williamson. After a relapse, his illness was identified as typhoid fever. He died on 27 March. Newspapers reported that his estate would amount to £100,000, and there was surprise when the sum proved to be £36,600. The discrepancy reflected no loss in earning power in the last years, but rather the fact that he had earned less and spent more than people knew. His novel* Dream of Destiny *was incomplete; he had left off writing it before the visit to Davidson. It was published the following year by Cassell. The proposed filming of* Imperial Palace *came to nothing.*

During the next few years the full effect of the Depression was felt in the book world. In America in particular, the book trade dwindled by about 40 per cent. The Pinker firm, launched so successfully there, was soon in trouble, and collapsed in 1939. The English office went into bankruptcy in 1941. The field was left to old rivals, old associates, and newcomers.

INDEX

Abraham Lincoln, 251, 275

Academy, xiv, xv, 16–17, 31, 33–34, 37–38, 42, 76

Accident, xxii, 364–5, 404

'Advanced Woman, The', 12

'Adventures of Jack Stout, The', 56–57, 118–20

Ainley, Henry, 186, 227, 232, 338

Albany Review, 102

Alden, W. L., 34

Allen, Grant, 10

Allen, James Lane, 16

All-Story Magazine, 174

Amalgamated Press, 131, 181

American Magazine, 163–5, 171, 174, 201, 222, 355

Ames, Winthrop, 206

Angell, Norman, 211

Angel Unawares, An, xv, 59

Angus, Ian, ix

Anna of the Five Towns: composition, 18–21, 363; publication, xv, 31, 33–34, 37–38, 46, 52, 67, 124, 126, 141–2; criticism, 33–34, 49, 288; dramatization, xvi, 95

Appleton, D., & Co., 124, 126–7, 150–151

'Are Scotsmen Really Mean?', 349

'Are We a Thrifty Race?', 249

Argosy, 174

Arnold, Matthew, 163

Arnold Bennett and H. G. Wells, xxiii, 42

Arnold Bennett, A Portrait Done at Home, xxiii

Arnold Bennett Calendar, The, 159–60

Arnold Bennett's Letters to His Nephew, xxiii

Art, Georges, 37–38, 46

Art and Letters, 265–6

'Artist and the Public, The', 180, 192–193

'Artist's Model, The', 11

Art of E. A. Rickards, The, 286

Ashdod, 89

Asquith, Lady Cynthia, 26

As You Like It, 275

Athenaeum, 41, 143

Atkins, J. B., 170, 205

Atlantic Monthly, 278

Atwill, Lionel, 167

Audoux, Marguerite, 128, 158

Austin, Frederic, xxi, 352–3

Austin, L. F., 185, 189

Author, The, 187–8

Authors and I, 16–17

Author's Craft, The, xix, 180, 182–5, 192, 220, 223, 285–6

Authors' League, 302, 342

Authors' Syndicate, 21–22

'Baby's Bath, The', 63, 83–84

Background with Chorus, 167

Bailey, Vernon Howe, 280

Baker, Augustus, ix

Ballad of Reading Gaol, The, 23, 58

Bandits, The, xxi, 352–3

'Barber, The', 203

Barker, H. Granville, 186–7

Barrett, Frank, 40

Barrie, J. M., 106, 264

Barrymore, John, 287

Barton, Violet, ix, 27–28

Bâtisseurs de ponts, Les, 199–200

Baum, Vicki, 410

Bear, Archie de, 167

Beardmore, Frank, 202

Beardmore, George, ix

Beaverbrook, Max: 285, 295; trips with A. B., xxii–xxiii, 368, 397; at Ministry of Information, 263; novel about father, 280, 286, 296; A. B. published in his newspapers, 356, 364–5, 375

Beerbohm, Max, 6–7

Beggar's Opera, The, xx, 274–5, 285, 352

'Beginning the New Year', 83–84

Bell, Moberly, 84–86

Belloc, Hilaire, 125

Belmont Book, The, 89

Benn, Ernest, Ltd., 361–2, 384–5, 398, 402

Benn, Sir Ernest, 362, 385

Bennett, Dorothy Cheston, ix, xx, 1, 298, 371, 395, 397, 410

Bennett, Emily, 171

Bennett, Enoch, xiii, xv, 6–7, 13, 31, 95

Bennett, Frank, 59, 95, 160, 166, 171, 202–3

Bennett, Marguerite: 95, 97–98, 125, 244; marriage, xv, xx, 2, 91–92, 205–206, 297–8; comments by, 115, 230, 264, 297; residences and travels, 116, 134, 143, 152, 155, 172, 174, 177–8, 196, 266, 276; recitations, 281–2

Bennett, Richard, xix, 1, 166, 303, 321, 341, 387–8, 410

Bennett, Sarah Ann, xiii, xix, 31, 59, 72, 97

Bennett, Tertia, 20, 72, 92, 97, 121–2, 146–7, 171, 247

Bennett, Virginia, xxi

Benson, A. C., 140

Bernhardt, Sarah, 262

Besant, Sir Walter, 24

Best of Bennett, The, 277

Best of Life, The (see *How to Make the Best of Life*)

Bierce, Ambrose, 225

B.I.P. (*see* British International Pictures)

Birmingham Gazette, 341

Bishop's Apron, The, 80

Bisland, Mrs., 133–4

Black & White, 20, 22–23, 64, 102, 124

Blattner, Ludwig, Corporation, 380

Blue Bird, The, 135

Body and Soul, xx, 166, 274, 276, 308–309

Boll, T. E. M., ix

Bomb, The, 106–7

Bookman, The, 154, 270, 272–3, 278, 313, 368

Bookman's Journal, 338

Book of Carlotta, The (see *Sacred and Profane Love*)

Book of the Month Club, 410

'Books and Persons', xvii, xxi, xxiii, 13, 360–1, 411

Books and Persons, xix, 245, 278

Boston Evening Transcript, 134

Boucicault, Dion, 143, 263–4

Bourchier, Arthur, 309–11

Bourget, Paul, 60–61

Bowden, Mrs. Ann, ix

Brade, Reginald, 268

Braithwaite, Lilian, 338

Brandt, Carl, 314, 319, 359–60

Brentano's, 139

'Bridge-Builders, The', 199–200

Bright, Golding, 240–1, 322–3, 325, 337–8, 367

Bright Island, The, xxi, 270, 274, 276, 284–5, 308, 338

British Amalgamated Films, 368

British Authors Productions, 356, 384

British Film Institute, x

British International Pictures, 378, 381, 384, 392–5, 408

British Weekly, 140

Brothers Karamazov, The, 345

Brown, Curtis : 26, 64; and *Hugo*, 66–68; *Sinews of War*, 66–68, 85; *The Statue*, 88–90, 92–94, 103; Pinker on, 124–5

Browne, Maurice, 255

Brugmans, Linette F., 401

Buchan, John, 18

Buckles, F. M. & Co., 67

Buhrer, Albert, 294

John Bull, xx

Buried Alive: composition, xvii, 12, 100–101, 123; publication, xvi, 100–1, 104–5, 109, 131, 133, 139, 148–9, 220; novel modelled on, 157, 231, 256; dramatization, xviii, 186; film, 323

Butler, Dr. Lafayette, ix, 5

Butler, Miss, 381

Butler, Patricia, ix

Butt, Alfred, 316, 323

Bystander, 63–64

Calthrop, Donald, 298, 308

Cambridge Magazine, 261–2

Campbell, Mrs. Patrick, 368–74, 376

Candid Friend, The, 107

'Can the Doctors Be Cured?', 349

Capek, K. and J., 275

Card, The: composition, 109, 116, 118–120; publication, xvii, 125, 127, 132–133, 143–4, 150; film, xx, 315, 323; and *The Regent*, 148, 157, 165–6

Case of the Plain Man, The (see *The Plain Man and His Wife*)

Cassell & Co. Ltd.: publishing *The Statue*, 92–93, 103; *Journals*, 204, 399; *The Lion's Share*, 257; *The Pretty Lady*, 261–262; *Lord Raingo*, 280; *Lilian*, 318; *Riceyman Steps*, 325–8, 339, 341–2; *Elsie and the Child*, 341–2, 399; *The Vanguard*, 356; *Venus Rising from the Sea*, 399; *Journal*, *1929*, 399; *Imperial Palace*, 404; contracts with, 336, 356, 404

Cassell's Magazine, 117–18, 267, 289, 316

Casson, Sir Lewis, 198–200

Cazenove, C. F., 64

Century Co., 206, 280

Century Magazine, 206, 219, 222, 224, 331–2, 339

Century of Books for Bibliophiles, A, xiii–xiv, 9–10

Chancellor, The, xiv, 59

Chapman & Hall Ltd.: publishing *The Grim Smile of the Five Towns*, 67, 83, 86–87; *The Old Wives' Tale*, 87–88, 94, 109–10, 131; *Helen with the High Hand*, 96, 134; *Buried Alive*, 109–10; reputation of, 77–80; A. B. leaves firm, 131

Chatto, Andrew, Jr., 245

Chatto, Andrew, Sr., 40, 43–48, 50–53, 62, 68–69, 79, 141–2

Chatto & Windus : publishing *Anna of the Five Towns*, 31, 33–34, 142; *The Gates of Wrath*, 38; *A Great Man*, 41, 47; *Savoir Faire Papers*, 46; *A Novelist's Log-Book*, 46; *The Ghost*, 47, 77–80, 83–84, 95–96, 110–11; *Teresa of Watling Street*, 47; *The City of Pleasure*, 72, 83–84, 86–87, 95–96, 110–11; *The Grim Smile of the Five Towns*, 79–80, 86–87, 110–11; *Ashdod*, 89; *Tales of the Five Towns*, 110–11; *Hugo*, 155; *Books and Persons*, 245, 247; *Art and Letters*, 265; *The Best of Bennett*, 277; *How to Become an Author*, 283–4; 'The Death of Simon Fuge', 347; *The Return Journey*, 383; contracts with, x, 58, 63; as publishers, 40–41; A. B. leaves firm, 124

Cherry Orchard, The, 275

Chester, J. & W., 386

Chesterton, G. K., 129–30, 185, 189–190, 225

Cheston, Dorothy (*see* Bennett, Dorothy Cheston)

Chicago Tribune, 215, 408

Children of the Mist, xiv, 59, 94

Christina, xv, 39, 44, 59, 67–68, 72

Chronicles of Barabbas, 126, 148, 258

City of Pleasure, The: 109; composition, 37–38, 54–55, 62–63; publication, xvi, 67, 72, 78, 83, 86–87, 91, 95–96, 110–11; criticism, 55; film, 390

'Clatter and Racket', 268

'Claudius Clear' (*see* Nicoll, Sir W. Robertson)

Clayhanger: setting, xiii, 128; composition, 125, 132–5, 232, 405; publication, xvii, 135–8, 140–1, 145–6, 151; criticism, 143

Clayhanger Family, The, 345–6

Clayhanger Trilogy: composition, 125, 127, 148; publication, 136, 150, 158–159, 220, 230, 251, 253, 345–6

Cliff, Laddie, 315

Clunie, bookseller, 348

Clutton-Brock, Arthur, 281

Cochran, Charles, 261–2, 316

Cohen, Harriet, 2

Colles, William Morris, 21–22, 38, 107–8

'Common Sense About the War', 215

Compton, Fay, 297

Conrad, Jessie, 24–25, 289–90, 303

Conrad, Joseph: 118, 173, 217, 406; relations with Pinker, 3, 23–26, 28, 289–90, 303; opinions on, 95, 106, 192–3, 288; as playwright, 284, 317

Constable, Archibald, & Co., 35, 134

Cooper, Gladys, 167

Coppet, Marcel de, 400, 402–3

'Cornet Player, The', 351

Cornhill Magazine, 165

Correspondence College (*see* Literary Correspondence College)

Correspondance André Gide—Arnold Bennett, xxiii

Cosmopolitan: administration, 157, 249, 295; A. B. does serials for, 159–60, 283–4; stories, 164, 201–2, 276, 288, 295–6; essays, 246, 267; *Riceyman Steps*, 319

Cosmopolitan Book Corporation, 406

Country, 32

Country Life, 117

Country of the Blind, The, 173

Courlander, Alphonse, 64

Courtney, W. L., 261–2

Craft of the Story Teller, The (*see The Author's Craft*)

Craig, Frank, 168–9

Crane, Stephen, 3, 23

Credit to Human Nature, A (*see Christina*)

Crime, The, xv, 59

Criterion, The, 346, 366–8

Crockett, Samuel Rutherford, 106

Cupid and Commonsense, xvi–xvii, 60, 94–95, 122, 129–30, 182, 193
Curwen Press, 399–400

Daddy-Long-Legs, 242
Dagnall, Evelyn, letters to, 368–9, 371, 381–2
Dagnall, T. C., 369
Daily Chronicle, 41, 129–30, 147, 154, 213, 227, 265
Daily Dispatch, 97, 129–30
Daily Express, xx, 273, 290, 292, 363–5, 385, 396–7, 411
Daily Mail, 128, 131, 402
Daily News: war articles for, xviii–xix, 211, 213, 215, 234–5, 237–8, 264–5, 268; review of novel in, 118; other articles, 130, 354–5; and Chesterton, 130; and Shaw, 215; and Masterman, 237; and Milner, 268
Daily Telegraph, 261–2, 396, 399, 402
Dance Club, The (see *Flora*)
David, Dr. Albert, 384–5
Davidson, Jo, 363, 406, 411
Davis, Robert H., 174, 204–6, 246, 250–8
Davis, Tom B., 191–2
Davray, Henry, 58, 61
Dean, Basil, 270–1, 276, 282, 322–3, 325, 337–8
'Death of Simon Fuge, The', 84, 86–87, 134, 152, 221, 346–7
Débats, 37
Deeds of Denry the Audacious, The (see *The Card*)
Delage, Maurice, 199–200
Delineator, The, 276, 284, 293, 302
Denny, Ernest, 263–4
Denry the Audacious (see *The Card*)
Dent, J. M., 32
'Desire for France, The', 35
Divorce, Un, 60–61
Dodd, Mead & Co., 127, 270
Donald, Sir Robert, 129–30, 265
Don Juan de Marana: composition, 115, 181–2, 186–7; production, 181–2, 186–7, 242, 270, 287; publication, xxi, 262–3, 319–21; opera, xxiii, 409
Doran, George H., Co., 136–8, 142, 151, 153–4, 296, 323, 363
Doran, George H.: becomes A. B.'s publisher, 125–8; publishing *A Great Man*, 94; *The Old Wives' Tale*, 126–7,

143, 361–2; *Helen with the High Hand*, 135–6; *These Twain*, 135–6, 223; *How to Live on Twenty-Four Hours a Day*, 138; *The Truth About an Author*, 143; *Sacred and Profane Love* (*The Book of Carlotta*), 143, 149; *The Feast of St. Friend*, 146, 159; Tertia Bennett's books, 146–7; *Buried Alive*, 148–9; *The Grand Babylon Hotel*, 161–2; *The Regent*, 163; *Milestones*, 171; *Books and Persons*, 245; *Our Women*, 268; *Lilian*, 316; 'The Death of Simon Fuge', 347; editions of A. B.'s works, 138–9, 292, 350, 388–9; negotiations with Munsey and others, 145–50, 174, 201–2, 250, 252, 254–8, 262, 328–9, 350–1, 359; A. B. with in America, 161–3; and Equitable Life Assurance, 197; and *Bookman*, 270, 272, 278, 313, 368; relations with Doubleday and Hearst, 385–6, 404–8, 410
Doran, Mrs. George, 126, 406–7
Doubleday & Co., 386, 399, 405–8
Doubleday, Nelson, 406–7, 410
Doubloons (see *The Sinews of War*)
Douglas, James, 261–2
Doyle, Sir Arthur Conan, 106, 225
'Dream, The', 407–8
'Dream of Armageddon, A', 42
Dream of Destiny, xxiii, 407–11
Drinkwater, John, 250–1, 275
Duckworth & Co., 130
Dumas, Alexandre, 70
Du Maurier, Sir Gerald, 381–2
Dupont, A. E., 378–81, 389–90, 392–395, 397
Durell, of British International Pictures, 389–90
Dutton, E. P., & Co., 127, 136, 144–145, 151, 159–61, 223
Dutton, George D., 138, 149–50
Dyall, Franklin, 270
Dyson, Miss, 27

Eadie, Dennis, 117, 167, 186, 263–4, 276, 367
East Anglia Daily Times, 216
East of Suez, 106–7
Eclipse Cinema Company, 214
Écho de Paris, 46
Edge, Emily (*see* Bennett, Emily)
Edwards, Aaron, 80
Eliot, T. S., 266, 346, 366–7

'Elsie and the Child', 330, 338–9
Elsie and the Child, xxi, 277, 288, 341–342, 398–400
English Review: articles for, 32, 128–9, 147, 173; story, 106–7; review of *The Old Wives' Tale*, 106–7; serial novel, 111; 'The Matador of the Five Towns', 118–19, 123, 134; *What the Public Wants*, 121, 130; *The Author's Craft*, 180, 192
'Entirely Reasonable' (*see* 'Mr. Jack Hollins and Destiny')
'Epidemic, The', 354
'Episode in Room 222, The', 36
Equitable Life Assurance Society, 196–197, 223
Ervine, St. John, 274–5, 279
Evening News, 101, 195–6, 262, 290, 292, 329
Evening Standard, xxi, 13, 342, 356, 360–1, 363, 375
Everett, P. W., 288–9, 324
Everybody's Magazine, 128, 213
Everybody's Weekly, 152
Experience Has Taught (see *How to Make the Best of Life*)

Faber, Leslie, 319–20
Fame and Fiction, xv, 16, 20, 33
Famous Players Lasky, 285, 388
Farley, Agnes, 89
'Farrls and a Woman, The', 36
Faust (film), xxii, 357–8
Feast of St. Friend, The, xvii, 146–7, 159–60, 166–7
Feipel, Louis N., 2–3
'Fiction and Happiness', 130
Film Weekly, 383
'Fish, The', 276, 295
'Five Towns Xmas, A', 83–84
Flaubert, Gustave, 17, 288
Flecker, James Elroy, 323
'Flight, The', 409–10
Floating Home, A, 205
Flora, xxii, 346, 368–74
Florentine Journal, 366–8
Flower, Sir Newman: position in Cassell firm, 280; and *Lord Raingo*, 280, 349, 352, 355–6; *The Old Wives' Tale*, 326; *Riceyman Steps*, 326–30, 342; 'Elsie and the Child', 330, 338–9; *Elsie and the Child*, 342, 399; *The Vanguard*, 356–7; 'The Hat', 366; *Mediterranean Scenes*,

386; *Imperial Palace*, 398–9, 403; *Venus Rising from the Sea*, 399; *Journal, 1929*, 402; *Accident*, 404; biography, 302; contract, 356–7; and *Evening Standard*, 375
Food of the Phagocytes, The, 89–90, 94
Ford, Ford Madox (Hueffer), 3–4, 27, 106–7, 111, 116–21, 137
Ford, Hugh, 286, 299–300, 302
Ford, John, ix, 80
Fortnightly, 107, 249
Free Solitude, A, 78, 80
Friendship and Happiness (see *The Feast of St. Friend*)
Frohman, Charles, 245
'From One Generation to Another', 134
From the Log of the 'Velsa', xix, 206, 219, 222, 280, 363

Gaige, Crosby, 379–80
Galsworthy, John, 118, 211, 225, 237, 261, 285
'Games and Pastimes', 332
Ganguli, Professor, 277
Gardiner, A. G., 235, 264–5
Gardner, Fitzroy, 13–15
Garnett, Edward, 1
Gaspar Ruiz, 26
Gates of Wrath, The, xv, 38, 53, 163–4
Gaumont British Films, 384
Gentleman Dash, 147
George, W. L., 137
Gerber, Helmut E., ix
'Getting Level with Life', 351
Ghost, The: composition, xiv, 19, 51–53, 67; publication, xvi, 43–45, 47–48, 54, 59, 68–69, 77–80, 83, 87, 89, 96, 111, 162, 401
Gibbon, Percival, 225
Gide, André, xxiii, 400–1, 403
Gilchrist, Murray, 107–8
Gissing, George, 16, 37, 192–3
'Glimpse, The', 102, 106, 407
Glimpse, The: theme, 102, 115; composition, 118–19, 124, 407; publication, xvii, 124, 127, 150–1, 223; criticism, 151
Glyn, Elinor, 144
Godal, Edward, 368, 375–6
Golden Cockerel Press, 338
Golden Penny, 45
Goldwyn Pictures Corporation, 261, 277

Gollancz, Sir Victor, 361–2, 398
Goncourt brothers, 17
Goodall, Edyth, 276
Good Housekeeping, 295
Goossens, Eugene, xxii–xxiii, 386–7, 409
Gosse, Edmund, 25
Gowers, Sir Ernest A., 238–9
Grand Babylon Hotel, The: quality, 12, 37, 39, 48, 357, 385; composition, 21, 45, 50; publication, xv, 44–45, 52, 54, 55, 68, 98, 161–2; film, 214, 323, 380, 392
Grand Hotel, 410
Grand Magazine, 79–80, 230
Graphic, 118
Grasset, Bernard, 279–80
Gray, Gilda, 389–90
Great Adventure, The: production, xviii, 63, 186, 193, 206, 264, 309–10, 320; publication, 178; film, xix, 227, 232–233, 323
'Great Huntress, The', 350–1, 353
Great Man, A: quality, 109; composition, 39, 41–42, 44–45; publication, xv, 43–45, 47–50, 53, 59, 90, 93–94; reviewed, 55
Green, Anne, 74
Green, Eleanor, xvi, 71–74, 89, 226
Green, Julian, xvi, 72
Grim Smile of the Five Towns, The: publication, xvi, 54, 79–80, 83–84, 86–87, 105, 111, 134; stories in, 64, 67, 83–84, 86–87, 152, 226
Grossmith, George, 316
Guinness, Alec, 315
Guy Domville, 245

Hackett, Francis, 126
Haggard, Rider, 4
Haight, Gordon S., ix
Hammerton, J. A., 152
Hanson, Charles L., 376–8
Harden, Hubert, 242
Hardy, Thomas, 22, 118, 203
Harmsworth, Alfred (*see* Northcliffe, Lord)
Harmsworth organization, 108, 111, 116, 144, 168
Harper & Brothers: refuse *Anna of the Five Towns*, 31; publishing *Your United States*, 156–9; *The Price of Love*, 157–9, 164; other negotiations, 202, 246–7, 253, 268, 351, 359–60, 366

Harper's: articles for, 128, 222, 278–80, 331–2, 396; *The Price of Love*, 157–158, 195; *Your United States*, 162, 166; A. B.'s opinion of, 128, 248, 278; review of A. B., 151
Harper's Bazaar, 157, 280
Harper's Weekly, 213, 221
Harris, Frank, 106–8, 225
Harrison, Austin, 128, 192
Harrison, Frederick, 59–60
Hart-Davis, Rupert, ix
Hassan, 323
'Hat, The', 366
Hawtrey, Charles, 117, 242
Haye, Helen, 263–4
Hearst, William Randolph, publications, 156–7, 160, 405–6, 408
Hearst's International, 157, 277, 295
Hearth and Home, 16, 31, 34, 44, 107
Heath, Major-General Sir Charles Ernest, 218
Heinemann, William, 22, 79, 292, 307
Helen with the High Hand: quality, 110; composition, 66, 75–76, 79–80, 86–87; publication, xvii, 91, 96, 100–1, 125, 133, 135–6; dramatization, xviii, 190–1, 204, 298; criticism, 100–1
Her Grace's Secret, xv, 59
Hilda Lessways: composition, 125, 132–133, 144, 156; publication, xvii, 133, 136, 154, 157, 160, 345
Hind, C. Lewis, 16–17, 33–35
Hirth, Mary M., ix
His Hour, 143–4
'His Worship the Goosedriver', 55–56, 79–80
Hitchcock, Alfred, 388, 391–2, 397
Hodder & Stoughton: publishing *The Human Machine*, 104; *A Man from the North*, 139, 141; *The Old Wives' Tale*, 142–3, 153, 155, 296, 313, 342–3, 348, 361, 399–400; *The Feast of St. Friend*, 146–7, 166–7; Tertia Bennett's books, 146–7; *The Author's Craft*, 285–286; *The Plain Man and His Wife*, 285–6; *Paris Nights*, 288; *How to Make the Best of Life*, 320–1; and George Doran, 126–7; and Claudius Clear, 140
Hodder-Williams, Sir Ernest, 153–4, 167, 296, 320
Hoey, Iris, 270
Holt, Henry & Co., 127

Home Chat, 347

Honeymoon, The: theme, 12, 211; composition, 75–76, 79, 122; production, xviii, 142–3, 193, 244, 264; publication, 135–6, 171; story based on, 144–6, 158

Hooley, Arthur, xiv, 21, 59

Hopkinson, Sir Alfred, 262

Horne, A. B., 309

Horniman, Annie E. F., 193–4, 197, 199

Hotten, John Camden, 40

'How a Case is Prepared for Trial', 10

Howard, Leslie, 264

Howard, Sydney, 369

Howells, William Dean, 126, 151

How to Become an Author, xv, 35, 39, 42, 74–75, 161, 178, 283–4

'How to Live on Sixty Minutes an Hour', 207

How to Live on Twenty-Four Hours a Day, xviii, 101, 121, 138

How to Make the Best of Life, xxi, 289, 293–4, 320–1, 323–4, 332

How to Write for the Magazines, 111

Hubbard, Esmé, 242

Hudson, W. H., 118

Hueffer, Ford Madox (*see* Ford, Ford Madox)

Hugo, xvi, 48–50, 52–54, 56–58, 60–61, 66–69, 72

Human Machine, The, xvii, 104, 121, 123, 138

Human Nature Notes, 129

Hundred Years of Publishing, A, 80, 131

'Hungarian Rhapsody', 36

Hunt, Violet, 22, 48, 63–64, 89

Hutchinson & Co., 271, 276, 280–1, 294, 296

Huxley, Aldous, 261, 266

Ideal Film Company, 296–7, 315

I Have This to Say, 64

Illustrated London News, 13, 130, 185, 189–90, 230

Imperial Palace: composition, 12, 256, 307, 385, 388, 398–9, 403–5; publication, xxiii, 398–9, 403–5; film, 409–411

'In a Hospital', 12–13

'In Calais Harbour', 212

Ingram, Sir Bruce, 185, 190

Inner Shrine, The, 125

Insect Play, The, 275

International Magazine Company, 295

International Variety and Theatrical Agency, 390

'In the Film World', 323

Ionides, Cyril, 205

'Is Love-Making a Lost Art?', 349

I.V.T.A. (*see* International Variety and Theatrical Agency)

Jackson, of Ludwig Blattner Corporation, 380

Jack Straw, 63

Jacobs, W. W., 106

'Jacob Tonson', xvii, 108, 122, 140, 245

James, Henry, 14–15, 22–24, 117–18, 177, 192–3, 217, 245

Jerome, Jerome K., 173

Jerrold, Mary, 338

Jessup, of Putnams, 37

'Jock-at-a-Venture', 158

John Ferguson, 274–5, 279

Johnson, L. G., 346–7

Johnson, Samuel, 24

'Jolly Corner, The', 118

Jones, Jefferson, 359–60

Joseph Conrad and His Circle, 289–90

Journal, 1929, xxiii, 396, 399, 402

Journalism for Women, xiv, 111

Journals of A. B.: composition, 320–1; published extracts, 204, 278, 320–1, 366–8, 396, 399, 402; *Journals of Arnold Bennett* published, xxiii, 379–380; quoted, 18–20, 77, 101, 134, 136–7, 151, 157, 163, 177, 232–3, 346, 351, 357, 387, 408

Joyce, James, 313

Judith, xx, 270, 274, 387–8; opera, xxii, 386–7, 409

Just as It Happened, 329–30

Kahn, Otto, xxii, 363

Kauffer, E. McKnight, 399, 410

Kauser, Alice, 167, 175–6, 227

Keane, Doris, 232–6, 239, 242–4, 270

Keddie, James, Jr., ix

Keeble, Lady (*see* McCarthy, Lillah)

Kennedy, James G., ix

Kennerley, Mary, ix

Kennerley, Mitchell, 406

Kennerley, W. W., 92, 97, 121–2, 247, 406

Kennerley, Mrs. W. W. (*see* Bennett, Tertia)
Keys, Nelson, 232
King, Basil, 125
Kingsley, Charles, 77, 80
Kipling, Rudyard, 40, 106, 199–200, 225, 285, 295
Knoblock, Edward: also Knoblauch, 5; collaborates with A. B. on *Milestones*, xviii, 167, 240–1; *London Life*, xxi, 314, 316; *Mr. Prohack*, xxii, 346, 367; films, 240–1, 315
Komisarjevsky, Theodore, 367
Kommer, Rudolph, 363–4

Lady Frederick, 63
Lafourcade, Georges, 92
Lanchester, H. V., 128–9, 287
Landon, W. Eric, 290–1
Lane, John, 18, 111, 138, 142, 144
Langton and Passmore, 241
Lanoire, Maurice, 279–80, 400–2
Lasky, Jesse, 285–6, 298–9, 301–2, 313–15, 321–3
'Last Love', 276
Last of Mrs. Cheyney, The, 382
'Last Words on Conscription', 268
Laughton, Charles, 367–8
Laurie, T. Werner, 65–66, 69, 90, 263, 319–21
Lawrence, D. H., 1, 26, 28, 259–61, 288, 406
Lawrence, Frieda, 261
'Lawyers and Their Costs', 10
Le Bas, Sir Hedley, 282–3, 324, 344–6
Lebert, M., 60–61, 102
Le Brasseur and Oakley, law offices of, 6, 9
Ledward, Olive, 130
Leonora, xv, 38–39, 41–42, 49, 52, 90, 107
Le Queux, William, 100
'Letter and the Lie, The', 64
'Letter Home, A', xiv, 12–13
Letter That Was Never Sent, A, 197
'Let us Realise', 214
Levant Herald, 22
Lever Brothers, 108
Levy, Ben, 368
Lewis, Wyndham, 266
Liberty!, xix
Liberty Magazine, 366

Library Press, Ltd., 292
Life and Letters, 97, 396
'Life of Nash Nicklin, The', 201–2, 219–23, 225–6
Lilian, xx, 316, 318–19
'Lion's Share, The', 63, 67, 83–84, 86–87, 134
Lion's Share, The, xix, 165, 223, 226, 228–9, 231, 257
Lippincott, J. B., Co., 359–60
Literary Agency of London, 64
Literary Correspondence College, 74–75, 111, 123
Literary Taste, xvii, 101, 121–3, 206
Liverpool, Bishop of (*see* David, Dr. Albert)
Living Age, 129
Lloyd George, David, 185, 211
Lloyd's Sunday News (see *Lloyd's Weekly Newspaper*)
Lloyd's Weekly News (see *Lloyd's Weekly Newspaper*)
Lloyd's Weekly Newspaper, xix, 262, 264–265
Locke, W. J., 151
London Bookman, A, 386
London Life, xxi, 314–16, 321–3, 325, 337–8
London Magazine, 144–6, 165–6, 169
London Mercury, 250, 278
Long, John, Ltd., 106–7
Long, Ray, 295–6, 322–3
Loot of Cities, The, xvi, 36, 38, 43–44, 49–50, 53, 58
Lord Raingo: theme, 280, 286, 355–6; composition, 307, 348–50; publication, xxi, 280, 352, 355–6, 360
Lorimer, George Horace, 229–30
'Lost Girl, The' (*see* 'Nine O'Clock Tomorrow')
Lost Girl, The, 288
Love and Life (see *The Ghost*)
Love and Riches (see *Helen with the High Hand*)
Love Match, The, xx, 274, 276, 298, 309–11
Lowndes, Mrs. Belloc, 22–23, 124–5, 307–8
Lowndes, F. S. A., 125, 188, 262
Lucas, E. V., 31, 48, 123, 155–6, 172–173, 204, 345–6
Lyric Theatre, Hammersmith, xx, 251, 274–6, 284–5, 309

MacAlarney, Robert E., 299–302
MacCarthy, Sir Desmond, 396
McCarthy, Lillah, 270, 387
MacCrae, John, 160
MacDonald, Pirie, 163
Machen, Arthur, 261–2
Mackenzie, Sir Compton, 217–18
Mackenzie, W. A., 22
McClure, S. S., 33, 36, 70, 164, 339
McClure, Phillips & Co., 33, 66
McClure Newspaper Syndicate, 339–340, 351
McClure Syndicate, 33–34
McClure's Magazine, 128, 133–5, 230
McKinnel, Norman, 191, 298
MacManus, Seumas, 26
Macmillan & Co., Ltd., 77, 80
Macmillan, Alexander, 80
Macmillan, Daniel, 80
MacWhirter, W. A., 331, 349
Mair, G. H., 227–8, 237
Make Believe, 275
Malone, J. A. E., 316
Manchester Guardian, 227, 281
Man from the North, A, xiv, 17–18, 20, 126, 138–42, 167, 363
Man with Red Hair, A, 368
M.A.P. (*Mainly About People*), 72
Marie-Claire, 128, 158
'Marie Marguerite', xx, 295
Markham, Lady (Lucy), 227
Marmaduke, 263–4
Married Life (see *The Plain Man and His Wife*)
Marston, Maurice, 314
Martin du Gard, Roger, 400–1
Massie, Hughes, 90
Masterman, Rt. Hon. C. F. G., 236–238
'Matador of the Five Towns, The', 116–20, 123, 134, 152, 221
Matador of the Five Towns, The, xviii, 64, 102, 118, 143, 158
Mathews, William Lee: as A. B.'s agent, 161, 169–70, 175–6; and *Don Juan*, 186–7; *Helen with the High Hand*, 190–1; *What the Public Wants*, 198; *Milestones*, 257
Maugham, W. Somerset, 4, 63, 78, 80, 108
Maupassant, Guy de, 17, 37
Maxwell, John, 381, 384, 389
Mediterranean Scenes, xxii, 363–5, 386

Mercure de France, Le, 58, 107–8
Meredith, George, 77, 80, 192–3
Merezhkovsky, Dmitri, 367
Merry Wives of Windsor, The, 275
Methuen & Co.: and D. H. Lawrence, 26; and E. V. Lucas (*see* Lucas); and Eden Phillpotts, 71; as A. B.'s publisher, 131–2; publishing *Helen with the High Hand*, 75; *The Statue*, 90, 103; *The Truth About an Author*, 134; *Clayhanger*, 136, 145; *A Man from the North*, 138–9, 167; *The Old Wives' Tale*, 141–3, 155; *The Matador of the Five Towns*, 152; *Whom God Hath Joined*, 156, 196, 274; *The Regent*, 194; *Methuen's Annual*, 204; *The Clayhanger Family*, 345–6; other negotiations, 108, 120, 162, 180–1; 212, 280
Methuen, A. M. S.: as A. B.'s publisher, 40, 61–62, 78, 150, 312; negotiations with, 69, 122–4, 132–3, 141, 177–81; publishing *The Card*, 148, 150; *The Old Wives' Tale*, 155–6; *Methuen's Annual*, 204; *The Price of Love*, 206–7; *These Twain*, 231; *Whom God Hath Joined*, 274; *Mr. Prohack*, 312
Metropolitan Magazine: publishing *The Plain Man and His Wife*, 162–4, 172–3, 175–6, 196; *The Author's Craft*, 162–4, 180–2, 184–5; *The Roll-Call*, 164–5; *The Lion's Share*, 164–5; stories, 206, 219–23
Milestones: composition, 167; production, xviii, 63, 167, 181, 186, 257, 271, 296; publication, 171; film, 240–241, 261, 323; and *Romance*, 232
Miller, Gilbert, 242, 287, 369, 373, 381–2
Milne, A. A., 275, 346
Milner, Alfred, Viscount, 268
'Mimi', 143
Ministry of Information, 262–3, 265–6
Mirror of the Sea, The, 95
Miser's Niece, The (see *Helen with the High Hand*)
Moffat, John, 232
Mond, Lord Alfred, 128, 250
Moore, Eva, 264
Moore, George, 17, 225
Moore, Mary, 59–60
Morley, Charles, 85–86, 88
Morning Leader, 136

Morrison, Arthur, 106
Morrison, Miss, 226
Moulin Rouge, 378
Morton, Michael, xxi
'Mr. Jack Hollins and Destiny', 276
Mr. Prohack: 314; composition, 274,
    276, 283–4; publication, xx, 283–4,
    292–3, 302; criticism, 312; drama-
    tization, xxii, 346, 367–8
Mrs. Dot, 63
Munsey, Frank A., 174, 250–8
Munsey's Magazine, 171, 174, 201–2, 254
Munsey Syndicate, 174, 201–2, 206,
    223, 246, 250–8
Murray, John, 132
'Muscovy Ducks, The', 219, 226
'Music Lesson, The', 59
Mycroft, Walter C., 389–90
My Garden, 71
'My Religion', 385
'Mysterious Destruction of Mr. Lewis
    Ipple, The', 276
Mysterious Uncle, The, 147
'My Wild Adventures in Watling
    Street', 32

Nares, Owen, 242
Nash, J. Eveleigh, 207
Nash's and Pall Mall Magazine, 246,
    276–7
Nash's Magazine, 207
Nation, The, 212
National Press Association, 91, 98,
    100, 116
National Provident Institution, 122
Needham, Sir Raymond, 238, 295–6
Nerney, Winifred: recollections, x, 2,
    303; gift to A. B. Museum, 4; hired
    as secretary by A. B., 4, 167, 263;
    work, 263, 326–7, 366, 391, 393, 397
Nethersole, Louis, 233–4, 239, 242
New Age: publishing 'Books and Persons',
    xvii, 13, 83, 107–8, 115, 121–2, 137,
    140, 143, 165, 177, 361; *Books and
    Persons*, 245, 247; 'The Glimpse', 102;
    reviewing *The Old Wives' Tale*, 107;
    'Why They Rule Us', 130
New Age Press, Ltd., 101, 104, 121–2,
    143, 247
Newnes, George, Ltd., 70–71, 155,
    163–4, 181, 289
Newnes, Frank, 288–9, 293
'New Novel, The', 177, 217

New Republic, 278
News of the World, 342
New Statesman, xix, 23, 27, 215, 249–
    250, 261, 272–3, 278, 382
New Weekly, 203
New York Herald Tribune, 360
New York Times, 34, 214–15, 238–9
Nicoll, Sir W. Robertson, 140, 152, 155
Night Visitor, The, xxiii, 351, 366, 408
'Nine O'Clock Tomorrow', 276, 288
'Nineteenth Hat, The', 133–4
N.N.S. (*see* Northern Newspaper
    Syndicate)
Noble Essences, 321
'Nocturne at the Majestic', 33, 37–38,
    45, 47, 122
'Nonsense About Belgium According
    to Bernard Shaw, The', 215
Northcliffe, Lord, 108, 195
Northern Newspaper Syndicate, 61,
    75–76, 87, 91
Northwestern University, 5
Nostromo, 95
Nouvelle Revue Française, La, 401, 403
Novelist's Log-Book, A, xv, 40, 46–50,
    54, 129–30
N.P.A. (*see* National Press Agency)
Nutt, Alfred, 60–62, 67, 69, 71, 75–77,
    79–83, 110, 156, 195–6
Nutt, David, 61

Observer, The, 290, 292
O'Connor, T. P., 47–48, 54–55, 57,
    72, 143
Odd Volume, The, 158
O. Henry (William Sydney Porter),
    225
Old Wives' Tale, The: theme, 3, 7, 135;
    composition, xv–xvii, 12, 41–44, 61,
    87–88, 94–97, 101–2, 104, 123, 405;
    publication, xvii, xxii, 87–88, 102,
    104–5, 109–10; dedication, 92; pub-
    lication in America, 126–7, 150, 220,
    223; new editions and translations,
    120, 131–2, 141–3, 152–6, 296, 313,
    342–3, 348, 361–3, 398–403; film,
    xx, 296–7; criticism, 106–7, 115, 118,
    134, 140, 401; compared to other
    novels of A. B., 316, 319, 326–7
Olson, Richard D., ix
'Onyx', xix
Oppenheim, E. Phillips, 173
Orage, A. R., 101, 104, 108, 247

Otto, Curt, 141–2
'Our Greatest Blunder in the War', 349
'Our Notebook', 185, 189–90
Our Women, xx, 12, 267
Outcry, The, 245
Outlook, 313
Over There, xix, 211, 227–30
Overtures and Beginners, 387

Paget, Lady, 227
Pain, Barry, 158
Pall Mall Gazette, 55, 207
Pall Mall Magazine, 67, 83–84, 86–87
Palmer, Frank, 122, 129–30, 138–9, 143, 165
'Paper Cap, The', 277
Paramount Pictures, 285
Paris Nights, xviii, 32, 128–9, 288
Parsons, Leonard, Ltd., 314
Paul I, 367
Pawling, Sydney S., 292
Payn, James, 189–90
Payne, Iden, 193–4
Pears' Annual, 222–3
Pearson, C. Arthur, Ltd., 21, 31, 34–35, 289, 332
Pearson's Magazine, 23
Peel, Mrs. C. S., 15–16
'People of the Potteries, The', 117
'Perfect Girl, The', 277
Perrin, Alice, 77–78, 80, 105–7, 173
Perris, G. H., 64
'Phantom', 44
Phillips, A. F. Palmer (*see* Palmer, Frank)
Phillips, J. S., 163–4, 168, 170
Phillips, Roland, 164
Phillpotts, Eden: collaborates with A. B. on *Children of the Mist*, xiv, 21, 59; *Christina*, xv, 39, 41, 44, 59, 67–68, 72; *An Angel Unawares*, xv, 59; *The Sinews of War*, xvi, 12, 54, 64–66, 68, 70–72; *The Sole Survivors*, xvi, 12; *The Statue*, xvii, 70–72, 74, 76, 84–86, 88–89, 92–95, 102–3; *The Food of the Phagocytes*, 89–90, 94; *The Bandits*, xxi, 352–3; influence on A. B., 19; works on *Black & White*, 20; A. B. visits and spends holidays with, 38, 44–45, 74; writing habits, 50, 70–71; A. B.'s opinion of, 50–51, 76–78, 225; opinion of A. B.'s work, 66, 78, 106–7; A. B. quarrels with, 76, 88–89, 92–95,

102–3, 352–3; letter to *The Times*, 86; and Murray Gilchrist, 108
Piccadilly, xxii, 378, 380–1, 383–4, 389–391
Pinker, Elizabeth Seabrooke, 22
Pinker, Eric S.: acknowledgements to, ix, xii; at his father's death, 25, 303, 307; joins firm, 218; in the war, 218, 267–8; expands the business, 307; letters to, 274–6, 279–81, 290, 296–8, 307 ff.; letters from, 322, 325, 330, 333–4, 339–40, 354, 405–6
Pinker, Mrs. Eric, 325, 334, 386
Pinker, J. B., & Co., contracts with, 160–1, 175–6, 307–8, 329, 332–6, 339–40, 354–5, 357
Pinker, J. B.: biographical sketch, 22–28; becomes A. B.'s agent, xv, 22, 31; places of business, 125; letters from, 124–5, 145, 149–50, 154, 160–1, 176, 185, 187–8, 192, 217, 250–1, 254–9, 267, 272, 274, 284, 289, 291–2; references to after death, 307, 321, 329, 332–5, 411
Pinker, Mrs. J. B., 156, 289–90
Pinker, Ralph: position in firm, 307, 334, 362; A. B. on, 406–8; letters to, 361–5, 375, 384–6, 396–400, 402–5, 408–9
Plain Man and His Wife, The: composition, 172, 176; publication, xviii, 162–3, 168–9, 172, 185, 196–7, 285–286; criticism, 220–1, 223, 229
Platt, Taylor, 296
Playfair, Nigel, xx, 264, 275–6, 279, 308–9
Poacher's Wife, The, 71
'Police Station, The', 36
Polite Farces, xiv, 59–60, 216
Pollinger, Laurence, 26
Portreve, The, 71
Post Mistress, The, 59
Pound, Ezra, 266
Pound, Reginald, ix, 74, 92, 154
'Present Crisis, The', 130
Preston, Harry, 232
Pretty Lady, The, xix, 212, 227, 259–63, 265, 320
Price, Nancy, 191
Price of Love, The, xix, 115, 157–8, 164, 195, 206–7, 217–18
'Prize Fight, The', 278
Pryce, Richard, xviii, 191, 204

P.T.O., 72
Publishers' trust, 85–86
Pugh, Ralph, 355–6, 384, 408
Punch and Judy, xxii, 380–1, 384, 388–395, 397, 408

Queen, The, 36
Que Faire?, 58
Question of Sex, A, 216
Quiller-Couch, Sir Arthur, 4, 106

Railroad Man's Magazine, 174
'Railway Station, The', 43–44
Rainbow, The, 26, 261
Rank, J. Arthur, 315
'Rat-Trap, The', 235
Ravel, Maurice, 200
Raven-Hill, Leonard, 168–9
Raymond, Ernest, 318
Readers Library, 381
Reasonable Life, The, xvi, 54, 72
Reburn, John, 100
Rees, Leonard, 273–4
Regent, The, xviii, 48, 157, 163–8, 194, 223
Reinhardt, Max, 364
Resist Not Evil (see *Riceyman Steps*)
'Restaurant Spooks', 12
Return Journey, The, xxii, 358, 381–3
Revue de Paris, 37
Reynolds, Paul, 3, 126–7, 162–4, 182, 184, 219, 319
Riceyman Steps: composition, 307, 314, 318–20; publication, xxi, 322–3, 345; errors in American edition, 2–3; quarrel over with Cassell, 325–30, 341–2; A. B.'s opinion of, 339; dramatization, xxi
Richardson, Frank, 53, 55
Rickards, E. A., 128–9, 286–7
Ricketts, Charles, 387–8
Rinehart, Stanley, 406
'Risks of Life, The', 197
Rivals, The, 275
Roberts, Harry, 32
Roberts, Thomas R., ix
Roch, Walter, 344
Roll-Call, The: composition, 159, 212; negotiations over, 159, 162, 164–5; publication, xx, 271, 296; quarrel over with Munsey, 246, 250–8
Romance, 232
Romeo and Juliet, 369

Rosenfeld, Sybil, x
Rosmer, Milton, 193–4, 197–200
Rota, Bertram, x
Royal Magazine, 330–2
Rutter, Frank, 265–6
Religious Interregnum, The, xxii, 384–5

Sacred and Profane Love: composition, 39, 41–42, 62; publication, xvi, 50, 52–54, 58–59, 61–62, 68–69, 90, 143, 148–9; dramatization, xx, 233–6, 242–4, 270–1, 374
St. James's Gazette, 17
Salmon, Eric, x
Samuelson Film Company, 241, 260–1
Sanity of Art, The, 101
'Sardonyx', xix, 272–3
Saturday Evening Post, 154, 229–30, 356
Saturday Review, 107
'Saturday to Monday', 43–44
Savoir Faire Papers, xv, 40, 46–50, 54
Savoir Vivre Papers, xvi, 72
Savour of Life, The, xxii, 323
'School-days in the Five Towns', 203
Schwob, Marcel, 37–38
Scott, Joseph W., ix
Scott, Sir Walter, 70
Scott-James, R. A., 203
Scribner's, Charles, Sons, 127, 279–80
Sea and the Jungle, The, 336
Sears, of Appleton & Co., 124
Secker, Martin, 157
Secret Agent, The, 55, 284, 317
Sedgwick, Ellery, 278, 281
Self and Self-Management, xx
Selwyn, Archibald, 277
Selwyn, Edgar, 169–70, 175–6, 205–6, 285, 380
Sera, La, 44–45
Service, F. Stanley, 34–35, 39
Sharpe, Herbert, 172
Shaw, Bernard: and literary agents, 4; and New Age Press, 101; and Court Theatre, 186; and the war, 215, 217; on Henry James, 245; and Mrs. Patrick Campbell, 374; and music, 387
Sheffield Telegraph, 129
Sheldon, Edward, 233
Sheppard, Robert, 65–66
'Silent Brothers, The', 63, 83–84
Silver Cord, The, 369
Sinclair, May, 261

Sinews of War, The, xvi, 54, 64–66, 68, 70–72, 76
Singleton, Frank, x
Sinister Street, 217–18
Sisley's Ltd., 85, 89
Sisson, Edgar Grant, 249
Sitwell, Edith, 266
Sitwell, Osbert, 265–6, 321
Sketch, The, 41
Sloane Productions, 366–8
Smith, C. Aubrey, 263–4
Smith, Greenhough, 173, 221, 228–9, 249, 350–1, 353–4
Smith, Pauline, 1–2
Smith, W. H., & Son Ltd., 262
Smith, Elder & Co., 132, 165
Smithers, Leonard, 23
Society for Theatre Research, x
Society of Authors: acknowledgement to, x; and literary agency, 21–22, 175–6, 321, 403; A. B. consults, 142, 144, 215, 251, 254–5, 342; letter to, 187–8
Sole Survivors, The, xvi
Solon, Léon Victor, 168–9
'Some Impressions of Portugal', 278–9, 332
Soulie, Marguerite (*see* Bennett, Marguerite)
Spalding, Percy, 245, 283–4
Spectator, 143, 170, 205
Spender, J. A., 297
Sphere, 36
Spielmann, M. H., 22
Squire, Sir John, 250
Staffordshire Knot, xiii, 7–9
Staffordshire Sentinel, 7, 55, 107
Stage Society, xvii, xxi, 94–95, 116–117, 193, 244–5, 261, 285
Stanley, Sir Albert, 272–3
Star, 11, 48, 91, 101, 261–2, 342
Statue, The, xvii, 72, 76, 84–86, 88–94, 102–3, 135
Stevenson, R. L., 22, 37, 68
Story of the Lyric Theatre, Hammersmith, The, 275–6
Storyteller, The, 276, 339, 356
Story Teller's Craft, The (see *The Author's Craft*)
Straight, Sir Douglas, 55
Strand: publishing *The Regent*, 165; *The Plain Man and His Wife*, 168–9, 173, 175–6; *The Author's Craft*, 173; *The*

Lion's Share, 228–9; *How to Make the Best of Life*, 288–9, 294–5, 332; article, 249; stories, 350–1, 354
Strange Necessity, The, 347
Strange Vanguard, The (see *The Vanguard*)
Sullivan, Sir Arthur, 302
Sullivan, Herbert, 302
Sun, 12, 17
Sunday Chronicle, 129
Sunday Express, 364–5
Sunday Pictorial, xxi, 23, 294–5, 331–2, 343, 349, 363
Sunday Stories Journal, 122
Sunday Times, 273–4, 293–4
Sutherland, Duke of, 80
Swinnerton, Frank: acknowledgement to, x; A. B. travels with, xx, 278; letters from A. B. to, 2, 126, 356; opinions of, 27, 167, 211, 329; represents Chatto & Windus, 245, 247, 262, 265, 283, 347, 383; and Doubleday, 386

Taffs, C. H., 169
Tales of the Five Towns: publication, xvi, 39, 43–44, 47, 49–53, 58, 61, 111; stories in, 33, 36, 79
Tauchnitz, publishers, 38, 109, 120, 134, 141–2, 206
Tayler, Alistair, xx, 275, 311
Tell England, 318
Tempest, Marie, 143
Temps, Le, 46
Teresa of Watling Street, xv, 43–44, 47–48, 52–53, 58, 163–4
These Twain: composition, 166, 201–2, 212; publication, xix, 125, 158–9, 201–2, 206, 223, 229–31, 251, 254, 256, 258, 345; criticism, 253–4
Things That Have Interested Me, xx, 203, 212, 283–4
Things That Have Interested Me, Second Series, xxi
Things That Have Interested Me, Third Series, xxi, 350–1
Things That Interested Me, xvi, 278
Things Which Have Interested Me, Second Series, xvi, 278
Things Which Have Interested Me, Third Series, xvii, 278
39 Steps, The, 388
'Thirty Years On', 347

Thomas, Jameson, 389–90
Thomson, Andrew, 170–1
Thorpe, J. C. A., 357–8, 378–81, 384, 388–95, 397, 408
Those United States, xviii, 156–7, 166, 169, 377–8
Three Sisters, The, 367
Thring, G. Herbert, 144, 175–6, 257
Tibbett, Lawrence, 409
Tillotson Syndicate: publishing *The Ghost*, 19; stories, 36–37, 41, 43–44, 79, 83–84, 87–88, 118–19, 133–4; serial, 44–45, 64–66; *The City of Pleasure*, 54–56, 59, 62, 72, 75; *The Card*, 116; articles, 147
Tillotson, Lever, 36, 44–45
Times, The: Chatto & Windus advertise in, 68; Times Book Club, 77–78, 84–86, 88; letters to, 86, 216; serializes *The Card*, 132; reviews in, 143, 311, 338; and F. S. A. Lowndes, 262; and A. Clutton-Brock, 281
Times Book Club, 77–78, 84–86, 88
Times Literary Supplement, The, 143
Times Weekly Edition, The, 132
Tiptail, 147
Tit-Bits, 10–11
Title, The, xix, 260–1, 263–4, 266, 271, 275
Today, 61–62
Tolstoy, Leo, 118, 345
Tomlinson, H. M., 336
T. P.'s Magazine, 143
T. P.'s Weekly: publishing *Savoir Faire Papers*, xv, 36–38, 40, 46–49; *A Novelist's Log-Book*, xv, 40, 42, 46–49, 129–30; *Savoir Vivre Papers*, xvi, 72; *The City of Pleasure*, 36–38; *A Great Man*, 47–48; *The Sinews of War*, 65–66, 71; *Literary Taste*, 101, 122; *The Human Machine*, 104; other journalism, 34, 36, 43–44, 54–55, 331; and *T. P.'s Magazine*, 143
Train de Luxe (see *Accident*)
Tree, Sir Herbert, 181–2
Tree, Viola, 308
Trench, Herbert, 122, 135–6
Tribune, 65–69, 79–80
Trood, Charles, 117
Truth About an Author, The: composition, 34–35; publication, xv, 33–35, 39, 46–47, 134, 138, 143, 153, 206; autobiographical detail from, 6–9, 12–20;

quoted, 7–10, 12–14, 17–18, 35–36, 115
Turgenev, Ivan, 16–17
Turnbull, Miss, 300–2
Turner, Florence, 297
Turner, W. J., 382
Tweedale, Violet, xv, 59
Twelve Stories and a Dream, 42

Ufa Films, 357–8
Under Western Eyes, 24
University College, London, 5
University of Texas, 5
Unlucky Number, The, 71
Untitled play, xxii, 382
Up-Along and Down-Along, 71

'Vados', 89
Vallentin, Hugo, 262–3
Vallombrosa (see *The Bandits*)
Vanbrugh, Irene, 263–4
Van Dieren, Bernard, 281
Vanguard, The, xxii, 356–7
Vanity Fair, 108
Vaudeville, 378
Vedrenne, J. E., 186, 191–2, 194, 197–200, 232–3, 263–4, 276, 282
'Velsa', xviii, 170, 172–3
Venus Rising from the Sea, xxiii, 398–9
Vernon, Frank, 181–2, 186, 191, 193–194, 282, 298, 310–11
Victory, 284

Walker, Martin, 308
Walpole, Hugh, 245, 262, 307–8, 368, 385, 406
Ward, Lock & Co., Ltd., 43–44, 89
War and Peace, 345
Wardour Films, 357–8
Esther Waters, 34
'Watling Street: A Memory', 32
Watson, Nan Marriott, 308
Watt, A. P., & Son, 4, 22, 24, 63
Watt, A. S., 199–200
Waugh, Arthur: opinion of Pinker, 27, 131; as A. B.'s publisher, 78–80, 131; publishing *The Grim Smile of the Five Towns*, 86–87, 152; *The Old Wives' Tale*, 87–88, 104–5, 107–10, 118, 120, 131, 140–1; *Buried Alive*, 104–5, 109; *The Glimpse*, 120, 124, 127
Way of the World, The, 275
Wayward Duchess, A, xiv, 59, 94

Webster, Alexander, 164

Webster, Ben, 117

Webster, George, 123–4, 178

Wedding Dress, The, xx, 286, 298–302, 322–3

Wells, H. G.: collaborates with A. B. on *The Crime*, xv, 59; correspondence with A. B., xxiii, 18, 107; and literary agents, 4, 22, 31, 187–8; takes A. B. to Pinker, 22, 31, 188; writings of, 42, 118, 213, 215, 297, 341; A. B. on, 56–57, 76–77, 155, 173, 225; on A. B.'s work, 106–7, 151; Pinker on, 192; takes A. B. to Cassell, 257; editing A. B.'s novels, 282–3, 324; and films, 285; and Ray Long, 295; bust of, 406

Wells, T. B., 157–9, 248, 359–60, 396

West, Rebecca, 346–7, 385

Westminster Gazette, 272, 276, 294, 297, 341

Westward Ho!, 80

Wharton, Edith, 3

'What Marriage Will Be Like One Hundred Years Hence', 354–5

'What's Bred in the Bone', 10–11

What's Bred in the Bone, 10–11

'What the German Conscript Thinks', 213

What the Public Wants: composition, 108, 116–17, 123; production, xvii, 117, 191–4, 197–200, 224, 242, 244, 250–251; publication, 121, 129–30, 135

Whelen, Frederick, 191

'When the Truce Comes', 215

Whigham, Henry James, 182–4, 219–26, 229

Whirlwind, The, 86, 90

Whishaw, Fred, 40

White Rose of Weary Leaf, 64

Whitten, Wilfred, 40–43, 47–48, 54–55, 104

Whom God Hath Joined: composition, 60–62, 71, 74; publication, xvi, 54, 62, 67, 69, 72, 75–77, 81–83, 141, 156, 196–7, 274; criticism, 75–76, 78, 87

'Why I Don't Live in London', 152

Whyte, Frederic, 22

'Why the Clock Stopped', 118

Wicken, Frederick C., letters to, 214, 341–2, 363–4, 368, 375–6, 378–81, 383–4, 388–95, 397, 401–2

Wilde, Oscar, 23, 58

Wile, F. W., 215

Williamson, A. M., 23, 145–6, 411

Williamson, C. N., 22–23, 145–6

Willison, Ian, ix

Wilson, Harris, 42

Winawer, Bruno, 303

Windsor Magazine, 33, 36, 38–41, 43–45, 47, 83–84, 110, 122

Winwood, Estelle, 369–71, 376

With Much Love, 74

Woman: A. B. on staff, xiv, 13–19, 31; writing for, 13–19, 59; and W. M. Colles, 22; and H. G. Wells, 42; and Mrs. Perrin, 80; and F. C. Bennett, 95; and Mrs. Patrick Campbell, 369

Woman's Home Companion, 410

Woman's Journal, 398

'Woman Who Stole Everything, The', 356

Woman Who Stole Everything, The, xxii, 351, 356

Women in Love, 261

Wong, Anna May, 389–90

Wooden Horse, The, 245

Woolf, B. A., 392

'Work and Worry', 140

World Today, The, xxii

Wounded Allies Relief Committee, 226–7, 231–2, 239

Wright, Haidée, 167

Wright, John, 277

Wyndham, Sir Charles, 60

X, 249–50

'Yacht, The', 276

Year of Prophesying, A, 341

Yellow Book, 13

Yonge, Charlotte M., 16

Your United States (see *Those United States*)

Youth's Companion, 169, 203, 222

Zola, Émile, 7

Zukor, Adolph, 285